An Expanding World
Volume 27

European and Non-European Societies, 1450–1800

AN EXPANDING WORLD
The European Impact on World History, 1450–1800

General Editor: A.J.R. Russell-Wood

Please note titles may change prior to publication

An Expanding World
The European Impact on World History 1450–1800

Volume 27

European and Non-European Societies, 1450–1800

Volume II: Religion, Class Gender, Race

edited by
Robert Forster

Ashgate
VARIORUM

This edition copyright © 1997 by Variorum, Ashgate Publishing Limited, and Introduction by Robert Forster. For copyright of individual articles refer to the Acknowledgements.

Published in the **Variorum Expanding World Series** by

Ashgate Publishing Limited
Gower House, Croft Road
Aldershot, Hampshire GU11 3HR
Great Britain

Ashgate Publishing Company
Old Post Road
Brookfield, Vermont 05036–9704
USA

ISBN 0–86078–521–1

British Library CIP data
  European and Non-European Societies, 1450–1800.
  (An Expanding World: The European Impact on World History, 1450–1800: Vol. 27). 1. Culture conflict–History. 2. Imperialism. 3. Ethnic relations–History. 4. Culture diffusion. I. Forster, Robert. II. The Longue Durée, Eurocentrism, Encounters on the Periphery of Africa and Asia. III. Religion, Class, Gender, Race. 305. 8' 009.

US Library of Congress CIP data
  European and Non-European Societies, 1450–1800/edited by Robert Forster. p.cm. – (An Expanding World: The European Impact on World History, 1450–1800: Vol. 27). Includes bibliographical references. Contents: Vol. I. The Longue Durée, Eurocentrism, Encounters on the Periphery of Africa and Asia. Vol II. Religion, Class, Gender, Race. 1. Social classes–Europe–History. 2. Social classes–Latin America–History. 3. Indians–First contact with Europeans. 4. Indians, Treatment of. 5. Europe–Colonies–America–Administration. 6. Europe–Politics and government. 7. Europe–Race relations. 8. Latin America–Politics and government. 9. Latin America–Race relations. I. Forster, Robert, 1926–   . II Series.
  HN373. E88   1997   96–53597
  305. 5' 094–dc21   CIP

This book is printed on acid free paper.

Printed and bound by Athenaeum Press, Ltd.,
Gateshead, Tyne & Wear.

AN EXPANDING WORLD 27

Contents

Volume II: Religion, Class, Gender, Race

14

"Inquisition of the Indians?":
The Inquisitorial Model and the
Repression of Andean Religion
in Seventeenth-Century Peru

Nicholas Griffiths

The task of repressing native Andean religions in the vice-royalty of Peru during the colonial era was not undertaken by the traditional defender of orthodoxy, the Holy Office of the Inquisition, but rather by a separate organization, deriving from archiepiscopal authority, which has come to be known as the "Extirpation." Despite the separation of jurisdictions, both the intellectual bases and the procedure of the Extirpation derived greatly from the model of the Inquisition to such an extent that historian Pierre Duviols has called the Andean variant "the bastard child of the Inquisition" and a "true Inquisition of the Indians."[2] In 1571, Philip II formally removed the native inhabitants of the Spanish colonies from the jurisdiction of the Inquisition. The Spanish crown refused to subject the neophyte Indians to the rigors and intimidation of the Holy Office on the grounds of their "simplicity and poor understanding" and too recent instruction in the faith.[3] From the 1520s to the 1560s, native religious offenders in the viceroyalty of New Spain had been tried (and before 1540, some had

---

[1] The author would like to thank the late Professor Derek Lomax for stimulating observations on the ideas in this article.

[2] Pierre Duviols, *Cultura andina y represión: procesos y visitas de idolatrías y hechicerías, Cajatambo, siglo XVII* (Cuzco: Centro de estudios rurales andinos "Bartolomé de las Casas," 1986), lxxiii; Duviols, *La lutte contre les religions autochtones dans le Pérou colonial: "l'extirpation de l'idolâtrie" entre 1532 et 1660* (Lima: Institut français d'études andines; Paris: Editions Ophrys, 1971), 221-24.

[3] For the grounds for Indian exclusion from inquisitorial jurisdiction, see Duviols, *La lutte*, 217; José Toribio Medina, *Historia del Tribunal de la Inquisición de Lima: 1569-1820*, 2nd ed., 2 vols. (Santiago: Fondo histórico y bibliográfico J.T. Medina, 1956), 1:27-28; Juan de Solórzano Pereira, *Política indiana*, Biblioteca de autores españoles, 5 vols. nos. 252-56 (Madrid: Compania Ibero-Americana de Publicaciones, 1972), 3:364.

20   COLONIAL LATIN AMERICAN HISTORICAL REVIEW   WINTER 1994

even been executed) under inquisitorial jurisdiction.[4] In Peru, however, there is no evidence that Indians were ever tried by the Inquisition. Instead, the prohibition of 1571 was circumvented by the establishment of a parallel organization, which was truly quasi-inquisitorial in that it shared the goal of enforcing orthodoxy through institutionalized intimidation. Thus, if the jurisdiction of the Holy Office was not to be directly applied to the Indians, at least the inquisitorial model could be adapted to the Andean situation. It is hardly remarkable, of course, that the repression of native religion should take the Inquisition as its prototype. It is more significant to appreciate how the Extirpation diverged from its model as a result of the wholly different context within which this "bastard child" was forced to function. The most striking difference between the two organizations was that the Andean variant was never as effective in the task of imposing religious orthodoxy; indeed, the evidence of idolatry trials indicates its failure to suppress native religious deviance by means of retribution and repression. The paradox is that, despite imitating a highly effective example, the Extirpation remained a fundamentally flawed structure. Its flaws will be the subject of this paper.

The essential characteristic which the Andean Extirpation shared with its parent organization was that it was principally an instrument of judicial repression. In order to root out and punish native

---

[4] The Franciscan friar inquisitors, Martín de Valencia and Friar Juan de Zumárraga, tried and executed Indian religious deviants in Central Mexico during the 1520s and 1530s. Although the death penalty for Indians was prohibited by royal decree in 1540, inquisitorial persecution of native delinquents continued under Francisco Tello de Sandoval, among the Mixtec Indians of Oaxaca in the 1540s, and reached a climax with the trials under the Franciscan Diego de Landa in Yucatán between 1559 and 1562. Even after the royal decree of 1571, the tribunal continued to act as a fact-finding agency in the uncovering of Indian transgressions. However, jurisdiction over prosecutions of Indians fell to the local *provisors* (vicars-general) of the dioceses and archdioceses. See Richard E. Greenleaf, "The Inquisition and the Indians of New Spain: A Study in Jurisdictional Confusion," *The Americas*, 22 (1965):138-66; Greenleaf, "Historiography of the Mexican Inquisition: Evolution of Interpretations and Methodologies," in *Cultural Encounters: The Impact of the Inquisition in Spain and the New World*, Mary E. Perry and Anne J. Cruz, eds. (Berkeley: University of California Press, 1991), 260-62; J. Jorge Klor de Alva, "Colonizing Souls: The Failure of the Indian Inquisition and the Rise of Penitential Discipline," ibid., 3-22; Roberto Moreno de los Arcos, "New Spain's Inquisition for Indians from the Sixteenth Century to the Nineteenth Century," ibid., 23-36.

religious deviance, the Extirpation borrowed from the Holy Office a sophisticated repressive apparatus. The principal instrument was the *juez visitador* (visiting judge) or *visitador general de las idolatrías* (visitor-general of idolatry), an office modeled on that of the inquisitorial judge.[5] The visitor-general presided over investigations into local religious practices and conducted idolatry trials against perceived offenders. It was his responsibility not only to direct the inquiry and question witnesses and suspects, but also to pass judgment and execute the sentence. He was granted all the powers of the archbishop: jurisdiction over ecclesiastical judges; the right to visit all *doctrinas* (missionary indigenous parishes), whether religious or secular; the right to check the level of linguistic knowledge of priests; and the right to remove *doctrineros* (parish priests of indigenous communities) from their offices.[6]

The visitor-general had a specialized team which was also modeled on that of the Inquisition. It comprised, as a core group, the visitor-general himself, the *fiscal* (public prosecutor),[7] and a notary or scribe. Since at least the appearance of a true legal process was maintained, the Indian accused was entitled to a defense.[8] This clear demarcation of responsibilities was an indication of the relative professionalism of the repressive apparatus of the Extirpation. A further loan from the Inquisition was the issue of an "edict of grace" by the visitor-general on his arrival in a native village, allowing three days during which individuals could denounce themselves or their fellows. This measure was derived from the inquisitorial practice of according

---

[5] The title was first conferred on Father Francisco de Avila in 1610. See Duviols, *La lutte*, 156.

[6] For the powers and methods of procedure of the visitor-general, see Duviols, *Cultura andina*, xlvii-xlviii, and *La lutte*, 201-10. His account is largely based on Pablo José de Arriaga, "La extirpación de la idolatría del Perú," *Crónicas peruanas de interés indígena*, Francisco Esteva Barba, ed., Biblioteca de Autores Españoles, no. 209 (Madrid: Atlas, 1968), 240-56.

[7] The *fiscal* was in charge of communication with the Indians and the arrest of the guilty; he might also act as an interpreter.

[8] This role did not necessarily merit a specialist in his own right and, in many cases, was a mere token gesture. The post could be filled by a member of the team's entourage or a local person of standing, such as the priest, an educated Spaniard, or even a hispanicized Indian.

22   COLONIAL LATIN AMERICAN HISTORICAL REVIEW   WINTER 1994

absolution in exchange for a spontaneous confession or denunciation within a fixed period of time.[9]

Like the inquisitorial trial, the idolatry visitation culminated in the traditional *auto de fe*, which provided a ritual context for the destruction of the objects of worship, the abjuration and absolution of offenders, and the administration of punishment of the *camayos* (religious leaders). The penalties inflicted upon the convicted also echoed those of the Inquisition. There were punishments of reform (for example, service in the local church) and punishments of separation and isolation (such as long-term or perpetual confinement to a house of correction, or exile from the community). But those which most clearly drew on the inquisitorial tradition were the punishments of infamy and shame by means of public humiliation and ridicule: dressing in the robes and headdress of the penitent, whipping, cropping of the hair, and passage through the streets half-naked on the back of a llama. In all these ways, inquisitorial practice served as a paradigm for the Andean context.

While much of the Extirpation modeled itself upon the Inquisition in terms of procedure, it could not replicate the most important achievement of the Holy Office: it failed to institutionalize itself. The Extirpation never became an institution of colonial life because its very existence relied excessively on the will and initiative of individual archbishops or viceroys. The first campaigns of extirpation in the seventeenth century were summoned into existence by the triumvirate of the archbishop of Lima, Bartolomé Lobo Guerrero (1608-22), the Jesuit provincial, Pablo José de Arriaga, and the viceroy, Francisco de Borja, Príncipe de Esquilache (1615-21). Without the guiding inspiration of these three individuals after 1622, the momentum of the Extirpation vanished and concerted campaigns of repression of native religion ceased. The new archbishop, Hernando Arias de Ugarte (1630-38), was unconvinced of the need for repressive measures against the Indians.[10] Consequently, the efforts of the

---

[9] Duviols, *La lutte*, 221.

[10] There were campaigns of extirpation under Archbishop Gonzalo de Campo (1625-26) but his untimely death brought them to a rapid end. Arias's correspondence with the king indicates that he believed that idolatry was more a myth than a reality and that the Indians were exempt from it. Letters of Archbishop Hernando Arias de Ugarte to the king, May 27, 1632, and May 13, 1633, Archivo General de Indias, Sevilla (hereinafter cited as AGI), Lima 302.

advocates of repression, Francisco de Avila and Hernando de Avendaño, were frustrated by the lack of a sponsor. The second wave of campaigns of extirpation of the seventeenth century (1649-70) also sprang from the initiative of the chief prelate, this time Archbishop Pedro de Villagómez (1641-71). It was Villagómez who, in 1649, appointed seven new visitors-general of idolatry and instigated the extension of the campaigns throughout the archbishopric during the next fifteen to twenty years.[11] After his death, there were no more campaigns of extirpation until the short-lived revival in 1725 under Archbishop Diego Morcillo Rubio de Auñon (1724-30).

Emphasis upon the key role of the ecclesiastical hierarchy should not obscure the fact that idolatry investigations at the local level sprang from the social tensions of the particular native communities in which they took place. Idolatry trials were invariably initiated either by the local *doctrinero* or by powerful native authorities such as the *kuraka* (chieftain or headman), *alcalde*, or *fiscal*, in order to assert their power over dangerous rivals or to settle old scores. In effect, idolatry denunciations served to elevate fundamental social conflicts to the judicial sphere. Even so, not all local idolatry investigations led to campaigns of extirpation. Although local trials might provoke centrally-organized campaigns, they could also operate autonomously and exist in isolation; as the case of Francisco de Avila illustrated, a denunciation of "idolatries" was of little consequence beyond the confines of the priest's own *doctrina* unless there was the resolve in Lima to launch a campaign in response. Thus, if the existence of campaigns of extirpation depended upon the close interaction of local *doctrineros* and the ecclesiastical hierarchy, their timing was determined by the center rather than by the locality.[12]

---

[11] For further details of these campaigns, see Duviols, *La lutte*, 164-65.

[12] It is also worth noting that the intermittent character of the campaigns of extirpation did not necessarily reflect the "objective" frequency of native religious practices. It is not true to say that the campaigns of idolatry occurred between 1609 and 1622, and between 1649 and 1670, because these years witnessed an empirical and measurable recrudescence of native beliefs, independent of the actions of the colonial authorities. In this sense they are probably different from the wave of extirpation unleashed by discovery of the *Taki Ongoy* movement in the sixteenth century. Whereas the 1560s was a time of revolution in native religious beliefs centered around the significance of the date 1565, there is no reason to believe that the years around 1609 and 1640 were significant from the native point of view.

Since it remained forever under the jurisdiction of the bishops, the Extirpation failed to develop a body of committed careerists who would have conferred an independent existence. It lacked a permanent council comparable to the *suprema* (supreme council) of the Inquisition. It had no local bodies to represent it in the provinces. It had no permanent staff of officials. Above all, it was without a financial base. The visitors-general remained dependent on the resources that the archbishop could make available to them. Because of this excessive reliance upon powerful patrons, the Extirpation always remained a collection of individuals rather than becoming a genuine institution. Lacking a firm bureaucratic base, it never attained the self-perpetuating power of the Inquisition. Thus, if the Extirpation achieved considerable professionalization in terms of its repressive methods, its organization remained profoundly amateurish.

This amateurishness was particularly noticeable in its inability to resolve certain points of practice which its model, the Inquisition, had satisfactorily settled. The most important weakness of the Extirpation was its failure to exclude from its trials the testimony of known enemies of the accused. Inquisitorial hearings disallowed such testimony because its source would be suspect and, most important, it would undermine a conviction.[13] To ensure the exclusion of malicious testimony, the accused was required to submit a list of potential enemies whose evidence should not be admitted. An inevitable corollary was that he could not know the names of his accusers since, by adding their names to his list, he could have disqualified any evidence against him. The Extirpation was not so punctilious. Some visitors-general, far from excluding enemies, actively exploited them in order to secure denunciations of individuals. The defendant was not only permitted to know the identity of his accuser, he was also often physically confronted with him. The extirpators found that in this way they could extract information from both witness and defendant in a spiral of mutual denunciation.[14] Convinced of the collective guilt of all Indians, the extirpators accepted evidence from any source. It mattered

---

[13] Henry A. F. Kamen, *The Spanish Inquisition* (London: Weidenfeld & Nicolson, 1965), 179.

[14] See Karen Spalding, *Huarochirí: An Andean Society Under Inca and Spanish Rule* (Stanford: Stanford University Press, 1984), 257-58, for an example of the use of this tactic by the visitor-general Juan Sarmiento de Vivero.

little that the accusation was motivated by enmity as long as it brought to light otherwise hidden religious deviance.

This practice provided an excellent lever to open up cracks in the testimony of declarants who were reluctant to cooperate, but it had one great disadvantage. It removed an essential safeguard. A victim of the Inquisition could not add names to his list of enemies retrospectively. If testimony against him derived from a source omitted from his list, he could not contest the evidence on the grounds of enmity. A victim of the Extirpation, on the other hand, could attempt to disqualify any witness against him as soon as he learned his identity. The result was that many idolatry trials were invalidated by the accused's charge of capital enmity against key witnesses. Since it was clear in many cases that the witnesses were indeed manipulating the idolatry charge in order to settle old scores with the defendant, many cases were dismissed and the defendant absolved.

For example, the idolatry accusation leveled against the *kuraka* Tomás de Acosta was dismissed as soon as it became clear that it had been motivated by enmity. There was no proof that he had made offerings to *huacas* (native deities). However, there was evidence to indicate that the prime mover in the case, the *kuraka's* younger illegitimate brother, Antonio Pomalibiac, intended to exploit the idolatry charge in order to deprive his brother of the *cacicazgo* (native chieftainship) and secure it for himself. The defense rejected the accusation against Acosta on precisely the grounds that it was the result of a conspiracy to unseat the *kuraka*. Since the evident malice of the witnesses had nullified the accusation, Acosta was absolved and freed.[15]

Similarly, the idolatry accusation against the *kuraka* Gerónimo de Auquinivin was dismissed on the grounds that the charge had been made by his own nephew, whose ambition was to replace his uncle as native lord. The explicit confession of the fabrication of testimony on the part of the witnesses for the prosecution led to the absolution and

---

[15] "Causa de idolatría contra Don Tomás de Acosta, cacique de segunda persona de este repartimiento de Checras, Santiago de Maray, Provincia de Chancay," 1647, fols. 1-4, 10-11, 57, 61-64, 77, Archivo Arzobispal de Lima (hereinafter cited as AAL), Idolatrías 2 (4:13).

release of the accused.[16] Likewise, the idolatry trial against the two *kurakas* Miguel Menacho and Juan de Guzmán was suspended since it originated in the accusation made by a rival for the *cacicazgo*. When the case was transferred to Lima, Menacho pointed out that he had been in litigation with the chief witness against him for more than ten years over the *cacicazgo*. In the absence of clear proof of idolatry, Menacho's defense that the denunciation was motivated by animosity was upheld and he was absolved.[17]

Such an outcome was the rule in cases where ill will was perceived to be the primary determinant of an accusation of idolatry. The dismissal of such charges became more frequent in the later seventeenth century and early eighteenth century as more cases were transferred from the provinces to Lima. In the capital, at the hearings under the auspices of the *provisor*, greater emphasis was accorded to empirical evidence and legal formalities, a process which encouraged an increasingly explicit rejection of denunciations motivated purely by personal enmity. Whereas the most zealous visitors-general of the mid-seventeenth century, such as Juan de Sarmiento and Bernardo de Noboa, had been indifferent to the motives of witnesses as long as idolatry was uncovered, the authorities in Lima were increasingly unprepared to convict on testimony clearly rooted in malice. Unlike the visitors-general, the archbishop's officials had no vested interest in proving the existence of idolatry in order to justify their enterprise and reap the rewards. The rejection of evidence inspired by personal enmity undermined the foundations of the Extirpation. The failure even to convict offenders, let alone reform them, hardly represented a serious method of enforcing religious orthodoxy. Native exploitation of idolatry trials as a means of attacking their enemies and settling their own

---

[16] "Autos hechos por Juan Gutiérrez de Aguilar, cura de Pira y Cajamarquilla contra indios por idolatría, San Gerónimo de Pampas, Provincia de Huaylas," 1646, fols. 10, 17v, 26v, 45, 76, 85-91, AAL, Idolatrías 2 (6:8).

[17] "Causa contra Don Miguel Menacho y Don Juan de Guzmán, caciques principales del repartimiento de Huamantanga, Provincia de Canta," 1696, fol. 3, AAL, Idolatrías 12 (2:33). See also Biblioteca Nacional, Lima, B1400, "Por las preguntas siguientes se examinan los testigos que fueron presentados por parte de Don Juan de Campos Vilcatapayo, principal del pueblo de San Pedro de Quipan del repartimiento de Huamantanga, Provincia de Canta, en los autos que sigue con Don Juan de Guzmán y Don Miguel Menacho sobre el cacicazgo y gobierno de dicho repartimiento," Lima, 1695.

scores rendered the Extirpation ineffective in its primary purpose: the control and punishment of deviant religious behavior.

If the failure to forbid the testimony of known enemies created the opportunity for Indians themselves to pervert the original purpose of the trials, such a problem had not been entirely unanticipated. Those who had opposed the subjection of the Indians to the Inquisition had based their objections precisely on the fact that, since the Indians were so tempted to lie and avenge themselves on their enemies, they would use the institution for these purposes, and the tribunal would be overwhelmed with denunciations based on hatred. This is exactly the fate which befell the Extirpation, a fate from which it could have been saved by more professional rules. Thus, one of its fundamental weaknesses was that it failed to model itself sufficiently upon the Inquisition.[18]

As well as procedural anomalies, the Extirpation also suffered from ideological inconsistencies which did not beset the Inquisition. The first derived from the application of a model of the repression of heresy to victims whose status as heretics was never satisfactorily settled. Those who considered the Indians to be apostates believed that repression was a justifiable (though not exclusive) means of separating them from their idols, and thus, logically, argued for their subjection to the Inquisition. Francisco de Toledo, the viceroy of Peru (1569-81), advocated, in vain, the submission of native priests to the jurisdiction of the Inquisition. The mastermind of the first campaigns of extirpation of 1609-22, the Jesuit provincial Pablo José de Arriaga, clearly considered that the Indians' idolatries amounted to apostasy. The first edition of his extirpation manual drew upon the *Directorium inquisitorum* (1376), or inquisitors' manual, of the Catalan inquisitor Nicolás Eymerich, which linked idolatry with heresy and argued that all heretics should be under the jurisdiction of the Inquisition.[19] If Arriaga himself did not call upon the crown to revoke its decision and allow the subjection of the Indians to the Holy Office, he may have been prevented only by the traditional distrust between the Jesuits and

---

[18] For the arguments of the opponents of the Inquisition for the Indians, see Ruben Vargas Ugarte, *Historia de la iglesia en el Perú*, 5 vols. (Burgos: Aldecoa, 1953-62), 3:319.

[19] Nicolás Eymerich, *Directorium inquisitorum* (Montpellier: Impr. de F. Aviñon, 1821). See Duviols, *Cultura andina*, lxvii-lxviii.

the tribunal. Although the Jesuit generals had always opposed the tribunal's persecution of *conversos* (converts), the open hostility between the company and the Inquisition dated from the trial of the Jesuit Luis López in 1578. Since that time, no Jesuit in Lima had been allowed to take part in inquisitorial activities without the authorization of the superior. The creation of a parallel tribunal for the repression of native religion was an effective means of sidestepping both this controversy and the king's decrees on the Indians and the Inquisition. At the same time, an alternative tribunal entirely under archiepiscopal control must have seemed the most attractive option to Archbishop Lobo Guerrero since inquisitorial jurisdiction would have impinged upon his own freedom of action.

Even so, later advocates of the Extirpation urged the king to confer jurisdiction over the Indians to the Holy Office. In 1626, the archbishop of Lima, Gonzalo de Campo (1625-26), advised the king to place Indian idolatries under the jurisdiction of the Inquisition. He recognized that the tribunal's procedures and punishments in Indian cases would naturally vary from those in Spanish cases, so he considered it appropriate to inspire in the Indians "fear and terror." Indeed, this was the only method by which the "plague of idolatry" would be extinguished.[20] Hernando de Avendaño wrote to the king in 1651, and again in 1653, asserting that the most effective method of extirpation would be to subject the Indian *kurakas* to inquisitorial supervision. He insisted that his purpose was not to deprive the bishops of their jurisdiction but to persuade them to share it with the Holy Office.[21] If the Indians never were transferred to inquisitorial jurisdiction, it was because the ambiguity of their status was never resolved. Throughout the colonial period, despite the passage of several generations, they never ceased to be regarded as "New Christians."[22]

---

[20] Letter of Archbishop Gonzalo de Campo to the king, October 8, 1626, AGI, Lima 302.

[21] Letter of Hernando de Avendaño to the king, August 5, 1653, AGI, Lima 332.

[22] As late as 1686, Sancho de Andrade, the bishop of Huamanga (1682-87), wrote to Pope Innocent XI, requesting that, as more than one and a half centuries had passed since preaching had begun in Peru, the Indians should no longer be considered neophytes and should be subjected to the jurisdiction of the Inquisition along with the Spaniards. The request was not granted. See Vargas Ugarte, *Historia de la iglesia*, 3:13, 319-20.

Because the Indians were neophytes, religious repression had to be accompanied by pastoral instruction. Thus, the Extirpation differed from the Inquisition in that it attempted to combine a repressive function with a didactic one. The campaigns of 1609-22 were accompanied by a well-organized pedagogic policy, with preaching in the vernacular and persuasive pastoral activity. The visitors-general were always accompanied by two or three Jesuit priests and the ecclesiastical trials were preceded by a popular mission consisting of twelve sermons on the principal themes of Christianity. Arriaga gave details of the missionary work of the Jesuits and discussed the need of both visitors-general and Jesuit priests to persuade the Indians to surrender their idols.[23] However, these two functions sat rather uneasily together and left the true purpose of the Extirpation highly ambiguous.

Pedro de Villagómez revealed in his own writings the unresolved contradiction between these two aspects of the Extirpation. In his *Carta pastoral* of 1649, he observed that the visitations were more about "hearts" than "bodies," about "hard work" than "force," and "pity" rather than "justice," and so it would be better to replace the use of "judicial apparatus and authority" with teaching, sermons, and confessions. In this way the visitors-general could act as "fathers and teachers" rather than "judges or investigators."[24] Yet, in 1654, in a letter to the king, he explained that the function of the visitors-general was not to be "preachers" but "principally to be judges" and that "they should proceed in the manner of the Holy Office, publishing their edicts, carrying out their enquiries, compiling their cases, listening to declarants, and pronouncing and executing their sentences."[25]

As long as the aim of the judicial process remained the physical destruction of *huacas* and the punishment of native priests, the priority ultimately lay with repression rather than pedagogy. Since these two goals were fundamentally incompatible, the pedagogy inevitably became

---

[23] Arriaga, "La extirpación," 242.

[24] Pedro de Villagómez, *Carta pastoral de exhortación e instrucción contra las idolatrías de los indios del arzobispado de Lima*, Colección de libros y documentos referentes a la historia del Perú, vol. 12, Carlos A. Romero and Horacio H. Urteaga, eds. (Lima: Sanmartí, 1919), 180.

[25] Letter of Archbishop P. de Villagómez to the king, August 24, 1654, AGI, Lima 303.

"a pedagogy of fear."[26] Despite its pastoral pretensions, the Extirpation always lay closer to the Inquisition than to missionary activity. This exposed the fundamental contradiction at its heart: whereas the decision to profess Christianity was recognized to be a voluntary choice, the Extirpation used repression to force the Indians to be good Christians.

If the first fundamental contradiction underlying the ideology of the Extirpation was the ambiguity of the Indians' status as heretics, the second was the assimilation of native religious offenders to the Spanish category of *hechicero* (sorcerer). The *hechicero* was the practitioner of *hechicería*, the superstitious manipulation of occult forces in order to secure effects in the real world that were beyond the realms of natural science. Because, from the earliest days of evangelization, Andean native priests and shamans were classified as *hechiceros*, they assumed in the eyes of their persecutors the typical characteristics of the peninsular *hechicero*. In Spain, the *hechicero* was considered by most educated clerics to be a fraud and a trickster; his claim to possess genuine supernatural powers was largely treated with derision and contempt. Hence, when this classification was imposed upon the Andean priest, he too acquired the status of charlatan. The Spanish persecutors of Andean religion were characterized by the same scepticism and incredulity that was typical of the repressors of the peninsular *hechicero*. While on the one hand native practitioners were labeled as heretics, which should have demanded severe penalties, on the other hand they were designated as *hechiceros*, who, by common consent, were not heretics but charlatans. This inconsistency subverted the association of idolatry with heresy, and of native practitioners with both.

Unlike experts in much of the rest of Europe, the inquisitors of metropolitan Spain exhibited profound scepticism as to the reality of the supernatural powers which *hechiceros* attributed to themselves. Although the peninsular Inquisition rigorously pursued blasphemers, bigamists, Judaizers, and Protestants, it devoted very little of its time to *hechiceros*. Those offenders who claimed to possess diabolical

---

[26] For the "pedagogy of fear," see Bartolomé Bennassar, "Modelos de la mentalidad inquisitorial: métodos de su 'pedagogía del miedo,'" in *La Inquisición española y mentalidad inquisitorial*, Angel Alcalá, ed. (Barcelona: Ariel, 1983), 174-79.

powers were treated by the Holy Office as relatively trivial. The comparatively light punishments imposed upon them demonstrate that the Inquisition implicitly denied the reality of many of the accusations against them.[27] Similarly, the Andean branch of the orthodox Inquisition treated *hechiceros* as deceitful tricksters rather than genuine practitioners of diabolical arts. The account of trials by the Tribunal of Lima for the years 1647-48 referred to "frivolous superstitions and sorcery which tend more to be feminine tricks and deceptions to cheat people out of their money and do not imply any suspicion of heresy or pact with the Devil."[28]

The Extirpation inherited from the Inquisition this tradition of incredulity and scepticism about the supposed powers of *hechiceros*, but applied it to a fundamentally different type of practitioner, the native Andean shaman. All commentators concurred in designating the native religious practitioner as *hechicero*. As early as the 1580s, the first extirpator of native religion in Peru, the secular priest Cristóbal de Albornoz, identified the native Andean priest with the figure of the *hechicero*, attributing the responsibility for the preservation and evangelization of native religion to the *hechiceros huacamayos*, those individuals charged by their communities with the upkeep of the native deities.[29] The native chronicler, Felipe Guaman Poma de Ayala, followed Albornoz in assimilating priests of native religion to the

---

[27] For inquisitorial scepticism and incredulity concerning the powers of *hechiceros*, see, for example, Gustav Henningsen, *The Witches' Advocate* (Reno: University of Nevada Press, 1980); the works of Julio Caro Baroja: *Las brujas y su mundo*, 9th ed. (Madrid: Alianza, 1990), *El Señor Inquisidor y otras vidas por oficio*, 3rd ed. (Madrid: Alianza 1983), and *Vidas mágicas e Inquisición* (Madrid: Taurus, 1967); Carmelo Lisón Tolosana, *Brujería, estructura social y simbolismo en Galicia* (Madrid: Akal, 1987); H. A. F. Kamen, "Notas sobre brujería y sexualidad y la Inquisición" in Alcalá, *La Inquisición española*, 226-36; Juan Blázquez Miguel, *Inquisición y brujería en la Yecla del siglo xviii* (Yecla: Ayuntamiento patr. cultura, 1984). Caro Baroja has identified the background of the inquisitors as the determinant of their scepticism. Possibly it was their training in canon law rather than in pure theology which made rationalism rather than speculation their strength. C. Baroja, *Vidas mágicas*, 20-21; *El Señor Inquisidor*, 194-95.

[28] Archivo Histórico Nacional, Madrid, Inquisición Lima, libro 1031, fol. 338.

[29] Cristóbal de Albornoz, "Instrucción para descubrir todas las huacas del Perú y sus camayos y haciendas," (1583, 1584) *Fábulas y mitos de los incas*, Henrique Urbano and P. Duviols, eds., Crónicas de América 48 (Madrid: Historia 16, 1989), 172-73.

32   COLONIAL LATIN AMERICAN HISTORICAL REVIEW   WINTER 1994

category of *hechicero*, characterizing them as *hechiceros mentirosos* (false sorcerers).[30] The Jesuits Pablo José de Arriaga and Bernabé Cobo refused to acknowledge a real demonic presence in the work of *hechiceros* and considered that the vast majority of practitioners were merely ineffective charlatans.[31]

This scepticism became the most important factor in determining how Andean religious deviants were to be tried and punished. The healing activities of native *curanderos* (folk healers), for example, were not worthy of serious punishment because they were considered inefficacious. The principal accusation against native *curandero* Agustín Carbajal was not healing with herbs but "leading other Indians to believe" that he was a fortune teller and a clairvoyant. His defense argued that Indians very often cured and availed themselves of "other tricks" in order to alleviate their poverty. The sentence against him confirmed that his offenses had been mere lies with no pact with the devil, and he was condemned to only six months service at the hospital of Huánuco. If scepticism about the reality of diabolical contracts led Carbajal's interrogators to discount the likelihood of a genuine diabolical pact, his actions could only be judged as hollow and ineffective. His healing activities became simply one example of a monstrous fraud he had perpetrated upon the Indians.[32]

Another defendant, Pedro Guamboy, was admonished for his belief that his communications with a sacred rock had enabled him to fly through the air. He was also reprimanded for his conviction that he could deprive people of their lives by making magic with the earth where they had left their footprints. His co-defendant María Inés was similarly censured for having "given the impression" that she was a diviner and for "leading innocents to believe" that she had done them some harm by occult means. The guilt of these offenders lay not in any genuine demonic pact, but in their superstitious beliefs about their own capabilities. The characteristic scepticism of the extirpators manifested

---

[30] Felipe Guaman Poma de Ayala, *El primer nueva corónica y buen gobierno*, John V. Murra and Rolena Adorno, eds., 3 vols. (Mexico D.F.: Siglo Veintiuno, 1980), 1:253.

[31] Arriaga, *La extirpación*, 205-9, 249; B. Cobo, *Historia del nuevo mundo*, in *Obras*, Biblioteca de Autores Españoles, 2 vols., no. 91-92 (Madrid: Atlas, 1956), 2:227-30.

[32] "Causa contra Agustín Carbajal, León de Huánuco," 1662, no folio nos., AAL, Idolatrías 6 (3:3).

itself in an emphasis upon the sinful beliefs of the defendants rather than upon the alleged outcome of their acts.[33]

Other declarants were similarly ridiculed by their incredulous interrogators. When Felipe Cupeda recounted how he had entered a *huaca* and maintained conversations with the spirits therein, he was instructed not to believe in foolish dreams which could only have originated from sunstroke. Cupeda's interrogator was convinced of the man's sincerity but discounted the possibility of genuine supernatural intervention. The only alternative was a sleeping fantasy induced by the hot sun, in which case the sin lay in the subject's belief in the reality of imaginary events, rather than any genuine contact with supernatural beings.[34]

If the practitioner of Andean religion was equated with the *hechicero*, it is logical that, in practice, he was not punished as a dangerous heretic but rather as a deceitful fraud. But the willingness of prosecutors to impose lighter punishments on native offenders who admitted to the fraudulent character of their practices undermined the function of legal trials as an effective deterrent to religious deviance, and convictions for religious offenses were subverted by official scepticism.

By their insistence on interpreting the actions of native offenders exclusively according to the dichotomy of fraud/diabolical pact, the extirpators signaled the limits of their ability or willingness to comprehend indigenous religious experiences on their own terms. Trickery or alliance with Satan were the only two alternative explanations available to the defendants. There was no third possibility of considering their claims as valid in their particular context. It was precisely this option which the extirpators sought to eradicate, because, in their view, it allowed the offender to remain on dangerously ambiguous ground. For, if the native religious system was to be replaced by Christianity, the psychological hold of the native priest over the mass of the population had to be destroyed. After all, if the Indians remained convinced of the literal reality of the priest's powers, it would be very difficult to overcome the sense of fear and respect that

---

[33] "Causa de hechicería contra los indios de San Gerónimo de Sallan," fols. 10r-13v, 57r-58v., AAL, Idolatrías 6 (5:8).

[34] "Causa de hechicería contra los indios del pueblo de San Gerónimo de Sallan," fols. 1v-2r, 18v-19r., AAL, Idolatrías 6 (5:7).

he commanded. So the exigencies of evangelization encouraged the devaluation of the significance of the indigenous priest and the exclusion of the possibility that he manipulated genuine supernatural powers.

The flaw of such a strategy was that it failed to recognize that Andean realities might be different from European ones. Native priests, by virtue of their privileged status as intermediaries with the supernatural, could not be so easily divested of their powers. There always remained a fundamental difference between the European witch/sorcerer and the South American shaman which made the imposition of the category of *hechicero* wholly inappropriate. By definition, European witchcraft was deviant; witches were thought to be those whose acts were abhorrent and the very negation of everything decent. But while the European witch was an outcast of society, the Andean priest, on the contrary, lay at its very center. In Europe, witchcraft was attributed to the marginalized members of society: the weak, the poor, the old, the disadvantaged. By contrast, the Andean shaman was neither marginalized nor weak, but powerful and influential. By definition, he was (and is) "the one who possesses an extraordinary amount of what is most desirable," a quality in the Andes which is often called *sami* or *samay*.[35] The power of the Andean shaman would never be broken by denying an efficacy of which the Indians themselves were never in any doubt. Since official incredulity encouraged Spaniards to perceive the Andean native priest as a powerless, self-deluded individual, the very real power which he possessed as the spiritual intermediary of his community remained unacknowledged and hence unchallenged.

Thus, the Andean terrain did not quite fit the map of the extirpators' intellectual constructs. Ultimately the Extirpation was flawed, not only because the model of the Inquisition was poorly applied, but, more profoundly, because it was not appropriate for the different task which lay before the repressor of Andean religion. The most fundamental difference between the Inquisition and the Extirpation lay in the identity of their victims. The Inquisition functioned mainly in towns and pursued individuals (Spaniards, mestizos, Blacks, mulattos) who, by definition, were already substantially integrated into

---

[35] Frank Salomon, "Shamanismo y política en la última época colonial del Ecuador," *Revista cultural del Banco Central del Ecuador* 21b (1985):505-6.

Spanish culture. As a percentage of the total population, their numbers were small and hence controllable. As a considerable minority, they comprised a "natural" class of religious deviants, whom it was relatively easy to isolate from the mainstream of their society. The small numbers of unrepentant heretics (those who denied, boasted of, or relapsed into their activities) could be liquidated in order to prevent the contamination of the bulk of good Christians; the contrite offenders (including *hechiceros*) could be rehabilitated. Bartolomé Bennassar has indicated that the power of the Inquisition lay less in the severity of its physical punishments than in the psychological weapons it could employ. The most potent elements of its armory were the use of secrecy, the threat of misery (the threat of deprivation of life and material goods was more effective than its application), and the memory of infamy.[36] The bestowal of infamy exploited the offender's fear of exclusion from society and became a powerful incentive to conform. At the same time, it clearly demarcated the deviant from the non-deviant and established social sanctions for crossing the divide. Because offenders had departed from the norms generally accepted by their fellows, they were despised by the general population, and so, while their fate might excite curiosity as a public spectacle, it aroused little sympathy. The public punishment of an offender acted as an exemplary warning to others not to stray from the religious practices prescribed by elite society. Thus, the status of the heretic as outcast encouraged him to return to the fold before it was too late and discouraged others from falling into religious deviance. The success of the Inquisition lay in the fact that its norms were recognized both by the elite which imposed conformity and by the society of which the offender formed a part.

These conditions were not replicated in the context within which the Andean Extirpation was forced to function. First, the Extirpation differed from the Inquisition in terms of the sheer numbers of its potential victims. Almost the entire native population of the viceroyalty practiced some form of native religious ceremonies, and so, paradoxically, every Indian was a religious deviant. However, it was impossible to "relax" (the transfer of prisoners to the secular arm for punishment) the entire population without causing a rebellion which

---

[36] For the techniques of the Inquisition, see Bennassar, "Modelos de la mentalidad inquisitorial," 174-79.

would destroy Spanish rule. Nor was it possible to remove the deviant from his society without imprisoning all the Indians, so in the attempt to replicate the stark opposition of heretic and Christian community, the Extirpation was forced to drive a theoretical cleavage between the mass of the Indians and the figure of the *hechicero*. But this figure was a Spanish invention and its abstract differentiation from the rest of the community did not reflect Andean realities. Whereas the heretic in peninsular Spain was a genuine outsider, reviled by society, the Andean religious specialist lay at the center of his community. Subjection to an idolatry trial did not provoke the ostracism by the community which was characteristic of the treatment given to the victim of the Inquisition. Indeed, the victim's reputation might instead only be enhanced. The very fact that he had challenged the Christian hegemony sufficiently to provoke the wrath of the visitors-general may have convinced his potential clients that he was clearly a force with whom to reckon. The attempt to expose the specialist to the stigma of infamy could backfire. Furthermore, by contrast with Spain, where the punishment of the heretic evoked rejection of the nonconformist, in the Andes the punishment of the native priest evoked a sense of identification with the victim. Designation as an outcast by the dominant elite did not imply rejection by the offender's peers, since the victims of the Extirpation did not share the cultural norms of their persecutors.

As has been shown, the Extirpation differed fundamentally from the Inquisition in that it primarily persecuted individuals who inhabited rural communities and who, by definition, were not culturally integrated. Hence, the persecution suffered by its victims (which in itself was never as harsh as that of the heretical victims of the Inquisition) was negated, or at least counterbalanced, by the spiritual sustenance provided by the solidarity of the community behind the individual offender. Whereas the victim of the Inquisition suffered twice over, firstly from the rejection of the elite and secondly from that of his peers, the victim of the Extirpation suffered while fortified by the moral support of his society. Indeed, it was better to break the norms of the alien elite rather than those of his own community, for which the consequences, in terms of both human and divine wrath, were infinitely more terrifying. For these reasons, the technique of infamy, so effective for the Inquisition, was not a weapon which could be easily employed in the Andean context. The alternative cultural inheritance of the victims of the Extirpation conferred a communally accepted validity on their religious behavior which was not available to the victims of the Inquisition. The failure of the Extirpation lay, then, in the fact that the norms of the Spanish dominant elite and those of Indian society did not coincide, but contradicted one another. If the victims of the Extirpation chose to conform to the norms of their own society, it could hardly be otherwise when, in reality, it was the Spaniards who were the true religious "deviants" in Peru, and not the Indians.

The strength of Andean religious norms not only neutralized the effectiveness of the weapon of infamy but also eliminated the weapon of secrecy. If the extirpators dispensed with the juridical safeguards of the Holy Office (the anonymity of accusers, the exclusion of testimony of enemies), it was because these restrictions would have paralyzed the repression of such a ubiquitous phenomenon as native religious practices. Such practices were not the preserve of an isolated few, but were the common inheritance of most of the indigenous population. In a sense, the Extirpation could not afford the Inquisition's scruples if it was to uncover the "true" extent of departure from Christian norms. Klor de Alva has stressed that the inquisitorial techniques of random investigation and selective punishment rendered the institution a poor mechanism for effectively regulating vast numbers of unacculturated Indians. It was for this reason that the "Indian Inquisition" in Mexico was abandoned.[37]

A mere technology of repression was wholly inadequate to create a comprehensive "disenchantment" of the Andean religious world. The native religious universe could not be divested of its meaning without the transfer of "mystery" to other spheres, in particular the rites of the church—something which could only be achieved by intense missionary activity. The physical destruction of *huacas* did not prevent their survival in purely spiritual form, or through association with those indestructible repositories of divine power which lay in natural phenomena. The Jesuit Francisco de Patiño highlighted the dilemma facing the extirpators when he recounted how an Indian asked him: "Father, are you tired of taking our idols from us? Take away that mountain if you can, since that is the God that I

---

[37] See Klor de Alva, "Colonizing Souls," 12-15.

38   COLONIAL LATIN AMERICAN HISTORICAL REVIEW   WINTER 1994

worship."[38] Mountains have remained, until this day, receptacles of irresistible forces, whether benevolent or hostile, and whether of Andean or Spanish origin. The sacred Andean landscape could not be obliterated.[39] The last redoubt of the native religious system lay not in the purely physical world but in the imagination. The failure of the Extirpation to breach this fortress and "colonize the imaginary" ensured the failure of the enterprise.[40] The construction of a new sacred universe to replace the old one was a task that was well beyond the competence of the inquisitorial model.

---

[38] Letter of Francisco de Patiño to Archbishop P. de Villagómez, October 14, 1648, printed in Villagómez, *Carta pastoral*, 278. The planting of crosses on such indestructible numinous sites merely confirmed their sacred status in the eyes of the Indians. See Michael J. Sallnow, *Pilgrims of the Andes: Regional Cults in Cusco* (Washington, D.C.: Smithsonian Institution Press, 1987), 52.

[39] William Christian spoke of a process of "paganization" of Christianity whereby rural pre-Christian notions of a sacred landscape reasserted themselves over an initially cathedral-, parish-, and church-centered religion. See Christian, *Apparitions in Late Medieval and Renaissance Spain* (Princeton: Princeton University Press, 1981), 20. In the Andean context, Sallnow has shown how the numinous power of ancient sacred peaks of the Andes is manifested in the cult of advocations of Christ which lie upon them. For example, the cult of *Señor de Qoyllur Rit'i* is explicitly associated with the great mountain peak and deity, *Apu Ausangate*. Similarly, the sanctuary of *Señor de Wank'a* in the Vilcanota valley lies on the slopes of *Apu Pachatusan*. The hallowing of such rocks through miraculous theophany has assimilated unique sites of the Andean sacred into the Catholic cult. Thus, the landscape was not de-sacralized in the colonial period, but, on the contrary, re-sacralized. Sallnow, *Pilgrims*, 54, 79, 235-59, 269.

[40] Serge Gruzinski coined the expression "the colonization of the imaginary." See Gruzinski, *La colonisation de l'imaginaire: sociétés indigènes et occidentalisation dans le Mexique espagnol XVI-XVIII siècle* (Paris: Gallimard, 1988); Carmen Bernand-Muñoz and S. Gruzinski, *De l'idolâtrie: une archéologie des sciences réligieuses* (Paris: Seuil, 1988), 161, 176.

15
Pachacuti:
Miracles, Punishments, and
Last Judgement—Visionary Past and
Prophetic Future in Early Colonial Peru
Sabine MacCormack

THE SPANISH INVASION OF PERU, WHICH BEGAN IN 1532, and the resulting collapse of the Inca empire, initiated a long process of still continuing political, religious, and cultural transformation. Equally long lasting has been the process of reflection and questioning by both the conquered peoples of the Andes and the conquering Spaniards concerning the rationale and the import of this transformation. Having mastered their complex natural environment and created a series of advanced civilizations without contact or interference from the outside world, Andeans were for the first time in their long history exposed to ideas and styles of action entirely new and alien. The Spanish newcomers on their side had become aware of the sharp contrast between themselves and the peoples of America during their earlier occupation of the Caribbean and invasion of Mexico. Yet, in the Andes, they found forms of religious expression and political organization for which neither the Caribbean nor Mexico had prepared them. Within a century of the invasion, however, the newcomers in Peru had acquired a knowledge of Andean thought and conduct that enabled them to exercise effective political control. Andeans, for their part, had not only adjusted to the new dominant culture but had also taken initiatives in adapting many of its elements for their own use.[1]

It is all too easy to view the outcome in straightforward and simple terms, and to suppose that elements of Christianity and Hispanic culture and politics came to coexist with an Andean substratum in some kind of syncretism. As I will endeavor to demonstrate, this is not what happened. First, the convergence of Andean and Spanish ideas and strategies of political action was riddled throughout by tensions and conflicts that are still alive today. Second, while Andeans did accommodate

Research contributing to this article was funded by the Center for Latin American Studies of Stanford University, which made available to me a grant from the Andrew W. Mellon Foundation, and by the Pew Memorial Trust. To both, I extend my thanks. I would also like to thank Professor Paul Robinson, who commented on an earlier draft of this article, and the four anonymous scholars who evaluated it for the *AHR*. Their corrections and comments were most helpful in preparing this final version.

[1] For the connection between knowledge and power, or political control, especially over colonial societies, see Edward W. Said, *Orientalism* (New York, 1978); for the Spanish impact on the Andes, see P. Duviols, *La Lutte contre les religions autochtones dans le Pérou colonial: "L'Extirpation de l'idolatrie" entre 1532 et 1660* (Lima, 1971); N. Wachtel, *La Vision des vaincus: Les Indiens du Pérou devant la Conquète espagnole 1530–1570* (Paris, 1971); Steve J. Stern, *Peru's Indian Peoples and the Challenge of Spanish Conquest: Huamanga to 1640* (Madison, Wis., 1982); K. Spalding, *Huarochirí: An Andean Society under Inca and Spanish Rule* (Stanford, Calif., 1984).

Pachacuti: *Miracles, Punishments, and Last Judgment*   961

themselves to the invaders by sheer force of necessity, they also persisted in constructing their own logically coherent and complete interpretation of their world and their experience. Andean culture remained intelligible from within itself after the invasion, just as it had been before that event.[2] At the same time, a deeper understanding of the complex process whereby Andeans confronted the realities of alien invasion and government can be achieved by taking into account the mental furniture those aliens brought with them. I here study one aspect of this process. I juxtapose the Andean concept of *pachacuti*, which describes the termination and reversal of an established order whether past, present, or future, with the Christian concept of the Last Judgment, a definitive day of reckoning at the end of time. When thinking of *pachacuti* after the invasion, Andeans took cognizance of the Last Judgment, but they did so on their own terms.

Evidence presented here comes from Andean and Hispanic as well as European sources. Applying to this field a methodology I have developed elsewhere, I consider historical, mythic, and theological texts side by side with visual images so as to arrive at a three-dimensional representation of the complex reality that speaks to us from the Andean past.[3] The period covered extends from 1532 to the early nineteenth century, when the Peruvian viceroyalty gained independence from Spain. But the core of my argument focuses on the years between 1565, when the Spaniards successfully suppressed the first major revolt in the Andes, and 1615, when the Andean noble and historian Phelipe Guaman Poma de Ayala completed his *Corónica*. This work, a history of Peru from the Creation to the author's own time, is one of the most important available sources for the study of Andean thinking during the early colonial period and is central to this inquiry.[4] While the passing of every generation removed the empire of the Incas to an ever more remote past, Andean ways of thought, forms of social and political organization, and strategies of political action remained continuous with that past. This is not to say that they did not change profoundly. Continuity of Andean traditions stood in constant tension with radical discontinuity. The juxtaposition of *pachacuti* with Last Judgment constitutes one aspect of this tension. We will begin with the event that initiated the tension, the death of the Inca ruler Atawallpa in Cajamarca in

---

[2] On syncretism in the Andes, see M. Marzal, *La Transformación religiosa Peruana* (Lima, 1983); see also his *Estudios sobre religión campesina* (Lima, 1977), esp. 108–30. Anthropologists in particular have disagreed with such an interpretation. See, for instance, J. W. Bastien, *Mountain of the Condor: Metaphor and Ritual in an Andean Ayllu* (Prospect Heights, Ill., 1978); Gary Urton, *At the Crossroads of the Earth and the Sky: An Andean Cosmology* (Austin, Tex., 1981); B. Condori and R. Gow, *Kay Pacha* (Cuzco, 1982); T. Bouysse-Cassagne and P. Cassagne, "Volcan indien, volcan chrétien: A propos de l'éruption du Huaynaputina en l'an 1600. Pérou méridional," *Journal de la Société des Américanistes*, 70 (1984): 43–68; M. J. Sallnow, *Pilgrims of the Andes: Regional Cults in Cuzco* (Washington, D.C., 1987); T. Platt, "The Andean Soldiers of Christ: Confraternity Organisation, the Mass of the Sun and Regenerative Warfare in Rural Potosí (18th–20th Centuries)," *Journal de la Société des Américanistes*, 73 (1987): 139–91.

[3] S. MacCormack, *Art and Ceremony in Late Antiquity* (Berkeley, Calif., 1981); "Christ and Empire, Time and Ceremonial in Sixth Century Byzantium and Beyond," *Byzantion*, 52 (1982): 287–309; and "From the Sun of the Incas to the Virgin of Copacabana," *Representations*, 8 (1984): 30–60.

[4] See the study of R. Adorno, *Guaman Poma: Writing and Resistance in Colonial Peru* (Austin, Tex., 1986); see also R. Adorno, ed., *From Oral to Written Expression: Native Andean Chronicles of the Early Colonial Period* (Syracuse, N.Y., 1982); and S. Jakfalvi-Leiva, *Traducción, escritura y violencia colonizadora: Un Estudio de la obra del Inca Garcilaso* (Syracuse, N.Y., 1984).

962   *Sabine MacCormack*

1533. Nearly forty years later, when he was an old man, Pedro Pizarro, brother of the conqueror Francisco Pizarro, wrote down what he remembered of that time.

PEDRO PIZARRO RECALLED THAT, before the Inca Atawallpa was executed, he told some followers and ladies of his court, "even if the Spaniards were to kill him, he would return to them if only his body were not burned, because his Father the Sun would resurrect him." Indeed, Atawallpa allowed himself to be baptized lest his body be burned. In the normal course of events, a deceased Inca, his body carefully embalmed and clothed, continued his existence among the living. In Cuzco, the embalmed bodies (*mallqui*) of dead Incas all had their palaces and were assembled regularly to feast with the members of their lineages in the main square. However, matters did not turn out as Atawallpa had anticipated. As Pedro Pizarro recalled in haunting detail:

Once the Inca was dead . . . after some people had hanged themselves along with one of his sisters and other Indian ladies, saying that they were going to the other world to serve Atawallpa, two sisters remained alive and went about in deep mourning with drums and singing, telling the deeds of their husband. Then they awaited the time when the marquess left his dwelling and went to where Atawallpa used to be, and asked me to allow them to enter. Once inside, they began to call Atawallpa, looking for him everywhere, very carefully. But seeing that he did not answer them, they uttered a great cry of grief and left. I asked them what they were looking for, and they replied as I have told. I undeceived them and said that the dead did not return until the day of judgment.

Without fully realizing it, Pedro Pizarro had witnessed part of the long-established courtly ritual of an Inca's obsequies, curtailed though it had been by the unusual circumstances. During the first phase of this ritual, the lords and ladies of Cuzco searched and called out for the deceased in all the places he used to frequent when alive. After fifteen days, the most eminent of those present announced that the Inca was now dwelling with his Father the Sun. Later, certain individuals close to the deceased would kill themselves—which is what Pizarro witnessed. The ceremonial order also prescribed a procession of mourning ladies, their faces blackened with llama grease and ash and playing drums.[5] These were the ladies with whom Pizarro talked, and the same ladies had earlier performed an abbreviated version of the search for the dead Inca.

The supposition that the Inca could return was thus supported by the customary ceremonial. But Pizarro superimposed on this ceremonial and the Inca's abiding with his Father the Sun the Christian promise of resurrection at the end of time.

[5] Pedro Pizarro, *Relación del descubrimiento y conquista de los reinos del Perú*, G. Lohmann Villena, ed. (Lima, 1978), chap. 11, pp. 63 and 69–70; on Inca *mallquis* in Cuzco, see Miguel de Estete, "Relación del descubrimiento y conquista del Perú," in *Colección de libros y documentos referentes a la historia del Perú*, 2d ser., 8 (1924): 47, 54 and following; Pizarro, *Relación*, 10: 53. It was only as one generation of deceased Incas was added to the preceding that a specific deceased ruler would begin to recede into the past and become impersonalized. The process was identical for non-Inca lords; see R. T. Zuidema, "La Parenté et le culte des ancêtres dans trois communautés péruviennes," *Signes let langages des Amériques: Recherches amérindiennes au Québec*, 3 (1973): 129–45, 133. On Inca funerary ceremonial, see Juan de Betanzos, *Suma y narración de los Incas* (Madrid, 1987), Book 1, chap. 31, 145; Book 1, chap. 39, 177; Juan de Santacruz Pachacuti Yamqui, *Antigüedades deste reyno del Perú*, in M. Jimenez de la Espada, ed., *Tres relaciones de antigüedades Peruanas* (Madrid, 1879), 278.

Indeed, since the Inca had been buried in the ground by a Christian cleric, to expect for him a resurrection of the Christian kind was not unreasonable.[6] But this is not what Andeans expected. One of Atawallpa's brothers stole his body from its grave in Cajamarca and bestowed on it the honors a *mallqui* traditionally received, hoping thereby to establish his own title to succeed the deceased as Inca. Although the troubled times foiled this plan, a cluster of events and ideas associated with Atawallpa suggested that his presence in the world would continue, though not necessarily as a *mallqui* and not in any Christian sense. Some of Atawallpa's followers remembered after his death that he had instructed them to await him in his capital city of Quito, where he would appear to them as a serpent. This promise originated in an episode some three years earlier when Atawallpa had been captured by his Cañari enemies but was able to escape from the prison because, so he maintained, his god had turned him into a serpent, *amaru*. Possibly, this was why Atawallpa's palace in Cajamarca, inside which was a serpent carved in stone, was known as the House of the Serpent. Atawallpa was not the first Inca to be associated with *amaru*. The divine double of the eighth Inca, Viracocha, bore the name Inca Amaru, and one of the Inca myths of origin recorded that the first Inca was a "son of the serpent, *amaru*." In Andean cosmology, *amaru* augured the disruption of order by political or natural catastrophe.[7] Atawallpa's capture first by the Cañari and then by the Spanish amounted to such catastrophes. At the same time, his promise to return as *amaru* suggests that catastrophe was not final.

A preoccupation with the death and return of the Inca continues in the Andes and has been formulated in a variety of ways. In the early seventeenth century, Guaman Poma de Ayala struggled to conceptualize the death of the Inca without a successor. Guaman Poma recorded separately both the death of Atawallpa, who was strangled, and the death of the Inca Tupa Amaru, who was beheaded in the main square of Cuzco in 1572, after centrally organized Andean resistance against the invaders had finally broken down. But, at the same time, he conflated these two events, by depicting both Atawallpa and Tupa Amaru as being decapitated (see Figures 1–2). He thus created a stereotyped, generalized representation for the Inca's death. This is the earliest surviving formulation of what was to become an ever-recurring theme in Andean drama and myth. A Quechua play, *The Tragedy of the Death of Inca Atawallpa*, extant in several different versions, was possibly

    [6] Pedro de Cieza de León, *Descubrimiento y conquista del Perú*, F. Cantú, ed. (Rome, 1979), hereafter, Cieza, *Descubrimiento*, chap. 54, compare 55; Betanzos, *Suma*, Book 2, chap. 26, 285.
    [7] On the fate of Atawallpa's body, see Betanzos, *Suma*, Book 2, chap. 26, 285–86. Atawallpa promises to return as serpent, Cieza, *Descubrimiento*, chap. 54; turns into serpent, Pedro de Cieza de León, *Señorío de los Incas*, C. Aranibar, ed. (Lima, 1967), chap. 72; on Atawallpa's palace, see F. Xerez, *Verdadera relación de la conquista del Perú*, C. Bravo, ed. (Madrid, 1985), 108; on the Inca as "son of serpent," see Phelipe Guaman Poma de Ayala, *Nueva corónica i buen gobierno*, eds. J. V. Murra and R. Adorno, 3 vols. (Madrid, 1987), 82. See also C. Bravo, "Revitalización del mito de origen en la etapa final de la historia incaica," *Proceedings of the 42nd International Congress of Americanists*, 4 (1976): 327–33. On the Inca Viracocha's double, see Pedro Sarmiento de Gamboa, *Historia Indica, Biblioteca de Autores Españoles*, 135, chap. 25, p. 230. On Andean cosmology, see J. Earls and I. Silverblatt, "La Realidad física y social en la cosmología andina," *Proceedings of the 42nd International Congress of Americanists*, 4 (1976): 299–325, 314 and following; Bouysse-Cassagne and Bouysse, "Volcan indien," 57–59.

964   *Sabine MacCormack*

CONQVISTA
CORTALE·LACAVESA·A
ATAGVALPA·INGA·VMATACVCHV

murio atagualpa
enla ciudad de caxa marca   jecomo

FIGURES 1–2. The end of the Inca empire as seen by Guaman Poma:
1. Death of Inca Atawallpa in Cajamarca, 1533. The executioners are soldiers of Pizarro's invading
army. *Nueva corónica*, 390.

Pachacuti: *Miracles, Punishments, and Last Judgment*   965

2. Death of Inca Tupa Amaru in Cuzco, 1572. Here, the executioners are the civilian administrators of the Spanish viceroyalty of Peru. But this difference to one side, Guaman Poma regarded the two executions as identical. In both cases, the Inca, wearing the imperial headband, holds a cross and dies as a Christian, that is, innocently. *Nueva corónica*, 451.

966   *Sabine MacCormack*

performed as early as 1555 in Potosí and is still performed in Andean villages.[8]
In many of these plays, the Inca Atawallpa dies by the sword, and the action ends
with a promise of his return. Similarly, the myths of Inkarrí—the King Inca—
promise that the Inca will return when his severed head will have rejoined his body
or grown a new body.[9]

These expectations, which arise specifically from the Spanish invasion of the
Andes, were continuous with an overall Andean system of ordering time that
predated the invasion. A variety of myths collected by the Spanish in different parts
of the Andes during the early colonial period described the Andean past and
future in terms of distinct epochs, each of which terminated in an upheaval.
Colonial sources often refer to these upheavals as *pachacuti*, and it is likely that the
term was also current before the invasion, even though this particular upheaval
endowed the concept of *pachacuti* with much greater prominence in Andean
awareness. The historian Garcilaso de la Vega, who was the son of an Inca royal
lady and a *conquistador*, and thus grew up speaking both Quechua and Spanish,
wrote of "*pachamcutin*, which is to say the world turns around. For the most part
[Andeans] say it when great things are turned from good to ill, and sometimes they
say it when things change from ill to good." The seventeenth-century lexicogra-
pher of Quechua, Diego Gonzalez Holguin, listed the term as *pachacuti* and
translates it as equivalent to *pacha ticra*, "the end of the world, or great destruction,
pestilence, perdition or loss." These Andean epochs were marked by the departure
and return of founding deities; the myth of the return of the Inca thus had
counterparts in the divine world. The Creator, Viracocha, had departed over the
ocean but promised to return. Christian missionaries, in an endeavor to make their
message more convincing, identified Tunupa from the Titicaca region, another
beneficent deity whose return was expected, with the apostle Thomas, who, so it
was suggested, had in former times preached in the Andes.[10]

[8] For the performance in Potosí in 1555, see Arzans de Orsua y Vela, *Historia de la Villa imperial de Potosí*, eds. L. Hanke and G. Mendoza, 3 vols. (Providence, R.I., 1965), Book 4, chap. 2 (2: 98). For an edition of one manuscript and translation into Spanish, see Jesus Lara, *Tragedia del fin de Atawallpa* (Cochabamba, 1951). Rogger Ravines, *Dramas coloniales en el Perú actual* (Lima, 1985), surveyed a number of contemporary performances; see also E. Gonzalez Carré and F. Rivera Pineda, "La Muerte del Inca en Santa Ana de Tusi," *Boletin del Instituto frances de estudios andinos*, 11 (1982): 19–36; M. Burga, *Nacimiento de una utopia: Muerte y resurreccion de los incas* (Lima, 1988), especially Part 1.

[9] See the remarkable study by Jan Szeminski, *La Utopía tupamarista* (Lima, 1984), 139–46; and R. T. Zuidema, "The Lion in the City: Royal Symbols of Transition in Cuzco," *Journal of Latin American Lore*, 9 (1983): 39–100, 68 and following. Different versions of the myth of Inkarrí appear in Juan M. Ossio, ed., *Ideología Mesiánica del mundo andino* (Lima, 1973), 217 and following, 461 and following; A. Ortiz Rescaniere, *De Adaneva a Inkarrí: Una Visión indigena del Perú* (Lima, 1973); F. Pease, "Una Version ecológica del mito de Inkarrí," in R. Hartmann and U. Oberem, eds., *Amerikanistische Studien: Festschrift für Hermann Trimborn*, 2 vols. (St. Augustin, 1979), 2: 136–39; and D. D. Gow, "The Roles of Christ and Inkarrí in Andean Religion," *Journal of Latin American Lore*, 6 (1980): 279–98. In general, A. Flores Galindo, *Europa y el Pais de los Incas: La Utopía andina* (Lima, 1986).

[10] On *pachacuti*, see Garcilaso de la Vega the Inca, *Comentarios reales de los Incas*, Biblioteca de Autores Españoles, 133 (Madrid, 1963), vol. 1, Book 5, chap. 28, p. 188; Diego Gonzalez Holguin, *Vocabulario de la lengua general de todo el Perú llamada lengua Quichua o del Inca* (Lima, 1608), "el fin del mundo, o grande destrucción, pestilencia, ruyna o perdida o daño común"; similarly, the *Vocabulario y phrasis en la lengua general de los Indios del Perú, llamada Quichua*, published by Antonio Ricardo (1586; rpt. edn., Lima, 1951), "ticra" being the noun of "ticrani," "bolver lo de dentro a fuera o bolver el rostro atras," s.v. "ticrani"; on the apostle Thomas in Peru, see Santacruz Pachacuti Yamqui, *Antigüedades deste reyno del Perú*, 236.

Pachacuti: *Miracles, Punishments, and Last Judgment*   967

Accounts of epochs ruled by different deities varied from place to place, although they shared certain features, in particular, the cataclysmic nature of the shift from one epoch to the next. Thus the historian Agustín de Zárate, who was in Peru as inspector of the imperial finances and who published his *History* in 1555, collected a myth from near the great oracle and sanctuary of Pachacamac on the coast of Peru, according to which Pachacamac had displaced the original Creator, Con, converted the people that Con had made into animals, and brought forth a new generation of men. Pachacamac "endured for many generations, until the Christians arrived in Peru, and then he never appeared again." The cycle of myths from Huarochirí, written down in the early seventeenth century, also describes conflicts between deities who ruled during succeeding epochs. Pariya Qaqa, who was identified with water and received sacrifices of *mullu* (sea shells), coca, and *tiqti* (maize), displaced Wallallu, who was identified with fire and received human sacrifices. The narrator of the myth identified this supernatural conflict with political and cultural upheaval, because he thought that Wallallu's people were the Yunga and that they had been expelled to Antisuyo along with their deity.[11]

The most detailed account of Andean epochs was composed in the early seventeenth century by Guaman Poma and was reiterated by the Franciscan historian of Peru, Fr. Buenaventura Salinas y Cordoba, who appears to have had access to Guaman Poma's text.[12] By that time, Andean concepts of time and history had already been modified by Hispanic and Christian concepts, so that Guaman Poma begins with a Christian vision of the Creation. Nonetheless, Guaman Poma saw the past in Andean terms. The last of the Andean historical epochs before the coming of the Spanish was that of the Inca, *Inca pacha runa*. "From their lineage and country the world was renewed," according to the Jesuit missionary José de Acosta.[13] Indeed, in one sense, each Inca brought on a new epoch. Thus, in 1542, the Inca keepers of historical records (*quipucamayos*), whom the royal official Cristóbal Vaca de Castro questioned, described the outset of Atawallpa's reign as a time when "they had to begin a new world afresh." This new beginning was also made explicit in one of Atawallpa's titles, Ticci Capac, "Original Ruler." An Inca's

[11] M. Bataillon, "Zárate ou Lozano? Pages retrouvées sur la religion peruvienne," *Caravelle*, 1 (1963): 11–28, 23; these chapters were omitted from all but the 1555 edition of Zárate and were rediscovered by Bataillon. For a collection of colonial texts on Andean origins, see H. Urbano, *Wiracocha y Ayar: Héroes y funciones en las sociedades andinas* (Cuzco, 1981), 3–31. For the myths of Huarochirí, see ed. and trans. G. Urioste, *Hijos de Pariya Qaqa: La Tradición oral de Waru Chiri* (Syracuse, N.Y., 1983), hereafter, *Waru Chiri*, 1.6, 6.73, 8.95–109. On the Yunga, and the conflict between Pariya Qaqa and Wallallu, see *Waru Chiri*, 1.6; 8.96 and following.

[12] Fr. Buenaventura was a page in the viceregal household from the age of nine in 1601, until 1615. In this capacity, he could have been approached by Guaman Poma to arrange for the transport of his manuscript to Spain. In this way, the numerous parallels between Guaman Poma's and Fr. Buenaventura's accounts of Andean origins, which involve many details not found in other sources, could be explained. See Buenaventura de Salinas y Cordova, *Memoriál de las historias del nuevo mundo Pirú* (1630; rpt. edn., Lima, 1957), *discurso* 1, chap. 1. On the Andean epochs, see J. Imbelloni, "La Tradición Peruana de las cuatro edades del mundo en una obra rarísima impresa en Lima en el año 1630," *Anales del Instituto de Etnografía*, 5 (1944): 55–94; and his *Religiosidad indígena americana* (Buenos Aires, 1979), 73–115.

[13] On the *Inca pacha runa*, see Guaman Poma, *Nueva corónica*, 79 and following, 367 [369]; José de Acosta, *Historia natural y moral de las Indias*, Edmundo O'Gorman, ed. (1590; Mexico, 1962), Book 1, chap. 25, "de su linaje y de su patria se abia renovado el mundo."

accession could thus be understood as a return of the world to its origins. So, apparently, could an Inca's death. Guaman Poma recorded that, when Tupa Amaru was executed, the Indians grieved for him, "Inca Vana Cauri, where have you gone?" The name by which they invoked their dead ruler, Guanacauri, was also a holy place, *huaca*, near Cuzco, which was associated with the first advent of the Incas in that region; moreover, a statue of Manco Capac that the Incas took with them into battle was also known as Guanacauri.[14] To call Tupa Amaru by the name that was borne both by an image of his earliest ancestor and by a primordial holy place makes clear the intimate connection and tension Andeans perceived between the origin and the overthrow of the established order.

A notable new beginning in the history of the Incas occurred in the mid-fifteenth century. At this time, the ruler Inca Yupanqui, renamed as Pachacuti because he saved Cuzco from the Chancas, laid the foundations of the Inca state as an empire.[15] Of this second founder, it was told that he had reentered the rock of Pacaritambo, the "place of emergence" of the Incas, and had come forth from there anew to inaugurate his governance. In this way, he imitated the example set by his mythic ancestor and predecessor, Manco Capac, who had also come forth from Pacaritambo. The name Pachacuti was thus explained to signify "he who turns or turns around or transforms the world," or "the turning about of time or the world." Another author called him "Pachacutec Yupanqui Capac Indichuri . . . turning about of the time, King Yupanqui, Son of the Sun."[16]

The term *pachacuti* thus not only described the duration and content of historical epochs but also interpreted present events as either restatements or reversals of the past. Faithful to this ordering principle, Guaman Poma observed that some kings are called Pachacuti because of the upheavals occurring in their reigns. Similarly, Pachacuti *runa* were the men who fought out the war between Guascar and his brother Atawallpa, which preceded the Spanish invasion. In effect, *pachacuti* in Guaman Poma's text is a synonym for disaster.[17] It was thus with good reason that Andeans used the concept of *pachacuti* when confronted with the

[14] *Relación de la descendencia, gobierno y conquista de los Incas*, J. J. Vega, ed. (Lima, 1974), 20, "de nuevo habian de comenzar"; for Ticci Capac, see *ibid* and p. 49; also Santacruz Pachacuti Yamqui, *Antigüedades deste reyno del Perú*, 322; on Tupa Amaru's death, see Guaman Poma, *Nueva corónica*, 451 [453]; on the statue of Manco Capac, see Santacruz Pachacuti Yamqui, *Antigüedades deste reyno del Perú*, 269. For the "beginning afresh" with each reign, see R. T. Zuidema, *The Ceque System of Cuzco: The Social Organisation of the Capital of the Inca* (Leyden, 1964), to be consulted along with J. H. Rowe, "La Constitución Inca del Cuzco," *Histórica* (Lima), 9 (1985): 35–73. *Huaca*, Quechua for holy place or object, is also spelled *guaca* in colonial sources. In the text of this article, I use *huaca* regardless of the spelling used in the original.
[15] See the study by Maria Rostworowski, *Pachacutec Inca Yupanqui* (Lima, [1953]).
[16] On the Inca Yupanqui at Pacaritambo, see Sarmiento de Gamboa, *Historia Indica, Biblioteca de Autores Españoles*, 135 (Madrid, 1965), chap. 30, p. 236; on the name Pachacuti, see Garcilaso de la Vega, *Comentarios*, 5, 28, "el que vuelve o el que trastorna o trueca el mundo"; Bernabé Cobo, *Historia del Nuevo Mundo, Biblioteca de Autores Españoles*, 92, Book 12, chap. 12 (Madrid, 1964), "vuelta del tiempo o del mundo"; Betanzos, *Suma*, 1.17, 83.
[17] Guaman Poma, *Nueva corónica*, 94, 109; see, further, the excellent discussion by R. Adorno, "The Rhetoric of Resistance: The 'Talking' Book of Felipe Guaman Poma," *History of European Ideas*, 6 (1985): 447–64, 456–57; Guaman Poma, 911 [925] with Szeminski, *La Utopía tupamarista*, 124 and following; Guaman Poma, 94, 109, 911 [925]; for a rebel lord in the time of Tupa Inca Yupanqui calling himself Pachacuti, see J. H. Rowe, "Probanza de los Incas nietos de conquistadores," *Histórica* (Lima), 9 (1985): 193–245, 198, 214, 225.

Spanish invasion, for the invasion marked the end of an epoch more radically than any preceding upheaval had done.

EUROPEANS, ON THEIR SIDE, WERE BLIND TO THIS ASPECT of Andean experience. Nonetheless, they in their own right were engaged in speculations about the nature of the last times and the end of history. According to a historiographical principle pioneered in the Western Roman empire by Augustine of Hippo and still widely used in seventeenth-century Europe, the incarnation of Christ had inaugurated the sixth age, which was to come to an end with Antichrist and a period of tribulation. This vision of history was graphically depicted in the German world chronicle of 1493, which circulated widely in the Spain of Charles V. Having brought the sixth age to its conclusion with portraits of the pope and emperor of the day, the illustrators added three further pictures referring to the seventh age. Here we see the fall of Antichrist: he descends to earth along with three devilish creatures, while a swordbearing angel bars any return to heaven. Below, the preaching of Antichrist is juxtaposed with that of the prophets Enoch and Elijah. Next, there is the resurrection of all flesh, represented, however, as the dance of death. Finally, at the Last Judgment, in an iconographic scheme that had earlier been used by some late medieval Flemish painters, whose work was greatly admired in Spain, the good enter heaven, and the wicked are driven into hell, the scene being dominated by Christ enthroned on a rainbow with the earth as his footstool (see Figures 3–4).[18] The message of these images is a moral one, exhorting the beholder to conduct life in such a way as to be found on the last day among the saved rather than the damned. Specific historical references are omitted.

But the last things and Antichrist could also be represented within a concrete context of current events, such as the capture of Constantinople by the Ottomans in 1453. The Ottoman sultan could thus be regarded as Antichrist, and this theory was capable of being underpinned by referring to the prophet Daniel's account of Gog and Magog.[19] In the eyes of the German reformers, however, Antichrist was the pope. In 1527, when the troops of Charles V sacked Rome, Protestant descriptions of Rome as the whore of Babylon and the pope as the incarnation of

[18] R. Schmidt, "*Aetates mundi*": Die Weltalter als Gliederungsprinzip der Geschichte," *Zeitschrift für Kirchengeschichte*, 67–68 (1955–57): 288–317. Hartmannus Schedel, *Liber Chronicarum* (Nurenberg, 1493), translated as *Register des Buchs der Croniken und Geschichten mit Figuren* (1493); rpt. edn., *Die Schedelsche Weltchronik*, R. Portner, ed. (Dortmund, 1979), fols. 263v–264; the Last Judgment, Fig. 4 of this article. For the rainbow throne, a pictorial rendering of Ezekiel 1.28 and John the Divine, *Apocalypse*, 4.3, see J. Fournée, *Le Jugement dernier: Essai d'exégèse d'une oeûvre d'art: Le Vitrail de la cathédrale de Coutances* (Paris, 1964), 28 and following. For Rogier van der Weyden's "Beaune Last Judgment" and the closely related "Last Judgment" in Gdansk attributed to Hans Memling, see K. B. McFarlane, *Hans Memling* (Oxford, 1971), 16–27. For an example of this Flemish iconography in sixteenth-century Spain, see E. Bermejo, *La Pintura de los primitivos flamencos en España* (Madrid, 1980), 1: 139–41, on Vrancke van der Stockt's "Redemption," Prado inventory 1888–1892, formerly attributed to van der Weyden; inventory 1891 is the "Last Judgment," Fig. 3 of this article. A useful survey and discussion of depictions of the Last Judgment is by C. Harbison, *The Last Judgement in Sixteenth-Century Northern Europe: A Study of the Relation between Art and the Reformation* (New York, 1976).

[19] See, for example, Genebrardus, *Chronographia . . .* (Paris, 1567) *ad annum* 3586 (after the Creation); interestingly, the passage about Gog and Magog was deleted from the 1585 edition.

970   *Sabine MacCormack*

FIGURE 3. A late medieval vision of the Christian life. Christ seated on the cosmic rainbow, his feet resting on the earth, with the Virgin Mary and John the Baptist interceding, judges humankind. The good (left) are led to heaven by an angel, the wicked (right) are driven into hell. On the arch are depicted the works of mercy a Christian should perform to merit salvation. Left wing of the "Redemption" triptych by Vrancke van der Stockt. Prado, Madrid.

Pachacuti: *Miracles, Punishments, and Last Judgment* 971

Ultinia etás mundi

FIGURE 4 (cover illustration). Last Judgment and resurrection of the dead from Hartman Schedel's Latin history of the world, printed in 1493. The work enjoyed wide circulation in Spain. Similar engravings were later used as models by painters in colonial Peru. (See Figs. 15–17.) Photo courtesy of Biblioteca Nacional, Madrid.

972   *Sabine MacCormack*

EL SANCTISSIMO PADRE

**De fu padre el diablo recibe el Antechrifto las leyes,
Con que tiraniza cófciencias de vaffallos y Reyes.
1. a Timotheo. 4.**

FIGURE 5. "From his father the devil Antichrist receives the laws with which he tyrannizes the consciences of vassals and kings." The pope is represented as Antichrist in a Reformation treatise entitled *Image of Antichrist*. Photo courtesy of Biblioteca Nacional, Madrid.

Antichrist seemed to have been validated (Figure 5). It was in response to such theories that in 1533, the year Atawallpa died, Pope Clement VII commissioned Michelangelo to paint the Last Judgment in the Sistine Chapel, which, by way of counteracting Protestant propaganda, omitted specific references to contemporary events.[20]

While, in those times, many people thought of the end of the world in terms of punishments for the wicked, others looked forward to a final age of spiritual men such as had been prophesied by the twelfth-century visionary Joachim of Fiore. Between 1516 and 1527, the Augustinian hermit Silvestro Meuccio published in Venice five of Joachim's works. In his preface to Joachim's commentary on the *Apocalypse (Expositio in Apocalipsim)*, Silvestro recorded the interest expressed in his

[20] André Chastel, *The Sack of Rome, 1527* (Princeton, N.J., 1983), 199 and following; F. Saxl, "A Spiritual Encyclopedia of the Later Middle Ages," *Journal of the Warburg and Courtauld Institutes*, 5 (1942): 82–142, 131 and following. An apparently anonymous anti-papal treatise of the Reformation translated into Spanish is *Imagen del Antechristo conpuesta primero en Italiano y despues traduzida en Romançe por Alonso de Peñafuerte* (n.p., n.d.), Biblioteca Nacional, Madrid, U 11097; it depicts the pope as Antichrist, Fig. 5 of this article. I would like to thank Gladys White for pointing out this publication to me.

work by Giles of Viterbo, the reforming general of the Augustinian order of hermits.[21] Even earlier, in 1506, Christopher Columbus had already quoted Joachim in his *Book of Prophecies* to document the claim that his discoveries had inaugurated Joachim's age of the holy spirit. Jerusalem was to be rebuilt, that is, recovered from the Ottomans, and this would be done, so Columbus had read in a work attributed to Joachim, by a Spanish sovereign.[22] Here, Columbus saw himself as God's instrument, because his voyages had opened a new route to Zion. He expected the end of the world to come at the end of the seventh millennium after the Creation, which he calculated to be 155 years from his time of writing. By then, all prophecies would have been fulfilled, and the gospel would have been preached everywhere, in particular in the newly found lands. "Our Lord is hastening in this matter," Columbus added to one prophecy about the conversion of the gentiles, suggesting that this last phase of human history had already begun. In the mid-seventeenth century, the Peruvian missionary and extirpator of idolatries Fernando de Avendaño still thought that the preaching of the gospel throughout the world was a sign of the fulfillment of the times, of the approaching second advent of Christ.[23]

Throughout the sixteenth century and beyond, some members of the missionary orders of Mexico and Peru—Franciscans, Dominicans, Augustinians, and Jesuits—saw themselves as God's chosen instrument in the work of evangelization.[24] However marginal such individuals were to the main thrust of their orders' endeavors, the expansion of Christianity overseas supported the Catholic claim of universality and truth, and these same arguments fired the debates of the Counter-Reformation. In the 1630s, in distant Lima, Antonio de la Calancha, the historian of the Augustinian order in Peru, read and pondered Silvestro Meuccio's edition of Joachim's treatise on the Apocalypse, and the ancient text convinced him that his order in particular had been chosen to preach to the Indians. Yet Calancha

[21] M. Reeves, *Prophecy in the Later Middle Ages: A Study in Joachimism* (Oxford, 1969), 262 and following; on the millennial hopes of Giles of Viterbo, General of the Augustinian Order, see John O'Malley, S.J., "Fulfillment of the Christian Golden Age under Pope Julius II: Text of a Discourse of Giles of Viterbo 1507," *Traditio*, 25 (1969): 265–338. On his influence in Spain, see Catherine Swietlicki, *Spanish Christian Cabala: The Works of Luis de Leon, Santa Teresa de Jesús, and San Juan de la Cruz* (Columbia, Mo., 1986), 22 and following, 34.

[22] Christopher Columbus, *Libro de las Profecías*, in *Autografi di Cristoforo Colombo*, C. de Lollis, ed., Part 1, vol. 3. (Rome, 1892), 110, 147; an excellent study of Columbus's thought on these matters is by Pauline Moffitt Watts, "Prophecy and Discovery: On the Spiritual Origins of Christopher Columbus's 'Enterprise of the Indies,'" *AHR*, 90 (February 1985): 73–102. See also A. Milhou, *Colón y su mentalidad mesiánica en el ambiente franciscanista español* (Valladolid, 1983). On Joachimism in the New World, see M. Reeves, *Joachim of Fiore and the Prophetic Future* (New York, 1977), 116–35.

[23] On fulfillment of prophecies, see de Lollis, *Autografi di Cristoforo Colombo*, 106 and following; on gospel, de Lollis, 130, 142; compare Moffitt Watts, "Prophecy and Discovery," 94; de Lollis, 106; Fernando de Avendaño, *Sermones de los Misterios de Nuestra Santa Fé Catolica . . .* (Lima, 1648), sermons 1, 2.

[24] John L. Phelan, *The Millennial Kingdom of the Franciscans in the New World: A Study of the Writings of Geronimo de Mendieta (1525–1604)* (Berkeley, Calif., 1970); M. Reeves, "The Abbot Joachim and the Society of Jesus," *Medieval and Renaissance Studies*, 5 (1961): 163–81; compare Anello Oliva, *Historia del reino y provincias del Perú . . .* (Lima, 1895), 1.5, referring the vision of S. Brigid to the Jesuits in Peru; M. Reeves, "Joachimist Expectations in the Order of Augustinian Hermits," *Récherches de théologie ancienne et medievale*, 25 (1958): 111–41.

974   *Sabine MacCormack*

was cautious in his statements: apocalyptic speculation was frowned on by the colonial church—indeed, it was dangerous to speculate on the prophetic future.[25]

But perhaps such ideas were more widely discussed in Peru at this time than is readily apparent. We may consider here Guaman Poma's vacillations in explaining the origin of the Incas. He had his own reasons for ambivalence. While in Guaman Poma's eyes, the rule of the Incas had been exemplary compared to colonial government, the Incas had nonetheless displaced his own ancestors as rulers of Lucanas. Guaman Poma's resulting hostility to the Incas had found expression in his interpretation of the myth that the Inca dynasty had sprung from *amaru*, a serpent. He recorded that the originator of the royal line, Manco Capac, was the offspring of a sorceress and of *amaru*, which he translated as "devil." This translation matched the Christian image of the devil as a serpent but was at variance with the Andean and Inca conception of *amaru*. On further thought, Guaman Poma therefore crossed out this statement. The statement is revealing, however, beyond the general Christian identification of devil with serpent and its supposed Andean equivalent because, according to sixteenth and seventeenth-century speculations, Antichrist was to be a son of the devil and a corrupted woman. Indeed, José de Acosta, whose *Historia* Guaman Poma referred to, wrote a Latin treatise on Antichrist that explains this genealogy.[26] The reign of Antichrist was to inaugurate a new epoch, what Andeans would consider a *pachacuti*. With some hesitation, and only at this one point in the *Corónica*, Guaman Poma viewed the origin—and by implication the fall—of the Incas analogously.

Guaman Poma repeatedly pondered the connection between the missionaries' exhortation to a perfect Christian life and the violent onslaught by representatives of the colonial state on the old Andean order. He was torn between Andean and European ways of understanding these events and endeavored to translate between the two cultures. Sometimes, however, he attempted no explicit translations but simply used the Christian vocabulary of perfection to highlight its absence in his own society. As seen by Guaman Poma, missionary orders and secular clergy all fell far short of the ideal that they themselves advocated and that Calancha had read about in Joachim's commentary on the *Apocalypse*. Guaman Poma therefore invariably described relations between clergy and Indians as relations of oppression. The Indians submit in "obedencia"; they offer alms and more alms but are always punished and afflicted. There is a single clear-cut exception to this refrain. It is the "holy hermit, sinner, and the other hermits of this kingdom." Guaman Poma describes two encounters between Andeans and the

[25] On Catholic propaganda, see Thomas Bozius, *De Signis ecclesiae libri xxiiii* (Rome, 1591); Gregorio Garcia, *Predicación del evangelio en el Nuevo Mundo, viviendo los Apostoles* (Baeza, 1625), 1.3; Luis de León, *In Abdiam prophetam explanatio* (Salamanca, 1582), 660; Swietlicki, *Spanish Christian Cabala*, 112 and following. Antonio de la Calancha, *Corónica moralizada del orden de San Augustín en el Perú* (1639; rpt. edn., Lima, 1983), 1.3, 9–10. On Fr. Francisco de la Cruz, see M. Bataillon, *Estudios sobre Bartolomé de las Casas* (Madrid, 1976), 353–67; on millenarian unrest in Peru during the later sixteenth century, see A. Milhou, "Du pillage au rêve édénique: Sur les aspirations millenaristes des 'soldados pobres' du Pérou (1542–1578)," *Caravelle*, 46 (1986): 7–20.

[26] On the *amaru* as devil, see Guaman Poma, *Nueva corónica*, 82; on Antichrist, see José de Acosta, *De Temporibus novissimis* (Rome, 1590).

holy hermit. In the first, an Andean of low status kneels behind the holy hermit saying, "obedience, saint; I respect you, saint" (Figure 6). In the second encounter, it is the hermit who kneels before a high-status Andean who says, "here is the alms, Father," and the hermit replies "for God" (Figure 7). In the later sixteenth century, Pedro de Quiroga, Canon of Cuzco Cathedral, had already proposed that a hermit, an individual without vested interests in church or state, should figure in a truly Christian relationship such as could be the norm in Joachim's age of the holy spirit, even though, so both Quiroga and Guaman Poma implied, this was unlikely to happen in the Peru of their own time. Since Joachim's writings circulated in Peru, one may perhaps find in these holy hermits an echo, however distant, of the spiritual men who had figured prominently in those writings and in the works of Joachim's sixteenth-century successors. In this case, Guaman Poma's drawing of King David playing a ten-stringed psaltery (Figure 8) could be understood as a reminiscence of the schematic drawings of ten-stringed psalteries illustrating the Venice edition of Joachim's *Psaltery of Ten Strings* (Figure 9).[27]

In their teaching addressed to Indians, however, most missionaries during the late sixteenth and the seventeenth centuries, far from hastening the age of the holy spirit, sought to support the colonial order of society.[28] It was not up to the Christian faithful to look for either the incarnation of Antichrist or for a millennial kingdom. It was only on the last day that God's activity throughout human history would be fully revealed, although this activity was frequently made partially manifest in the miracles with which God favored his servants and the punishments he meted out to the wicked. In the footsteps of missionaries, some historians of the New World therefore found in the events they chronicled examples of both miracles and punishments. God had miraculously aided the conquerors, it was held, so as to replace from among the Indians the souls that the Catholic church had lost to the reformers. This providentialist claim appeared to be at loggerheads not only with the economic and political constraints of colonial government but also with the demographic collapse, the "wasting away," as early colonial writers expressed it, of the Indian population that characterized the first decades after the

[27] On the hermit, see Guaman Poma, *Nueva corónica*, 480 [484], 631 [645]. On King David, see Guaman Poma, 28 (unnumbered), with Joachim of Fiore, *Psalterium decem choradrum* (1527; rpt. edn., Frankfurt, 1965). Guaman Poma admired the Jesuits (see 635 [649] and following; note the drawing on 637 [651] in which the Jesuit is followed by a Franciscan and, significantly, the holy hermit holding his skull and cross). Both Franciscans and Jesuits considered Joachim's prophecies to be applicable to themselves; A. Prosperi, "America e Apocalisse," *Critica Storica*, 13 (1976): 1–61, with M. Reeves, "The Abbot Joachim and the Society of Jesus," *Medieval and Renaissance Studies*, 5 (1961): 163–81. Perhaps Guaman Poma had access to Joachite writings from his Jesuit contacts. On the *Psalterium* and its imagery, see M. Reeves and B. Hirsch-Reich, *The Figurae of Joachim of Fiore* (Oxford, 1972), 23 and following, 50–61, 199–211, 217; also compare the bust of God the Father in Guaman Poma, 28 (unnumbered) with Reeves and Hirsch-Reich, Fig. 45, bust of God the Father above ten-stringed psaltery: the gesture of God's right hand and the cross-bearing globe in his left hand are almost identical in the two drawings. The *Coloquios*, which seem to have been written in about 1562 (see 81, "treinta anos que ya gocais de libertad"), are conversations between three Andeans and two Spaniards, one of whom is a soldier and the other a hermit. Antonio de Quiroga, *Coloquios de la Verdad* (Seville, 1922). On Pedro de Quiroga himself, see "Libro de la visita general del Virrey Don Francisco de Toledo," *Revista histórica* (Lima), 7 (1921): 123.

[28] S. MacCormack, "'The Heart Has Its Reasons': Predicaments of Missionary Christianity in Early Colonial Peru," *Hispanic American Historical Review*, 67 (1985): 443–66.

976   *Sabine MacCormack*

FIGURES 6–7. "Good government" and Christian social relations as they ought to be, according to Guaman Poma: an Andean of low status kneels behind a Spanish hermit, but, when this hermit meets an Andean lord, it is he who kneels to receive a gift of alms. *Nueva corónica*, 480, 631.

Pachacuti: *Miracles, Punishments, and Last Judgment*   977

FIGURE 7.

conquest. However, at the time, these events were usually analyzed in a cursory fashion, which easily gave way to the theological hypothesis that the Indians were being punished for past sins, just as the people of Sodom and Gomorrah, among others, had been punished in the Old Testament. In early colonial Peru, the idea of divine punishment was used by missionaries not only to urge conversion to

978   *Sabine MacCormack*

FIGURE 8. Guaman Poma's "fourth age of the world" as recorded in the Bible: King David plays a ten-stringed psaltery before God the Father in heaven. *Nueva corónica*, 28 (unnumbered).

Pachacuti: *Miracles, Punishments, and Last Judgment*   979

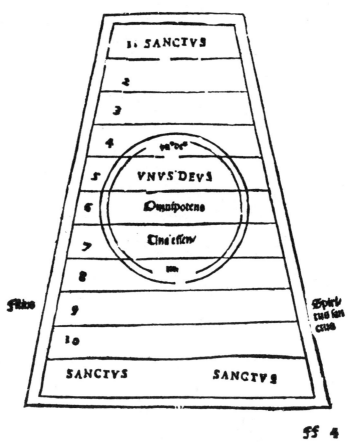

FIGURE 9. Psaltery of ten strings in Joachim of Fiore's *Psalterium decem cordarum* (Venice, 1527), representing the Trinity (God the Father at the top of the instrument, Son left lower corner, Spirit right lower corner). The strings stand for the hierarchy of created beings and for the virtues to be cultivated by holy men. A design of this kind may have inspired the psaltery played by Guaman Poma's King David.

Christianity but also to enforce submission to the new social and political order.[29]

In their different ways, during the early generations after the conquest, both Andeans and Spaniards were looking for an interpretive framework within which to understand the events of their time. Andean myths of ancient cataclysms invited comparison with European equivalents. The soldier-historian Cieza de León, who traveled extensively in the lands of the Incas during the early years after the invasion, outlined myths of the flood from Chucuito, Jauja, and the lowlands. But, unlike subsequent less critical observers, he suggested that these accounts could not refer to the universal flood of Noah but rather reflected distant memories of "some flood particular to this land, like that of Thessaly."[30] In this way, Cieza, like late antique Christian chronographers, made allowance for accounts of the past that differed from scripture but at the same time left the absolute truth of scripture unquestioned. Andeans in their turn applied their own categories to biblical history. While European historians and scholars of the sixteenth and seventeenth centuries investigated the precise year of Noah's flood, Andeans could classify this event without reference to the year of its occurrence either as a *pachacuti* pure and simple or else as the end of the first and beginning of the second age of human history.[31] Andeans understood Noah's flood as a marker in time, not a date.

Yet Andean and Christian theories of time and history did not simply run side by side without mutual interpenetration. Stories about Andean prophecies of the end of the Inca empire occur in most colonial histories of Peru. Cieza, with his characteristic sobriety, observed that such prophecies "could be fable," or possibly, he thought, they had been inspired by demons.[32] On a more factual level, however, the idea of a predestined end of the Inca empire corresponded to the Spaniards' conviction of their providential mission. Yet, however much visions of the end articulated purposes germane to the colonial state, they also expressed authentic Andean expectations. Like the mythic creator who, according to Zárate, had turned an earlier generation of men into animals, the destroyers of the Incas were to be newcomers. Garcilaso de la Vega and the Jesuit historian Anello Oliva, whose *History of the Kingdom and Provinces of Peru* received its ecclesiastical approbations

---

[29] Francisco López de Gómara, *Historia de las Indias, Biblioteca de Autores Españoles*, 22, prologue to the emperor; A. Vazquez de Espinosa, *Compendio y descripción de las Indias Occidentales, Biblioteca de Autores Españoles*, 231, chap. 2. N. D. Cook, *Demographic Collapse: Indian Peru 1520–1620* (Cambridge, 1981); on divine punishment for idolatry, see G. Dumezil, "'El Buen pastor': Sermon de Francisco Dávila a los Indios del Perú (1646)," *Diogenes* (Buenos Aires), 20 (1957): 85–103.

[30] Cieza, *Señorío de los Incas*, chap. 3; for different views, see Sarmiento de Gamboa, *Historia Indica*, chap. 6, p. 207; Oliva, *Historia del reino*, 1.2.1, 23; further, Guaman Poma, *Nueva corónica*, 51 with Szeminski, *La Utopía tupamarista*, 104. Compare Guaman Poma, 24, where two Andean animals, a llama and a jaguar, appear in Noah's ark, along with the European animals. For *pachacuti* and Andean epochs, see, further, Zuidema, *Ceque System of Cuzco*, 228 and following.

[31] Sarmiento de Gamboa, *Historia Indica*, chap. 6, p. 207a; Guaman Poma, *Nueva corónica*, 24–25, but note, the second Andean age is different; see Guaman Poma, 53–54 with N. Wachtel, "Pensamiento salvaje y ac20ó20: El Espacio y el tiempo en Felipe Guaman Poma de Ayala y el Inca Garcilaso de la Vega," in his *Sociedad e ideología: Ensayos de historia y antropología andinas* (Lima, 1973), 163–228; and J. Szeminski, "Las Generaciones del mundo segun Don Felipe Guaman Poma de Ayala," *Histórica* (Lima), 7 (1983): 69–109.

[32] Cieza, *Señorío de los Incas*, chap. 68; compare his *Crónica del Perú* (orig. pub. Seville, 1553), the only one of Cieza's works to be printed in his lifetime, chap. 44; López de Gómara, *Historia de las Indias*, chap. 115, believed that the Incas had prophesied the end of their empire.

in 1631, attributed the prediction of their advent to Viracocha Inca, who, in the traditional accounts of the Inca dynasty, was the father of Inca Pachacuti, originator of a new religious and political order. According to Guaman Poma, on the other hand, the prophesying Inca was Tupa Inca Yupanqui. This Inca, in his capacity of visionary of the past and prophet of the future, adopted the name of the god Viracocha, who had ruled in a past epoch and was to return in a future one.[33] According to Garcilaso, Andeans called the Spaniards "Viracochas" after the Inca who had foretold their coming. This explanation attempts to translate Andean theory into European fact. If instead we follow the argument of Guaman Poma, we see that the Spaniards were to be called Viracochas because they inaugurated a new epoch. What had formerly been prophetic future became present reality thanks to a *pachacuti*; Viracocha the Creator revealed another of his several faces, that of Viracocha the destroyer.[34]

Garcilaso and others relate that the prophecy of the coming invasion was repeated by the Inca Guayna Capac, father of Atawallpa, who advised his followers not to fight the invaders, because they would bring with them a better law. The prophecy, according to Garcilaso's principal Inca informant, was "more effective in overcoming us and depriving us of our empire than the arms your father and his companions brought to this country."[35] Diverse versions of this story were told to many Spaniards in Peru. The Incas themselves, it was repeatedly asserted, had known of a new law and a better religion, and were merely waiting for both.[36] Andean prophecies could thus be seen to have converged with European ones in foretelling the universal triumph of the Catholic church. Much of this was European wishful thinking, expatiating on the assumption that the "New World" was passively waiting for revelation to be mediated by divinely appointed European exponents. This, at any rate, was the message conveyed to Andeans by missionaries. Nonetheless, there was an Andean core to Inca prophecies of the end. These prophecies envisioned the age of the Incas coming to an end in the same way earlier ages had done.

The catastrophic nature of this ending is spelled out in Guaman Poma's repeated description of the colonial order as "mundo al rreves," or world upside down. The catastrophe also speaks in a quite different account of the Inca's prophecy by Juan de Santacruz Pachacuti Yamqui, an Andean lord from the region of Canas and

---

[33] Garcilaso de la Vega, *Comentarios*, 1.5, 28; Oliva, *Historia del reino*, 1.2, 13; Guaman Poma, *Nueva corónica*, 262 [264]: "Topa Ynga Yupanqui hablava con las *vacas* y piedras y demonios y savia por suerte de ellos lo pasado y lo venedero de ellos y de todo el mundo y de como avian de venir espanoles a governar y aci por ello el *Ynga* se llamo *Viracocha Ynga*." See R. Randall, "Qoyllur Rit'i, an Inca Fiesta of the Pleiades: Reflections on Time and Space in the Andean World," *Boletín del Instituto frances de estudios andinos*, 11 (1982): 37–81, 61.

[34] Garcilaso de la Vega, *Comentarios*, 1.5, 28; Guaman Poma, *Nueva corónica*, 378 [380] with J. Benzoni, *La Historia del Mundo Nuevo*, trans. C. Radicati di Primeglio (Lima, 1967), 64 and following. Cieza, *Señorío de los Incas*, 5, explained that, initially, the future to be inaugurated by the Spanish was projected to be a reversal for the better, thus justifying calling the invaders messengers and sons of Viracocha.

[35] Garcilaso de la Vega, *Comentarios*, 1.9, 15; compare Guaman Poma, *Nueva corónica*, 386 [388], which draws a moral lesson; Oliva, *Historia del reino*, 1.2, 12; Calancha, *Corónica moralizada*, 1.16, 7.

[36] Salinas y Cordova, *Memoriál*, 1.6; 1.7, 58, 71, respectively; Santacruz Pachacuti Yamqui, *Antigüedades deste reyno del Perú*, 254; compare 256, 260, 261 and following.

Canchis, near Cuzco. According to him, one midnight near Quito, Guayna Capac saw himself surrounded by the souls of all those who would die as a result of the Spanish invasion, and those souls were his enemies. Soon afterward, an unknown messenger from the Creator, wearing a black cloak, brought the Inca a box that he was to open himself. When he did so, a host of phantoms like butterflies or little pieces of paper flew from it—this was the pestilence that preceded the invasion, and soon Guayna Capac himself died of it. These two visionary events epitomize the reversal of established order that is *pachacuti*: the Inca was surrounded by souls of his subjects, but they were his enemies, and the Creator, who was implored in prayer for good, sent evil.[37]

Like Garcilaso, Santacruz Pachacuti Yamqui and Guaman Poma wrote in the early seventeenth century; by then, the colonial order had been established definitively, and this reality was reflected in the writings of these three authors. All three consciously and deliberately constructed bridges between European and Andean ideas in matters of chronology, religion, and ethics. Andean was integrated with European time, Andean religion was said to foreshadow Christianity, and Andean ideals of goodness were described in juxtaposition and comparison with Christian ones. Simultaneously, at a much more pervasive but less consciously articulated level, the three writers, especially Guaman Poma and Santacruz Pachacuti Yamqui, drew on European ideas and artifacts to articulate Andean realities. Thus the *amaru* of the Incas is capable of sliding into the identity of the Christian devil, and the Inca Guayna Capac opens a Pandora's box of evils represented by butterflies, which were an Andean token of ill omen, and papers, which could only be European.[38] Indeed, Andean realities themselves changed with the presence of Spaniards in the Andes, so that Andean concepts, one of which was *pachacuti*, were expanded to apply to states of affairs formerly unimaginable.

IN THE 1560s, ANDEANS IN MANY PARTS OF PERU joined together in an organized movement known as Taqui Onqoy, "Dance of Disease," to reverse this process of change and adjustment that, a generation after the death of the Inca, was clearly discernible in Andean society. An early and persistent Andean reaction to missionary endeavors at spiritual conquest had been to reject Christian ideas wholesale whenever possible. Thus, in 1560, Augustinian friars noticed that, in Guamachuco, Andean religious leaders instructed their people not to obey missionary priests and to avoid going to Mass. The Taqui Onqoy transformed local rejection of things Hispanic and Christian into a coordinated body of theory and practice. The movement appears to have been organized by the Incas exiled in Vilcabamba and was in part religious, in part military. Rejection extended not only

---

[37] On the "world upside down," see Adorno, "Rhetoric of Resistance," 451; on Guayna Capac's vision, see Santacruz Pachacuti Yamqui, *Antigüedades deste reyno del Perú*, 307. For the prayers, see Cristóbal de Molina, *Fábulas y ritos de los Incas*, in F. A. Loayza, ed., *Las Crónicas de los Molinas* (Lima, 1943), 38 and following; see esp. the prayers for the Inca, 41 and following.

[38] On butterflies, see Guaman Poma, *Nueva corónica*, 281 [283]; for papers as an adverse augury, compare my article "Atahuallpa y el libro," forthcoming in *Revista de Indias*.

Pachacuti: *Miracles, Punishments, and Last Judgment*   983

to all Christian rituals but also to Spanish food, clothes, and other matters of daily life. The Taqui Onqoy marked the time when "the world was turning round." In terms reminiscent of Andean myths of creation, Andean leaders asserted that the victory of the *huacas* over the Spaniards and their god would shortly inaugurate a "new world" of "other people" and that the Spanish would be swallowed up in the sea.[39] As reported by the inquisitor Albornoz, the teachers of the Taqui Onqoy explained that "they were the messengers of the *huacas* Titicaca and Tiaguanaco, Chimboraco, Pachacamac, Tambotoco, Caruauilca, Caruaraco, and another sixty or seventy *huacas* . . . The . . . apostates said that they were warring against the god of the Christians and that soon he would be conquered and that his *mita* of command would come to an end."[40]

The Quechua term, *mita*, here describing the unique turning point when the Spanish invaders would be driven from the land, originally referred to certain annual festivals of the Andean calendar. One of these was Onqoymita, celebrated in early June, near the beginning of the Inca year. The festival marked the heliacal rise of the Pleiades. Among the Quechua names of this constellation was Onqoy, or "illness." Illness was expected in the Andes while the Pleiades were not visible, during late April, May, and early June. For, at this time, after a period of rain, and after the harvest had been collected and put into storehouses, the earth was sterile. Storehouses for the crops were known as *colca*, and *colca* was at the same time another name of the Pleiades.[41] In colonial times, the festival of Onqoymita continued being celebrated under the guise of Corpus Christi, the date of which roughly coincided with it.[42]

---

[39] "Relación de la religion y ritos del Peru, hecha por los primeros religiosos Agustinos que alli pasaron," in *Colección de documentos inéditos relativos al descubrimiento, conquista y colonisación de las posesiones españolas en America y Oceania* III (Madrid, 1865), 5–58, 45 and following; for the date, 55. On "daba la vuelta el mundo," see Molina, *Fábulas y ritos de los Incas*, 79. On a "new world," see L. Millones, *Las Informaciones de Cristóbal de Albornoz, Sondeos* 79 (Cuernavaca, 1971), 2/109; on the Spanish to be swallowed by the sea, see Molina, 79–80. Zuidema, *Ceque System of Cuzco*, 234–35, points out that 1565 was exactly 1,000 years after the date posited for the beginning of the Inca empire by Sarmiento. Also see Duviols, *La Lutte*, 112–20. Guaman Poma served the extirpator of the Taqui Onqoy as interpreter; see R. Adorno, "Las Otras fuentes de Guaman Poma," *Histórica* (Lima), 2 (1978): 137–58, 151 and following.

[40] Millones, *Informaciones*, 2/53; see also 8, 62, 88; compare Molina, *Fábulas y ritos de los Incas*, 78 and following; A. Yaranga Valderrama, "Taki Onqo ou la vision des vaincus au XVIᵉ siècle," *Les Mentalités dans la Péninsule Ibérique et en Amérique Latine aux XVIᵉ et XVIIᵉ siècles: Histoire et problématique: Actes du XIIIᵉ Congrès de la Société des Hispanistes Français de l'Enseignement Supérieur, Tours 1977* (Tours, 1978), 119–79, 154, 160.

[41] Molina, *Fábulas y ritos de los Incas*, 25, "comenzaban a contar el ano mediado Mayo, dia mas o menos"; R. T. Zuidema, "Catachillay: The Role of the Pleiades and of the Southern Cross and α and β Centauri in the Calendar of the Incas," in A. Aveni and G. Urton, eds., *Ethnoastronomy and Archaeoastronomy in the American Tropics* (New York, 1982), 203–31, 211 and 208, respectively; Randall, "Qoyllur Rit'i," 41 and following, 59; for the celestial storehouse, see Urton, *At the Crossroads*, 113 and following.

[42] Jose Arriaga, *Extirpación de la idolatría del Perú, Biblioteca de Autores Españoles*, 209 (Madrid, 1968), chap. 5, p. 213; in a letter of 1564, the Taqui Onqoy is described as *cuyllur oncoy* (disease of stars); see Yaranga Valderrama, "Taki Onqo," 167. This evidence makes explicit the connection between the Taqui Onqoy and the June festival of the Pleiades; for a different explanation, see Yaranga Valderrama, 131, 169 and following. For an important discussion of the issue, see Bruce Mannheim, "The Virgin and the Pleiades: Poetic and Religious Syncretism in Colonial Peru," forthcoming in T. Abercrombie, ed., *Civil Administration, Ecclesiastical Indoctrination and the Transformation of Andean Politics*.

Another Andean name for the Pleiades was Catachillay. The Pleiades shared this name with the constellation of the celestial llama, the lower culmination of which was noted in the Inca calendar in September and October. In September, the Incas celebrated the festival Coya Raymi, also known as Citua, when diseases and other evils were ceremonially expelled from Cuzco. Guaman Poma, first having described the ceremonies of Citua as celebrated in Cuzco, continues: "These [rites] were performed in the entire kingdom along with many other ceremonies, so as to drive out *taqui oncoc* [him who is sick from dance] and *sara oncuy* [disease of the maize], and *pucyo oncuy* [disease of springs]." The Incas thus performed rites relating to illness on two annual occasions, in June and September. In addition, Guaman Poma's account of Andean ritual specialists contains a list of ills to be remedied that is almost identical to his list of ills expelled during Citua, and is also headed by *taqui onqoy*.[43] *Taqui onqoy* was thus a recurring condition. The celebration of cures for *taqui onqoy*, observed twice a year, suggests that the movement of 1565 may be understood as a heightened expression, brought on by the conquest, of a perennial Andean theme. Yet this theme had been modified by invasion, conquest, and colonial government on two levels. First, as the leaders of the Taqui Onqoy saw clearly, the presence of the Spanish newcomers, speakers of a foreign language, bearers of alien ideas and modes of conduct, and above all of alien technology, had no precedent in earlier Andean history. Pre-Hispanic Andean history had seen a great deal of war and conflict, but these had been wars and conflicts among neighbors known to each other for millennia. Second, the behavior and thinking of Andeans was changed and modified irreversibly by the intrusion of Spaniards into their world, irrespective of such countermeasures as the leaders of the Taqui Onqoy might take to reject Spanish ideas and artifacts.

Nonetheless, this movement was attempting to cure the disease of invasion as expressed in the alien government of Spain and the alien religion of Christianity. Andean rituals and beliefs that articulated both the Taqui Onqoy and subsequent responses to Hispanization accordingly confronted and refuted the arguments and propositions of missionaries. For instance, in one Andean ceremony around 1565, a cross was set up along with certain *huacas* (here, holy objects), which, according to participants in the ceremony, "responded" to the cultic actions addressed to them while the cross did not. This was proof that "the *huaca* who speaks to us is our god and creator," while the cross was a mere "stick." This description of the cross is evidently a retort to missionaries who perceived the *huacas* as mute sticks and stones that, like the idols reviled in the Letter of Jeremiah, were incapable of speaking to their worshipers, let alone of granting them favors. For Andeans, by contrast, the *huacas* were givers of prosperity and life, while worship of Christian holy objects was, quite cogently, associated with death and the reversal and destruction of the established order. As some teachers of the Taqui Onqoy explained in about 1564:

[43] On the celestial llama, see Zuidema, "Catachillay," 221 and following, 211; on Citua, see Miguel Cabello Valboa, *Miscelánea Antárctica* (Lima, 1951), 2.19, 351; Guaman Poma, *Nueva corónica*, 252 [254]; but note Molina, *Fábulas y ritos de los Incas*, 29 and following, places this festival in August. See Guaman Poma, 252 [254], 280 [282] with 676 [690], on the extirpation of the Taqui Onqoy of 1565.

While they worshiped the *huacas*, they would prosper in all their affairs, they themselves and their children and their fields. But if they did not worship the *huacas* or perform their ceremonies and sacrifices . . . they would die and would walk with their heads to the ground and the feet above, and others would turn into wild guanacos and vicuñas and into other animals and would throw themselves over cliffs and . . . these same *huacas* would make another new world and other people.[44]

This account, even though given by a Spanish observer, does capture the process of adaptation of Andean vocabulary and concepts to new circumstances and indeed to the end of the known order of things. For, when human beings are changed into wild animals, civilization as a whole ends.

Andean religious terminology thus expanded in its range of meanings; at the same time, new terms were incorporated into the Andean vocabulary. For example, some women teachers of the Taqui Onqoy called themselves by the names of "Santa Maria, Santa Maria Magdalena and by the names of other saints, so as to be revered as saints," while others described themselves as the messengers of the great *huacas* of Peru, just as the Spanish missionaries referred to themselves as messengers of the Christian god.[45]

The teachers of the Taqui Onqoy conceded to missionaries that the Christian god was indeed powerful, seeing that he had conquered the Inca at Cajamarca. But this did not mean that his power encompassed everything. Rather, even in the mid-seventeenth century, over two generations after the Taqui Onqoy had been ferociously suppressed by ecclesiastical and secular authorities, Andeans still argued that the Christian god was indeed the creator of Spain and of the Spaniards but that they themselves and their world had been created by the *huacas*. A map by Guaman Poma displaying Peru above and Castille below, in the Andean hierarchy of *anan* (upper) and *urin* (lower), also stresses the distinctness of the two worlds (Figure 10).[46]

Even in the middle and later seventeenth century, there were still Andean religious leaders, many of them women, who inculcated a systematic rejection of alien products and ideas. Such leaders considered it sinful for Andeans to attend Mass and catechism class, insisting that offenders confess and atone for their

[44] On the cross as a "stick," *palo*, see Millones, *Informaciones*, 2/136; the argument against idols is repeatedly outlined in the first three councils of Lima; Vargas Ugarte, ed., *Concilios Limenses*. Avendaño, *Sermones de los Misterios*, sermon 4, fol. 48, comments on the Letter of Jeremiah (printed after Lamentations in the Greek Old Testament). The quotation is from Millones, 2/109; see also 1/22, if the *huacas* were not believed, "los harian tornar a los yndios en guanacos e vicunas e otros animales." For the interdependence of cult of the *huacas* and wellbeing, see *Waru Chiri*, 140.

[45] Millones, *Informaciones*, 2/46; compare 2/62; on the absorption of Christian into Andean vocabulary, see H. Urbano, "Dios Yaya, Dios Churi y Dios Espiritu: Modelos trinitarios y arqueologia mental en los Andes," *Journal of Latin American Lore*, 6 (1980): 111–27; Urton, *At the Crossroads*, 129–50; and T. Gisbert, *Iconografía y mitos indígenas en el arte* (La Paz, 1980); on messengers of the *huacas*, see Millones, 2/53; on messengers of the Christian god in the *requerimiento*, see Duviols, *La Lutte*, 75 and following.

[46] Millones, *Informaciones*, 1/17, "Dios era poderoso para aver fecho a Castilla e a los espanoles . . . pero . . . las guacas avian sydo poderosas para aver fecho esta tierra e a los yndios . . . e quel Marques Pizarro quando . . . subjeto este rreyno avia sydo porque Dios entonces avia vencido las guacas e pero que agora todas avian rresuscitado para dalle batalla e vencelle"; Molina, *Fábulas y ritos de los Incas*, 78; with Avendaño, *Sermones de los Misterios*, sermon 4; with Duviols, *La Lutte*, 280–85. For the map, see Guaman Poma, *Nueva corónica*, 42; on Guaman Poma's geographical ideas, see N. Wachtel, in L. Bethell, ed., *Cambridge History of Latin America* (1984), 1: 234 and following.

986 *Sabine MacCormack*

FIGURE 10. The system of the world according to Guaman Poma: "The Indies of Peru above Spain, Castille below the Indies." In both Peru and Castille, the central capital city is surrounded by four provincial capitals. This model of organizing space was derived from the Incas, whose empire, Tawantinsuyo, "the four parts" of Peru, had its center in Cuzco. Mountainous Peru illumined by the sun is set above a sunless Castille in the plains in accord with the Andean hierarchy of *anan* (upper) and *urin* (lower). *Nueva corónica*, 42.

actions.[47] Furthermore, the expectation of another *mita*, which would cause the times to turn about, endured far beyond the suppression of the Taqui Onqoy. Andeans kept stone figures of the Inca among the domestic holy objects that safeguarded and embodied the generative energy of plants, animals, and humans. Sometimes, the Inca appeared in dreams and visions, explaining that he himself had sent the ills from which his people were suffering so as to induce them to "recover their senses," that is, to return to their old religion and to avoid the use of Spanish artifacts and objects of worship. This explanation formed a direct response to missionaries attributing the suffering of Andeans to God's punishment for Andean idolatry. In expectation of the return of the Inca, Andeans continued using quipus to account for the contents of state storehouses in the seventeenth century, and by this time also, some Andean communities had ritualized the anticipated return of the Inca in annual performances of the *Tragedy of the Death of Inca Atawallpa*.[48] Such statements of Andean identity notwithstanding, missionary preaching, reinforced by the coercive action of the state, penetrated everywhere and forced Andeans into debate, compromise, submission, and the reformulation of their values. Andeans, the most articulate being Guaman Poma, thus found inescapable the notion that the *pachacuti* of the conquest had brought on a permanent state of chaos, a "world upside down" that could not generate any return to order.[49]

GUAMAN POMA EXPLAINED THIS WORLD UPSIDE DOWN by juxtaposing the Christian concepts of miracles and divine punishments. These figured regularly in missionary preaching and in the early historiography of Peru, but Guaman Poma had found his own authority for the juxtaposition in Fr. Luis de Granada's *Treatise on the Christian Life*. Guaman Poma accepted the paired concepts of miracle and punishment unconditionally: the idea that the Christian god intervened in history both positively and negatively presented no difficulties for him. Quite the reverse: miracles and punishments listed interchangeably enabled him to articulate his bewilderment at the random injustice of colonial life. In repeating or alluding to the Christian examples of miracle and punishment, Guaman Poma therefore changed the scope and effect of both. For, on the one hand, he regarded as historical and theologically meaningful many episodes from the Bible and from the history of the conquest. But, on the other hand, he explained the moral significance or, rather, the absence of it in these episodes from an exclusively Andean standpoint.

---

[47] Millones, *Informaciones*, 1/17, 2/25, 2/52 and following; Molina, *Fábulas y ritos de los Incas*, 78; Archivo Arzobispal, Lima, Idolatrias 4.19, 5.15; Arriaga, *Extirpación*, chap. 5, p. 212. Also see Irene Silverblatt, *Moon, Sun and Witches: Gender Ideologies and Class in Inca and Colonial Peru* (Princeton, N.J., 1987), 198 and following.

[48] Polo de Ondegardo, "Relación de los fundamentos acerca del notable daño que resulta de no guardar a los Indios sus fueros," *Libros y documentos referentes a la historia del Perú* III (Lima, 1916), 77; S. MacCormack, "'The Heart Has Its Reasons,'" 458. For stone figures of the Inca, kept among domestic holy objects, see *Tercer catechismo* (Lima, 1585), sermon 18; on visions and dreams of the Inca, see *Monumenta Peruana* (Rome, 1970), 4: 208 and following.

[49] See the prayer cited by Spalding, *Huarochirí*, 262, "You see that the times are all in reverse, and you take no heed of us, and we give you all this . . . because we are persecuted and in another time."

988   *Sabine MacCormack*

Accordingly, Guaman Poma accepted as historical the intervention of the Virgin Mary on behalf of the Spaniards during the siege of Cuzco in 1534.

Saint Mary of Peña de Francia, a very beautiful lady . . . and when they saw her, the Indians were afraid and they say that she threw earth into their eyes, who were infidel Indians. For thus God performed a miracle to do . . . a favor for the Christian Spaniards, or rather, the Mother of God wanted to do a favor for the Indians so that they might become Christians and the souls of the Indians might be saved.[50]

The story echoes a frequent argument of missionaries, who explained that while the miracles of the Christian god advanced the conquest they also led to the salvation of Indian souls.[51] Another story Guaman Poma heard from the missionaries was about the activities in the Andes of one of Christ's original apostles. He termed the advent of this apostle in the Indies a miracle and associated with it a series of divine interventions in the world. These are described interchangeably as miracle, punishment, or judgment:

The fall of that angel was a great judgment . . . the fall of all the human race and the punishment of all the world in the waters of the flood. A great judgment was the election of Jacob and the reprobation of Saul and the perdition of Judas Iscariot, and the vocation of Saint Paul and the reprobation of the people of the Jews and the election of the gentiles along with other miracles and punishments that pass among the sons of the people of this world. And thus, there have been many other miracles and punishments in the time of the Inca . . . and so we write the sum of them all. Therefore the punishment of God is called *pachacuti, pacha ticra*. And hence some kings were called Pachacuti, and in this life we have seen the outbreak of the volcano and a rain of the fire and dust of hell on [the] city of Arequipa.[52]

This survey of world history led Guaman Poma to enumerate further disasters in his own time—earthquake, unseasonable snow and hail, plagues of noxious animals, failure of the harvest, and the depopulation of the Indies—all of which he describes as miracle, punishment, or pestilence. A very similar list occurs in his account of ecclesiastics and their activities in Peru. Consistent with this convergence of miracle and punishment, Guaman Poma described Arequipa as a

---

[50] Santa Maria de Peña de Francia, una señora muy hermosa . . . De velle se espantaron los yndios y dicen que le echava tierra en los ojos a los yndios ynfieles. Como hizo Dios milagro para hazelle merced . . . a los espanoles cristianos, por mejor dezir que mas quizo hazer merced la Madre de Dios a los yndios porque fuesen cristianos y salvasen las animas de los yndios." Guaman Poma, *Nueva corónica*, 403 [405]. The story was first told by Betanzos, *Suma*, 2.32, 300.

[51] Garcilaso de la Vega, *Historia general del Perú, Biblioteca de Autores Españoles*, 134 (Madrid, 1960), Book 2, chap. 25, reports and discusses the Virgin's appearance at the siege of Cuzco; for related arguments, see Avendaño, *Sermones de los Misterios*, sermon 1.

[52] "Gran juicio fue la cayda de aquel angel . . . la cayda de todo el genero humano . . . el castigo de todo el mundo con las aguas del diluvio. Gran juicio fue la eleccion de Jacob y la rreprovacion de Sau y el desanparo de Judas Escariote y la bocacion de San Pablo, la rreprobacion del pueblo de los Judios, la elicion de los gentiles y como otros milagros y castigos que pasan en los hijos de los hombres del mundo. Y anci avido otros muchos milagros y castigos en el tiempo del Ynga . . . Y aci se escrive toda la suma; por eso el castigo de Dios le llaman pachacuti, pacha ticra. Y anci algunos rreys fueron llamados Pachacuti. Y en esta vida como emos visto el rreventar el bolcan y llover fuego del ynfierno y arena solar una ciudad." Guaman Poma, *Nueva corónica*, 94–95. As Rolena Adorno has discovered, the biblical episodes in this passage are quoted from Fr. Luis de Granada, *Memorial de la Vida Cristiana* 2.3, 4; see R. Adorno, "El Arte de la persuasión: El Padre de Las Casas y Fray Luis de Granada en la obra de Waman Puma de Ayala," *Escritura* (Caracas), 8 (1979): 167–89; and Adorno, *Guaman Poma*, 257 with n. 31.

god-fearing city that displayed "much charity," and saw no incompatibility between such an assessment and the divine judgment that fell on Arequipa in the volcanic eruption of 1600, when God punished the city and "wished to burn it with fire from hell" (Figure 11). Other Andeans considered this eruption as a sign of turning times, while the Spanish were quick to point to the hand of their god.[53] But the problem was that nothing changed in the political and social order of Peru.

According to Christian teaching as reiterated by Guaman Poma, the good are rewarded in heaven and the wicked punished in hell. But in the world upside down he described, in which all social and moral order had been so obliterated that the humble Andean steward could wear the tunic (*uncu*) of an Inca lord, and the actions of Spanish figures of authority flagrantly violated their own precepts, there was no room for such straightforward justice. While Guaman Poma hoped that Christ might return again "to judge and punish the wicked and give glory to the good," he realized that in effect there was, as he so often repeated, "no remedy."[54] Guaman Poma reached the conclusion that "there are no Christians or saints because they are all in heaven." But were the saints really in heaven? Guaman Poma depicted a "city of heaven" with no inhabitants other than the Trinity and Mary (Figure 12). His hell by contrast is crowded (Figure 13).[55] There could be no more graphic testimony of the depth of his despair.

The lessons of Christianity did not cohere for Guaman Poma in the way that the missionaries had intended.[56] He expressed the aspect of the Catholic theological and moral system that is articulated in the concepts of God's miraculous intervention in history, and in God's punishment and final judgment of human actions, as experienced by Andeans, not as explained by missionaries. In the eyes of the missionaries, miracles and divine punishments had a twofold purpose: they were didactic, and they achieved a particular outcome. For Andeans, on the other hand, while the outcome—the conquest and its results—was inescapable, the lesson to be learned remained highly dubious. As an explanatory system underpinning colonial moral and social values, miracles and punishments were therefore a failure. Thus Guaman Poma, like other Andeans before and after his time,

---

[53] For a list of disasters, see Guaman Poma, *Nueva corónica*, 95, 640 [654] and following; on Arequipa, see Guaman Poma, 1053 [1061] and following, 1077 [1087]; see also T. Bouysse-Cassagne and P. Bouysse, "Volcan indien."

[54] On reward and punishment, see Guaman Poma, *Nueva corónica*, 938 [952] and following; see also Murra and Adorno, eds., *Nueva corónica*, p. 1355, note on 954; on Inca *uncu*, see Guaman Poma, 800 [814]; I would like to thank Professor Zuidema for bringing this drawing to my attention; on the Spaniards, see Guaman Poma, 643 [657] and following; on "no remedy," see Guaman Poma, 1106 [1116], compare 902 [916].

[55] Guaman Poma, *Nueva corónica*, 923 [937], 938 [952] and following.

[56] MacCormack, "'The Heart Has Its Reasons'"; see also T. Beidelman, *Colonial Evangelism: A Socio-Historical Study of an East African Mission at the Grass Roots* (Bloomington, Ind., 1982). The conclusions of this book, which offers a critical evaluation of missionaries' descriptions of their own work, as well as an assessment of the impact of Christianity on African converts, are also relevant to Latin American missions. Contrast P. Borges, *Métodos misionales en la cristianisación de América, siglo XVI* (Madrid, 1940); F. de Armas Medina, *Cristianisación del Perú (1532–1600)* (Seville, 1953); and even the seminal work of R. Ricard, *La Conquète spirituelle du Mexique* (Paris, 1933), in which the self-evaluation of missionaries is taken as a guideline; thus the contradictory, and even destructive, impact of Christianity on converts and potential converts fails to emerge. On the other hand, Duviols, *La Lutte*, confronted this problem.

990   *Sabine MacCormack*

FIGURE 11. Miracle and punishment as understood by Guaman Poma: the eruption of the volcano Huaynaputina in the year 1600 engulfs the city of Arequipa in a rain of fiery ashes. A penitential procession moves across the main square in the apparently forlorn hope of appeasing divine wrath. *Nueva corónica*, 1053.

Pachacuti: *Miracles, Punishments, and Last Judgment*   991

FIGURES 12–13. Guaman Poma's heaven and hell.
12. The "City of Heaven for good poor sinners" with "water of life [in the] Upper World" is empty. The plan of the city, with buildings surrounding a central square, follows the layout of Peruvian cities of Guaman Poma's time. (Compare Figs. 11, 14.) *Nueva corónica*, 938.

992 *Sabine MacCormack*

13. "City of Hell," for "the punishment of proud sinners and the rich who do not fear God." The mouth of hell, drawn according to the traditional European iconography, contains a cross-section of colonial society headed by a Spaniard. *Nueva corónica*, 941.

retained the explanatory system of the old religion, describing radical change quite simply as the turning about of *pachacuti*, which was miracle, punishment, and judgment all in one. *Pachacuti*, unlike for instance the destruction of Sodom and Gomorrah in the Hebrew Bible, occurs irrespective of human merit. This is made plain in an Andean myth recorded by the missionary Martin de Murúa, whom Guaman Poma knew. During the reign of the first Inca, Manco Capac, the earth "wanted to turn about and destroy itself" in torrential rains. At this time, Ynga Yupangui, one of Manco's sons, encountered at Sapi above Cuzco a huge person who was about to blow a trumpet. Ynga Yupangui begged this person to desist, lest "the earth turn about."[57] The desire of the earth to turn in this myth has nothing to do with humans. Similarly, Guaman Poma's divine punishments, miracles, and judgments occur for reasons that require no explanation.

Even so, Guaman Poma wrote from a Christian viewpoint because overtly, at any rate, he accepted Christianity as true. Other Andeans, although they shared a similar vocabulary, did not. Thus, in 1613, a Jesuit extirpator of idolatries heard from an Indian of Huamantambo that his arrival had been foretold to the village by a *huaca* that the extirpator identified with the devil. According to the extirpator, the devil had said to his worshipers, "For me has now arrived the *cutipacha*, which is the judgment, because these clerics and fathers who are coming will destroy my *huacas*, churches, and places of worship. Woe unto you, for ill is going to befall you and you have to suffer hunger, pestilences, and deaths, because you have revealed my secrets." Similarly, in Chavin, the rock that was the principal *huaca*, Auqui Chanca told the Indians that "for the *huacas* the day of judgment had come and that the Indians should no longer worship them in their churches and other appointed places, nor, out of respect for the visitor, should they gather together as a community, because he was a great enemy of the *huacas*. And they should not reveal anything to the visitor . . . or make confession, because he would consume them with travail and deaths."[58] The term *cutipacha*, as used by the speaker from Huamantambo, is synonymous with the Quechua *pachacuti* and the Spanish *juicio*. It describes the overthrow of the existing order, which in the speaker's mind was Andean religion and society. In Chavin, on the other hand, the overthrow of *huacas* and their worshipers was described by the Christian term "day of judgment." Guaman Poma, for all his Christian and Spanish erudition, also continually intertwined the imported ideas with Andean ones, as in his speculations about a restoration of the Inca empire and the eventual remedy to the ills of his time. In a drawing adumbrating an Inca restoration, the hoped-for new Inca, dressed in the traditional regalia, stands surrounded by the rulers of the four parts of his empire on top of the mountain of Potosí. But this drawing is not an antiquarian reconstruction of an iconography of power belonging to the past. The Inca is endowed not only with Andean but also with Spanish symbols of royalty, being sheltered beneath the coat of arms of Castille and León and flanked by the two columns of

[57] Martin de Murúa, *Historia general del Perú*, M. Ballesteros-Gaibrois, ed., 2 vols. (Madrid, 1962–64), 1: 86, 2: 3.
[58] Carlos Romero, "Idolatrías de los Indios Huachos y Yauyos," *Revista histórica* (Lima), 6 (1918): 192, 196–97.

994   *Sabine MacCormack*

FIGURE 14. Guaman Poma's vision of Peru's mining capital, the "rich imperial city of Potosí," overlooked by the mountain where in 1545 the first silver mine was discovered. The Inca standing on the mountain's peak is surrounded by the lords of the four parts of his empire (compare Fig. 10) who hold over his head the crowned coat of arms of Castille and León on two columns symbolizing Gibraltar, the terminus of the known world before the discovery of America. *Nueva corónica*, 1057.

Charles V's Plus Ultra (Figure 14). The description of this drawing spells out its composite message: "The rich imperial city of Potosí. Thanks to this mine exists Castille, Rome is Rome, the pope is pope and the king is monarch of the world, and holy mother church is defended and our holy faith is preserved by the four kings of the Indies and by the Inca emperor."[59] Andean symbols are here integrated with European ones into one coherent image of empire, but the empire is Andean.

Simultaneously, Guaman Poma had absorbed Christian and European millenarian thinking to the extent that the idea of "the Last Judgment" entailed a Christian ethical message, that is, the ultimate righting of the social and political ills of his time. Even here, however, he set aside Christian terminology in favor of the old Andean vocabulary of turning about: "There is no one who turns for the poor of Jesus Christ, if it is not that he himself turns about and returns for his poor ones." The return mentioned here may be read both in general terms as Christ's return in the Second Coming, when "God shall wipe all the tears from their eyes,"[60] and in a specifically Andean sense as a return inaugurating the political and social reform of colonial society.

A LATE CONTEMPORARY OF GUAMAN POMA, the Cuzqueño painter Diego Quispe Tito, was possibly thinking along similar lines when he painted his great picture of the Last Judgment in the Convent of San Francisco in Cuzco (Figure 15). The iconography of this epic depiction is derived from European prototypes inspired by the visions of the prophet Ezekiel and John the Divine. In these paintings and engravings, Christ enthroned on the rainbow, his feet resting on the globe of the earth as his footstool, was represented presiding over the Last Judgment (above, Figures 3–4).[61] In the upper center of Diego Quispe's painting in Cuzco, accordingly, Christ judging the living and the dead is enthroned on an arch colored in the hues of the rainbow, while beneath, the archangel Michael defeats the devil in the shape of a dragon. Some years later, a follower of Diego Quispe Tito painted a simplified version of this work for the church of Urubamba.[62] Other renderings of Christ seated on the rainbow include Marcos Zapata's painting of the Last Judgment for Cuzco Cathedral and a further Judgment done in a more popular style that is now in the Convent of Santa Catalina (Figure 16).

[59] "Ciudad la villa rica enpereal de Potocchi. Por la dicha mina es Castilla, Roma es Roma, el papa es papa y el rrey es monarca del mundo y la sta madre yglesia es defendida y nuestra santa fe guardada por los quatro rreys de las Yndias y por el enperador Ynga." Guaman Poma, *Nueva corónica*, 1057 [1065]. But note also Guaman Poma's ambiguities on the subject of sovereignty in Peru: 1111 [1122], and the complaint of three poor women against the extirpator of idolatries, Francisco de Avila: "Quisa se dolera nuestro Ynga que es el rrey," as opposed to 904 [918], "Quien es el Ynga? El rrey catolico."

[60] "No ay quien buelba por los pobres de Jesucristo, cino que torne otra ves, buelba al mundo por sus pobres"; Guaman Poma, *Nueva corónica*, 485 [489]; John the Divine, *Apocalypse* 7.17 and 21.4; reminiscences from Isaiah 25: 8.

[61] See above, n. 18. Among major depictions of the Last Judgment not cited by Harbison, *Last Judgement*, are Albrecht Dürer's *Die Heimliche Offenbarung Johannis*; see F. van der Meer, *The Book of Revelation in Western Art* (New York, 1979), 283 and following; also, Jehan Duvet, *L'Apocalypse figurée* (1561; rpt. edn., London, 1962), engraving for John the Divine, *Apocalypse*, chap. 6 with 9.

[62] For Diego Quispe Tito's painting, see T. Gisbert and J. de Mesa, *Historia de la Pintura Cuzqueña* (Lima, 1982), Fig. 171, and, for the imitation by a follower, Fig. 187.

996 *Sabine MacCormack*

FIGURE 15. The beginning and end of history according to Diego Quispe Tito from Cuzco. Christ on the rainbow judges the world. Below him, the archangel Michael fights the devil, below whom (left) Adam and Eve are expelled from Paradise. At the bottom, the condemnation of the wicked. Convento San Francisco, Cuzco. Photo courtesy of World Monuments Fund, by kind permission of the Archbishop of Cuzco.

Pachacuti: *Miracles, Punishments, and Last Judgment*   997

FIGURE 16. Last Judgment by an anonymous eighteenth-century painter from Cuzco. Christ on the rainbow flanked by the saints is adored by angels. Below, the devil masquerading as St. Michael presides over hell. At left, a glimpse into purgatory. Convento Santa Catalina, Cuzco. Photo courtesy of the Instituto Nacional de Cultura, Cuzco.

An eighteenth-century anonymous picture, also from Cuzco, depicts St. Jerome in his study (Figure 17). The saint, holding a book, sits at his table beneath which is the customary lion, while Jerome's other attribute, the ascetic's skull, has been transformed into a desiccated corpse such as might have been extracted from a pre-Hispanic Andean burial. An angel next to Jerome points into the distance, where Christ is enthroned on a rainbow while resting his feet on a globe. This painting, like its European prototypes, employs the traditional iconography of the Last Judgment to represent a visionary experience such as was appropriate for Jerome the commentator on the prophet Daniel.[63]

But Andean painters did not always follow European models so closely. A picture belonging to a series on the life of Catherine of Siena shows this saint sitting on a rainbow (Figure 18). An inscription informs the beholder that St. Catherine had a vision while searching for solitude but mentions no rainbow, which would in any case be incompatible with the terminology of traditional piety in which the inscription is couched.[64] Here, then, the Cuzqueño painter departed from conventional Catholic iconography. His intention evidently was to convey a Catholic message, but he did so in a language of images that diverged from what a European model or even the inscription of the picture would prescribe. Another painting of this type, possibly dating from the eighteenth century, hangs in the museum of Riobamba, Ecuador. It shows the Virgin and Child seated under a rainbow. At the Virgin's feet are four of her devotees, while below, five further devotees are shown as souls in purgatory. Here also, the rainbow is an alien element in what for the rest was a traditional Catholic iconography.

However, when understood in broader terms, the rainbow may be seen to enhance and add to such Catholic iconographies in two respects. If, on the one hand, we consider the rainbow as an indicator of the Christian Last Judgment and the end of time, the Virgin's rainbow at Riobamba points to the final destiny of the Christian souls that she is depicted as protecting. And St. Catherine's rainbow spells out the glorious future of a saint of God. We may thus conclude that in these two pictures, the Andean painter has simply used an established Christian image more freely or independently than a Spanish or European painter would have done. On the other hand, rainbows also have an Andean meaning that is distinct from, though not incompatible with, their Christian one. An Andean meaning cannot be excluded when interpreting these paintings. In the Andes, the rainbow, like the *pachacuti*, indicated a new beginning or the reversal of a given order. According to the myths of Huarochirí, a rainbow thus appeared when, clothed in a red puma skin, Wathiya Uquri, son of the powerful deity Pariya Qaqa, defeated his enemy. Similarly, Sarmiento de Gamboa and Santacruz Pachacuti Yamqui recorded that, before Manco Capac founded Cuzco, he saw a rainbow at

---

[63] Eugene F. Rice, *Jerome in the Renaissance* (Baltimore, Md., 1985), 111 and following, 148; Harbison, *Last Judgement*, 84–88.

[64] The painting belongs to Santa Catalina, Cuzco. The inscription reads: "Estando N[uestr]a M[adr]e S. Catalina contemplando en las vidas de las Santas que las pasaron en los desiertos se salio de su casa en busca de la soledad a poco trecho fuera de la ciudad se paso en orasion y arrebatada en extasis a las oras de nona bajo una nube que la puso en las puertas de la ciudad de donde se fue a su casa sinque en ella la uviesen echado menos."

Pachacuti: *Miracles, Punishments, and Last Judgment* 999

FIGURE 17. St. Jerome, absorbed in study, is shown by an angel a vision of Christ on the rainbow throne at the Last Judgment. Eighteenth-century anonymous painter from Cuzco. San Cristobal, Cuzco. Photo courtesy of the Instituto Nacional de Cultura, Cuzco.

Sabine MacCormack

FIGURE 18. St. Catherine of Siena seated on a rainbow is removed beyond space and time in a state of **ecstasy**. Anonymous painter, eighteenth century. Convento Santa Catalina, Cuzco. Photo courtesy of **the** Instituto Nacional de Cultura, Cuzco.

Pachacuti: *Miracles, Punishments, and Last Judgment*   1001

Guanacauri and interpreted it as a sign of greatness to come.[65] The late colonial version of the Inca coat of arms that is reproduced in the Betancur dossier (Figure 19) displays a rainbow sustained by two serpents; this composite image may be understood to refer to the origins of the Incas, that is, both to the rainbow of Guanacauri and to the descent of the Incas from *amaru*.[66] Similarly, in his drawing of the universe, Santacruz Pachacuti Yamqui depicted a large rainbow above the image of the earth, which he labeled as both "mother earth" and "lord earth."[67] It was thus possible to connect the rainbow not only with Inca origins but also with the origin of humankind at large.

Like the *pachacuti*, Andean rainbows could carry a negative as well as a positive meaning. An eighteenth-century painting depicting the death of Atawallpa in the Museo Arqueologico, Cuzco, shows, beneath a rainbow, the beheaded Inca placed behind a structure resembling a Christian altar, from which blood streams down (Figure 20). This scene is also described by an eighteenth-century Quechua poet in an elegy addressed to Atawallpa, with only one change: the rainbow is black.

> What rainbow is this black rainbow that rises?
> The horrible thunderbolt of Cuzco's enemy flashes,
> And everywhere a sinister hailstorm strikes.

There follows an extended and slow-moving description of the death of the Inca and the grief of his people. Only at the very end is there a hint of consolation:

> Will your heart allow, o powerful Inca,
> that we may be completely lost, separated,
> dispersed, subjugated by others, trampled on?

> Come and open your sweet eyes that dart beams of light;
> come and stretch your generous hands;
> and comforted by that happiness, bid us good-bye.[68]

---

[65] Sarmiento de Gamboa, *Historia Indica*, chap. 6, p. 207a; Cabello Valboa, *Miscelánea Antárctica*, 3.9, 262, used the same source, which perhaps is Cristóbal de Molina's lost history of the Incas; Santacruz Pachacuti Yamqui, *Antigüedades deste reyno del Perú*, 241; *Waru Chiri*, 5.63; this text, along with the Quechua elegy cited below at n. 68, is the least likely to have been contaminated by biblical and European ideas about rainbows (see, beyond material discussed here, Genesis 9:13–14 on Noah; possible connections made in colonial Peru between Manco Capac's rainbow and that of Noah are left aside here, but note Nuremberg Chronicle, Latin text (Schedel, *Liber Chronicarum*, f. xi r), in which Noah's rainbow is said to betoken both the Flood and the Last Judgment, and is therefore of interest to the present argument. Further, R. T. Zuidema, "La Imagen del sol y la huaca de Susurpuquio en el sistema astronómico de los Incas en el Cuzco," *Journal de la Société des Américanistes*, 63 (1974–76): 199–230, 214 and following.

[66] *Genealogia de Don Diego Felipe de Betancur y Tupac Amaru Hurtado de Arbieto*, vol. 1, Archivo Departamental, Cuzco; and above notes 7 and 26. The importance of the Andean rainbow was recognized by Avendaño, *Sermones de los Misterios*, sermon 4, asserting that the rainbow, like springs, sun, moon, lightning, and rivers, "no es dios." Andeans worship the rainbow: see Polo de Ondegardo, "Instrucción," *Revista histórica* (Lima), 1 (1906): 192.

[67] Biblioteca Nacional, Madrid, MS 3169, fol. 144v, reproduced in Jimenez de la Espada, *Tres relaciones*, 257.

[68] Translation cited from M. Lopez Baralt, "The Quechua Elegy to the All-Powerful Inka Atawallpa," *Latin American Indian Literatures*, 4 (1980): 79–86.

1002   *Sabine MacCormack*

FIGURE 19. "Coat of arms bestowed by his Caesarian Majesty our King and Lord Don Carlos I, King of Castille and León, on May 9, 1545, to Don Juan Tito Tupa Amaro, his sons and descendants, and their sons and descendants." The claim here declared was false, but aspects of the iconography displayed on the coat of arms, in particular, the rainbow supported by two serpents, depict authentic Andean concepts. Betancur Genealogy, vol. 1, Archivo Departamental, Cuzco. Photographed by the author, reproduced here by kind permission of Don Horacio Villanueva Urteaga.

Pachacuti: *Miracles, Punishments, and Last Judgment*   1003

There is, then, a hint that the Inca might return. Expectations of such a return were also aroused by performances of the *Tragedy of the Death of Atawallpa*, which represented the death of the Inca as a wrong that must be avenged and reversed. In the play's last scene, the king of Spain recognizes his own countenance in that of the decapitated Inca and orders vengeance on the house of Pizarro. The play was performed regularly in colonial Peru. During one such performance in Lima, a riot broke out and the site was closed to further performances.[69]

The play envisages that vengeance for the dead Inca will be taken in some mythic, nonspecific time. At the same time, however, hopes for an Inca restoration became concrete and entered the realm of explicit political action when they focused on descendants of the Incas among Andean aristocrats. Thus, in 1667, Don Alonso de Arenas Florencia Inca, corregidor of Ibarra near Quito, claimed to have been descended directly from the Inca dynasty and substantiated his claim by means of a genealogical painting. Andeans knelt before him, and triumphal arches were erected to grace his arrivals in towns and villages of his *corregimiento*. In due course, the colonial authorities, fearing a rebellion, arrested Don Alonso and sent him to Lima for trial.[70] But other revolts led by descendants of the Incas followed, culminating in the uprising of José Gabriel Tupa Amaru in 1780, which covered Peru, Bolivia, and parts of Argentina. Although this uprising also failed, the Andean countries eventually gained their independence from Spain. A painting by Santiago Juarez in the Museo Histórico in Cuzco affords a small glimpse of an Andean interpretation of these events. The picture, dated July 5, 1825, is entitled "Homage to the Liberator Simon Bolivar" (Figure 21). Amid portrait busts of Bolivar himself and other generals of the wars of independence appears a circle containing the sun, moon, and stars, and inside it a schematic depiction of a landscape surmounted by a large rainbow. According to the painter, Bolivar had brought about the *pachacuti* that had been awaited for so long. In 1825, it was still too early to see clearly that, for Andeans, the benefits of independence were ephemeral.

WE MAY NOW RETURN TO DIEGO QUISPE and the other Andean painters who depicted rainbows in a Christian context, whether they did so in the accepted and traditional imagery of the Last Judgment or whether they created images independent of explicit European prototypes, such as the portraits of the Virgin in Riobamba and St. Catherine in Cuzco. The image of the rainbow links the Christian Last Judgment and Christian visions of the seventh age to the Andean *pachacuti*. As we have seen, Guaman Poma understood judgment, miracles, and

---

[69] See above, n. 8. For a description of the play as performed in eighteenth-century Trujillo, see Baltasar Jaime Martinez Compañón, *Trujillo del Perú a fines del siglo XVIII* (Madrid, 1936), plate 66 taken from vol. 2 of the manuscript in the Biblioteca del Real Palacio, Madrid. I was unable to consult the recent facsimile edition of this volume. On the riot, see A. F. Frézier, *A Voyage to the South Sea and along the coast of Chili and Peru in the years 1712, 1713 and 1714 . . . with a postscript by Dr. Edmund Halley* (London, 1717, I was unable to consult the French original), 273. Further, Wachtel, *La Vision des vaincus*, 255 and following.

[70] I would like to thank Carlos Espinosa for showing me this document on which he is currently working in the Archivo Histórico Nacional in Quito.

1004   *Sabine MacCormack*

FIGURE 20. The death of Inca Atawallpa according to an anonymous eighteenth-century painter from Cuzco. Beneath a rainbow of ill omen, the headless body of Atawallpa leans over an altar-like structure flanked by Fr. Vincente de Valverde, who baptized the Inca before his death, and by Francisco Pizarro. Museo Arqueologico, Cuzco, photograph by R. T. Zuidema by kind permission of the Director.

divine punishment as a single whole, which he described as *pachacuti*. The colonial "mundo al rreves," like the death of the Inca, were intelligible to him only insofar as they could be integrated into an Andean conceptual universe.

From the very beginning, some Andeans had linked the death of the Inca to some kind of return: after Atawallpa's death, certain individuals anticipated his return as a serpent. Later, the Inca's return was foretold in some versions of the *Tragedy of the Death of Inca Atawallpa* and in the myths of Inkarrí. The very idea of the return of an Inca was, however, the product of the colonization of the Andes; for, in the normal course of events, an Inca would be succeeded by one of his kin. The idea of the Inca's return thus conjoins the old with the new, the Tawantinsuyu of the Incas with Spanish Peru.

At the same time, to think of the return of Atawallpa implied thinking of

FIGURE 21. Painting by Santiago Juarez honoring Simon Bolivar. The heraldic iconography is that of republican Peru, but the central image, a landscape surmounted by a rainbow of auspicious augury, is a traditional Andean one. Museo Historico, Cuzco. Photographed by the author, reproduced here by kind permission of the Director.

alternatives to the status quo, such as were also adumbrated in the Christian Last Judgment. In Andean terms, Diego Quispe Tito's painting can be read as incorporating an allusion to the death of Atawallpa. This death was the *pachacuti* that had inaugurated the colonial epoch, when the established order of the Incas was reversed, just as in Christian thought, the Last Judgment will reverse the established order of the world. The Andean rainbow could convey an auspicious meaning: thus, for Manco Capac, it had been an augury of Inca glory. In Diego Quispe Tito's painting of the Last Judgment, this auspicious aspect of the rainbow points on the one hand to the reward of the just, the punishment of the wicked, and to the future reign of the City of God, and, on the other hand, it points to the return of the Inca. Yet Tito's was in no sense a subversive painting, for it depicts

1006   *Sabine MacCormack*

the Christian Last Judgment in an iconography that would have satisfied the ecclesiastical censor but that, for the Andean beholder, was capable of conveying a very different message.

Colonization transformed Andean religious thinking and brought into existence a new religious vocabulary. In this new vocabulary, Andeans posited alternatives to the dominant religion, while the dominant religion contributed to defining and describing those alternatives. Andeans looked back to their pre-Hispanic past but in doing so were capable of expressing themselves in the ancient terminology of Christian apocalyptic. However, a shift occurred in the meaning of this Christian and European terminology as used in the Andes. In Europe, from late antiquity onward, Christian apocalyptic had been a means of articulating programs of political and ecclesiastical reform.[71] These programs of reform tended to look back to a state of perfection in the long distant past and deployed the moral imperatives of Christianity in order to affirm as tonegiving the practices and values of the primitive church. In the Andes, by contrast, it was the past of the Incas that inspired the present and lent purpose and significance to the religious ideas that lay at the root of *pachacuti*, even in its new Christian guise. As a result, perceptions of this Inca past changed. Guaman Poma, in his account of the Inca empire, had voiced numerous criticisms of its governance. When he reached the colonial period, however, he set aside these criticisms and made the Incas into the yardstick to measure the failures and injustices of Spanish government.[72] Similarly, the portrait of Atawallpa as a gentle ruler of his people in the *Tragedy of the Death of Atawallpa* is incompatible with the historical figure of this monarch. It is a well-known commonplace of Andean historiography that the Spanish conquest fragmented Andean historical awareness. But this is not the whole story. For it was also the Andean people themselves who reformulated their past so as to contend with their present, and this they continue to do.[73]

---

[71] N. Cohn, *The Pursuit of the Millennium* (Oxford, 1970); and G. B. Ladner, *The Idea of Reform: Its Impact on Christian Thought and Action in the Age of the Fathers* (Cambridge, Mass., 1959).

[72] Guaman Poma, *Nueva corónica*, 339 [341], "no avia tanto dano como agora"; 657 [671], priests from Spain should have the status of conquered peoples (*mitimaes*), as they would have done under the Incas; the Inca and Spanish moral order compared, 914 [928].

[73] Franklin Pease, *Del Tawantinsuyo a la historia del Perú* (Lima, 1978), 31–114 and literature there cited; R. Gow, "Inkarrí and Revolutionary Leadership in the Southern Andes," *Journal of Latin American Lore*, 8 (1982): 197–223. O. Harris, "De la fin du monde: Notes depuis le Nord-Potosí," *Cahiers des Amériques Latines*, n.s., 6 (1987): 93–118.

16

Landscape and World View:
The Survival of Yucatec Maya
Culture Under Spanish Conquest

Inga Clendinnen

The religions of contemporary Middle American Indian communities fall neatly enough under the descriptive category we call 'syncretic'. Myths and rituals, integrated experiences for the participant believers, betray to the outside observer their Spanish and Indian antecedents. This indicates a methodology of analysing the ongoing flow of religious life into its smallest constituent parts—colours and gestures, sacred objects and sacred locations, the structure and language of invocations—the more precisely to identify the ingredients of the 'mixed' religion we see being lived out. When enquiry moves to the process of imposition and selection by which the mix was initiated, in the early days of Spanish-Indian contact, the same familiar methodology lies ready to hand: Spanish Catholicism, and what is known of the traditional Indian religion, can be analysed into elements, those elements arranged in parallel, and the likely ease of transference inferred, being judged to be the highest where a match seems good and where evidence from the ethnographic present appears to offer confirmation.

The method has its utility, not least in that it facilitates comparison between cases and allows some estimation of degrees and rates of acculturation. Its defects lie in its assumptions that the Spanish presence was a constant and was identically perceived by all Indian groups, and (more important) in the 'mosaic' models of religion and of culture on which such an analysis rests.

This paper explores another approach. Spanish invasion and colonisation was very differently experienced by different native American groups. The Yucatecan situation presents a distinctive form of the encounter. The military phase of conquest extended over twenty years in Yucatan. In most

A preliminary version of this paper was offered as part of the subsection 'Interpreting Past Environments' in the History section of the 48th ANZAAS Congress at the University of Melbourne, August to September 1977. The subsection was devised and coordinated by my friend and colleague Rhys Isaac, whose intellectual vigour and infectious passion for the problems of social history are a constant delight and stimulus to all who work with him.

of the other settled regions of Spanish America (including Central Mexico and Peru), *congregación* and *reducción*—the forced resettlement of Indian communities—was carried out by civil authorities 40 or more years after initial conquest, in response to an already massive population decline; in Yucatan it was implemented by missionary friars a decade after conquest and involved the dislocation and transplantation of still viable native communities. Early in the next decade came a sustained inquisition into 'idolatries'; in this, the friars again displayed their dominance. This sequence of events might well lead us to expect a quite rapid breakdown in traditional patterns of thinking and action among the Maya. What we find instead is a remarkable persistence of old patterns and a highly self-conscious cultural conservatism which persists even into this century.

While generations of scholars have noted the remarkable conservatism of the Maya, few have as yet sought to account for it, and those few have tended to concentrate on the post-Caste War Maya of the Quintana Roo region. The richness of the sixteenth-century documentation permits us to start the enquiry earlier, in the crucial early years of Spanish-Maya contact. How was it that among the traumas of conquest, colonization, and an unusually vigorous, coherent, and ruthless conversion campaign, the Maya were able to maintain a high sense of autonomy and of the legitimacy of their traditional account of the world? The documents permit the identification of those concepts of the old religion consciously and conscientiously preserved by the Maya and the tracing of the processes by which particular Christian elements were selected and incorporated within that familiar frame. It is possible to glimpse the Mayan conceptualisation of the generic features of their landscape through which they were able to recreate their traditional social worlds within the physically restructured villages imposed on them by the friars. Further, we may see how their conceptualisation of time and of their own history permitted them to sustain a sense of autonomy in face of defeat and subjugation by the Spanish conquerors.[1]

THE FRANCISCAN OFFENSIVE

The handful of Franciscan missionaries who offered themselves in the mid-1540s for the task of converting the Maya Indians of Yucatan were faced with a discouraging landscape. In Mexico, their brothers had found an obvious focus for missionary action in the great centres of Indian

---

[1] Work done in Papua New Guinea, where the introduction of Christianity has been sufficiently recent to permit the 'native response' to be traced in some detail, demonstrates the extraordinary flexibility of native cognitive systems, and the various and to us startling ways in which Christian teachings have been misunderstood. E.g., see Peter Lawrence, *Road Belong Cargo* (Manchester: Manchester University Press, 1964), and Peter Worsley, *The Trumpet Shall Sound* (London: Schocken Books, Inc., 1957). For developments in African studies, see Robert Strayer, 'Mission History in Africa: New Perspectives on an Encounter', *African Studies Review* 19 (1976): 1–15.

376   INGA CLENDINNEN

population. In Yucatan, the combination of slash-and-burn agriculture and dependence on natural wells, or cenotes, for reliable water supplies, together with the need for protection from interprovincial raids and the attractive power of a developed collective ritual and social life, had dispersed the Indian population in villages and hamlets distributed fairly evenly over the whole rocky surface of the peninsula. In the vales and hillsides of Mexico, Franciscans had seized the chance to knit the agricultural cycle into the web of Christian ritual, organising masses and processions for rain in direct competition with native agricultural gods. In Yucatan, the milpas or cornplots were littered, apparently haphazardly, through the dry, dense grey forest which hemmed the villages, and the dim paths which led to them blurred easily into bush, at least to European eyes. The friars recognised that the forest could not be controlled: it had masked the preparations for the last desperate uprising of the Maya of the southern and eastern provinces in 1546, when they had destroyed all things Spanish, including the dogs and cats and even the trees of Castile, until their final and bloody suppression, and it was to serve as the last refuge of the most recalcitrant Maya until the end of the colonial period and beyond.[2] After gathering up the sons of the native lords, to be sequestered within the mission schools attached to each monastery until they could be transformed into 'Christians' and assistants in the teaching of the faith, the friars turned their attention to the villages. Understanding from their experience within their own order the efficacy of a minutely regulated environment in shaping behaviour into desired forms, they studied the patterns of traditional village life in order to effect their transformation.

In Maya villages, the line between public and private, family and social was vaporous. The long, multiple-family houses, where sons brought their wives after they had worked their years of bride service, denied in their very structure the social proprieties of Christian marriage and Christian parenthood. The private familial area was restricted to the dark sleeping quarters: public space began with the long verandah-like chamber running the length of the house. The houseyard was the women's privileged place. There, many household tasks were performed, as were devotions to the household gods. Through the long hours of the afternoon they could visit together, weaving the slow intricate patterns on their backstrap looms in the fruit

[2] The best account of the prolonged conquest of the peninsula and of the Great Maya Revolt, as the Spanish named it, remains that of Robert S. Chamberlain, *The Conquest and Colonization of Yucatan 1517–1550*, Carnegie Institution of Washington Publication no. 582 (Washington, D.C., 1948). For a succinct discussion and useful bibliography on the vexed question of the peninsula's population, and the impact of conquest, see Sherburne F. Cook and Woodrow Borah, *Essays in Population History: Mexico and the Caribbean* (Berkeley: University of California Press, 1974) II, ch. I, esp. pp. 62–65. Cook and Borah estimate the population of the peninsula (excluding Uaymil-Chetumal) in 1543 at 476,200, and in 1549 to have been 233,776. Those six years saw the final 'pacification' of the peninsula. Note also the comment on Uaymil-Chetumal, scene of the bitterest fighting, on pp. 47–48.

trees' shade, free from the restrictions imposed by formal modesty when they left the houseyard to enter the village streets, to visit kin, to barter, or to pursue the endless task of fetching water from the village cenote.

It was while engaged in that task that Maya girls had most opportunity to practice their pretty routines of avoidance of men's glances, for around the wells clustered the spaces and edifices which provided the stages for significant male activity. There stood the temple-crowned pyramid, flanked by the storehouse for the masks, plumes, drums, and flutes required for the great ceremonial performances. In the long warrior house the youths of the village lived from puberty to marriage, learning the chants, dances, and stories which taught them what it was to be a Maya man. The house of the village chief, like those of the lords, was more public building than private residence. In the oratories of the chiefs were preserved the images and the inlaid skulls of specially revered ancestors. Their courtyards and reception chambers were sometimes courts of justice and sometimes the venue for the great feasts which saw the celebration of bonds of mutual dependence, where to meet an obligation was to strengthen rather than to extinguish it. They also provided the setting for major religious performances. Women played little part in those ceremonies—only old women, safely past menopause, were permitted to dance before the gods in the temple—but for the men, the cluster of edifices and framed spaces at the heart of the village provided the setting for the activities we distribute between church, school, court, theatre, and club. This was the focus of their social and religious life. In all the villages, the four ceremonial entrances to the village were linked to this centre by paths wide enough to accommodate the processions which laced them during the elaborate ceremonies ushering in each new year.[3]

This was the world the friars put to the torch. Seizing on the shaky warrant of a series of ordinances issued by the visiting royal judge Tomas Lopez Medel in 1552, a bare six years after the final 'pacification' of the Maya, the Franciscans embarked on an ambitious and ruthlessly implemented programme for the relocation of existing communities, despite bitter protests from Spaniards and Indians alike. At times with no more warning than the unheralded arrival of a solitary friar, Indians were ordered out of their houses, which were then set burning, along with their carefully nurtured fruit trees and their meagre possessions. Then the dazed and weeping Indians were herded off to new sites, which were too often

[3] Most of this information is found in Fray Diego de Landa, *Landa's Relación de las Cosas de Yucatan. A Translation Edited with Notes by Alfred M. Tozzer*, Harvard University, Peabody Museum of American Archaeology and Ethnology Papers, XVIII (Cambridge, Mass.: Peabody Museum, 1941), esp. pp. 85–106, 124–25, 138–49. Hereafter cited as Landa, *Relación*, or as Tozzer, *Relación*, when the reference is not to the text but to the editor's notes. For an attractive and reliable secondary account, see Ralph L. Roys, *The Indian Background of Colonial Yucatan* (Norman: University of Oklahoma Press, 1972; first published in 1943).

378   INGA CLENDINNEN

inadequately prepared for them. Some died of hunger and exposure, and others, we are told, from 'the great sadness of their hearts'.[4]

In the villages built to replace those familiar worlds, there were significant spaces, but they spoke very differently of man's relation to man and of man's relation to the gods. The Christian church stood at the centre, but it was not to provide the focus for community action: placed in the charge of the schoolmaster, or another 'reliable' Indian, it was to be kept immaculately clean and, except for brief and specified times, locked, and so safe from unauthorised use. Close to the church stood the municipal building, where the chief and his leading nobles still appeared, but now in the guise of municipal officers in the Spanish system. The whipping post, that eloquent symbol of the new regime, spoke of the chief's new role: no longer custodian of traditional justice, he was permitted to mete out punishment to his followers for petty infractions of Spanish law. In this shrunken world, there was to be no stage for communal action; all feasting was forbidden, as were meetings of any kind after nightfall, and with the sounding of the bell for the souls in purgatory all were to withdraw to the single-family domestic prisons built to replace the traditional multiple-family structures. In place of the old complex religious round, from the constant small gestures of thanks and propitiation offered in the milpas to the great collective performances before the temple, there was to be solitary prayer, morning and night, and passive attendance at the church on Sundays and feast days, and at the occasional special exhortations delivered by visiting friars.[5]

It is something of a convention among historians of culture contact to deride the cultural myopia of missionaries, but it will not do to underestimate the understanding, the energy, and the psychological astuteness of the Yucatan friars. They were determined to turn religious energy inwards, away from collective and existential expression, to the anxious scrutiny of individual conduct and so to the scrutiny of the individual soul. They knew much of the complex interactions which structured the old social system; most of the material in the preceding pages is drawn from Fray Diego de Landa's great 'Account of the Things of Yucatan', and some of his fellow

---

[4] Relaciones de Yucatan, in *Colección de documentos ineditos relativos al descubrimiento, conquista y organización de las antiguas posesiones españolas de Ultramar*, 2nd series, vols 11, 13 (Madrid: Real Academia de la Historia, 1898–1900). Hereafter *R.Y. 1* and *R.Y. 2*. *R.Y. 2*: 209–210. See also 30–31; 68–69; 187. For the ordinances, see 'Ordenanzas del Lic. Tomas Lopez' in Fr. Diego Lopez (de) Cogolludo, *Historia de Yucatan escrita en el siglo XVII por el reverendo padre Fr. Diego Lopez Cogolludo*, 2 vols, 3rd edition (Merida: Manuel Aldana Rivas, 1867–1868). Lib. V.Caps. XVI–XIX, esp. Cap. XVI. Orders for the gathering of Indians into convenient locations occur from the earliest days of Spanish settlement in the Indies, but the policy of *congregación* or *reducción* was not systematically implemented elsewhere, at least among settled Indian populations (e.g., in Peru and Central Mexico), for forty or more years after conquest, when it was executed by civil authorities in response to massive Indian population loss, and the consequent debilitation of communities.

[5] For the prescriptions for the structures of the new villages, and the behaviours approved within those structures, see 'Ordenanzas del Lic. Tomas Lopez', Cogolludo, *Historia*.

missionaries were as fluent in Maya, and as tireless observers, as he. The friars knew what they were doing when they set the villages to burn and forced the Indians to watch; they knew those locations were thickly inscribed with the social and sacred meanings of a way of life and with a view of life they were determined to destroy. Their energy was formidable: we cannot be certain as to the percentage of villages and the percentage of Indians actually relocated, but we can be confident that few villages under Spanish control escaped substantial reorganisation, at least in external forms. Every village had its church and school, however modest, and by the end of the century multiple-family houses were rare, being common only where Spanish presence was intermittent.[6]

The friars also understood the effectiveness of more ritualised statements of power. In 1562, after seventeen years of missionary effort, a chance discovery revealed that idolatry was being practised on a massive scale in the province of Mani, home of the Spaniards' most reliable allies the Xiu, site of the first mission to the Indians and heartland of the mission enterprise. The friars responded to this shocking blow with characteristic energy. The chiefs and lords were hastily rounded up, to be kept close in Merida, the Spanish capital, until they could be interrogated at proper length. The commoners, bereft of their traditional leaders, were strung up by the wrists and flogged, until they 'confessed' not only the extent of their own wickedness but also the involvement of their lords. For three long months terror reigned in Mani and the two adjacent provinces of Sotuta and Hocaba Homun, where the enquiry had been extended. Dread spread across the land: at the news of the friars' coming, men fled into the forests or hanged themselves in fear and despair.

Many Indians died under the torture. Others were maimed. One Spaniard recalled that when the penitents were delivered to the whipping post for their prescribed number of lashes, their bodies were already so torn by the tortures inflicted by their interrogators that 'there was no sound part of their bodies where they could be flogged'.[7] But despite the mounting

[6] Ralph L. Roys, France V. Scholes, and Eleanor B. Adams, 'Census and Inspection of the Town of Pencuyut, Yucatan in 1583 by Diego Garcia de Palacio, Oidor of the Audiencia of [Mexico]', *Ethnohistory*, 6 (1959): 195–225, esp. 204–05; 'Report and Census of the Indians of Cozumel, 1570', *Contributions to American Anthropology and History*, 6, Carnegie Institution of Washington Publication no. 523 (Washington D.C., 1940), pp. 5–30.

[7] Testimony of Juan de Villalobos, 27 January 1565, in France V. Scholes and Eleanor B. Adams, eds., *Don Diego Quijada, alcalde mayor de Yucatan, 1561–1565*, 2 vols., Documentos sacados de los archivos de España. Biblioteca Historica Mexicana de Obras Ineditas, nos. 14–15 (Mexico City: Antigua Libreria Robredo, 1938), I, p. 66. An official enquiry conducted in 1565 established that 157 Indians had died under torture, and 32 remained crippled. Some 4,549 men and women had been put to the torture, and a further 6,330, who had confessed voluntarily, had been shorn or flogged as penance. Thirteen Indians had committed suicide, and 18 others, who had disappeared, were presumed to have done so. Information collected by Sebastian Vasquez on the abuses committed and tolerated by Dr. Diego Quijada, 25 March 1565, *Don Diego Quijada* II, pp. 213–14. For an account of the trials, see Ralph L. Roys and

protests of the local Spaniards and their insistence that the Indians in their anguish were 'confessing' to offences they had not committed, the friars held to their course. It was only the arrival of the new Bishop which brought the Inquisition to an abrupt end.[8] Bishop Toral, although himself a Franciscan, was appalled by his brothers' proceedings. Discounting lurid stories of multiple human sacrifice, with preliminary crucifixion of the victims and other grotesque 'Christian' embellishments, he imposed light penances for idolatry on the imprisoned chiefs and sent them back to their villages and their offices. I have argued elsewhere the difficulties in the way of treating extorted 'confessions' as directly descriptive of reality, but despite the inflations and distortions inseparable from the friars' methods of interrogation, there can be no doubt that the leaders of a number of villages, with the cooperation of the native 'Christian' schoolmasters, had continued to practise their old rituals as well as they were able and, worse, had brought their idols and sacrifices into the Christian church and to the foot of the cross itself.

For the Indians the events of 1562, following so close on a prolonged and bloody conquest and the wrenching relocation of the villages, ought to have been traumatic indeed. The houses of the lords had stood empty, their oratories rifled, while on the patios before the churches great mounds of idols—thousands, eyewitnesses said—slowly burned. The jewelled skulls of the great dead of the ruling lineages were smashed. It had been discovered that Nachi Cocom, territorial chief of Sotuta, redoubtable enemy of the Spaniards, and later friend and informant of the Franciscan Diego de Landa, had been a secret idolator until his death, so his corpse was exhumed and flung on the fire to burn with the idols. Through the strange new rites of judicial torture and *autos de fe*, profound loyalties had been tested, and broken. Landa himself, who had headed the Inquisition, believed it had been effective, and that punishment had brought the Indians to true repentance and a full recognition that the old ways were irretrievably gone.[9] Certainly on the Spanish side there was a fairly rapid decline in the attention given to the conversion programme in the peninsula, the last decades of the century seeing the development of a comfortable consensus,

France V. Scholes, 'Fray Diego de Landa and the Problem of Idolatry in Yucatan', *Co-operation in Research*, Carnegie Institution of Washington Publication no. 501 (Washington D.C., 1938), pp. 586–620. For a revisionist view, see Inga Clendinnen, 'Fray Diego de Landa and the Problem of Human Sacrifice in Yucatan', Master's thesis, University of Melbourne, 1972.

[8] The head of the secular administration in Yucatan, the *Alcalde Mayor* Don Diego Quijada, had taken up his office only in June or July of the previous year. He officially committed himself to the support of the Franciscans in their inquisitional proceedings, but only, it seems, under pressure. Petition of Fray Diego de Landa to Don Diego Quijada, 4 July 1562, *Don Diego Quijada* I, pp. 69–71. For Quijada's early identification of Fray Diego de Landa as a man to be wary of, see Don Diego Quijada to the Crown, 15 April 1562, *Cartas de Indias*, LXVII.

[9] Landa, *Relación*, p. 80.

challenged by very few voices, that the Indians were—for Indians—well enough converted and—for Indians—good enough Christians.

THE MAYA RESPONSE

Historians chronicling the collapse of other native cultures under what sometimes seems no more than the fatal breath of European intrusion grope for metaphors of exquisite fragility; of tender flowers wilting and shrivelling, of shimmering spun-glass vessels shattering at a rude touch. For Maya culture the inelegant image that thrusts itself forward is of a tough, webby, dense sponge, elastic and, given the intricacy and multiplicity of its interconnections, almost impossible to tear. The Maya had suffered savage blows, and some of those blows were intelligently directed, yet a hundred years after the conquest they were reading the world much as they had a hundred years before. To understand the durability of that vision, it is necessary to understand Maya conceptualisations of space and time and how those conceptualisations were figured forth in their experienced world and in their account of their own human past.

The Maya conceived the world as quadrilateral. At each of the cardinal points a Sky-Bearer god sustained, like Atlas, his quarter of the world. Each Direction was identified by its own colour—red for the east, white for the north, black for the west, and yellow for the south—and possessed its own deities of wind and rain. At each corner of the world grew a tree, of the appropriate colour, while at the centre, or the Fifth Direction, rose the great green silk-cotton tree, the Tree of Life, whose branches pierced the thirteen layers of the heavens. Below the world lay the nine levels of the Underworld, a chill, bleak, shadowy place where all Maya, save those fortunate few whose manner of death exempted them, were doomed to wander endlessly.[10]

That quadrilateral shape was replicated throughout the seen world in the spaces made by men to frame human activity and in those 'natural' formations of special significance to men. In the Maya language, the classifier AC, which as a noun means turtle or turtle shell, was applied to all things which were recognised as sharing a certain basic shape. We would tend to see them as 'hollow objects', but for the Maya they were rather 'enclosed spaces'. The word was used for cenotes, caves, milpas (enclosed by the walls of the forest), villages, which were 'human' spaces in the forest, houses, temples, and (in time), churches.[11] Each of these significant spaces had its four orientations, with their appropriate colours and influences. When a house was to be built, its four corner posts, and the centre post

---

[10] Landa, *Relación*, p. 132; J. Eric S. Thompson, *Maya History and Religion*, Civilization of the American Indians Series Vol. 99 (Norman: University of Oklahoma Press, 1970), esp. pp. 194–304.

[11] For the classifier 'ac', see Thompson, *ibid.*, XIX.

382   INGA CLENDINNEN

which marked the Fifth Direction, were carefully blessed. In the temples, and in the courtyards of the lords, the shape was repeated. The shape was sketched in the air in the purification ritual preliminary to all religious ceremonial, when four old men held cords stretched tight between them, while the priest cleared the space within of dangerous spirits. Each milpa was guarded by its four spirits, very present to the milpero as he worked in the silent forest, which he propitiated again and again in rituals that traced and retraced that significant shape. The village itself was located firmly in the same frame, its four ceremonial entrances aligning it with the great orientations of the universe and marking the boundary between the unsafe, because not ritually controlled, world of the forest and the relative security of the village—a security preserved by the tireless vigilance of the priests. There were few witches in Yucatan villages: significant danger, the Maya knew, lay outside.

Round this four-cornered world moved the endlessly changing procession of deities which for the Maya constituted Time. The smallest unit recognised was the day, probably measured from sunset to sunset. The main sacred calendar, used for divination and prognostication, was based on a cycle of 20 named days, interacting with a numbers cycle from 1 to 13 and so forming a larger 260-day cycle, known as the Sacred Round. (There was also a 'week' of 9 nights, the precise significance of which is lost to us.) The solar year controlled another calendar, which consisted of 18 months of 20 days, along with a nineteenth 'month' comprising 5 unnamed and dangerously unlucky days, the *Uayeb*. Given that structure, only 4 of the 20 named days could begin the 'new year'; they were designated 'Year Bearers', and the influence of the particular Year Bearer was felt throughout his year.

During the *Uayeb* days, the gods were pausing, some slipping off their burdens of time, others readying themselves for the slow onward march. Those days were thus in a sense 'out' of time, and outside the influence of the gods. They were therefore days of peculiar terror for the Maya. Men ventured out of their houses only for ritual purposes and out of the village not at all, fearing the assault of uncontrolled forces in the form of wild beasts and serpents.[12]

During those hushed days, lords, priests and commoners together wove an elaborate ceremonial pattern, linking temple, lord's house, and village entrances, until the image of the incoming Year Bearer god was finally installed at his appropriate entrance, to serve for the next year as guardian, compass, and clock to villagers who passed and repassed, telling them, in the endless spirals of time, and the mindbaffling expanses of land and sky, 'where they stood'.[13]

[12] Cogolludo, *Historia*, Lib. IV, Cap. V.
[13] Michael Coe has presented an elegant and ingenious model of a complex rotational

Longer periods of time the sixteenth century Maya measured by a calendar based on a year or *tun* of 18 months each consisting of 20 days each. Twenty *tun* equalled 1 *katun*, or 7200 days, and 13 *katuns* (approximately 256 years) comprised the cycle in terms of which human history was located and understood. Each of the 13 *katuns* was identified by the particular named day and number with which it ended. As the names and numbers identified the gods influencing that particular slice of time, each *katun* was identified with characteristic events, which would reoccur with the return of the 'same' *katun*. Thus 'history' was, simultaneously, prophecy, and prophecy became history again with the next swing of the cycle.[14]

It was this conviction of the endless repetition of history which enabled the Maya to grasp and to render intelligible, in their own terms, their defeat and subjugation by the Spaniards. At the time of the Spanish intrusion, the Maya knew that the peninsula's political fragmentation and its endemic interprovincial warfare was a decline from an earlier period of harmonious and unified government. That harmony had been the outcome of foreign invasions. Throughout the peninsula, the noble caste based its claim to rule on descent from the lords who had once ruled at Mayapan, the Camelot of the Maya past. The real events are misty indeed, but it seems that sometime towards the end of the tenth century Yucatan was conquered by invaders of Mexican origin led by the Captain Kukulcan, the Feathered Serpent, who established their capital at what was later to be called Chichen Itza. That great city was abandoned in a *Katun* 6 Ahau, which ended in 1224. Then another group of foreigners, the Itza, possibly Mexicanised Chontal-Maya from Tabasco, took over the site, naming it 'the well of the Itza'. Led by a new 'Kukulcan', the Itza transferred their capital to the new city of

political system which he claims perhaps operated within Maya communities and replicates the transference of responsibility between deities. His argument is seductive, but I am troubled that Landa, so acute an observer, leaves no account of such a system. M. D. Coe, 'A Model of Ancient Community Structure in the Maya Lowlands', *Southwestern Journal of Anthropology*, 21 (1965): 97–114.

[14] The best discussion of the Maya calendars remains that of J. Eric S. Thompson, *Maya Hieroglyphic Writing: An Introduction*, Carnegie Institution of Washington publication no. 589 (Washington D.C., 1950). For a series of *katun* prophecies, see Ralph L. Roys, *The Book of Chilam Balam of Chumayel*, Carnegie Institution of Washington Publication no. 438 (Washington D.C., 1933), pp. 144–63. The elegance of the interlocking systems is indicated in Father Avendano's 1696 account of the sacred books of prophecy of the Peten Maya. These, he tells us, showed 'not only the count of the said days and months and years, but also the ages (*katuns*) and prophecies which their idols and images announced to them, or, to speak more accurately, the devil by means of the worship which they pay to him in the form of some stones. These ages are thirteen in number; each age has its separate idol and its priest, with a separate prophecy of its events. These thirteen ages are divided into thirteen parts, which divide this kingdom of Yucatan and each age, with its idol, priest and prophecy, rules in one of these thirteen parts of this land, according as they have divided it'. Philip Ainsworth Means, *History of the Spanish Conquest of Yucatan and of the Itzas*, Harvard University, Peabody Museum of American Archaeology and Ethnology Papers, vol. VII (Cambridge, Mass.: Peabody Museum, 1917), p. 141.

Mayapan, 'the Banner of the Maya'. Kukulcan continued to rule for a time before his mysterious withdrawal from Yucatan, but Mayapan was remembered in the native histories as a confederation of Maya chiefs ruling together with acculturated Itza. Within the walled city the chiefs and nobles of the peninsula had lived a harmonious round of ritual, feasting, and hunting, activities which expressed the highest human conformity to the great principles which moved the cosmos. In those golden days the peninsula was at peace, the commoners working in their dispersed villages to sustain the exemplary centre. When that world of order collapsed into conflict as, in the Maya view of history, all worlds must, the chiefs and nobles, fleeing in bitterness to their respective provinces, carried with them the esoteric knowledge, inscribed in the sacred books of hieroglyphs which only they could read, which was their warrant and proof of their right to rule.[15]

The Spanish intruders the Maya identified with the Itza. Like the Itza, they were lascivious and unmannerly, but also like the Itza, they had brought new and useful knowledge. Their coming did not abrogate the authority of the native rulers but merely eclipsed it: in time they would either withdraw, as had some of the Itza, or would recognise the legitimacy of the rule of the native lords, as had happened at Mayapan. The failure of the great uprising of 1546 made clear that the Spaniards could not be destroyed and demonstrated to those Maya who had doubted that a period of foreign domination was upon them. That domination they knew they must endure, but they also knew that their authority—enhanced by what they could learn from these intruders—would survive it and that they would rule again.

Much of what seems puzzling in the glimpses we have of Maya behaviour is rendered intelligible by this reading. Nachi Cocom, the formidable territorial chief of Sotuta and long a mighty fighter against the Spaniards, nevertheless was ready to discuss matters of religion with the young friar Diego de Landa. He was even ready to show Landa one of the sacred hieroglyphic books which were the treasure of his lineage, not in submission, but as part of an exchange between men of special wisdom versed in high matters.[16] The early friars had been as much puzzled as outraged to

[15] Landa, *Relación*, pp. 20–39. See also Tozzer's copious notes on the same pages. The mysteries surrounding the identity of the Itza are engagingly rehearsed and partially clarified by Eric Thompson, 'Putun (Chontal Maya) Expansion' in *Maya History and Religion*, ch. 1.

[16] 'The successor of the Cocoms, named Don Juan Cocom after [he became] a Christian, was a man of great reputation, learned in their affairs, and of remarkable discernment and well acquainted with native matters. He was very intimate with the author of this book, Fray Diego de Landa, and told him many facts concerning the antiquities. He showed him a book which had belonged to his grandfather. . . . In this [book] was a painting of a deer, and his grandfather had told him that when large deer of this kind should come to that country (for this is what they call the cows), the worship of the gods would cease; and this was fulfilled since the Spaniards brought large cows with them'. Landa, *Relación*, pp. 43–46. Landa's steady pen is

find that native lords who obstinately persisted in their traditional rituals also readily set up illicit schools and churches where they pretended to teach the Christian doctrine to their followers and to baptise and marry them in fine disregard for the friars' monopoly in that area; those lords were doing no more than maintaining their traditional role as custodians and administrators of knowledge and authority. The friars also complained of other Indians who, while urging commoners to hide their children to protect them from the dangerous and perhaps fatal rite of baptism, themselves contrived to be baptised time and again. These were clearly sorcerer-priests, 'men of power', who, having recognised on excellent empirical grounds the danger of the rite (did not the ailing children and adults the friars most urgently rushed to baptise usually die?), nevertheless submitted themselves to it again and again, to test and augment their own spiritual force.[17]

The small worlds briefly illuminated in the 1562 trial records reveal chiefs, lords, and priests pursuing their traditional roles as well as the exigencies of their situation permitted, incorporating as they went the new structures of the church, the new prominence given the traditional symbol of the cross, and those elements of the new teaching which illuminated the old.[18]

The new skills introduced by the friars were also called upon by the chiefs to serve traditional ends, as the mission-trained schoolmasters were recalled to traditional loyalties and traditional self-identifications. The chiefs engaged in arranging and sustaining the ceremonies designated illegal by the new regime communicated not by messengers but by letters, written and read by the mission-schooled. Indeed it is possible that the native schoolmasters were not initially fully aware of the friars' requirement that they should choose between the two faiths; as nobles and sons of nobles, it was fitting that they should have been selected to have privileged access to the new knowledge, and control of its dispersal among the commoners. One, who while installed as schoolmaster underwent the

to be admired, given that he had watched the corpse of his old friend burn, along with his treasured idols, in 1562. Landa was later to burn as many of the 'books' as he could lay his hands on, which, he noted, the Indians 'regretted to an amazing degree, and which caused them much affliction', Landa, *Relación*, p. 169.

[17] 'Ordenanzas del Lic. Tomas Lopez', Cogolludo, *Historia*, lib. V. cap. XVII.

[18] Late in the enquiry, some Indians confessed to having participated in rituals in which victims suffered crucifixion preliminary to sacrifice by the excision of the heart. The identification of the actual events through the double distortion of forced testimony and interrogators' perceptions is too complex a problem to unravel here, but there can be no doubt that, from the array of Christian symbols presented to them in those early days, the Maya recognised the cross as meaningful. Even today the cross is ubiquitous in Yucatan, while the elaborated cult of the saints which flourishes in mainland Mexico is lacking. For the significance of the cross to the Maya before the arrival of the Spaniards, see Merle Green, Robert L. Rands, and John A. Graham, *Maya Sculpture* (Berkeley: Lederer, Street, Zeus, 1972). See also Tozzer, *Relación*, p. 42, n. 211.

386   INGA CLENDINNEN

training to become a priest of the old religion, probably did so to enrich rather than to repudiate his Christian learning.[19]

Scattered reports down through the rest of the century and into the next make clear that chiefs, lords, and schoolmasters remained active idolators, even within the structures of the new order, and actively sustained their old ceremonies.[20] Sanchez de Aguilar, a Yucatan-born secular priest, was sufficiently roused by what he saw as the Maya passion for their old ways to write an elaborate account of the 'idol worshippers' of the bishopric in 1613. He was particularly angered by the 'audacity' and 'wickedness' of one Indian who identified himself as Moses and another pair who presented themselves as pope and bishop. What we notice about these chosen identities is that they are all lawgivers.[21]

The clearest evidence of the Maya lords' tranquil and continuing conviction of the legitimacy of their authority comes from the extraordinary compilations of Maya history, ritual, and customs to which scholars have given the generic title of 'the Books of Chilam Balam'. Their beginnings lay in the Maya recognition of the vulnerability of their treasured hieroglyphic books to confiscation and destruction by the friars. Therefore, the books were transcribed into European script and kept jealously hidden. New material was added as the years passed. Through multiple recopying by inadequately informed scribes, the original meanings, deliberately rendered obscure to the uninitiated, have been further obscured, but they remain a rich source of information on the values and ideas of the Maya ruling caste.[22]

Two of the handful of the Books of Chilam Balam which have come to the attention of scholars contain a set of esoteric questions and answers, called 'the Language of Zuyua'. The Language of Zuyua originated in the preconquest period as 'a sort of civil service examination conducted by the *halach uinic* with the object of weeding out from the ranks of legitimate

---

[19] Scholes and Adams, *Don Diego Quijada*, I, pp. 104–05, 108–09, 114.

[20] E.g., *R.Y. 2*, pp. 28, 147, 190, 212; Cogolludo, *Historia*; F. V. Scholes, R. L. Roys, E. B. Adams, 'History of the Maya Area', *C.I.W. Yearbook* 43 (July 1943/June 1944); Eva Alexander Uchmany de De la Pena, 'Cuatro Casos de Idolatria en el Area Maya ante el Tribunal de la Inquisición', *Estudios de Cultura Maya*, 6 (1967): 267–300.

[21] Pedro Sanchez de Aguilar, 'Informe contra idolorum cultores del obispado de Yucatan', in Francisco del Paso y Troncoso, *Tratado de las idolatrias, supersticiones, dioses, ritos, hechicerias y otras costumbres gentilicas de las razas aborigenes de Mexico*, 2d ed. (Mexico: Ediciones Fuentes Cultural, 1953), Vol. II.

[22] Landa and Tozzer, *Relación*, pp. 27–29; Roys, *The Book of Chilam Balam of Chumayel*; Alfredo Barrera Vasquez and Silvia Rendon, *El Libro de los libros de Chilam Balam* (Mexico City: Fondo de Cultura Economica, 1948). One scholar claims that 'soon [after the conquest] almost every village or town in the northern half of the peninsula had a copy either of these early chronicles. . .or of later ones written by their own native priests. . .' Alfredo Barrera Vasquez in Alfredo Barrera Vasquez and Sylvanus Griswold Morley, 'The Maya Chronicles', *Contributions to American Anthropology and History*, 10, no. 48, Carnegie Institution of Washington Publication no. 585 (Washington, D.C., 1949), p. 10.

chieftainship the upstarts, pretenders, and those who had obtained office under false pretences'.[23] The test continued to be applied, secretly, during the colonial period, and was held in reserve as one of the main weapons to be used in the purge that would follow the return to power of the legitimate chiefs, when 'the offspring of the harlot, the two day occupant of the mat [or authority], the rogue of the reign' would be destroyed.[24]

Let us consider the following 'riddle', clearly a postconquest addition to the 'Language'. The candidate is instructed:

> Bring the sun . . . bring the sun, my son, bear it on
> the palm of your hand to my plate. A lance is
> planted, a lofty cross, in the middle of its heart.
> A green jaguar is seated over the sun to drink its
> blood.[25]

Resonant symbols indeed. What is actually brought? A 'very large fried egg', over which the sign of the cross has been made, with a green chile pepper sitting beside it. To us, there is something a touch pathetic in those grand images being contained in such lowly domestic objects. But in a society where knowledge was power, the concealment of the highly significant in the apparently mundane must have been intensely gratifying to those who held the key of understanding.

That the Maya lords had not been recruited by the Spaniards is not surprising; they were not asked to become the colleagues of the Spaniards but required to become their servants, and their very status as the defeated protected them from more delicate and seductive techniques of recruitment. They had, therefore, nothing to gain from embracing the Spanish definitions of their roles, as administrators of Spanish policy, or primary teachers of the Faith, especially as the Spaniards operated less by reward for service than punishment for noncompliance. Nor was a learnt desire for Spanish goods liable to erode their authority from within. Of the rather meagre array of Spanish artifacts the impoverished colonists of Yucatan were able to display, only the iron axe (later to evolve into the indispensable machete) seems to have aroused Maya covetousness. But axes were in sadly short supply, and the Maya were reduced to stealing them.[26] The prestige symbols of the Spaniards also appear to have been little coveted. The horse, which for the Spaniards made the difference between a *caballero* and a *peon* and which loomed so large for Bernal Diaz that at 80 he recalled as much about his equine as his human comrades in the great campaign for Mexico, failed to grip the Maya imagination. Some chiefs petitioned and received licenses to ride horses, but (as the Spaniards had discovered during the years of war) the beasts slipped and stumbled on the stony paths and keeping them watered was a bothersome problem. The Maya called the

[23] Roys, *Book of Chilam Balam*, p. 192.   [24] *Ibid.*, p. 93.
[25] *Ibid.*, p. 89.   [26] *R.Y. I*, p. 256.

388 INGA CLENDINNEN

horse 'the tapir of Castile', and were content to leave it at that. Their own
tapirs remained much more interesting animals, being regarded as such
tough quarry that huntsmen considered it 'an act of great bravery to kill
them, and the skins, or parts of it, lasted as a memorial down to the great
grandsons. . . .'.[27]

A problem remains: why, under the impact of foreign rule and given the
real diminution of their power, did the Maya lords continue to command
the loyalty of their followers?

We are familiar enough with the phenomenon of men, marginal in their
traditional societies, who in a period of alien rule are able to move swiftly to
positions of dominance precisely because of their freedom from traditional
obligations and restrictions. Yucatan yields few traces of such men.
Changes of course there were, and significant ones: there are hints of
substantial readjustments in the vulnerable area of sexual relations and in
child-bearing patterns, and subjugation sharply reduced the economic
distance between lord and commoner.[28] But the traditional social structure,
though compressed, survived. In Mexico the Inquisitorial records are
studded with cases of Indians opportunistically and voluntarily denouncing their superiors: Landa was persuaded that, among the Yucatec Maya,
'there was not an Indian man or woman who would dare to speak against a
lord or a *principal*, even if they were to be burnt alive'.[29] When the lords
returned to the villages after the convulsive trials of 1562, no hints of
reprisals or readjustments came to Spanish ears: the villages settled their
affairs silently.

The peculiar toughness of the bonds between ruling caste and commoners sprang in part from the uncertainties of the agricultural conditions
of the peninsula. Rainfall in Yucatan is notoriously unreliable; while the
'average' annual rainfall in Merida is 34.33 inches, records over a 30-year
period reveal a variation from 16 to 64 inches, and nothing indicates the
pattern was different in the sixteenth century.[30] For the agricultural Maya,
the timing of the rains was also crucial. For maximum 'burn', the cleared
scrub had to be left to dry as long as possible, but left too long, until the
coming of the rains, a man's labour and his milpa were lost for that season.
Thus time and labour spent in the service of those knowledgeable in the
swings of the seasons and the moods of the gods were time and labour

[27] Landa, *Relación*, p. 203.
[28] With the imposition of monogamy, a number of women with their offspring were cast
into a social void. Landa noted a decline in women's chastity and an increase in violence
between marriage partners. He also recorded a decline in the age of marriage from twenty to
twelve or fourteen with the likely consequence of earlier, more frequent, and less successful
pregnancies. Landa, *Relación*, pp. 100, 127.
[29] Reply of Fray Diego de Landa to charges made by Fray Francisco de Guzman, n.d., in
Don Diego Quijada II, p. 416.
[30] Roys, *The Indian Background of Colonial Yucatan*, p. 10.

sensibly invested. Only the calendar priest could determine the appropriate day for the communal hunt, for the firing of the felled timber on the new milpas, for the bending over of the stalks of the drying corncobs, to save them from unseasonably late rains. For aid in individual misfortune or sickness, the commoner would turn to the local curer or 'doctor', but for those great decisions, and others like them, on which the survival of the group depended, the calendar priest was essential.

Priest and lord were not aloof from the villagers. On those other occasions when calamity threatened the village, it was the priests who led the dances which would climax in the offering of a human life, but the commoners had also fasted, though not so austerely, and had also lacerated ears, tongue and thighs to offer the gods their blood. They knew their small offerings to the lords had helped the lords create the elaborate *mise-en-scene*, with the regalia, the sounds, the foods, most likely to please the gods, which consumed so much of their resources. In those experiences, when the life of the whole village was absorbed in the ritual process, men learnt that the differences between priest, lord, and commoner were less important than their shared dependence on the gods and the fragility of their human order. While the man-in-the-village-street could not be privy to the complexities of the Maya pantheon, or the bewildering permutations of the multiple calendars, he was aware that it was the priests' knowledge and the lords' largesse which, by making human action harmonious with the cosmos, were indispensable for the orderly and safe functioning of human life.

When the great Montezuma was prodded and peered at by grinning Spaniards, the highly elaborated mystique that had rendered his person sacred and validated his authority was deeply scarred. The simpler face-to-face communities of Yucatan had evolved more subtle and less vulnerable modes of eliciting and offering deference. In the shared understanding of proper precedence, in the nice calculation of the values of gifts exchanged between superior and inferior, in the throatily-murmured titles, in the very intonations of speech, rank—which is order—was coded and celebrated. Those routines were to prove durable when subjugation had swept the external material signs of rank away.[31]

[31] Landa, *Relación*, pp. 62, 97. By the end of the sixteenth century through most of Spanish America those native lords who continued to command deference did so by virtue of their position within the Spanish system. Charles Gibson tells us that in the valley of Mexico Indian lords retained *Tecuhtli* titles within their own communities into the sixteenth and even into the seventeenth centuries, but that by late colonial times cacique status of its own was no longer of any significance. Charles Gibson, *The Aztecs Under Spanish Rule* (Stanford: Stanford University Press, 1964), pp. 156, 163–65. In Yucatan the *almehenob*, members of traditional ruling lineages, even although otherwise indistinguishable from commoners, were accorded their titles by those commoners into the nineteenth century. Roys also notes that in the Chan Kom area territorial boundaries which had received no official validation since the sixteenth century were still known and acknowledged by the native inhabitants as late as the 1930s. Ralph L. Roys, *The Titles of Ebtun*, Carnegie Institution of Washington Publication no. 505 (Washington, D.C., 1939), pp. 47, 62.

390   INGA CLENDINNEN

There were other and more conscious connections, forged by the very experience of conquest. Today, in the remote villages of Quintana Roo, in the southeast of the peninsula, the Maya descendants of the insurgents of the Caste War continue to celebrate their high sense of autonomy in great annual ceremonies at which their shared 'history' is expounded and interpreted in prolonged performances by specially trained and specially respected old men. The anthropologist Allen Burns has brilliantly elucidated the ways in which the histories have been developed into a coherent cultural system, modelling and interpreting the world as experienced by the Maya, and providing modes of evaluating past and future action. Burns also describes the meetings at which the performances take place as 'times of unification and intensification' for the several thousand Maya who attend.[32]

I suspect that tradition of the celebration and affirmation of the community through the celebration of its history has very long roots. The enigmatic surfaces presented by the Books of Chilam Balam are not solely due to the deficiencies of copyists and the uncertainties of translation: they are, deliberately, gnomic. They are texts designed to be elucidated by skilled oral performers. 'Still he who comes of our lineage will know it, one of us who are Maya men. He will know how to explain these things when he reads what is here,' sings the Chilam Balam of Chumayel.[33] A series of Spanish observers tells us of the Maya practice of reading, or rather performing, at secret gatherings, their 'fabulous stories and injurious histories' through the first century after conquest and beyond.[34]

All the Books of Chilam Balam which survive deal with the shared history of the peninsula of the disruptive but fructifying invasions of the legendary Kukulcan and the mysterious Itza; of the great exemplary centres of Chichen Itza and Mayapan; of the diaspora which followed their collapse; and all these events are set within, and so explained by, the great cycles of the *katuns*. Each book also contains a local history. In the Chumayel, for example, we follow a wandering group which names water-holes and resting places, conferring significance on previously undifferentiated locations, so that, memorialised in place names, the group history was inscribed upon the landscape.[35] My guess is that the meetings Burns describes found their origins in the immediate postconquest period, when the pressures of the conquest situation led to a democratization of participation in what had perhaps previously been a more exclusive celebration of

[32] Allen F. Burns, 'The Caste War in the 1970's: Present Day Accounts from Village Quintana Roo', *Anthropology and History in Yucatan*, ed. Grant D. Jones, Texas Pan American Series (Austin and London: University of Texas Press, 1977), p. 261.

[33] Roys, *Book of Chilam Balam*, p. 78.

[34] 'Ordenanzas del Lic. Tomas Lopez', in Cogolludo, *Historia*, lib. V, cap. XVI; Sanchez de Aguilar, *Informe. . .*, 325; Cogolludo, *Historia*, lib. IV, cap. VI.

[35] E.g., Roys, *Book of Chilam Balam*, pp. 72–77.

the lords. The history of the dominant lineage was transformed into a statement and account of the identity of the local community, while the story of the Itza rendered intelligible and unthreatening the presence and behaviour of the Spanish overlords.[36]

Maya knowledge was demonstrated to be adequate to explain the intrusion of previously unknown foreigners and their dominance. Even more powerfully, the landscape itself attested the truth of the traditional account of the world. Like all agriculturalists, the Maya lived according to the rhythm of the yearly agricultural cycle and the lesser growing cycles it contained. The seasons were strongly marked: during April, the sun burned hotter and more cruelly day after day, until, at last, the flying ants began to swarm, signalling the crashing thunder which announced the coming of the Chacs, with their life-giving rain. But that yearly cycle was embedded in larger cycles. As a milpa could be planted for only two or three seasons before the yields grew too light and the scrubby forest regrowth too stubborn, each man tended milpas at different stages of their cycles, marking out a careful space in the forest at one place, and beginning the hard labour of felling the larger trees, gathering what he knew to be his last crop in another. All around him were the signs of this endless process: the blackened square of a milpa being created; the dim shapes of milpas in the course of reclamation by the forest. Even the tallest forest, he knew, had been milpa once, and would be milpa again. Those cycles within cycles the priests could discern in the majestic wheelings of the stars could also be read by the commoner, for they were inscribed upon the land.

Human settlement told the same story. Where population growth in the mother village enforced the dispersal of the milpas beyond the tolerance even of Maya legs, a few families moved to 'hive off' to form a temporary hamlet for a few years until that area of the forest had been exploited. All around were the traces of those brief habitations, in the slowly collapsing wattle and daub huts or in the slight elevations which marked the house mounds on which the huts had once stood. And, of course, there were the great stone structures, thrusting up through the forest, testifying to the much larger and more permanent habitations of the past. Some of the ruins were of cities the Maya knew from their myths, like Mayapan, Chichen Itza, and Uxmal, and recalled past conflicts, past invasions, past harmony. Regarding others the myths were either silent or confused. But as Indians, under Spanish orders, dragged the shaped carved stones from the ruins of Tihoo to build the city the Spaniards called Merida, or destroyed a pyramid

---

[36] E.g., Roys, *Book of Chilam Balam*, p. 79. 'Then with the true God, the true *Dios*, came the beginning of our misery. It was the beginning of tribute, the beginning of church dues. . .the beginning of forced debts, the beginning of debts enforced by false testimony. . .But it shall still come to pass that tears shall come to the eyes of our Lord God. The justice of our Lord God shall descend on every part of the world. . .'

392   INGA CLENDINNEN

to build a monastery, it is likely that the lesson they drew was not of the dominance of the new regime but of the transciency of all such human devisings.

In 1545, Nachi Cocom had carried out a prudent survey of the borders of his province. Although he and most of his entourage were still unbaptised, he readily utilised crosses as his boundary markers.[37] In later land maps of the sixteenth century, within the distinctive Maya circular form with the significant direction of the east to the top of the page, crosses identify boundaries, and churches identify villages. Through the landscape itself, crosses proliferated, in private houses, in front of churches, at village entrances, along the roads, at the corners of milpas. There is nothing to indicate the Maya were responsive to the specific resonances of the cross as Christian symbol: rather the cross was taken over—'encapsulated', in Vogt's useful word—to mark out, as idols and images had once done, significant locations and boundaries in the Maya map of the experienced world, just as it had been utilized, under Spanish direction, to designate locations and boundaries in the painted map of that world.[38] In the Books of Chilam Balam, the coming rule of the Lord Jesus Christ and of the Lord God is celebrated and welcomed, but the two lords of the new cycle take delight not in Christian offerings but in the jade, the precious green plumes, and the mead-like balche which delight the gods of the Maya. The 'Christian' deities are neatly inserted into a Maya scheme of things: the world they inhabit is the four-directional world of the traditional cosmology, and it is the Maya sacred numbers of four, nine and thirteen which reverberate through their ceremonies. For the Maya there was no tension between their repudiation of the Spanish claim to rule and assertion of a monopolistic control of Christian truth, and their acceptance of the Christian gods as deities whose time had come: when the Lord Jesus Christ entered at last upon his rule, it was the Maya lords who would rule under him.[39]

The world as the Maya experienced it, even in the relocated villages, remained the traditional world. For the women, rising in the grey light of dawn to pursue their round of women's tasks, grinding the sacred corn, weaving and spinning, nurturing their children and tending their animals, it was the familiar Maya goddess of fertility, sexuality, and things domestic whose protection they solicited, whatever name the friars gave her. House and houseyard, church and patio, echoed the four-sided shape of the world, and the new village, like the old, protected itself from the forest by guardian crosses at its four entrances. For the men too, making their swift offerings as they passed the crosses marking the traditionally dangerous and sacred

[37] 'Documentos de Tierra de Sotuta', appendix in Roys, *The Titles of Ebtun*, pp. 421–33.
[38] Evon Z. Vogt, *Zinacantan: A Maya Community in the Highlands of Chiapas* (Cambridge, Mass.: Belknap Press of Harvard University Press, 1969), p. 582.
[39] E.g., Roys, *Book of Chilam Balam*, pp. 98–107; 120–25.

places along the paths between milpa and village, the continuity of the old order was constantly pledged by the rhythms and shapes of daily experience.

To the Spaniards, colonists and friar alike, the only locations of significance in Yucatan's grey monotony of forest were the human concentrations of the villages. The idols they found in caves, cenotes and milpas, the secret meetings they stumbled upon in the forests, they saw as evidence of Maya inventiveness in deceit, for those areas the Spaniards had defined as mere terrain. The Maya read their landscape very differently. The small cleared spaces of village and milpa, linked by the narrow and perilous paths, still spoke at once of the mutability of human endeavour and of its glory, evoking as they did in their shape and orientations the great exemplary centres of Mayapan and Chichen Itza. Only the forests, the waterholes and the gods of the World Directions were constant. The friars of Yucatan had enjoyed in those first days after conquest an unusual freedom of action, but despite the intelligence and the ruthlessness of their assault on the imaginative universe of the Maya, they had crucially miscalculated. An account of the world which dismissed the forests as mere nature, and which postulated the progressive nature of time and the primary value of the individual human life, could not, in the ironic context of the Yucatan landscape, compel belief.[40]

[40] The conscientious conservatism of the Maya persists. In parts of modern day Yucatan where plantation henequen production has long dominated the milpas, many towns must import the *h-men* (Maya priest) from other areas for the annual Maya *cha chaac* ceremony. In some areas, where government redistribution of former plantation land has permitted the restoration of the milpas after a long hiatus, the milpa ritual has also been revived. Irwin Press, *Tradition and Adaptation: Life in a Modern Yucatan Maya Village* (Westport, Conn.: Greenwood Press, 1975), p. 34.

17

Race and Class in Colonial Latin America: A Critique

Robert McCaa, Stuart B. Schwartz
and Arturo Grubessich

The relationship of society to economy and the interplay of economic realities and social ideology remain central concerns in Latin American history. It is for this reason that the recent article by John K. Chance and William B. Taylor is so important. Nevertheless we believe that there are serious methodological flaws in their study which detract from the value of their results. The statistical errors they have committed and the measures we propose to overcome them should be of interest to all those concerned with the analysis of social systems. We therefore offer our criticisms and suggestions as part of an ongoing dialogue with social historians.

Chance and Taylor limit their analysis to one city at a single point in time—Antequera, Oaxaca, in 1792—but the implications of their findings and indeed the extrapolations from the data are used to suggest wider application for their model. The thrust of their argument is that, rather than a rigid system of estates based on color and juridicial definition, a system of socioeconomic groups reflecting the increasing "capitalist oriented economic class system" had emerged in Oaxaca by the late eighteenth century (p. 456). While we find ourselves in agreement with the broad direction of change they suggest, we believe that they have made conceptual and methodological errors that impair the validity and usefulness of their analysis. Their revisionary stance has overdrawn the neglect of class in the historiography of colonial Latin America, as is evidenced in works cited by the authors themselves.[1] In addition, a definition of class

[1] In addition to the works cited by Chance and Taylor, see Carlos S. Assadourian, Guillermo Beato, and Juan Chiaramonte, *Argentina de la conquista a la independencia* (Buenos Aires, 1972), pp. 309–49; Salvador de la Plaza, "La formación de las clases sociales en Venezuela," *Cultura Universitaria*, v. 87 (1965); José Miranda, *España y Nueva España en la época de Felipe II* (Mexico, 1962), pp. 94–103. That there were other hierarchies as well is pointed out in Germán Colmenares, *Historia económica y social de Colombia, 1537–1719* (Bogotá, 1973), pp. 408–460.

422   R. MCCAA, S. B. SCHWARTZ AND A. GRUBESSICH

based solely on occupation leads to serious errors in inference when not combined with information on wealth, residence or some other variable indicating economic position. More important, despite the authors' careful analysis and their ability to define the central questions, they have made a weak choice of statistical models for elaborating the relationship between race and occupation, as well as for the relationship between the race of brides and grooms. Their dependence on simple statistics (percentages) has led, we believe, to a series of unwarranted conclusions and to an emphasis on spurious relationships. Finally they exaggerate the economic basis of social stratification in colonial Oaxaca. We conclude that their data demonstrate just how little effect commercial capitalism had in the destruction of the racial and estate hierarchies of colonial society. The external pressures of capitalist expansion in Oaxaca and the dependent character of that growth reinforced the racial basis of the social structure in both behavioral and ideological terms.

Socioracial designations present the first problem. Chance and Taylor assume too much consistency in this regard. They note that both "passing" and changing socioracial classification were probably fairly frequent in colonial Oaxaca, although they make no attempt to assay this assumption quantitatively. A comparison of the racial designations in the census manuscripts and the designation of the same individuals in the marriage registers would prove enlightening. In an unpublished study of Valparaíso, Chile (1777–88), Arturo Grubessich using such a method, found considerable variation in socioracial labels over a person's lifetime. In fact, some 49 percent of male household heads altered their racial designations at least once within a twelve-year period.[2] Record linkage of parish registers, three

[2] Arturo Grubessich, "Social History of a Colonial Hispanic American City: Valparaiso (Chile) During the Last Quarter of the Eighteenth Century" (M.A. thesis, University of Minnesota, 1978), p. 34. Given the novelty of this kind of information, the deviations are reported here in detail.

Socio-Racial Variations for Male Household Heads as Derived from the Linkage of Censuses and Marriage Registers: Valparaiso, 1777–1788

	Spaniard	Mestizo	Mulatto	Indian	Total
Don	51	14	1	2	68
Spaniard		98	10	25	133
Mestizo			8	21	29
Mulatto				9	9

The chart shows that some two-thirds of the variations were between proximate groups in the socioracial hierarchy, such as "Spaniard-Don" and "Mestizo-Spaniard;" however, 30.5 percent of the variations, some 15 percent of all geographically stable male household heads, manifest large leaps or falls in their status. This kind of data may be generated only through minute linkage and systematic analysis of information on the lives of ordinary people from a wide variety of sources. See Grubessich, pp. 30–35.

RACE AND CLASS IN COLONIAL LATIN AMERICA   423

manuscript censuses, and other miscellaneous documents revealed considerable variation in the racial designations used by or ascribed to individuals on different occasions. Close analysis of these variations can reveal attitudinal and behavioral elements that determined racial designations at particular moments of contact with the state bureaucracy. The basic question is one of inference. Changing racial designations may indicate social fluidity and the existence of class, but the persisting importance of estate-based labels to both individuals and the state suggests to us the primary role of socioracial criteria. We argue that this position is supported by the quantitative analysis that follows.

The legal and practical disabilities that persons of darker phenotype suffered in colonial Latin America (as Chance and Taylor admit on p. 462) indicate to us the existence of estate or caste-like hierarchies reflected in attitude and behavior. The data from Valparaíso suggest that social norms demanded that individuals with certain economic attributes possess corresponding racial statuses. Therefore racial attributes changed as social circumstances and economic fortunes demanded. An attempt to analyze racial marriage patterns on the basis of marriage acts alone or occupational data with race as declared in the censuses will be conjectural because of the overwhelming need perceived by most peoples both to marry racial equals and to maintain a racial status appropriate to their social status. This phenomenon may be explained to some extent by the Royal Pragmatic of 1776, which gave parents juridicial grounds for denying consent to their children's marriages with partners of unequal status.[3] Then too it seems that the similarity of racial classifications for marriage partners reflects what people considered proper behavior, and therefore many couples harmonized their status at marriage in order to achieve this ideal. The transitory nature of racial or caste designations, recognized by Chance and Taylor in Oaxaca (p. 465) and by Grubessich in Valparaíso, indicates to us not so much the destruction of a hierarchy of estates as the continuing and powerful importance of the hierarchy in the face of economic change.[4]

To dissect the relationship race and class, Chance and Taylor rely exclusively on percentages, a strategy that prevents them from achieving their principal goal: to determine "*to what degree*" race and class determined social stratification (p. 483, italics in original). A more probing use of statistics—specifically endogamy measures, models of statistical independence, and correlation coefficients—produces a more accurate picture of marital and occupational structures. We believe that the inference from these statistics must be that socioracial criteria, as opposed to class, were the principal determinants of stratification in colonial Oaxaca.

[3] Richard Konetzke, *Colección de documentos para la historia de la formación social de Hispano America* (Madrid, 1953–62), 3:406–07.
[4] Grubessich, pp. 41–50.

First, the marriage data. Chance and Taylor present a marriage table in which the race of the bride is cross-classified with that of the groom and percentaged so that the race of the grooms sums to unity (Table 1). They then proceed to create a picture of Oaxaca marriage patterns on the basis of these percentages. Consequently their analysis ignores both the marginal distribution of nuptial partners by race and the imbalance of sex ratios

TABLE 1

Marriages by Socio-Racial Designation: Oaxaca, 1793–97

		Brides					
		Peninsulars	*Creoles*	*Mestizos*	*Mulattoes*	*Indians*	*Total*
Grooms	Peninsulars	0	19	1	0	2	22
	Creoles	0	144	48	12	7	211
	Mestizos	0	35	55	28	20	138
	Mulattoes	0	15	20	13	8	56
	Indians	0	33	45	26	183	287
	Total	0	246	169	79	220	714

SOURCE: Chance and Taylor (1977), Table 4.
NOTE: To simplify subsequent calculations, Negroes (2) are combined with the Mulatto group, caciques (4) with Indians, and unknowns (133) excluded. The authors refer to this information as a "complete sample" [*sic*] (p. 477) but at another point mention "1,318 brides and grooms" (p. 462).

(except for the extreme case of the peninsulars with twenty-two grooms and no brides). They emphasize the degree of intermarriage (or lack of endogamy) in Oaxaca without specifically indicating a standard for comparison. The implication is that an estate model would require all marriages to be between people of the same race. However, even in fully caste-like societies, such as certain Asian countries, marriage rules generally consist of prohibitions against unions within several lineages instead of total endogamy.

For purposes of measurement it is analytically useful to compare the observed marriage pattern with one to be expected solely from chance.[5] For example, in the case of Oaxacan Indians, Indian brides represent 30.8 percent of all brides (220 divided by 714). Therefore on the basis of random mating, 30.8 percent of Indian brides would be expected to marry with each

[5] The choise of a random model is made on substantive and statistical grounds. First, the estimates have an immediately understandable, intuitive meaning. Second, they facilitate further statistical elaboration (impossible where the expected values are 0 or 100 percent as in the implicit model used by Chance and Taylor). Most importantly, this approach advances comparative research independent of the actual racial structures and even of the stratification criteria being applied. It should be apparent that the expectation of random mating is a statistical hypothesis for purposes of measurement and not a substantive one that the researcher actually hopes to confirm.

group of grooms (e.g., 287 Indian grooms × 30.8 percent = 88.4 marriages expected between Indians; see Table 2). In contrast, Chance and Taylor calculate an intermarriage ratio, the percent of exogamous marriages for each race, which, given the heterogeneous racial structure of Oaxaca, principally reflects the racial distribution of brides and grooms rather than intermarriage rates or probabilities.[6]

TABLE 2

Marriages Expected from Random Mating

		Brides					
		Peninsulars	*Creoles*	*Mestizos*	*Mulattoes*	*Indians*	*Total*
Grooms	Peninsulars	0	7.6	5.2	2.4	6.8	22
	Creoles	0	72.7	49.9	23.4	65.0	211
	Mestizos	0	47.5	32.7	15.3	42.5	138
	Mulattoes	0	19.3	13.2	6.2	17.3	56
	Indians	0	98.9	67.9	31.7	88.4	287
	Total	0	246	169	78	220	714

Maximum likelihood estimates for $Cell_{ij} = (Brides_i/\text{Total Marriages}) \times Grooms_j$.

To draw firm inferences about the caste basis of marriage both substantive and statistical standards are essential. Statistically, norms based on probabilities take into account imbalances in the sexual and racial composition of brides and grooms. From these probabilities an overall measure of endogamy may be calculated. The difference between the observed and the expected endogamous unions indicates the relative importance of race for the selection of marriage partners. David J. Strauss recently proposed the statistic K* to measure endogamy.[7] For Oaxaca, K* is .46 (where 0.0

[6] They incorrectly refer to their measure as a rate while it is in fact a ratio, that is the proportion of grooms for each racial group who married brides of other groups. Actual rates, based on the marriageable population by race and sex, would be extraordinarily interesting for exposing the real marriage propensities and determining the relative importance of demographic (sex-ratio) and social (stratification) forces. Census data at their disposal, properly tabulated and related to the marriage acts, could be made to yield this important information. In communities where marriage probabilities by race vary greatly, failure to incorporate this feature could lead to spurious conclusions. This problem plagues all analyses of endogamy regardless of the substantive issue. Most researchers proceed with a warning and with little hope of obtaining the appropriate denominator. This is one of the few cases in which the relevant information for the population at risk may exist. See note 10 below.

[7] David J. Strauss, "Measuring Endogamy," *Social Science Research* 6 (1977): 225–27. The statistic K*, which measures the relative incidence of endogamy, is computed as follows:

Where,

P_o = Sum of Observed Endogamous Marriage/Total Marriages

P_e = Sum of Expected Endogamous Marriages (E_{ii})/Total Marriages

$E_{ij} = (Brides_i/\text{Total Marriages}) \times Grooms_j$

P^* = Sum of Minimum Number of Brides or Grooms for Each Group/Total Marriages

426   R. MCCAA, S. B. SCHWARTZ AND A. GRUBESSICH

indicated a completely random process and 1.0 signifies maximum endogamy). The figure has significance only in a comparative context. Two groups of Druz Arabs (with explicit lineage rules of intermarriage) show endogamy measures of .48 and .52. For Valparaíso the endogamy coefficient is .72. A more intuitively meaningful measure derived from the same approach is the percent of increase in observed endogamy above that expected by chance alone. For Oaxaca there were 112 percent more endogamous marriages than expected from random mating versus 130 percent for Valparaíso (1740–90) and 104 percent for León, Mexico (1782–85).[8] Clearly the selection of nuptial partners in Oaxaca was not a random process with respect to race. While a completely closed caste system did not exist, endogamy was very high—almost as high as in less dynamic outposts of the Spanish empire such as Valparaíso in the Captaincy General of Chile. In a comparative context these statistics indicate that racial endogamy in Oaxaca continued very strong until the end of the colonial regime, and indirectly they contradict the hypothesis that class was an important determinant of social stratification in Oaxaca.

The same measurement procedure (comparing differences between observed marriages and maximum likelihood estimates) can be applied to each racial group to analyze group marriage tendencies more accurately. According to Chance and Taylor, Creoles and Indians had the highest rates of endogamy while mulattoes and mestizos married out to such a degree that they "did not comprise groups in the sociological sense" (p. 481). The authors have confused arithmetic with sociology. Given their conclusion of unequal endogamy, it is appropriate to test the null hypothesis that endogamy rates are the same for all groups. In Table 3 we recalculate expected numbers of endogamous marriages for each group from the overall average of joint probabilities. The null hypothesis of equal endogamy may be accepted with a very high probability. Endogamous tendencies are virtually the same for all groups. The mestizos are slightly less endogamous

Then,

$$K^* = (P_o - P_e)/(P^* - P_e)$$
$$\Delta\%^* = ([P_o - P_e]/P_e/P^*) \times 100$$

Applying this procedure to the data for Oaxaca, we have;

$$
\begin{aligned}
P_o &= (0+144+55+13+183)/714 &&= 395/714 = .553 \\
P_e &= (0+72.7+32.7+6.2+88.4)/714 &&= 200/714 = .280 \\
P^* &= (0+211+138+54+220)/714 &&= 623/714 = .873 \\
K^* &= (.553-.280)/(.873-.280) &&= .459 \\
\Delta\%^* &= (.553-.280)/.280/.873 &&= 112\%
\end{aligned}
$$

(NOTE: Data may show some rounding effects; all calculations were performed with unrounded figures through the final step.) See also Yvonne M. M. Bishop, Steven E. Feinberg, and Paul W. Holland, *Discrete Multivariate Analysis: Theory and Practice* (Cambridge 1975), pp. 393–97.

[8] We prefer the percentage difference statistic because of its direct substantive significance and ease of interpretation. The K^* statistics, like most measures of association, are more difficult to interpret meaningfully.

RACE AND CLASS IN COLONIAL LATIN AMERICA   427

TABLE 3

Marital Endogamy in Oaxaca: 1793–97

Group	Total Marriages		Endogamous Marriages		Δ%	$(O-E)^2/E$
	Brides	Grooms	Observed	Expected		
Peninsulars	0	22	0	0	—	—
Creoles	246	211	144	143.6	0	0.0
Mestizos	169	138	55	64.5	−15	1.4
Mulattoes	79	56	13	12.2	6	0.0
Indians	220	287	183	174.7	5	0.4
Total	714	714	395	395.0		1.85

$\chi^2 = 1.85$; with 4 degrees of freedom, $P = .7$
with 3 degrees of freedom, $P = .6$.
Where $Expected_i = Brides_i \times Grooms_i \times$ Endogamy factor.
Endogamy factor = Total Endogamous Marriages/$\Sigma(Brides_i \times Grooms_i)$.
For method of calculation see Strauss, p. 241; Bishop, et al., pp. 393–98.

than other groups (with nine fewer intermarriages than expected, or −15 percent, while Indians appear to be slightly more endogamous (eight more or +5 percent). However, these differences are trivial. Given the observed frequencies and proportions, one would expect these slight differences to occur by chance in at least six instances out of ten. If the smaller racial groups in Oaxaca, the mestizos and mulattoes, had intermarriage ratios (measures used by Chance and Taylor) equal to those of the larger groups, that would in fact indicate much higher endogamy because the members of the small groups would have been rejecting a much larger proportion of exogamic partners. Whether the slight differences which we present are accepted as real or simply as random variations, the pattern indicates that all racial groups, whatever their sizes, were recognized as groups in a sociological sense, and marriage decisions and racial designations were influenced accordingly. Moreover if the designations in the marriage acts are accepted as valid, then the division of Oaxaqueño society by estates would have continued for many generations. Chance and Taylor were led astray when they ignored the marginal totals. The low endogamy ratio for the mulattoes and mestizos is almost wholly explained by their relative sparsity in the marrying population. In turn the fact that there were fewer mestizos is to be explained by the impressively high intramarriage and lower intermarriage propensities for the society as a whole.

Finally, with respect to the analysis of exogamy, the authors' analysis is similarly befuddled by their failure to consider marginal totals. The above statistical procedure may be used to generate a third set of estimates, but

428 R. MCCAA, S. B. SCHWARTZ AND A. GRUBESSICH

now the focus is exclusively on marriages between groups. Endogamous entries are dropped from the table and maximum-likelihood estimates are recalculated from the new marginal sums.[9] Table 4 reports the percentage differences of the observed pattern from that expected by chance.

TABLE 4

Intermarriage Patterns in Oaxaca, 1793–97: Percentage Difference Between Observed Exogamous Marriages and those Expected from Random Mating

	Brides (Δ%)				
Grooms (Δ%)	Creoles	Mestizos	Mulattoes	Indians	N
Creoles and Peninsulars	—	21*	−31	−25	70
Mestizos	−8*	—	5*	9	83
Mulattoes	9	−11*	—	20	43
Indians	6*	−12*	19*	—	104
N	83	114	66	37	300

SOURCE: Table 1.

NOTE: Entries marked "*" are based on expected values greater than 19. Peninsulars are collapsed with Creoles because of their very particular marriage pattetrn (total lack of peninsular brides). Figures indicate the relative attraction or repulsion of marriages between groups. For method of calculation, see note 9.

The contrast between conclusions based on percentages (pp. 479, 481) and those derived from Table 4 is noteworthy. While Chance and Taylor point to "the almost random mating behavior among many mestizos and mulattoes," more refined analysis shows that mulattoes more naturally paired with Indians and shunned mestizos and Creoles. Probabilistic analysis indicates that the society of castes was manifested both through high endogamy and a systematically ordered exogamous pattern. The authors' argument in respect to the exceptional frequency of marriages between couples of nonadjacent racial groups—cited as an indicator of the breakup of the caste system—is also contradicted when sex ratios and size of groups are controlled. The systematic preference for mates of adjacent groups and a rank ordering of marriage structure is impressive. The principal exception is that of Creole women who married relatively more mulatto and Indian

[9] The expected values are derived by a process of proportional iterative fitting. See Strauss, pp. 239–41, and Bishop et al., pp. 206–09, 398–99. Richard M. Bernard and John B. Sharpless, "Analyzing Structural Influence on Social History Data," *Historical Methods* 11 (Summer 1978): 113–121, use a similar but more refined approach to estimate the effects of demographic constraints but they neglect measures for analyzing social processes.

RACE AND CLASS IN COLONIAL LATIN AMERICA   429

men than expected. The problem is to distinguish sex-ratio induced exogamy from the effects of underlying principles of social stratification. At the same time that the severe imbalance of the sexes by race necessitated considerable exogamy, social norms strongly encouraged choices in agreement with a system of hierarchically ordered castes.

At this point the importance of true rates, as opposed to ratios, becomes apparent. There were too many Creole and mestizo brides for the number of white grooms and, at the other social extreme, too many Indian grooms for the number of Indian brides. Were there more (fewer) marriageable white (Indian) women than men in Oaxaca? True marriage rates by sex and race are essential to determine the relative importance of demographic as opposed to sociological factors.[10] While conclusions derived from inscribed marriages instead of true propensities must be conjectural, in this instance it seems clear that marriage patterns in one of the most dynamic regional economies of colonial Hispanic America were strongly conditioned by caste-like considerations from all viewpoints: with respect to overall endogamy, endogamy for specific groups, and even specific exogamy patterns. While the comparision between Oaxaca and León, on the one hand, and Valparaiso, on the other, indicates less endogamy for the former, the differences are small. They seem insufficient to signal a transition from a society of castes to some other stratification system, such as one of classes.

What evidence is there for stratification along class lines in Oaxaca? The occupational data presented by Chance and Taylor also contradict the thesis that Oaxacan society was ordered along class lines. The analysis is hampered by two shortcomings in the original data: the exclusion of Indians (which they fully discuss) and the apparent omission from the

---

[10] Marriage figures must be related to population data derived from a timely census indicating the number of unmarried adults by race and sex. A very rough indication of the variations can be derived from comparing the occupational data by race for adult males with marriages as follows:

Male Crude Marriage Rates by Race, Oaxaca

	Peninsulars	Creoles	Mestizos	Mulattoes	Indians	Total
Occupation 1792	218	1536	833	611	1543	4741
Marriages, 1793–97	22	220	152	69	315	778
% (M/O)	10.1	14.3	18.2	11.3	20.4	16.4

This suggests that Indian men married twice as frequently as peninsulars. In fact, aside from mulattoes, there is a pronounced inverse correlation between race and frequency of marriage. Similar but more refined data for both sexes are required to develop this line of analysis with confidence. Finally, one should not overlook the opportunity to analyze occupational and marriage data by broad age groups. Some differences may be due to structural differences in ages for each group; others may be due to life-cycle differentials by race.

430   R. MCCAA, S. B. SCHWARTZ AND A. GRUBESSICH

original enumeration of common laborers, carriers and simply the brute manpower needed to move goods and perform menial tasks.[11]

Moreover occupational information as contained in colonial censuses presents methodological and analytical obstacles for inferring class status. If data on property ownership or place of residence are not included or not used, then a false image of social hierarchies can result. In the 1778 census of Buenos Aires, for example, it can be demonstrated that while castas comprised 13.2 percent of those in trade and commerce, indicating relatively higher status in Chance and Taylor's unidimensional system, an examination of residence patterns shows that these groups were heavily concentrated in districts on the outskirts of the city, in poor areas where the majority of the population was nonwhite.[12] Sharing the same occupational designation is not in and of itself a sign of equality.

Finally the analysis of class and estate is obscured by the authors' statistical methods and insufficient attention to the interrelationships apparent in their principal table (Table 5). There is an obvious, strong and systematic association between estate and occupation, even if one leaves aside the problem of omitted categories. Most peninsulars were members of the elite; most mestizos and mulattoes were low-status artisans. Creoles were scattered more heterogeneously throughout all occupational categories; nevertheless, they were obviously concentrated in the middle layers and less well represented in the extremes. The coefficient of correlation between race and occupation is .44 (Somer's d with occupation dependent; .53 with race dependent), a moderately strong relationship.[13] Moreover the

[11] The authors lament the lack of occupational information for the Indians but nevertheless attempt to dissect the economic structure of the city without them (1543 were presumed to live there but their occupations were not specified). This omission means that a goodly proportion of the bottom half of the occupational pyramid must be ignored (1543 versus 3198 with known occupations). A related problem is that the survey reveals far too few common laborers, porters and the like. In a city with seventy-two high royal officials there were only ninety-three male servants listed. Similarly, 215 merchants required only fifteen muleteers. In an economy with many artisans there were virtually no laborers, odd-jobbers, carriers or simply unskilled hands to aid them, if the enumeration is accepted without adjustment. Moreover, unemployed males (102), farmers and farm laborers (172) and miners (14) are (unintentionally?) excluded from consideration (9 percent of listed workers; see p. 473, note 20). There is also a peculiar imbalance between merchants (215) and shopkeepers (18). Finally, Chance and Taylor classify all merchants as members of the elite (exactly two-thirds of the total) which seems excessive for the time and place. The result of these decisions and problems is to inflate the elite and make the lowest stratum of the working population disappear. In these circumstances analysis of the social structure is seriously distorted.

[12] This observation is drawn from Peggy Creider, "A Study of the Casta Population of Buenos Aires based upon the Census of 1778" (summa cum laude thesis, University of Minnesota, 1968), done under the direction of Stuart B. Schwartz. It should be noted that after 1778, when attempts were made in Buenos Aires to create guilds, the efforts to form a shoemakers' guild broke down exactly over the issue of race. In 1793 the *criollo* shoemakers finally received permission to create a guild that excluded both *castas* and foreigners. See also Lyman Johnson, "The Silversmiths of Buenos Aires: A Case Study in the Failure of Corporate Social Organization," *Journal of Latin American Studies* 8.2 (Nov. 1976): 181–213.

[13] See Robert H. Somers, "A New Asymmetric Measure of Association for Ordinal

TABLE 5

Distribution of Occupational Groups by Race: Oaxaca, 1792

		Race					
		Peninsulars	*Creoles*	*Mestizos*	*Mulattoes*	*Indians*	*N*
Group	Elite	87.6%	8.6%	0.4%	0.2%	—	327
	Professionals	6.9	17.9	1.3	1.0	—	307
	High-status Artisans	3.7	19.2	8.5	6.0	—	411
	Low-status Artisans	1.8	53.1	84.3	87.7	—	2058
	Servants & Peons	—	1.2	5.5	3.1	—	95
	N	218	1536	833	611		3198
	Not specified					1543	

SOURCE: Chance and Taylor (1977), pp. 468, 474, 475.

level of association would be even higher if the lower occupational groups (servants and peons) had been proportionately greater and racially distributed like low-status artisans. To test the extreme case, assume that all Indians were peons. The correlation jumps to .75 (.83 with race dependent). A more probable model for Indians might be to distribute them according to the pattern of the mestizos and mulattoes, but inverting the low artisan and peon ratios to generate sufficient unspecialized laborers. This hypothesis yields correlations of .73 and .67 (estate and occupation dependent, respectively). To summarize, there is clearly a systematic, ordered association between estate and class in colonial Antequera. The observed correlation is greatly attenuated by the omission of Indians and common laborers.

Our conclusions should be contrasted with those of Chance and Taylor (p. 473): " . . . with the exception of the peninsular groups, the racial divisions . . . did not coincide with the socio-economic hierarchy of the city." While the authors are correct in asserting that the association between estate and class is not so high with the peninsulars removed (d=.33 and .43; or .64 and .69 with Indians distributed among all occupational groups), the overall relationship continues strong.

The strength of the association is made more precise by comparing the observed occupational structure with that expected by chance (Table 6). The percentage differences between the observed pattern and the maximum likelihood estimates (in which cell frequencies are functions of row and column marginals and the total N) shows an extraordinarily systematic relationship. The peninsulars are the extreme example, of course. But note the pattern for mestizos and mulattoes. There were roughly 90 percent fewer in the professional and elite categories than one would expect on the

Variables," *American Sociological Review* 27 (1962): 788–811; or Herman J. Loether and Donald G. McTavish, *Descriptive Statistics for Sociologists* (Boston, 1974), pp. 221–29.

432   R. MCCAA, S. B. SCHWARTZ AND A. GRUBESSICH

TABLE 6

*Percentage Difference Between Observed and Expected Racial
and Occupational Structure*

	Race			
	Peninsulars	Creoles	Mestizos	Mulattoes
Elite	757	−16	−97	−98
Professional	−28	87	−86	−90
High Artisan	−71	49	−34	−53
Low Artisan	−97	−17	31	36
Servants	—	−61	86	71

$\%_{ij} = [(Observed_{ij} - Expected_{ij})/Expected_{ij}] \times 100.$
Where $Expected_{ij} = (Race_i/Total\ N) \times Occupation_j.$

basis of chance. Similarly they were overrepresented in the low artisan and servant categories. The group for which the relationship between class and caste is weakest is the Creoles. Nevertheless the pattern is very strong: Creoles are slightly underrepresented in the elites (but see note 10), strongly overrepresented in the professional and high artisan groups, and underrepresented in the lower categories.

The authors work with an implicit model demanding a perfect correlation between class and caste. However, few modern social historians paint colonial Spanish America in such sharply contrasting colors—even for the immediate postconquest epoch. From the earliest days of Spanish rule some Indians and castes advanced in the occupational hierarchy at the same time that some Spaniards performed lowly artisan jobs for want of other opportunities. What may be surprising about the Oaxaca data is that over 50 percent of Creole workers were low-status artisans. However, this is congruent with the thesis developed by historians of colonial society that Spaniards, regardless of social pretensions, entered any remunerative trade at which money could be made if more rewarding alternatives were unavailable (not, to be sure, without running a risk of suffering a loss of status and falling a step or more on the socioracial ladder).[14]

Scholars who believe that colonial Spanish America was wholly a caste system in which groups were rigidly constrained by racial origins should have their belief shaken by the Oaxaca data. Yet most scholars have for some time recognized the fluidity between racial groupings; they have never seriously questioned the importance of occupation as a determinant of status. The question has been to identify the relative weight of race and occupation in the determination of life chances and social standing.

[14] See, for example, James Lockhart, *Spanish Peru, 1532–1560* (Madison, 1968), Cf. Norman Martin, *Los vagabundos en la Nueva España* (Mexico, 1957).

RACE AND CLASS IN COLONIAL LATIN AMERICA   433

Chance and Taylor compare observed patterns against a statistically unspecified, but apparently extreme, model of a perfect caste system. Their conclusions correctly emphasize the disparities between reality and their fictive model. The statistical models we present, while also hypothetical, are explicit and more refined; consequently they permit an arithmetically precise assessment of deviations. They point to substantive inferences that differ markedly from the revisionist ones advanced by Chance and Taylor.

The problem must be examined with respect to both ideology and behavior: on the one hand, it is a question of values, esteem and perceptual identity, and on the other, behavioral realities as reflected in marriage and occupational patterns. Much of the documentation presented by Chance and Taylor points directly to a system of castes in terms of ideology and social values. It is significant that Indians and blacks were excluded from the census of 1792, but scribes and shoemakers were not. The political, economic and bureaucratic privileges and prohibitions conferred by racial origin confirm the caste-like basis of colonial Oaxaca's social ideology. Its underpinnings in terms of social customs, informal norms and juridical rulings were strongly racial. These ideological realities, whether imposed by the elite or embraced by the masses, were reflected in the marital and occupational behavior of the people at all levels of society. Few people from the higher estates needed realistically to fear or aspire to marriage with people of the lower estates. The rank correlation of occupation and estate adds support to the thesis that race remained a strong principle of social stratification even in the relatively commercial and proto-industrial economy of colonial Oaxaca.

Finally the fact that some, and perhaps many, individuals changed their racial identifications does not contradict these conclusions. On the contrary, it strengthens the argument that the people believed that their socioracial and socioeconomic statuses should agree. The class system purportedly found by Chance and Taylor must be considered incipient with respect to behavior and completely alien with regard to social values. We agree with their emphasis on "a multidimensional approach to stratification." Where we disagree is on the relative importance of estate and class criteria. Estate continued to be the predominant principle of stratification in Oaxaca through the end of the colonial era. Comparisons of structure and process in other areas of the empire with the statistical models proposed here should contribute to understanding the determinants and directions of social change and stratification in colonial Spanish America.

Estate *and* Class: A Reply

JOHN K. CHANCE AND WILLIAM B. TAYLOR

The critique of our article on Oaxaca in 1792 by Messrs. McCaa, Schwartz, and Grubessich reflects the rapid progress and increasing influence of statistically oriented demographic studies in Latin American history. At the same time it illustrates the dangers involved when the manipulation of numbers becomes an end in itself and the resulting statistics are not interpreted in terms of the social and cultural context that produced the numbers in the first place. We wish to thank our critics for the statistical reanalysis they have performed on the Oaxaca data, and we agree that their figures and measurements of endogamy and exogamy are probably more exact than ours. They have helped to convince us that simple arithmetic is not sufficient to carry out many types of quantitative analysis. In their zeal to achieve statistical rigor, however, it is apparent that McCaa and his associates have misinterpreted our argument and portions of the Oaxaca data. We remain unconvinced by the rather extreme, cut and dried conclusions they draw and disagree with the inferences and assumptions on which they are based.

Our purpose in the article is an admittedly ticklish one—to use census records and other sources on race, occupation, and economic position to show the declining importance of race in the stratification system. In such an enterprise, the parish and census data must be handled carefully and interpreted in conjunction with other sources, some of them qualitative rather than quantitative. Despite their statistically precise reworking of the data, we feel that McCaa and his associates stick too close to the marriage and census figures alone and are therefore led to mistaken conclusions. Among the issues raised by their critique, we see the most important ones as 1) how to interpret data from parish marriage registers; 2) how to interpret "racial mobility" or changes in the racial identification of individuals; and 3) how to assess the place and functions of the *sistema de castas* in colonial Oaxacan society. As McCaa, Schwartz, and Grubessich know, the basic questions involved in these issues are inferential rather than statistical.

The most compelling aspect of the critique is the application of Strauss's (1977) newly developed statistical method to our parish marriage data. We have no quarrel with their computation of the statistic K*, and they appear to have satisfactorily confirmed the null hypothesis that endogamy rates are roughly the same for all racial groups. While these findings certainly have a bearing on our argument, they also raise additional questions. Before considering these, let us briefly explain just what we did with the Oaxaca parish registers.

We chose the records for 1793–97 inclusive as our sample years, partly because the time we had to devote to this aspect of the research was limited and partly because the records for these years were relatively complete. During these years there were a total of 847 church marriages in Oaxaca, involving 1,694 people. In computing our marriage ratios, however, we had to eliminate 133 marriages (266 people) in which the race of one or both partners was not given (our Table 4 on p. 478 makes this clear). Also included among these 266 are a handful of individuals with "miscellaneous" classifications (like *mestindio*) that we weren't sure how to reclassify in terms of the major categories of the sistema de castas. In all, 151 people (68 men and 83 women) were not racially identified at all in the registers. Hence our sample is biased and not a random one, since we can't be sure why racial information was not given in these cases. This is a fascinating question in its own right, which a painstaking analysis of the registers and supporting census material might be able to answer. At any rate, since we were working with a biased set of figures, we thought it inappropriate to base our analysis on a Chi-square test, and of course at that time Strauss's work had not yet been published. Instead, in assembling and analyzing our marriage table we chose to follow the leads of Brading and Wu (Brading 1971, Brading and Wu 1973) who a few years earlier had worked with similar documentation from other regions of New Spain.

But historical statistics is a rapidly changing field, and we humbly accept the verdict of the statisticians that our analysis of the marrying habits of Oaxaqueños is inadequate. We would warn them, however, that their reanalysis is also shaky since the data were biased (nonrandom) to begin with. Furthermore, as our critics recognize, their new computations at best only "indirectly contradict the hypothesis that class was an important determinant of social stratification in Oaxaca." They apply a better measure of endogamy in Strauss's recent formulation, but their approach, as much as ours, is confounded by the limited evidence that allows them to measure endogamy only in narrow racial terms rather than by including relationships of marriage partners by wealth, occupation, neighborhood, etc.

Moreover our critics' reanalysis raises new doubts about the utility of the marriage records (the marriage acts themselves) for the study of race relations in Oaxaca. Even if we assume their analysis to be completely valid, it conflicts with other evidence (see below) indicating that many individuals who began their lives as *castas* appear as *españoles* in the marriage registers. How can we use such a source to study group affiliations when it seems likely that racial identification was transitory and subject to change for many of the people involved? Despite their faith in their computations, our critics are also aware of this problem and perceptively suggest that "the similarity of racial classification for marriage partners reflects what people considered proper behavior, and therefore many couples harmonized their status at marriage in order to achieve this ideal." We agree that this may have been the case, and would only add that population proportions show that most people were harmonizing upward to white (creole) status. Yet, recognizing these possibilities, McCaa, Schwartz, and Grubessich go on to claim that their reanalysis of the marriage acts shows that "all racial groups, whatever their sizes, were recognized as groups in a sociological sense. . . ." Here we must differ. If we accept the fact that "racial mobility" was common, it is difficult to understand how the categories of the sistema de castas operated as groups in the sociological sense. True, the elitist white bureaucracy (and probably the urban parish priests) tended to *perceive* their society in this way, for they had good reason to do so, given their dominant position. But just what the numerous nonelite brides and grooms were thinking when the curate recorded their racial designations is another matter, one we will take up in more detail in a moment.

As to the general endogamy rate as measured by the statistic K*, there remain serious problems of interpretation. Where 0.0 indicates completely random marriage and 1.0 signifies maximum endogamy, it seems difficult to argue that Oaxaca's coefficient of .46 demonstrates "high" endogamy. It unquestionably demonstrates that endogamy was present and significant, but it is still below the halfway mark and in itself does not negate our argument of decreasing endogamy. Admittedly we need more figures from different periods to substantiate our argument, but that is another matter. We must also disagree with our critics' assertion that the "very high" Oaxaca coefficient of .46 is "almost as high" as the Valparaiso coefficient of .72. It appears to us that there is a significant difference between these two figures, one that could be interpreted as supporting our argument about racial fluidity in Oaxaca. But here we rest our case, for the satisfactory resolution of this problem requires more comparative data, which only future studies in other colonial Latin American cities can provide.

The problem with using marriage acts to study race relations in Oaxaca, it appears, is that marriage was just one (albeit important) situation where racial designations were employed. In other situations the same people may have employed different ones. The basic issues raised by McCaa, Schwartz, and Grubessich, in our opinion, have nothing to do with statistics but involve assumptions and inferences regarding the significance of changes in individual racial classification. We argue that such changes were frequent in Oaxaca, though we have only indirect quantitative proof of this proposition in the form of population proportions, discusssd below. But there is little doubt that the phenomenon was a salient aspect of the social system and that most changes involved a move from darker to lighter status. We believe that such racial mobility was often linked with socioeconomic mobility within and across class lines and that both were largely stimulated by the emergent capitalist economy in the region. McCaa and his associates claim, on the other hand, that capitalism "reinforced the racial basis of the social structure in both behavioral and ideological terms." They continue: "Changing racial designations may indicate social fluidity and the existence of class, but the persisting importance of estate-based labels to both individuals and the state suggest to us the primary role of socioracial criteria." Thus our critics equate the "needs" of "the society" with a socioracial system. In doing so, they clearly attach too much significance to the process of racial labeling in Oaxaca. Significantly, in the eighteenth century racial terms appeared regularly only in tribute rolls, civil and ecclesiastical censuses, parish marriage records and transcripts of judicial proceedings. Except for the ubiquitous designation *indio,* racial labels were generally absent in other forms of documentation. Our analysis rests on the assumption that especially in a colonial society like Oaxaca where domination and repression were the order of the day, not all segments (such as classes) of the population perceived their society and their own place in it in the same fashion. There were most likely wide differences in ideology and social values, the ideology of race being a case in point. Because of the nature of the sources, it is difficult to find direct evidence on the racial ideology of Oaxaca's middle and lower groups. This is of course a common problem in historical investigation, and in this case we must be content with what we can infer from indirect evidence, especially from the behavior of the people.

As we see it, the basic function of the sistema de castas in colonial Oaxaca was to preserve the power base of the Spanish (white) elite. As reflected in the "official" statistics of the sort analyzed in our article, the sistema de castas represented the principal social strata *as defined by the elite.* Despite the fact that light status was a formal prerequisite for many jobs, there is no reason to assume that the rest of the population shared this elitist view or that jobs and wealth were distributed in this way. We sought to show that the phenomenon of passing as white (creole) was common and that many people realized that the racial hurdles devised by the Spanish could often be overcome by financial and other means. Capitalism and a shortage of skilled labor, and the chances for mobility they afforded, helped these individuals in their struggle to defeat the dominant ideology. Of course they never succeeded completely in overturning the racial hierarchy of status, but racial mobility was such that it did force some revisions in the terminological system over time (see below). According to elite ideology, one's "race" was an ascribed characteristic that could not be changed, while in practice change was frequently achieved and subject to considerable variation.

Colonial society in Oaxaca—as elsewhere in the colonies—was based on conflicting principles. While the elite clung to its racist view of society as embodied in the sistema de castas, socioeconomic factors had become important and were gradually acting to undermine the racial system. By the late eighteenth century, race mixture had blurred the social boundaries between the colonizers and the colonized, yet the elite could not psychologically accept this fact without undermining its own justification for colonial domination. We do not claim that analysis of marriage patterns alone is sufficient to support this interpretation of the Oaxaca racial system. Let us review briefly three other forms of evidence that support our argument. The third is found in the article; the first two come from Chance's other published work based on the same Oaxaca research.

1) The conflicting principles of the system are reflected in changes in the racial terminology itself. By the early seventeenth century, "mestizos" had become numerous enough that they were perceived as a threat to Spanish power and privilege. Part of the societal response to this was the introduction of a new racial category—*castizo*—intermediate between mestizo and creole, to help preserve white exclusivity. By the late eighteenth century this battle had essentially been lost, and the categories of mestizo, castizo, and creole had begun to fuse into one (see below). Now the threat to white exclusivity came from the mulatto sector. As mulatto infiltration of the ranks of the creoles increased, the lexicon was expanded once again to define the lighter skinned *moriscos* (see Chance 1978: pp. 176–77 for more details).

2) Further evidence of the weakening of the sistema de castas in Oaxaca is found in the few known *limpieza de sangre* proceedings carried out during the second half of the eighteenth century. Most Oaxaqueños did not have to resort to this legal procedure to legitimate their claims to white status. But those who did no longer had to prove pure Spanish ancestry in order to be legally of *casta limpia*. Frequently proof of castizo or mestizo heritage would do just as well, and one can argue that the mestizo, castizo, and español categories were well on the way to being merged into one (Chance 1978: p. 174).

3) Finally, in their statistical reanalysis of the data, McCaa, Schwartz, and Grubessich overlook the fact that the creole (white) sector of the city's population was always the largest and even increased in size during the eighteenth century. In contrast, the mestizo and mulatto sectors actually *declined* in proportional representation. Their suggested explanation for the low number of mestizos—that few were born because of a low intermarriage propensity—is clearly wrong and confuses biological with social race.

The large numbers of creole whites had to come from somewhere, and the evidence is clear that in-migration was not the source, nor were there sufficient peninsulars in Oaxaca to engender such a large creole group. In Oaxaca as well as elsewhere in New Spain, many individuals of mixed racial ancestry (mestizos, mulattoes, and others) were able to penetrate the ranks of the whites, a trend which Aguirre Beltrán (1972: p. 268) first identified some thirty years ago. In this regard, it is not surprising that the statistical association between Socio-Economic Group and race is weaker for the creoles than for other categories in the sistema de castas. It was precisely in this large creole group that the changes in the racial system were most evident. Our critics' assertion that creoles are "strongly overrepresented" in the high artisan group and "underrepresented in the lower categories" is exaggerated, judging by their own statistics and the guild election results which they choose to ignore.

Hence the numbers themselves do not tell the whole story, no matter what battery of tests may be applied to them. If not handled carefully and supplemented by other sources, they can be made to lie, like any other set of statistics. Of course in the censuses and marriage records most adults *are* racially labeled. But this was a requirement of the elite-controlled bureaucracy; it does not mean that everyone listed had the same faith in the sistema de castas. We suspect that the phenomenon of passing, like racial labeling, was largely confined to bureaucratic settings and that in many other social contexts racial identity, except for Indians and perhaps Negroes, was relatively unimportant for the middle and lower groups in late colonial Oaxaca.

In general we agree with our critics that "social norms demanded that individuals with certain economic attributes possess corresponding racial statuses. Therefore, racial attributes changed as social circumstances and economic fortunes demanded." This is only part of the story, however. The other part is that in the long run there was a "whitening" trend in the Oaxaca population as more people of mixed ancestry were able to enter the ranks of the creoles. Clearly this was a significant change in the functioning of the sistema de castas. It does not indicate the growing importance of the racial classification system, as our critics seem to think, but points to the fact that, with so many claimants to white status, race as an indicator of rank must have become increasingly unreliable and must have been supplemented increasingly with socioeconomic considerations. After all, there is only so much room at the top of the social pyramid, and when over 37 percent of the population is classified as white, other supplementary means of measuring rank are necessary on purely practical grounds. We do not argue that race no longer defined the status hierarchy in Oaxaca in 1792 but only that race no longer defined hierarchy so clearly and effectively as it once did. The sistema de castas *is* an important social fact of late colonial life but its importance comes not from its purported relationship to social stratification but from what it tells us about how Spaniards wished their society to be organized. Perhaps it is fair to say that incipient capitalism acted to strengthen racial ideology among Oaxaca's white elite but weakened it among the *castas*. This heightened sense of race in Spanish colonial legal forms fits well with our findings that the creoles' standing in the socioeconomic hierarchy was declining in the late eighteenth century. Admittedly we do not have quantitative data to support this point fully, but we have demonstrated, we believe, the general parameters of the process as a whole.

According to our critics, not only have we misread the data on race but we have botched our analysis of class as well. We are criticized for trying to infer class from occupations alone, for utilizing a deficient source (the 1792 census), and for making some dubious classifications of occupations. We are well aware of the problems raised by inferring class status from occupations, especially where data on wealth are absent, and we say so in the article. For this reason we use the term "Socio-Economic Group" for our occupational clusterings and argue only that "the occupational and ethnic patterns *imply a developing* system of preindustrial economic classes" (p. 469, emphasis added). It seems that McCaa, Schwartz, and Grubessich are attacking the thesis that the Oaxaca stratification system was ordered solely along class lines, a position we have not taken. We point out that we cannot accurately describe the class system with the limited data available to us and that in any case we infer a developing, rather than full-blown, system. In their response to our findings, our critics set up the either/or choice we took pains to avoid: capitalist oriented class system or socioracial estate system. They may wish to identify themselves with an estate interpretation but we did not claim to find a neat economic class system in Oaxaca. We posited a society less rigidly organized by socioracial criteria than is usually supposed, one in which a series of social hierarchies of status, power, and wealth existed. We did not, as our critics would have it, "admit" that there was discrimination based on race. We recognized discrimination based on race as an integral part of this society of multiple hierarchies. We said "the sistema de castas and the capitalist oriented class system were both integral parts of the Spanish colonial experience in Mesoamerica," (p. 486). Our main conclusion remains that "In the interplay between racial and economic criteria of rank in Antequera, the latter was definitely on the upswing in 1792. By the end of the colonial period the complexity and range of variation within the economic class structure rivaled that of the status hierarchy embodied in the sistema de castas, if indeed the latter had not been overtaken in this respect" (p. 485). We are puzzled that McCaa, Schwartz, and Grubessich accuse us of taking an extreme point of view, when in fact they appear to be the guiltier parties in this respect.

In asserting that we define class simply in terms of census occupation, McCaa, Schwartz, and Grubessich choose to ignore our efforts to supplement the census records in testing the relationship of race and social position. In our linkage of master craftsmen from guild election results (where they were *not* identified by race) and the census, we found that creoles occupied master status in the same guilds as mestizo and mulatto masters instead of being confined to certain "Spanish only" trades. We also distinguished between elite and nonelite in the important landholding group on the basis of property values, the prefix "don," and donations for the defense of Antequera against the Independence forces of Morelos in 1812. All three of these standards produced roughly the same number of elite landholders. Of course we would like to have applied similar standards of wealth, status, and "the smoking gun" of group behavior for all other groups. Except for residential patterns, the evidence simply is not available for Oaxaca. Perhaps for other places and times the written record is fuller, and we salute those who can produce the evidence and make sense of it.

As for the census itself and our classification of occupations, we freely admit the difficulties involved. The omission of Indians and most blacks from the census is a serious one indeed, but our rationale for using the manuscript is simply that no better source for the period is likely to be found. The apparent omission of common laborers is not serious since late colonial reports indicate that Indians—and not only city residents but seasonal workers and "commuters" from nearby villages—performed much of the construction and menial labor. Other day laborers and effectively unemployed men were undoubtedly hidden in the suspiciously larger low-status trades of carpenters, shoemakers, and blacksmiths (p. 480). At the top and the bottom—peninsular and Indian, Negro—the socioracial system has some explanatory power. But beyond this gross distinction between Indian and nonIndian, it is of limited use in analyzing the society of Oaxaca. With few models to go on (none at all for colonial Latin America), we puzzled over the classification of occupations innumerable times, and we are grateful to our critics for pointing out the problems involved as they see them. We would stress once again that the distribution of the creoles throughout the inferred class structure seems to us to be the most striking feature of the data, the one that gave us cause to rethink the relationship between race and stratification. We realize that our profile of SEG's has imperfections, but we expect that future work with similar sources will benefit from our experience with the 1792 Oaxaca census.

To conclude, we agree with our critics that statistical tests and models are important. But the role of basic assumptions and inferences is equally important, and it is here that we believe our critics have erred. If it is often necessary to "read between the lines" to interpret a written source adequately, it is just as important to "read between the columns" when

442   JOHN K. CHANCE AND WILLIAM B. TAYLOR

handling quantitative data. In the final analysis the utility of the Oaxaca study (and the statistics mustered by McCaa, Schwartz, and Grubessich) will depend on intracultural and crosscultural comparisons. Once we have additional comparable studies from Latin America and other areas, the merits and deficiencies of our work, and those of our critics, should come into clearer focus.

REFERENCES

Aguirre Beltrán, Gonzalo. 1972. *La población negra de México: estudio etnohistórico* (Segunda edición), Mexico City: Fondo de Cultura Económica.

Brading, David A. 1971 *Miners and Merchants in Bourbon Mexico, 1763–1810,* Cambridge: Cambridge University Press.

Brading, David A. and Celia Wu 1973 "Population Growth and Crisis: León, 1720–1860," *Journal of Latin American Studies* 5(1):1–36.

Chance, John K. 1978 *Race and Class in Colonial Oaxaca,* Stanford: Stanford University Press.

Strauss, David J. 1977 "Measuring Endogamy," *Social Science Research* 6: 225–45.

18

Spanish Society in Mexico City
After the Conquest

Ida Altman

THE approximately thirty-year period of Mexican history following the defeat of Tenochtitlán and conquest
of central New Spain witnessed the shift from patterns
and activities closely linked to the earlier Spanish experience in the Caribbean as well as the formation or evolution of institutions and forms of
organization that would shape society in New Spain itself. Nonetheless,
many aspects of Spanish activity in those years have yet to be examined
systematically, and our lack of knowledge has given rise to the impression
that the efforts of the first generation of Spaniards in Mexico served chiefly
as a backdrop and steppingstone to the prosperity and consolidation so
notable from around 1550 onward. Although that assumption may well
have some merit, the process of transition from the conquest generation
to the later sixteenth century remains obscure.

A reconsideration of the literature on the early postconquest period
pinpoints the shortcomings in our understanding. With some important
exceptions, such as the great demographic and economic studies by
Woodrow Borah and Sherburne F. Cook,[1] much of the work on early
Mexico has been primarily institutional in focus, although a number of key
studies reveal and incorporate much material on social structures, social
and cultural preservation and change, economic organization, and career

The author wishes to thank James Lockhart for his encouragement and advice in revising
this study and the readers of the manuscript for their valuable comments and suggestions.

1. See Woodrow Borah and Sherburne F. Cook, *The Aboriginal Population of Central
Mexico on the Eve of the Spanish Conquest* (Berkeley and Los Angeles, 1963); *The Popula-
tion of Central Mexico in 1548: An Analysis of the "Suma de visitas de Pueblos"* (Berkeley and
Los Angeles, 1960); *Price Trends of Some Basic Commodities in Central Mexico, 1532–1570*
(Berkeley and Los Angeles, 1958); and *The Indian Population of Central Mexico, 1531–1610*
(Berkeley and Los Angeles, 1962).

patterns.[2] For the encomienda and early estates we have the studies of
Leslie Byrd Simpson and Silvio Zavala, the monumental work of Charles
Gibson, José Miranda's brief but important examination of the early years
of the encomienda, G. Micheal Riley's study of the Cortés estates, and
Robert T. Himmerich's prosopographical study of encomenderos. For
architecture and construction there are the works of George Kubler and
John McAndrew. For many years our knowledge of the early church
and clergy went little beyond Robert Ricard's work on the mendicant
orders, but Richard Greenleaf's research on Zumárraga and the Inquisition and, most recently, John F. Schwaller's on the secular clergy and
church wealth have greatly expanded the picture of ecclesiastical activity
in early Mexico. The main chronological thrust of much of this literature,
however, lies well beyond the period in question.[3]

Despite the generally acknowledged hegemony of Mexico City, especially in the sixteenth century, few of the above works focus on patterns and trends in the capital.[4] Studies of other areas do reveal, at

2. An important recent addition to the bibliography is the work of Ethelia Ruiz
Medrano, "Gobierno y sociedad en México. Audiencia y Virreinato, 1530–1550" (Ph.D.
diss., Universidad de Sevilla, 1990), which uses the residencias and visitas of the 1530s and
1540s in the Justicia section of the Archivo de Indias to examine the economic activities of
some key governmental figures of the period and the early development of the corregimiento
system.

3. Lesley Byrd Simpson, The Encomienda in New Spain: The Beginning of Spanish
Mexico, 3d ed. (Berkeley and Los Angeles, 1966); Silvio Zavala, La encomienda indiana
(Madrid, 1935); Charles Gibson, The Aztecs Under Spanish Rule: A History of the Indians of
the Valley of Mexico, 1519–1810 (Stanford, 1964); José Miranda, La función económica del
encomendero en los orígenes del régimen colonial (Nueva España, 1525–31), 2d ed. (Mexico
City, 1965); G. Micheal Riley, Fernando Cortés and the Marquesado in Morelos, 1522–1547
(Albuquerque, 1973); Robert T. Himmerich, "The Encomenderos of New Spain, 1521–1555"
(Ph.D. diss., University of California, Los Angeles, 1984) (Himmerich's book of the same
title will be published by University of Texas Press, 1991); Ruiz Medrano, "Gobierno y socie-
dad," which includes a great deal of material on encomiendas and the relationship between
encomiendas and corregimientos; George Kubler, Mexican Architecture of the Sixteenth
Century, 2 vols. (New Haven, 1948); John McAndrew, The Open Air Churches of Sixteenth
Century Mexico (Cambridge, Mass., 1965); Robert Ricard, The Spiritual Conquest of Mexico
(Berkeley and Los Angeles, 1966); Richard E. Greenleaf, The Mexican Inquisition of the
Sixteenth Century (Albuquerque, 1969) and Zumárraga and the Mexican Inquisition, 1536–
1543 (Washington, 1961); John F. Schwaller, The Church and Clergy in Sixteenth-Century
Mexico (Albuquerque, 1987) and Origins of Church Wealth in Mexico (Albuquerque, 1985).

4. Gibson, Aztecs, and Kubler, Mexican Architecture, include a great deal of material
specifically on the city. Ross Hassig, Trade, Tribute and Transportation: The Sixteenth-
Century Political Economy of the Valley of Mexico (Norman, 1985), states that his book
concerns "the growth and maintenance of the city in the context of its sustaining hinterland" (4). His work is notable for its focus on the Valley of Mexico both before and after
the conquest. For Tenochtitlán after the conquest, see Edward Calnek, "Settlement Patterns
and Chinampa Agriculture in Tenochtitlán," American Antiquity, 37:1(Jan. 1972) and "Conjunto urbano y modelo residencial en Tenochtitlán," in Ensayos sobre el desarrollo urbano
de México (Mexico City, 1972). On Tenochtitlán in the period immediately preceding the
conquest, see Sonia Lombardo Ruiz, Desarrollo urbano de México-Tenochtitlán según las

SPANISH SOCIETY IN MEXICO CITY   415

least indirectly, a good deal about the function and centrality of Mexico City, although *Provinces of Early Mexico*, edited by Ida Altman and James Lockhart, which takes a regional approach to the history of colonial Mexico, still lacks its obvious counterpart, a systematic consideration of the capital. In any case, the studies included in the volume for the most part treat the period from the late sixteenth century forward.[5] One of the few studies that does focus on the capital in the early postconquest years concerns residential patterns and chinampa agriculture among the Indians of Tenochtitlán.[6] Notwithstanding the promising work of ethnohistorians, however, we know even less about Indians in Mexico City than about Spaniards for the period in question. In sum, the existing historical literature has set out the broad outlines of Spanish organization and activity in early Mexico (especially in the sense that we can discern the general direction of development from the early period, since the post-1550 historiography is stronger), with some and even considerable detail in many areas; but much is still lacking.

This study examines people and activities in early Mexico City to illuminate aspects of socioeconomic development up to around 1550, to relate the patterns identified both to the previous phase of Spanish experience in the Caribbean and to the future growth and consolidation of the capital and colony, and to draw comparisons with early Spanish Peru.[7] This examination is far from definitive. Because of the scarcity of documentation for the early years,[8] we may never have sufficient information on individual and collective patterns of association, mobility, and economic activity to reach solid conclusions on such developments. Nevertheless, looking at socioeconomic development from a noninstitutional point of

---

fuentes históricas (Mexico City, 1973) and José Luis de Rojas, "Cuantificaciones referentes a la ciudad de Tenochtitlán en 1519," *Historia Mexicana*, 36:2 (Oct.–Dec. 1986).

5. See, for example, articles by Leslie Lewis, "In Mexico City's Shadow: Some Aspects of Economic Activity and Social Processes in Texcoco, 1570–1620," and James Lockhart, "Capital and Province, Spaniard and Indian: The Example of Late Sixteenth-Century Toluca," in *Provinces of Early Mexico*, ed. Ida Altman and James Lockhart (Los Angeles, 1976).

6. See Calnek, "Settlement Patterns."

7. Comparisons with Peru are based principally on James Lockhart, *Spanish Peru, 1532–1560* (Madison, 1968). See also his *Men of Cajamarca: A Social and Biographical Study of the First Conquerors of Peru* (Austin, 1972).

8. For Mexico City and New Spain many of the early notarial records, which are a key source for Lockhart's study of early Peru, either have not survived or are in very poor condition; there are none before 1525. See Himmerich, "Encomenderos," 6–7, for a detailed discussion of the extant records. Most of the *protocolos* were summarized and published by Agustín Millares Carlo and José I. Mantecón in their *Índice y extractos de los protocolos del Archivo de Notarías de México*, 2 vols. (Mexico City, 1945–46). The extracts are for the periods August–December 1525, 1527, 1528, June 1536 to March 1538, and October–March 1553. All references to notarial documents in this article are to Millares Carlo and Mantecón, *Índice*, and will be noted as "MC" with the extract number.

view (and even at the personnel of institutions in socioeconomic terms) can point to some of the factors that must be taken into account in considering the formation of Spanish American society in Mexico.

That society had its roots in the Iberian peninsula, the experience of Spaniards in the islands and Tierra Firme, and the peoples, cultures, and ecology of Mexico itself. Ignoring long-term developments and earlier precedents when examining the history of Mexico and other Spanish American societies risks distortion by fostering inferences and conclusions that are made post hoc. The practice also masks or only partially accounts for processes of transmission and transformation that shaped the new societies of the Americas from cultures that had developed in isolation from each other.[9] The activities of the early years following the conquest are critical to those processes and should not be relegated to obscurity just because we know a great deal about their eventual outcome. Neither is it acceptable to assume that early Mexico will emerge as the exact counterpart of early Spanish Peru. Mexico is too central to the development of Spanish society in the Indies not to merit the scholarly attention that either would confirm the truth of that contention or, more likely, would modify it in some respects.

Government Officials and Institutions

The role played by governmental institutions and officials reflects how the rapidly expanding economy that tied Mexico City to the human and natural resources of the countryside proved substantial and dynamic enough almost from the beginning to satisfy most of the interests and elements that composed early Spanish society in Mexico. The imposition of royal rule and the early alleviation of overt and potentially destructive political conflict in New Spain also offer some contrasts to the situation in early Peru.

The fifteen-year period following the conquest of Mexico and the establishment of the capital of New Spain at the site of the center of the Aztec empire saw a steady increase in government agencies and the intensity of crown efforts to assert or maintain control over colonial administration. The cabildo of the Spanish capital came into existence almost immediately, its members—regidores and alcaldes—chosen by Cortés or his lieutenants until 1526. In that year the crown appointed two *regidores perpetuos,* and by the 1530s all appointments to the cabildo had to be

9. See Altman, "Emigrants and Society: An Approach to the Background of Colonial Spanish America," *Comparative Studies in Society and History,* 30:1 (Jan. 1988).

approved by the crown.[10] Royal treasury officials were present from the earliest years, and the first audiencia, under Nuño de Guzmán, was established in 1528. The first viceroy of New Spain, Antonio de Mendoza, arrived in 1535.

Mexico experienced nothing comparable in scale to the civil wars and turmoil of Peru's early period. Nonetheless, the first governor, Cortés, cabildo members, treasury officials, and audiencia judges in the 1520s became involved in factionalism, infighting, and often complicated alliances of political and economic interest. Such entanglements indicated both the existence of significant power struggles within the conquistador group and a high degree of involvement from the outset of government officials in the politics and economy of the new colony. If later the cabildo came to represent local and in particular encomendero interests, the substantial local interests of other officials during the period must also be borne in mind. Thus not only were the majority of cabildo members encomenderos, but so were most royal officials, including a number of judges on the audiencia, treasurers Alonso de Estrada and Juan Alonso de Sosa and other treasury officials such as the notorious factor Gonzalo de Salazar, the viceroy Antonio de Mendoza, and even the archbishop of Mexico, Fray Juan de Zumárraga. They not only held encomiendas but also acquired landholdings and invested locally in mining, stockraising, sugar cultivation, textile production, and commerce, and either they or their relatives married into local society.[11]

These involvements need not imply that royal officials and appointees necessarily circumvented royal policy or neglected the interests of the crown, although the members of the first audiencia were so notably corrupt and aggressively acquisitive that they created an uproar in local society.[12] But royal officials did enter fully into the local economy and

10. Peggy K. Liss, *Mexico Under Spain* (Chicago, 1975), 104. See also Gibson, *Aztecs*, 167.

11. John F. Schwaller, "The Secular Clergy in Sixteenth-Century Mexico" (Ph.D. diss., Indiana University, 1978), 34, notes, for example, that Viceroy Mendoza married his sister to a local encomendero. The documentation and literature on the local economic and social involvements of oidores and other officials is extensive. See Liss, *Mexico Under Spain*, 50–52, 55, 57, 62, 65–66; François Chevalier, *Land and Society in Colonial Mexico* (Berkeley, 1970), 75–76, 118, 123–124; Constance Carter, "Law and Society in Colonial Mexico: Audiencia Judges in Mexican Society from the Tello de Sandoval Visita General, 1543–1547 (Ph.D. diss., Columbia University, 1971); and Ruiz Medrano, "Gobierno y sociedad," especially chapter 3 on the extensive economic involvements of Lic. Lorenzo de Tejada, oidor from 1537 to 1550. For the holdings and investments of Cortés, the first governor, see Riley, *Fernando Cortés*.

12. See the residencia of the Nuño de Guzmán audiencia, begun in 1531, Archivo General de Indias (hereafter AGI), Justicia, legs. 226–229. See also Enrique Otte, "La Nueva España en 1529," in *Historia y sociedad en el mundo de habla española. Homenaje a José*

society, and the political struggles and clashes of the audiencia and other officials with the interests of Mexico City's cabildo and upper class must be viewed in light of these activities as well as of crown policy and prerogatives.[13] Even the role played in the early years by the Inquisition, never a powerful institution in New Spain, faithfully reflected the complex interplay of political and economic forces, which included the rivalry between Dominicans and Franciscans.[14] The political situation in Mexico City was hardly unique, of course; the patterns that emerged in the capital recurred elsewhere, as powerful political and economic interests converged.[15]

As early as the mid-1530s an increasing accommodation took place among the contending groups in New Spain. As the authority to grant land was centralized under the viceroy and audiencia after 1535 (in earlier years the cabildo made grants as far away as Michoacán), and as restrictions increased on the holding and perpetuation of encomiendas under the New Laws of the 1540s, the local upper class no doubt underwent a pragmatic readjustment to the regulation (if not absolute limitation) of its economic opportunities and the curbing of the prerogatives of its institution, the cabildo. Royal officials for their part showed greater willingness to respond in some degree to local interests. Viceroy Mendoza used political patronage to grant many Spaniards pensions or appointments as corregidors or alcaldes mayores; from the outset many corregidors were encomenderos or the sons or relatives of encomenderos.[16] Political infight-

---

Miranda, ed. Bernardo García Martínez et al. (Mexico City, 1970), 95–111. He points out that the oidor Lic. Diego Delgadillo, together with his brother Juan Peláez de Berrío (who was alcalde mayor of Oaxaca and received 25,000 Indians in encomienda) and their second cousin Luis de Berrío (who became captain and alcalde of the province of the Zapotecs), together with other Granadan-Andalusian relatives and compatriots, like Gonzalo de Salazar, formed a powerful new faction that all but displaced Cortés's Extremaduran clique (97).

13. See AGI, Justicia, leg. 107, no. 2, for the conflict between Alonso de Estrada and regidor Dr. Cristóbal de Ojeda. Despite the frequency of conflicts between royal and local officials it should not, of course, be assumed that the cabildo itself necessarily reflected the views and objectives of most local Spaniards. Diego de la Peña, a procurador who had more than one clash with cabildo scribe Antonio de Herrera, complained in 1536 that the cabildo's alcaldes were held in low esteem because they "do justice as between compadres and quarrel with one another. . . . People don't take off their hats when they talk with them. It's as if they were alcaldes of a village of 100 vecinos." Peña's testimony was part of a residencia taken of the cabildo and its officials in 1536–37 that also included complaints about the fixing of elections and purchase of votes; see AGI, Justicia, leg. 233, nos. 1–3.

14. See Greenleaf, *Mexican Inquisition*, 39.

15. See, for example, Peter Bakewell, "Zacatecas: An Economic and Social Outline of a Silver Mining District, 1547–1700," in *Provinces of Early Mexico*, 222–223, for cabildo membership, and Marta Hunt's discussion of the cabildo and the local social and economic ties of crown officials in seventeenth-century Yucatan in "The Processes of Development in Yucatan, 1600–1700," in *Provinces of Early Mexico*, 46–49. Stuart Schwartz has demonstrated a similar ambiguity in the roles played by the judges of Bahia's relação in *Sovereignty and Society in Colonial Brazil* (Berkeley, 1973), especially 176–184.

16. Liss, *Mexico Under Spain*, 59; Gibson, *Aztecs*, 83, 273. See Ruiz Medrano, "Go-

ing and clashes of interest did not disappear, of course; but by the 1540s major adjustments and accommodations, if sometimes uneasy, had been at least partially realized.[17]

Encomenderos and Encomiendas

There exist several fundamental works on the early encomienda. Himmerich's work, for example, not only provides a wealth of information on the individual histories of New Spain's encomiendas and their holders, but also shows the existence of a countrywide network of encomienda holding based in Mexico City, where nearly half the 506 encomenderos actually lived. The documentation that would make it possible to produce the kind of detailed analysis of a Mexican encomendero's enterprises that Trelles Aréstegui provides for Peruvian encomendero Lucas Martínez is mostly lacking.[18] Taken together, however, the existing studies and records do tell us a great deal about how the encomiendas functioned to underwrite Spanish enterprises in New Spain and concentrate wealth and resources in the hands of a relatively small group (mostly residing in Mexico City), while at the same time they contributed to the development of alternative forms of economic activity, use of Indian labor, and administrative organization that would long outlast the institution itself.[19]

The encomienda, or grant of Indian labor and tribute, was the principal economic and political institution of the early years in Mexico. Though almost from the beginning merchants, artisans, and humbler Spaniards far outnumbered the more visible and wealthy encomenderos, many or even most of them depended directly or indirectly on the wealth that the encomenderos extracted from the Indians or generated through their enterprises. Furthermore, Himmerich's work shows New Spain's encomendero group to have been more varied and broadly representative than gener-

bierno y sociedad," for the early close connections between encomenderos and corregimientos. An example of Mendoza's accommodation to local interests can be seen in the case of Gonzalo Ruiz, regidor of Mexico for thirty years, who in 1529 acquired an encomienda from the viceroy with 1000 pesos of annual income and was named a corregidor in 1538 and 1539. Ruiz had a store and seven house lots in Mexico City and an estancia and *huerta* in Tacubaya (131). See also Himmerich, "Encomenderos," 453–454.

17. See Carter, "Law and Society."
18. Himmerich, "Encomenderos," xi, 2; Efraín Trelles Aréstegui, *Lucas Martínez Vegazo: Funcionamiento de una encomienda peruana inicial* (Lima, 1982). Again the exception is the Cortés encomienda and Marquesado, studied by Riley, *Fernando Cortés.*
19. See Himmerich, "Encomenderos," 64; for the relationship between the encomienda and other forms of administration and exploitation of the countryside, see James Lockhart, "Encomienda and Hacienda: The Evolution of the Great Estate in the Spanish Indies," *HAHR*, 49:3 (August 1969); Robert G. Keith, "Encomienda, Hacienda and Corregimiento in Spanish America: A Structural Analysis," *HAHR*, 51:3 (August 1971); and Ruiz Medrano, "Gobierno y sociedad."

ally thought. The rather high rate of reassignment of grants (as many as thirty a year) meant that the number of individuals holding encomiendas at some time also was higher than often assumed.[20]

Probably the majority of the original conquistador group received encomiendas in New Spain, as did many other individuals—*pobladores*—who arrived some time thereafter; but not all grants were equal in size and value, nor did all individuals who obtained encomiendas succeed in keeping their grants. The encomendero group was heterogeneous both in its origins, ranging from artisans and miners to powerful political figures, and in its unequal access to capital, resources, and political favor. Encomiendas varied greatly in size and income. Thus while almost all wealthy and powerful individuals in early Mexico City were encomenderos, not all encomenderos were wealthy. Those encomenderos whose grants yielded only small incomes, or who lost their encomiendas with the eclipse of Cortés's authority in the late 1520s, tended to fall out of Mexico City's upper class entirely as they were forced to seek other sources of livelihood and income.

Nonetheless, the encomienda was crucial in providing labor for agriculture and mining enterprises and in generating a range of employment opportunities for Spaniards. The stewards and managers of encomiendas—the mayordomos—though ranking lower than their encomendero employers, could be figures of some importance and independence, particularly in the early years when managerial expertise and competence were at a premium, as Lockhart has shown for early Peru as well.[21] Riley's study of the Cortés Marquesado and encomienda in Morelos, which probably was atypical more in size than in organizational structure, suggests the variability of status within the encomienda system. Francisco de Terrazas, a close associate of Cortés who was a vecino of Mexico City and an encomendero in his own right, served as mayordomo of the Marquesado, as did Diego de Ocampo and Francisco de Herrera, also encomenderos. Another Cortés mayordomo, Francisco de Santa Cruz, was a vecino of Mexico City and held an encomienda in the Valley of Mexico through the 1550s, passing it on to his son.[22] The mayordomos of more modest encomienda establishments were, of course, humbler individuals, although they too could use their positions and rural base to develop their own enterprises.

The most successful encomenderos acquired other assets and expanded

20. Himmerich, "Encomenderos," 4, 22, 59.
21. Lockhart, *Spanish Peru*, 23–25.
22. Riley, *Fernando Cortés*, 68–69; Gibson, *Aztecs*, 413; Miranda, *Función económica*, 43. See Himmerich, "Encomenderos," for Herrera (326–327), Ocampo (394–395), Santa Cruz (480–481), and Terrazas (497–498).

their economic bases. They invested in sugar cane production, textiles, mining, and livestock enterprises; they acquired landholdings. Of 23 grants of land (excluding city plots for houses or gardens) made by the cabildo from late 1525 to mid-1528, 14 went to encomenderos; and of 218 such grants made by Mendoza in 1542–43, encomenderos obtained considerably more than half.[23] A large number of Valley encomenderos acquired landholdings within or near the areas of their encomiendas; they also obtained corregimientos and gained access to repartimiento labor.[24] New Spain's encomenderos were never able to channel encomienda labor as directly and effectively into mining operations as would their counterparts in Peru, but early mining in Mexico was closely related to the encomienda, as will be seen.

Beginning with its rather rudimentary origins in the islands of the Caribbean, the encomienda changed almost continuously in Spanish America. Given the greater size and wealth of Mexican provinces, the encomienda took on new substance when Spaniards transferred the institution to New Spain. Yet that same wealth had the effect of attracting many more immigrants than had moved to the islands.[25] Since the encomienda system was, after all, inherently limited by the number, size, and nature of the indigenous entities at its base, the growing numbers of Spaniards who were excluded from its benefits put the institution under increasing pressure. Himmerich has found that only five persons who received encomiendas in the period he studied arrived in Mexico after 1531.[26] The rapid reduction of Indian populations, especially after the epidemics of the 1540s, and the desire of the crown to check the development of a potentially powerful and politically independent upper class in New Spain also worked to modify the form and potential, and hence the significance, of the encomiendas by the midsixteenth century.

Miners and Mining

While the significance of the encomienda and the dynamics that worked to modify its function and position are now fairly clear, the importance of mining from the very earliest years in postconquest Mexico is often overlooked. Spaniards in Mexico first went into gold mining, just as they had

23. Miranda, *Función económica*, 26–27.
24. Gibson, *Aztecs*, 83, 275.
25. For analysis of emigration patterns, see Peter Boyd-Bowman, *Patterns of Spanish Emigration to the New World, 1493–1580* (Buffalo, 1973). Over the sixteenth century New Spain attracted the largest numbers of emigrants. For comparisons of figures for Mexico and Peru, see Boyd-Bowman, "Patterns of Spanish Emigration to the Indies Until 1600," *HAHR*, 56:4 (Nov. 1976), especially 601–602.
26. Himmerich, "Encomenderos," 56.

in the Caribbean and Tierra Firme, underscoring the similarities between early developments in Mexico and the Spaniards' previous experiences in the Caribbean.

Until the mid-1530s, mining interests in New Spain were relatively small-scale as well as mostly focused on gold, although some very small silver mines were being worked by the late 1520s.[27] Capital investment for gold mining was modest and went mainly to purchase tools, equipment (*bateas*, picks, hoes), and Indian and black slaves; nearly every mining operation had one black slave.[28] Even if not highly profitable, the gold mines, located in areas such as Oaxaca and Michoacán, formed an important link between Spanish society in Mexico City and the resources and population of the countryside. Encomiendas and mining interests were closely related; probably most, if not all, early encomenderos were involved in gold mining. Encomienda tributes provided encomenderos the income and supplies needed to acquire and maintain a slave labor force to work the mines, and encomienda labor might be illegally employed in mining or used indirectly to support the operation.[29]

The typical gold-mining enterprise of this period included a Spanish or Hispanized managerial-administrative staff and a large Indian labor force. The Spanish *minero* was assisted by one or more "mozos" and a black slave. The bulk of the labor force consisted of groups or gangs (*cuadrillas*) of Indian slaves (usually between forty and a hundred), sometimes replaced by encomienda Indians. In either case, capital investment in labor was not large; Indian slaves generally sold for three to five pesos each or even less. When encomienda labor was used, illegally in direct working of the mines or else in an auxiliary function, the required investment in labor was even less.[30]

Mining ventures frequently were joint undertakings of encomenderos or of encomenderos in partnership with other entrepreneurs.[31] Such partnerships to exploit Mexican mines and the use of encomienda labor for mining found their parallel in gold and silver mining in Peru, where

27. Rodrigo de Baeza and others mentioned silver mines in the province of Guachinango that were being worked on behalf of Nuño de Guzmán; see AGI, Justicia, leg. 226, no. 1.

28. Slaves and equipment were generally sold together. In a typical transaction recorded in 1527, one hundred Indian slaves with mining experience, together with the equipment, were sold for 550 pesos (MC 697). The equipment probably came to about 150 pesos. Prices for black slaves were considerably higher.

29. See Miranda, *Función económica*, 11, 22–23. The Indians of the town of Achiutla of the encomienda of Francisco Maldonado, for example, were obliged to maintain half of a mining cuadrilla (23). See Himmerich, "Encomenderos," 355–356, for Maldonado.

30. Miranda, *Función económica*, 12–14. See also Gibson, *Aztecs*, 77–78, 221, and Liss, *Mexico Under Spain*, 97.

31. See Miranda, *Función económica*, 20, 34–40, for examples of such arrangements.

once again the earliest mining operations involved gold. In Peru, as in New Spain, early miners most likely arrived with experience gained else-where—in the Caribbean or Tierra Firme or even in Mexico itself.[32] The black slaves assisting them may also have had prior mining experience; one Mexican slave named Antón is in fact called "minero" in a 1527 record.[33]

A large number of miners, identified as such, appear in the notarial records of the mid-1520s (a total of 45 for 1525, 1527, and 1528), but very few in the 1530s, likely because they were technicians of gold rather than of silver mining and refining. Almost never vecinos of Mexico City, they nonetheless came frequently to the city, usually to make year-long contracts, and then left for the countryside and the mines. Their work arrangements were almost always based on shares rather than salary,[34] yet on occasion they bought Indian slaves or tools, suggesting that they might have worked part-time on their own behalf.

With its more complex technology and greater capital requirements, silver mining soon eclipsed gold mining in early New Spain, but its rise was coincidental rather than directly contributing to the diminished im-portance of gold. High labor costs and falling returns had curtailed gold mining in one part of the Caribbean after another, and similar processes probably affected gold mining operations in New Spain as well.[35] The very low prices for which Indian slaves were being bought and sold strongly suggest that they were numerous in the early years, as well as suffering high mortality rates, but the use of Indian slave labor may have already been declining in the 1530s (at least in central New Spain) with increasing legal restrictions and prohibitions. The illegal and indiscriminate use of encomienda Indians in gold mines also came under control, although in the 1530s encomienda Indians were still being rented out for mine labor in Taxco.[36]

Following the discovery of silver mines at Taxco, mining began to take

32. Lockhart, *Spanish Peru*, 26, mentions a Sancho Tofiño who came to Peru from Mexico in the late 1530s and played an important role in the Carabaya gold mines, opened in 1542. See also Lockhart, 26, for a discussion of companies formed by encomenderos and other entrepreneurs for mining.

33. MC 612.

34. An apparently exceptional case was that of Francisco de Figueroa, miner, who in March 1527 agreed to work for sixteen months in the mines of Zacatula for 120 pesos and his keep (MC 411). According to Miranda, *Función económica*, 38, Esteban Miguel, who appears in MC 1692 as a "minero," was an encomendero; Himmerich, however, does not list him.

35. Carl O. Sauer, *The Early Spanish Main* (Berkeley and Los Angeles, 1966), 198.

36. See Liss, *Mexico Under Spain*, 53, for legislation. Indian slaves were, however, still being used in the silver mines in the 1530s; see, for example, MC 2028, 2051–2054. Juan Fernández rented forty Indians to work at Taxco from an encomendero for 550 pesos in 1536 (MC 1854). In 1537 Martín de Zavala, acting for the minor son of the encomendero Juan de Salcedo, rented the services of thirty Indians to work in mines at Taxco (MC 2317).

on a new dimension in New Spain. Investments grew larger, new technicians were needed, mine owners began to spend at least part of their time at the mines rather than sending out Spanish miners to supervise operations, and successful merchants began to invest.[37] Still tentative during the 1530s and 1540s, these developments emerged more clearly in the 1550s after the discovery of mines in the north.[38]

In the 1530s, mining operations, if not ownership as such, were assuming a certain independence from society in Mexico City, even before the major discoveries of silver in the north. Only four persons are identified as "mineros" in the notarial records of 1536–38, and one of these clearly owned mines in Taxco.[39] Nonetheless, ties between the mines and Mexico City persisted. Several individuals who claimed to be vecinos of Mexico City in the 1540s stated that they lived in Taxco or Zumpango; in 1539 Juan de la Peña Vallejo, who at one time served as alcalde mayor in Taxco, acted as representative of the mining interests in Taxco, protesting some of the new mining ordinances before Viceroy Mendoza. He claimed to be a vecino of Mexico City and was an encomendero from the late 1530s.[40] Cortés, the Marqués del Valle, made a substantial investment in mining in 1536, buying up shares in a mine and Indian and black slaves in Sultepec from three other men for a total of over 28,000 pesos; he then made one of the three, a vecino of Mexico City named Melchor Vásquez who had just sold his interests for 12,000 pesos, the mine's administrator. The royal treasurer, Juan Alonso de Sosa, also was involved, forming a partnership with Cortés in the 1530s to work mines in Sultepec.[41]

Merchants and Trade

The frequent appearance of merchants (*mercaderes*) in the notarial documents of the early years attests to a considerable degree of commercial

37. Taxco, southwest of Mexico City and a center for Indian tin mining, was the first major center for silver mining. Following the beginning of operations there, silver deposits were subsequently discovered in Zacualpan, Sultepec, and Temascaltepec. In the early 1540s a series of small mines was operating near Guadalajara. For discussion of gold- and silver-mining zones in Mexico, see Robert C. West and John P. Augelli, *Middle America: Its Lands and Peoples* (Englewood Cliffs, 1966), 258, 293.

38. Supply of the mines at Taxco began to take on a certain importance, foreshadowing the partial reorientation of regional supply networks toward Zacatecas after the 1540s. See Ruiz Medrano, "Gobierno y sociedad," 323.

39. MC 1854.

40. *Epistolario de Nueva España, 1505–1818,* 16 vols. (Mexico City, 1939–42), III, no. 190. See also Francisco A. de Icaza, *Conquistadores y pobladores de Nueva España* (Madrid, 1923), nos. 389, 694, 792; and Himmerich, "Encomenderos," 415.

41. MC 2051–2054, 2064. Vázquez bought a house in Mexico City for 1350 pesos the year following his deal with Cortés (MC 2273).

activity in Mexico City. Although the sources used do not provide a full description of the operation of commercial networks that linked New Spain and Mexico City to Spain and Seville, they certainly suggest that already-established networks and organizations that served Spaniards on the islands were extended or transferred to Veracruz and Mexico City. The presence of merchants and factors from northern Castile seems to have been still strong in the early years, as was true in the islands and in Peru at least in the 1530s. At the same time new individuals, firms, and organizations undoubtedly began to participate, particularly in the late 1530s and 1540s with the discovery of the silver mines.[42]

Fifty-six merchants are identified in the records for 1525 and 1527–28, and 107 for the period 1536–38.[43] Of the group of 56, 8 were vecinos of Mexico City; one of these was still present in the capital ten years later. Of the group of 107, 16 were vecinos during the period 1536–38, 4 more had become vecinos of the capital by the mid-1540s, and one appears in cabildo records of 1555 as a vecino.[44] In all, only 5 individuals from the second period were definitely present in Mexico City a decade later, suggesting transience and fairly rapid turnover. Such instability might be expected, given that most of the period in question antedated the discovery of substantial silver deposits in the north, which would bring the beginnings of real wealth to New Spain and attract and support a more stable— and better financed—commercial establishment in succeeding decades.

Merchants formed and dissolved numerous partnerships and desig-

42. For the participation of Castilian merchants in the American trade, see Ruth Pike, *Aristocrats and Traders: Sevillian Society in the Sixteenth Century* (Ithaca, 1972), especially 122–123, 128, and Lockhart, *Spanish Peru*, 78–79. See also Otte, "Mercaderes burgaleses en los inicios del comercio con México," *Historia Mexicana*, 18:1 and 2 (Jul.–Sep. and Oct.–Dec. 1968).

43. The merchants under discussion here are those who identified themselves as "mercader." The names of five merchants not found in the notarial records appear in the 1536–37 residencia of the Mexico City cabildo (AGI, Justicia, leg. 233, no. 1); Ruiz Medrano, "Gobierno y sociedad," 322, 326, mentions two others, one active in the late 1530s and one in the 1540s. The term "tratante" does not appear at all in the notarial extracts for the period and is not found in cabildo records until 1551. In that year two "tratantes," one a recent immigrant from Spain, obtained licenses to sell wine in the city. The *Actas de cabildo de la ciudad de México* have been published in 54 volumes (Mexico City, 1880–1916).

44. The term "vecino" may indicate only that a person maintained some kind of establishment or property in the city and had been there for about a year. In Spain the term had a specific legal meaning; one had to petition the city council for *vecindad* status which, if granted, conferred both obligations (such as liability for taxes) and privileges (such as the right to be granted municipal property and access to municipal common lands). While the practice of petitioning for and receiving *vecindad* status continued, it appears that at least in some places the strict legal meaning of the term was modified early. Furthermore, some individuals became vecinos of more than one city. See Julia Hirschberg, "A Social History of Puebla de los Angeles, 1531–1560" (Ph.D. diss., University of Michigan, 1976), 272–273, for vecinos of Puebla and Mexico City.

nated representatives in other towns or provinces. Their commercial dealings entailed a number of items common in the Indies trade at the time,
European cloth and clothing above all, but also wine, oil, black slaves,
and horses. Since they were not conquistadors or encomenderos, and only
infrequently vecinos of Mexico City, most of the available information
on merchants concerns their economic activities. Two merchants of the
1520s, the brothers Gonzalo and Diego de Morales, are familiar because
of the Inquisition trials of 1528, in the course of which they were tried for
heresy and blasphemy. Little is known about Gonzalo, who was burned
at the stake with the blacksmith Hernando Alonso. Diego, however, born
in Seville, was a vecino of Mexico at the time of his trial and was both a
merchant and a miner.[45]

Other individuals illustrate some of the possible involvements and
activities of the merchant group.[46] One Miguel de Ibarra, whose name
appears frequently in the records of 1527 and 1528, maintained rather
diverse commercial interests. Directly engaged in importing merchandise
and selling wholesale to other merchants, he formed a partnership with a
shipmaster based in Seville. Ibarra at some time owned property in the
capital, bought and sold small quantities of wine and pack animals, and
in 1528 purchased half of a caravel docked in Pánuco along with a hundred Indian slaves, who were probably to be sold in Hispaniola. Most of
his associates and business partners were from northern Spain, reflecting his own regional origins. Despite the diversity of his operations, most
were fairly small-scale and did not involve large capital investments. He
purchased the Indian slaves for 4 pesos each and half the caravel for 160.

Juan de Soldevila was a somewhat more substantial merchant than
Ibarra. Involved in internal trade, he first appears in the notarial records
in 1525, while trying to recover some money on the loss of merchandise
and houses (probably shops or warehouses) that had burned in Veracruz.
The scope of his business dealings during the next couple of years included
locations on the periphery of New Spain such as Colima and Zacatula. In
1527 he bought a black slave and hired a muleteer with five pack animals
to travel between Mexico City, Veracruz, and Medellín (the ephemeral
settlement near the east coast). The following year Soldevila purchased
nine shops in the capital for a fairly substantial sum (1,000 *pesos de oro de
minas* and 1,225 *pesos del corriente*).[47] The investment represented more

45. Greenleaf, *Mexican Inquisition*, 26–30.
46. The following discussion of individual merchants is based on a number of items in
the notarial extracts.
47. For monetary equivalents and standardization, see Borah and Cook, *Price Trends*,
9–10. See also their discussion of equivalents for weights and measures in use in Mexico,
11–12.

a real estate than a commercial venture, as he rented the shops shortly after purchase.

First called a *tendero* (shopkeeper), Pedro García Moreno was a fairly active entrepreneur who demonstrated a degree of upward mobility. In 1527 he formed a partnership with Juan de Salamanca to buy a shop and merchandise in the capital (he contributed 460 pesos, Salamanca 260), and the following year he was recorded as a *mercader*. In April 1528 he bought seven mules, a black slave named Pedro, and twenty wineskins for a little under 1,300 pesos. Then he hired an arriero named Gonzalo Gil, who agreed to travel between Mexico City and Veracruz with the mules and the assistance of Pedro, provided he could ride on one of the animals (if it could carry a burden of four arrobas in addition). The records for the same year show that Moreno bought up all the tallow from the slaughterhouses of Mexico City for the year 1528 at four pesos per arroba and agreed to sell the entire quantity to another merchant or his son to make candles.

Gregorio Yáñez de Burgos maintained a number of mining and commercial activities in the 1530s. He had silver-mining interests in Taxco, formed a partnership with Gregorio Montero in 1538 to buy additional mines and slaves, and rented forty Indians from the encomendero Francisco de Zamora in 1536 to work his mines. Evidently he was involved in the import business, because he had a representative in Veracruz to receive slaves and merchandise arriving from Seville and formed a partnership with a muleteer who traveled between Mexico City and Veracruz with eleven mules and a black and an Indian slave. In 1537 Gregorio Yáñez imported five black slaves from Seville, doubtless for resale. He also rented several shops in the *portales* of the city. Yáñez had extensive dealings with other merchants and a number of partners, most of whom were from northern Spain like himself.

A last interesting figure of this period was Juan Henche, also called Juan Alemán. His partners were two merchants named Lázaro Nurenberger and Cristóbal Reyser living in Seville, against whom Henche would write drafts for merchants returning to Seville. Henche and his partners had mining interests in Sultepec.

Evidence on merchants from the notarial records, albeit sketchy, suggests a probable increase in scale and sophistication of commercial activity in Mexico City over the ten-year period from the mid-1520s to the mid-1530s. This pattern is consistent with the initial postconquest lag in economic activity. Spaniards failed to find a very lucrative source of liquid wealth immediately after the conquest, but by the mid-1530s the discovery of silver mines at Taxco already had begun to change the economic picture. As commercial activity expanded and accelerated, merchants themselves became more directly involved in mining investments.

Commercial activities and investments were not, of course, limited to self-declared merchants. Audiencia judges Lic. Francisco Ceynos and Lic. Lorenzo de Tejada both were involved in the sale of wine in Mexico City, the latter with his nephew, the merchant Juan de Manzanares. Tejada had ties with other merchants as well, in particular Gerónimo de León, who maintained a store in Taxco. Tejada at one time assigned one hundred Indians from the jails of Mexico City to work in León's obrajes.[48] Juan de Mansilla, a vecino and regidor of Mexico City in the 1530s, was said to have a mercantile partnership with the merchant Luis de Córdoba to supply the mines in Taxco.[49] Such commercial arrangements involving officials were not at all unusual.

The conquest of Peru and its rising importance also stimulated commercial activity in Mexico.[50] Even the scanty evidence from the notarial records of the 1530s points to an early participation of Mexico City merchants in the Peruvian trade. Ventura del Espinar and Diego del Espinar entered the trade in 1536, the year when the Indian uprising in Peru brought urgent appeals to New Spain for supplies and help. Merchandise designated for Peru included horses, tools, and hardware, two black slaves, and two moriscas. Ventura financed the venture, and Diego agreed to make the trip to Peru.

Because of Mexico City's size, unique topography, and distance from both coasts, internal trade routes and transport activities were crucial from the outset. In addition to the Indian *tamemes*, or carriers, who remained an important means of transport for a number of years after the conquest,[51] a system of pack trains under Spanish muleteers came into existence almost immediately, followed by carters in the 1530s with the improvement of wagon roads. Nine major trade routes linked the central valley with the rest of New Spain and brought supplies to the capital.[52] Construction of inns and the increasing presence of Spaniards in Indian settlements were concomitants of the development and growth in importance of these trade routes.

48. See Ruiz Medrano, "Gobierno y sociedad," 321–322, 328, and MC 1867.

49. AGI, Justicia, leg. 233, no. 1.

50. See Borah, *Early Colonial Trade and Navigation between Mexico and Peru* (Berkeley, 1954), for the development of shipbuilding on Mexico's western coast and of trade and transport routes between Mexico and Peru.

51. See Hassig, *Trade, Tribute and Transportation*, 187–207, for discussion of the continued reliance on *tamemes* in the sixteenth century and attempts to regulate and limit their use.

52. Gibson, *Aztecs*, 361. See also Borah, *Early Colonial Trade*, 25–29; West and Augelli, *Middle America*, 299–302, for discussion of land transport and trade; David R. Ringrose, "Carting in the Hispanic World: An Example of Divergent Development," *HAHR*, 50:1 (Feb. 1970); and Hassig, *Trade, Tribute and Transportation*, 171–177, 193–197.

A total of 49 muleteers appear in the notarial records of 1525 and 1527–28, and 12 muleteers and 8 carters in the 1536–38 records; cabildo records of the 1540s and 1550s include an additional 2 muleteers and 3 carters. Most of the muleteers did not own their own animals or equipment but contracted with other individuals—merchants, miners, and encomenderos—to work for a year for a certain salary or to be paid a fixed amount per trip. Muleteers nevertheless showed signs of mobility and independence; many eventually did buy horses or mules, acquire black or Indian slaves, enter into partnerships, or become involved in renting and maintaining inns along the transport routes. Carters worked under similar conditions in the 1530s. Possibly by midsixteenth century Indians also had begun to enter into the transport trade previously monopolized by Spaniards, and a greater number of Spaniards engaged in these trades were able to work independently as the high costs of horses and mules in the early period began to decrease.[53]

Trades and Professions

From the beginning artisans were prominent in Spanish society in Mexico City. Their early presence and activity suggests that many came to New Spain from the islands. Artisans of all trades formed partnerships, bought or rented houses or shops in the city or rented out their own urban real estate, purchased black and Indian slaves, and invested in mining and stockraising.

Examination of the notarial records for 1525, 1527–28, 1536–38, and the very incomplete records of 1551–53, together with the cabildo records for the period, yielded a total of 440 artisans working in sixty trades (see Table 1). The table indicates the range of artisan trades found in Mexico City and the possible proportions in which these trades were represented, but the incompleteness of the records means that only part of the artisan group has been identified, perhaps as few as a third for the period. If the Spanish population of Mexico City grew to around 8,000 by 1550,[54] and the total number of Spaniards who arrived in the city during the entire period was at most twice the size of the 1550 population, then perhaps one in twelve individuals was an artisan. This estimate is somewhat lower than Lockhart's estimate of one in ten for Peru during the years 1532–1560 and lags well behind the figures for Puebla de los Ángeles—15 percent in the

53. Chevalier, *Land and Society*, 94, notes that by the midsixteenth century horses, following sheep and cattle, had begun to multiply rapidly in New Spain, and Indians also began to acquire pack animals. See also Hassig, *Trade, Tribute and Transportation*, 193–194, 200, 204.

54. Gibson, *Aztecs*, 380 (table 27). He gives a figure of 2,000 vecinos at around 1550.

TABLE 1: Artisans in Mexico City, 1525–1555

	Trade	Spanish term	Subtotal	Total
Clothing trades	Tailor	Sastre	60	
	Silk weaver, other fine cloth maker	Sedero, etc.	32	
	Hosier	Calcetero	28	
	Cloth shearer	Tundidor	8	
	Glove maker	Guantero	1	
	Hat maker	Sombrerero	1	
	Tapestry maker	Tapicero	1	131
Metalworkers	Ironsmith	Herrero	31	
	Swordsmith	Espadero	12	
	Horseshoer	Herrador	10	
	Locksmith	Cerrajero	6	
	Smelter	Fundidor	4	
	Refiner	Afinador	3	
	Armorer	Armero	2	
	Knife maker	Cuchillero	2	
	Dagger maker	Puñalero	1	71
Leatherworking trades	Shoemaker	Zapatero	18	
	Tanner	Curtidor	12	
	Saddler	Sillero	8	
	Wineskin maker	Odrero	7	
	Harness maker	Guarnicionero	3	
	Bit and bridle maker	Frenero	3	
	Ankleboot maker	Borceguinero	2	
	Leather embosser	Guadamacilero	1	54
Silversmiths	(Includes silver and gold workers)	Platero		52
Construction trades	Carpenter	Carpintero	15	
	Stonecutter	Cantero	10	
	Mason	Albañil	3	
	Street paver	Empedrador de calles	1	
	Bricklayer	Ladrillero	1	
	Sawyer	Aserrador	1	
	Cart maker	Maestro de hacer carretas	1	32
Barber-surgeons	Barber	Barbero	17	
	Surgeon	Cirujano	4	
	Others licensed to cure and treat		1	22
Pharmacists		Boticario		17
Food trades	Confectioner	Confitero	7	
	Baker	Panadero	4	
		Bizcochero	1	
	Butcher	Carnicero	2	14
Candlemakers		Candelero		
		Cerero		11
Gardeners		Hortelano		10

TABLE 1: Continued

	Trade	Spanish term	Subtotal	Total
Miscellaneous	Artilleryman	Artillero	3	
	Blaster	Cohetero	1	
	Potter	Tornero	2	
		Ollero	2	
	Batea maker	Bateero	4	
	Sieve maker	Cedacero	2	
	Brassworker	Latonero	1	
	Caldron maker	Calderero	1	
	Cooper	Tonelero	1	
	Mill builder	Maestre de hacer molinos	1	
	Gem worker	Lapidario	1	
		Perlero	1	
	Musician	Trompeta	3	
		Tañedor	1	
	Printer	Imprimidor	1	
	Bookseller	Librero	1	26
Grand total				440

Sources: *Actas de cabildo de la Ciudad de México*, Vols. I–VI (Mexico City, 1889); A. Millares Carlo and J. I. Mantecón, *Índice y extractos de los protocolos del Archivo de Notarías de México, D.F.* (Mexico City, 1945–46).

early 1530s and 18 percent in the 1550s.[55] Given Mexico City's key role as a center for trade and services from the time of the conquest, it seems unlikely that its share of artisans was notably lower than Puebla's. In any case the proportion of adult males who were artisans would have been greater than one in twelve, and more on the order of 15 percent—one in seven—or higher.

Cabildo records show that tailors in Mexico City began to regulate the examination and licensing of individuals in their trade in the early 1520s, and other artisan groups followed their example by the 1530s or 1540s. In 1525 three tailors—Gaspar Ramírez, Juan del Castillo, and Francisco de Olmos—complained to the cabildo that their authority to license new tailors was not being respected. In the following year the latter two, elected "alcaldes de los sastres de esta ciudad," requested two plots of city land to construct a hospice for the poor and needy, which would also serve as

55. See Lockhart, *Spanish Peru*, 96–97, for his estimate of the number of artisans in Peru, and 243 (table 5) for the breakdown of trades. For Puebla see Hirschberg, "Social History of Puebla," 116 (table 18) and 320 (table 71).

the gathering place for the city's tailors participating in the annual procession of Corpus Christi.[56] Some members of this group became active entrepreneurs. One Juan de Villarte, who lived in Mexico City from at least 1536 to 1553, owned black slaves and sheep, hired another tailor to work for him in 1536 for 65 pesos in salary, and was the principal investor in a partnership with two other men to sell goods in Santiago de Guatemala and buy cacao.[57] Tailors and hosiers were closely allied. In the 1540s silkweavers also formed a tightly knit group, organized on a trans-Atlantic basis. Records from Seville in 1542 show that one of them, Alonso Gómez, agreed in advance of his passage to New Spain to work for Juan Marín and Juan de Molina in Mexico City for two years; in 1543, also in Seville, Francisco Jiménez de Espinosa contracted to work for Juan Marín in Mexico.[58]

Members of the building trades—carpenters, stonecutters, masons, and bricklayers—were often key figures in local society, particularly in the first decade of intense construction in the new capital. Some of these men served the cabildo as *maestro de obras*, a position that involved supervision of the repair and maintenance of public works (roads, bridges, and water supply systems) and occasional new construction of municipal buildings. Besides supervising Indian labor in a spectrum of projects for the reconstruction and maintenance of the city, some of these artisans trained Indian artisans in Spanish construction techniques. When the Augustinians of Tiripitío (in Michoacán) began construction of a large church and monastery in 1537, they not only brought Spanish artisans from the capital to teach Indians stonecutting and joinery but also sent Indian artisans to Mexico City to be trained.[59]

Blacksmiths, horseshoers, silversmiths, and other metalworkers were prominent and active; not surprisingly, many were involved in mining, either as investors or as technicians. The well-known blacksmith Hernando Alonso, executed by the Inquisition as a heretic in 1528, was an associate of Cortés who arrived in New Spain via Cuba. A wealthy encomendero, he formed one partnership to exploit mining interests in Michoacán and another to raise livestock. In connection with these enterprises, he employed his nephew as a miner and in 1527 contracted to supply meat for the capital.[60] Another figure active in the 1520s, Pedro de Sepúlveda,

56. *Actas de cabildo*, I, 46, 71.

57. MC 1939, 1954, 2094, 2478, 2649.

58. *Colección de documentos inéditos para la historia de Hispano-América*, 14 vols. (Madrid, 1927–1932), XI, nos. 559, 638. A "silk" weaver produced many kinds of fine cloth, such as velvet, satin, and taffeta.

59. Kubler, *Mexican Architecture*, I, 110–114.

60. Greenleaf, *Mexican Inquisition*, 33–35; Miranda, *Función económica*, 19–20; Himmerich, "Encomenderos," 193–194. See MC 31, 600, 874, 1259, and other items.

limited his enterprises to metalworking. Variously identified as a *fundidor* (smelter) and blacksmith, in 1528 he bought a blacksmith's forge with three artisan slaves (two black, one Indian) for 300 pesos and then formed a partnership with another blacksmith, who agreed to work in the shop and supervise the artisan slaves and twenty Indian employees.[61]

A number of gardeners (*hortelanos*) worked or owned garden plots along the narrow canal that brought fresh water from Chapultepec, having obtained permission from the cabildo in 1527 to irrigate their plots from this source. Gardeners worked under a variety of arrangements, but few appear to have owned their *huertas* outright, normally the case in Castile as well. Irrigable land suitable for cultivating fruits and vegetables that was located within or very near to urban areas was valuable property, but gardeners themselves were fairly humble individuals; hence *hortelanos* typically leased rather than owned the plots they worked.[62] In 1525 Fernando Vásquez formed a year's partnership with Pedro Hernández de Plasencia to work a garden rented from Bachiller Alonso Pérez; Vásquez was to perform the gardening work and his partner to sell the produce in the city. Another gardener, Álvaro de Torres, made an agreement with Francisco de Lerma by which Lerma allowed Torres to use his house and *huerta* near the spring of Chapultepec for a period of two years; Lerma received two-thirds of the produce and Torres one-third, and the proceeds of the harvest were sold in Lerma's shop.[63]

Barbers, surgeons, and pharmacists (the first two groups often identical) were closely allied by their ties to the medical profession and at the same time used association with each other for various kinds of enterprise. In the 1520s the pharmacists formed partnerships for mining ventures, and their commercial investments suggest that a range of non-pharmaceutical items of merchandise was available in their shops.[64] But pharmacists and barbers, as well as surgeons, did administer medical treatment. In 1527 the cabildo of Mexico City authorized the wealthy regidor Dr. Cristóbal de Ojeda to visit the pharmacies of the city and license individuals for the practice of surgery and treatment of *bubas* (yaws, but probably meaning other diseases also, most likely including syphilis). In the same year a barber, Pedro Hernández, obtained from the cabildo a license to treat *bubas*, which the protomédico Pedro López had

---

61. MC 1373, 1702, and other items.
62. For a discussion of gardeners in Trujillo, Extremadura, see Ida Altman, *Emigrants and Society: Extremadura and Spanish America in the Sixteenth Century* (Berkeley and Los Angeles, 1989), 104.
63. *Actas de cabildo*, I, 117; MC 94, 1317.
64. An active participant in the "rescate" of slaves under the first audiencia was a barber named Salamanca, said to be a criado of Lic. Delgadillo, who would bring the slaves to Mexico City to be branded. AGI, Justicia, leg. 226, no. 1.

previously denied him; all evidence indicated that Hernández's treatment of the disease was successful.[65] Licensing to perform medical treatment was sometimes limited to the performance of certain procedures or the treatment of specified illnesses and generally fell under the supervision of professional medical practitioners; sometimes, however, officials set up by the barber-surgeons themselves were authorized to conduct examinations and inspections.

Early Mexico City did not lack formally educated physicians and lawyers. The majority were men of property, wealth, and status; some were even encomenderos. The prominent physician Dr. Cristóbal de Ojeda just alluded to was a member of the cabildo in the 1520s and had an encomienda in Michoacán; he may also have been involved in commercial imports.[66] Eleven physicians with degrees appear in the records, all but two in the 1530s; four of them held the licentiate and the rest the doctorate. Lawyers, almost three times as numerous in the records as physicians, frequently appeared before or were officials or judges of the audiencia. Most were *licenciados*, although some—especially in the 1520s—were only titled *bachiller*.[67] Despite diverse economic interests, almost all of those holding degrees in medicine and law seem to have engaged in the practice of their professions at least part of the time, in both private and public capacities.

It should be noted that the multiple economic involvements of artisans and professionals of all kinds in New Spain had well-established precedents among their counterparts in Castile. New opportunities encountered in the Indies doubtless contributed to the proliferation of economic activities. Nevertheless, typical of Castilian society were the blurring of lines between artisans and entrepreneurs and the diversification of investments on the part of professionals and tradesmen whose original occupation might position them to take advantage of economic opportunities with little direct relation to their vocation. These patterns repeated themselves

65. *Actas de cabildo*, I, 127, 119.

66. MC 554, 1341, 1552, and other items. Ojeda was an influential man in Mexico City in the 1520s. An antagonist of Alonso de Estrada, who at one time had him jailed, Ojeda had a less than sterling reputation. He supervised the branding of Indian slaves in the city and was known for poor treatment of the Indians of his encomienda of Capula in Michoacán. When reference was made to this mistreatment, his response was to bluster and joke about, rather than deny, the allegation. Ojeda said he shared the encomienda with the surgeon Maestre de Roa (Pedro Núñez), who collected the tribute and supplies for the mines. See AGI, Justicia, leg. 107, no. 2, ramo 2, and Himmerich, "Encomenderos," 393–394, 398.

67. As Lockhart has suggested for early Peru, lawyers holding a doctoral degree were a rarity, apart from some audiencia judges; see *Spanish Peru*, 60, for his discussion of levels of education and degrees among lawyers and physicians. A Dr. Valdivielso was appointed to serve as Mexico City's letrado in 1531; see *Actas de cabildo*, II, 83. Some ecclesiastics also held advanced degrees. The first treasurer of the Mexico City cathedral chapter, don Rafael de Cervantes, "held the largely honorary title of doctor of theology from the University of Sigüenza," according to Schwaller, *Church and Clergy*, 49–50.

not only in boom towns like Seville but also in smaller places where the local economies were far less dynamic.[68]

Royal and local government quite early generated a whole complex of legal technicians and minor officeholders in Mexico City, who were closely related to the professional and artisan groups. The cabildo, audiencia, visitadors, and other officials all employed the services of notaries.[69] Sometimes the turnover among them was rapid. Notaries were often active in commercial enterprises; some, by virtue either of prior political and personal connections or of their official capacity with the cabildo or audiencia, found themselves in a position to secure property grants or other concessions. Juan de Cuevas, the son of a lawyer and son-in-law of Lic. Diego Téllez, was an associate of Cortés who became *escribano mayor de las minas* in the 1520s, a position he held at least through the 1530s. A vecino of Mexico City, Cuevas acquired the encomienda of Cuitlahuac sometime before 1544 and held it for more than twenty years.[70]

Mexico City's many officials—appointed by the crown, viceroy, audiencia, or cabildo—ranged from the protomédico, assayers of the mint (silversmiths), and *alarifes* (masons or carpenters) to the more lowly constables (the *alguacil mayor* or chief constable, appointed by the cabildo, actually was an official of considerable authority), inspectors and guards of different kinds, and town criers. The petty officials, many of whom might have had no particular training or occupation and received low salaries, were most numerous and showed high rates of turnover.

Interpreters formed a sort of semi-official group whose abilities and functions could put them in positions of some influence. Three individuals who submitted depositions (*informaciones*) to the viceroy in the 1540s stated that they had served as interpreters for the audiencia: Juan Gallego, Francisco Muñoz, and don Hernando de Tapia. The last was an Indian, son of the *principal* don Andrés de Tapia.[71] A Juan Freyle served as interpreter for the audiencia in the 1550s. Two other interpreters, at least one of whom probably was an Indian, appear in the records of the 1520s, and three others in the 1530s. Apparently the linguistic skills of one of the latter, Pedro García, led the cabildo to employ him as a supervisor of Indian labor in repairing bridges and causeways in the city.

The background of most early interpreters is obscure. In the Tello de

68. See Pike, *Aristocrats and Traders*, 130–148, on artisans in Seville, and Altman, *Emigrants and Society*, 96–98, 119–122, for investments by artisans and professionals.

69. See Lockhart, *Spanish Peru*, 68, on the training and functions of notaries in the Spanish world.

70. See Gibson, *Aztecs*, 417; Greenleaf, *Mexican Inquisition*, 19; Icaza, *Conquistadores y pobladores*, no. 386; and MC 476, 2192.

71. Tapia was closely associated with Lic. Tejada. During Tejada's term in office he received a grant of land in Tacuba near Tejada's lands; see Ruiz Medrano, "Gobierno y sociedad," 267.

Sandoval visita an interpreter named Antonio Ortiz figured in the proceedings against the oidores; another interpreter, Pedro de Molina, lived in Ortiz's house. In a letter of 1547 Lic. Tejada, one of the oidores, complains about the procedures of the visita and specifically the part played by Antonio Ortiz, Marcos Romero, and Francisco Triana, whom he calls "moriscos e intérpretes." Triana was present in Mexico City from at least the 1530s.[72] In the 1540s and early 1550s interpreters—"lenguas" and "nahuatacos"—appear more frequently in the records, perhaps reflecting both an increasing frequency of bilingualism among Spaniards and Indians and a greater involvement of Indians in the Spanish legal system.

Activities of the regular orders in Mexico City and New Spain have been the subject of scholarly studies, as have more recently those of the secular clergy.[73] The latter tended to concentrate in particular in the centers of Spanish society, mainly Mexico City and nearby mining districts, in the early years, while the regular clergy were more active in the Indian countryside; but the distinction was not invariable.[74] Secular priests were present from the time of the conquest, and a number of them appear in the notarial records of the 1520s and 1530s, sometimes connected with the "Iglesia Mayor" of the capital, often seeking benefices in Mexico City "or any church in New Spain," as one unemployed priest put it. The records used furnish only one case of a priest who contracted to serve as *doctrinero* of an Indian parish. In 1536 Bernardo de la Torre, while in Mexico City, made an agreement with the representative of an encomendero holding a grant in Michoacán to serve as priest in the encomienda pueblos for a hundred pesos a year.[75] The clergy and religious orders more or less monopolized formal education; however, lay teachers not only tutored students but could obtain licenses to establish schools as well. Three such teachers appear in the records of the late 1530s and early 1540s.

Blacks, Moriscos, and Mestizos

Spaniards arriving in Mexico City from either the islands or the peninsula became part of an urban society whose members were heterogeneous not only socially and occupationally but also—and perhaps more strikingly—racially and linguistically. While contact with the indigenous peoples of

72. Carter, "Law and Society," 30, 45; Icaza, *Conquistadores y pobladores*, nos. 847, 739, 893; *Actas de cabildo*, I, 20; III, 6, 8; IV, 118, 191; MC 1390, 1959; *Epistolario de Nueva España*, V, no. 260. Ortiz was *teniente de corregidor* of Chinantla, and Molino held the same position in Tlapa (in Guerrero); the latter also might have been the encomendero of Santiago Camotlán in Oaxaca until 1545; see Ruiz Medrano, "Gobierno y sociedad," 267–268.

73. See note 3 above.

74. Schwaller, *Church and Clergy*, 75.

75. MC 1989.

New Spain was an entirely new experience for individuals coming directly from Spain, for most Spaniards the presence of Africans and persons of mixed racial descent would have been a familiar element, if not from their hometowns then certainly from the time virtually all emigrants spent in Seville before departing for the Indies.[76]

Black slaves were everywhere in early Mexico City. They almost invariably formed part of early mining operations and transport enterprises, working with Spaniards or under their supervision. They served as personal servants and housekeepers, in artisan shops, and under merchants, encomenderos, government officials, and entrepreneurs of all descriptions. The black slaves in Mexico from the early 1520s to the mid-1550s seem to have arrived from (or via) Seville or the islands but may have been African born in many or most instances.[77] The notarial documents record a number of slaves as being from "Guinea" and occasionally from other places in Africa.

Prices for slaves in the 1520s were generally between one hundred and two hundred pesos, although they sometimes rose much higher. A twenty-year-old slave named Catalina, for example, was sold for three hundred pesos in 1528. Origin in itself did not necessarily determine a slave's value, since a slave born in Africa still could be "ladinoized" or trained in a trade. In 1527 a slave named Cristóbal from Guinea was sold by a confectioner along with some tools of his trade, in which the slave obviously was skilled, for two hundred pesos; in contrast another slave from Guinea was sold in the same year for only seventy-five pesos, quite a low price.[78] In the 1530s prices for black slaves fell off somewhat, tending to average around one hundred pesos, but by the 1550s prices had climbed to over two hundred pesos.[79]

A black slave was valuable property. In several instances, as in Peru in the conquest period, runaway slaves who had not yet been recovered were sold for only slightly less than normal prices, and a slave named Alonso, described as a muleteer, was sold while still imprisoned for theft.[80]

76. For Seville, see Pike, *Aristocrats and Traders*, 154–192, on moriscos and African slaves. For discussion of ethnic diversity in the smaller cities of Trujillo and Cáceres, see Altman, *Emigrants and Society*, 122–124.

77. The data on the origins of black slaves in Gonzalo Aguirre Beltrán, *La población negra de México, 1519–1810* (Mexico City, 1972), are principally for the late sixteenth century on.

78. See MC 994, 626a, 862.

79. In Peru prices for black slaves rose from about 100–250 pesos in the 1530s to 150–300 pesos by the late 1540s; see Lockhart, *Spanish Peru*, 179. The low prices in New Spain in the 1530s might have reflected a very temporary excess of supply over demand preceding the initiation of larger-scale silver-mining operations, or it may be that conditions in Peru caused a major price rise, for prices in the early Caribbean had also been very low compared to Peru.

80. For discussion of such sales in Peru, see Lockhart, *Spanish Peru*, 189.

The need and ability to pay for slaves in Mexico City probably far exceeded the volume of the slave trade, especially in the 1520s. Officials and wealthy individuals pressed for greater freedom in the importation of black slaves.[81] In the 1530s and 1540s, while complaints about and fears of blacks and mulattos increased along with official attempts to restrict their activities and movements,[82] little or no action to curb imports was taken. The *contador* Rodrigo de Albornoz himself obtained a license to import one hundred black slaves in 1535, and fifty more soon thereafter.[83] Although Mexico City merchants as well as officials and other entrepreneurs were involved in the slave trade,[84] no overall figures on the volume of the trade are available, and those for the black population of the capital during the period may be questionable.[85]

The sparse records of manumissions of black slaves in the early period may in part reflect the limitations of the sources, but slave owners were unlikely to have given up such rare and valuable property without compensation. As elsewhere in the Iberian world, slaves were sometimes able to buy their freedom, usually either by working for employers other than their masters or by agreeing to serve someone for a certain period. A black woman named Bárbola contracted to work two years for the *confitero* Francisco de Lerma, who agreed to train her in his trade and buy her freedom for 130 pesos, the balance of what she owed her master, Hernando Cortés.[86]

Whether the few free blacks who appear in the notarial records were manumitted slaves or arrived in Mexico as free individuals is not clear. Probably the best known was Juan Garrido, who claimed to have been the first person to plant wheat in New Spain. Doubtless brought to Europe by the Portuguese, Juan Garrido became a Christian in Lisbon and lived six

81. See, for example, the deliberations of a meeting between the cabildo of Mexico City and representatives of other towns of New Spain held in 1525, in *Epistolario de Nueva España*, I, 87, no. 65.

82. See Liss, *Mexico Under Spain*, 65, 140; Aguirre Beltrán, *La población negra*, 23.

83. Aguirre Beltrán, *La población negra*, 22.

84. See, for example, MC 2163, 2216, 2251, and *Colección de documentos inéditos*, XIV, no. 618, in which Francisco de Almazán, vecino of Mexico City, arranged in 1548 to import 150 slaves to the Indies.

85. Liss, *Mexico Under Spain*, 140, states that "in 1553 Velasco reported 20,000 Negroes. The contraband trade in blacks made population estimates even more difficult." Colin A. Palmer, *Slaves of the White God: Blacks in Mexico, 1570–1650* (Cambridge, 1976), 133, estimates there might have been some 10,000 blacks in Mexico in 1537, the year of the first planned slave rebellion in the capital. Philip Curtin's estimates for total Spanish American imports of slaves in *The Atlantic Slave Trade: A Census* (Madison, 1969), 25 (Table 5), are 15,000 for 1521–50 and an additional 4,000 or so for 1551–55. Even assuming that the majority of slaves imported during the entire period 1521–55 went to Mexico and that Curtin's figures may be somewhat low, Palmer's (and Velasco's) estimates seem unrealistically high.

86. MC 1337 (contract made in 1528).

years in Castile before coming to the Indies. He lived in Santo Domingo and Puerto Rico previous to going to New Spain during the conquest. Whether he spent any or all of his pre-Mexican career as a slave is not known, but he was a free man in Mexico. A vecino of the capital, married with three children, by 1527 he owned a house and garden in the city. He worked for the cabildo in 1524 in some rather menial capacities. He was paid thirty pesos a year as the cabildo's porter, which involved summoning the council members and arranging tables and chairs, and he was hired for fifty pesos a year to guard the *acequia* that brought water from Chapultepec, keeping out animals and people. The latter duty was soon terminated; instead, a group of Indians was set to guard the water supply for five *mantas* and five fanegas (one and one-half bushels) of maize every ten days. In 1528 Garrido bought some slaves, some pigs, and equipment for panning gold, and in 1536 he dissolved a partnership with Francisco de Baena, together with whom he had owned Indian and black slaves.[87]

The moriscos were another slave group, possibly even closer to Spanish society than the blacks, who remained in some senses apart despite their often very high degree of acculturation. Numerically morisco slaves in Mexico were insignificant. Most were women who brought higher than usual prices, usually between two hundred and three hundred pesos. Often freed in wills, they were still being bought and sold through the 1530s. One reference to a morisco slave appears in records of 1540, when the encomendero Pedro Núñez de Roa arranged to have him brought from Seville.[88] The origin of moriscas was sometimes recorded. One was identified as being from "Berbería," another from "Oran" (both in 1528), and they were often called "white slaves." A 1551 record in which a slave named Ana was sold for 270 pesos, however, describes her as a "negra atezada, de tierra de Berberya."[89] Whatever their origin, the morisco slaves formed a minor group in the Spanish society of early Mexico City.

Mestizos were not highly visible in Mexico City in these years. Wills, evidence of Spanish-Indian marriages and more frequent informal liaisons, official comments, and the establishment of the San Juan de Letrán school for mestizo boys and of an orphanage or convent for girls all attest to the

87. MC 1263, 1674, 1889; *Actas de cabildo*, I, 17, 18; Icaza, *Conquistadores y pobladores*, no. 169. Garrido went with other vecinos of Salvaleón (on Hispaniola) to Puerto Rico with Juan Ponce de León as a free man; see Troy Floyd, *The Columbus Dynasty in the Caribbean, 1492–1526* (Albuquerque, 1973). Six other free blacks appear in the cabildo records. One, like Garrido, was a porter for the cabildo. The others, all vecinos, requested plots of city land.
88. *Colección de documentos inéditos*, XI, no. 505. See Pike, *Aristocrats and Traders*, 154–170, for moriscos in Seville, probably the source of most morisco slaves in the Indies, and Lockhart, *Spanish Peru*, 196–198, for discussion of moriscos in Peru.
89. MC 2551.

existence of mestizo children, but the word "mestizo" itself hardly appears in the documents of the period. Treatment of mestizo offspring—like the treatment of illegitimate children in general in Spanish society—probably involved considerable fluidity and variety, with some children remaining within Spanish society and others blending unobtrusively into the Indian world of their mothers.[90]

Some Spaniards made elaborate provisions for mestizo children. Diego de Sanabria left his illegitimate daughter in the care of two men from his native city of Cáceres who were to take her to Spain to live with his mother or brother. In her will of 1537 Inés Hernández provided a dowry of fifty sheep for one of two mestiza girls whom she had apparently raised in her home (they are called "mestizas" in her will), and she left various items of cloth and clothing to both. In 1527 another vecino of Mexico City sent a representative to Cuba to find his mestizo son, whose Indian mother had died.[91] Like Peru, Mexico had a small group of what might be called "mestizo aristocrats," such as the children of Moctezuma's daughters doña Leonor and doña Isabel.[92] Because of mestizos' relative invisibility, accurate population figures probably are not to be expected; a 1560 estimate suggests 2,000 mestizos in the city.[93]

Indians

With perhaps 75,000 Indian inhabitants in the mid-1550s, compared to a Spanish population of approximately 8,000, postconquest Mexico City was still very much an Indian entity, a fact the Spaniards must have recognized.[94] They were still calling their capital Tenochtitlán in the 1520s and Tenochtitlán-México in the 1530s. Nonetheless, if one looks for much detail or substance regarding Indian life and society in the Spanish records of the period, what is most striking is the scant mention made of Mexico's native inhabitants.[95]

---

90. See Altman, *Emigrants and Society*, 150–155, for discussion of the treatment of illegitimate children in Castile and their often intermediate or ambiguous status. For the situation in Peru, see Lockhart, *Spanish Peru*, 163–170.

91. MC 1331, 2370, 681.

92. See Gibson, *Aztecs*, 418–419 and 423–426, for the history of the encomiendas granted to doña Leonor and doña Isabel. For doña Isabel and her children by the Cacereño Juan Cano, see Altman, *Emigrants and Society*, 142, 253, 272–273.

93. See Gibson, *Aztecs*, 380.

94. Ibid., 377–380, for discussion of pre- and postconquest population figures for the city. Gibson notes (378) that the city "received an unusual influx of Indian peoples from all other areas during the colonial period," perhaps reflecting both the continuation of preconquest patterns of movement and the new circumstances created by the Spanish presence.

95. Recent and ongoing research based on Nahuatl documentation has increased greatly our knowledge of the Indians of postconquest Mexico. See, for example, S. L. Cline,

Indians appear in the notarial records of the 1520s and 1530s mainly as slaves or in connection with encomiendas. Mining operations in the 1520s and '30s possibly used the greatest numbers of Indian slaves, who also worked in such transport activities as pack trains and carting. Service by Indians in Spanish households or artisan shops was widespread throughout the period. Personal service embraced a wide spectrum of roles and activities—from women serving as part- or full-time housekeepers and mistresses, to men apprenticed and trained in Spanish crafts or trades—with concomitant implications for the degree and kind of acculturation. Prices of slaves and provisions in wills, while not extremely informative, are suggestive in this regard. In the mid-1520s, when groups of slaves were being sold for four or five pesos per slave, those selling for higher prices probably had more of the skills required by Spanish society. A slave named Juana was sold to a carpenter for twenty pesos in 1525; a muleteer bought another slave named Juana for thirty-one pesos in 1527; and in 1528 a twenty-year-old Indian woman named Catalina from Coatzacoalcos was sold for the unusually high price of one hundred pesos.[96] These women probably were moving toward acculturation into the Spanish world. Likewise Ochoa de las Rivas in a codicil to his will freed his ladino (Spanish-speaking) slave from Guatemala, Luisico, with the provision that he live with Bishop Juan de Zumárraga until his marriage, suggesting that Luisico would remain a part of Spanish society, perhaps as much because he was a foreigner in Mexico City as because he was ladino. But even extensive contact with and knowledge of Spanish society did not imply a complete break with Indian culture. Inés Hernández, in freeing her Indian slave Catalina and the latter's son Antonio in her will, left them a *carga* of cloth and specified that they were free to go wherever they wished. One might imagine that they turned toward the Indian world.[97]

If the available sources do not reveal much about the functions and roles of Indian men and women in personal household service, they say even less about Indians working in the Spanish crafts. A few Indian artisans appear in Spanish records. In 1528 a Guatemalan Indian slave and two black slaves were sold along with a blacksmith's forge; a notarial document of 1536 records the sale of an Indian, "Juan, silversmith," along with

Colonial Culhuacán, 1580–1600: A Social History of an Aztec Town (Albuquerque, 1986); Robert S. Haskett, "Indian Town Government in Colonial Cuernavaca: Persistence, Adaptation, and Change," *HAHR*, 67:2 (May 1987); and James Lockhart, *The Nahuas After the Conquest: A Social and Cultural History of the Indians of Central Mexico, Sixteenth through Eighteenth Centuries* (Stanford, forthcoming).

96. MC 407, 495, 1084. For discussion of the roles of acculturated Indians in early Peru, see Lockhart, *Spanish Peru*, 202–204.

97. MC 1896, 2370.

the silversmith's shop; and a will of 1538 specifically refers to Bartolomé González, "Indian blacksmith."[98] There are a number of examples of Spanish artisans buying Indian slaves in ones and twos whom they probably used as apprentices or assistants.

The merging of similar Spanish and Indian trades, practically if not formally, probably began early. Two Spanish candlemakers lost their guild offices in 1535 not only because of their monopolistic practices and the apparently overemotional behavior of one, but also because they were using Indian workers rather than doing the work themselves.[99] The secondary sources strongly suggest that Indians in Mexico City became involved in Spanish or Spanish-type trades early, a situation contrasting with that in Peru, where Indian practice of Spanish artisanry developed late and was not widespread even in the 1550s.[100] The official royal policy of separation of Indian and Spanish sectors, with its implications for protection of the former, was unsuccessful even from the earliest postconquest years in Mexico City, which was a setting for maximum contact.[101]

The failure of the policy of segregation and protection of Indian property rights and lands was hardly unique to Mexico City, but the process of Spanish infringement upon and dispossession of Indian lands and rights was accelerated because of the intense pace and strength of Spanish colonization in the capital. Still, the preconquest entities of Tenochtitlán and Tlatelolco maintained their political and legal existence throughout the colonial period, each with its own barrio organization, cabildo, and Indian governor, and both retained their jurisdiction over settlements (estancias) located outside the capital.[102] Calnek's findings on the re-creation of preconquest residential patterns in Mexico City during the sixteenth century also point to a high degree of continuity despite the massive demographic, political, economic, and ecological changes the Indians of Tenochtitlán experienced during and after the conquest.[103]

98. MC 1376, 2084, 2471. See Lockhart, Spanish Peru, 203–204, for the career of an Indian artisan slave named Francisco, who was born in Tenochtitlán and learned saddle- and harness-making from a Spaniard in Mexico, for whom he claimed to have worked as a free man. Around 1539, however, Francisco was sold in Lima to a Spanish shoemaker as a slave, and he spent subsequent periods both as a slave and as a free man.

99. Actas de cabildo, III, 108.

100. See Lockhart, Spanish Peru, 218, and Gibson, Aztecs, 399–400, for Indian participation in and organization of Spanish-type trades.

101. See Gibson, Aztecs, 368–369, on some of the immediate implications of the choice of the site for the Spanish capital. The cabildo appropriated urban land from Indian families to make property grants to Spanish vecinos in the 1520s and early 1530s (273), and from at least the mid–1530s Spaniards were living in Indian areas (376). See also Ruiz Medrano, "Gobierno y sociedad," chapter 3, which describes the process by which Lic. Tejada acquired lands in Tacuba and Chapultepec.

102. See Gibson, Aztecs, 371.

103. See Calnek, "Conjunto urbano."

Conclusion

The relatively few sources available for the study of early Spanish society in Mexico City suggest the rapid formation of an economically active community of Spaniards. Members of this community relied on the experiences and precedents brought from the islands and from Spain itself to organize mining, commercial networks, and agricultural and stockraising enterprises, mobilizing Indian labor and productivity in a variety of forms and using the skills and services of African slaves in intermediary positions. In doing so they quickly created the basis for economic prosperity and social stability for themselves. The small size of the Spanish community, fewer than 10,000 people at midcentury, and the availability and variety of economic opportunities (as well as, perhaps, their relative modesty, compared to Peru's) fostered considerable interpenetration of economic and occupational sectors, a pattern typical of the Caribbean as well, where a mixed economy of agriculture and mining developed from the outset. Merchants, artisans, miners, and encomenderos have been discussed here separately, but many individuals moved within and between such categories with ease. People from a range of occupations (including governmental and ecclesiastical officials) became involved directly and indirectly in the operation (and profits) of gold and silver mining, and almost everyone seems to have been at least a part-time entrepreneur, as was true in early Peru as well.

While the lines of social ranking within the Spanish group did not disappear in this context, the openness and flexibility of opportunity worked to foster coherence, prosperity, and an almost precociously rapid development of Spanish society. Full institutionalization took place by midcentury; the University of Mexico first offered classes in 1553. The first thirty years after the conquest of Tenochtitlán and founding of Mexico City represented not a period of tentative experiment or disorganization but rather one in which the enduring socioeconomic and institutional structures of New Spain, centered principally on Mexico City, took root and developed. Increased prosperity followed the discovery of silver mines in the north at the end of this period, but the changes of that time represented extensions and elaborations of forms of organization and activity that had already developed and crystalized.

Consideration of Spanish society in early Mexico City almost inevitably suggests parallels with Peru. Because of the fragmentary nature of records for early New Spain, in making comparisons to Peru one sets Mexico against an area that is both better documented and more thoroughly studied in its early decades of development. Mexico and Peru shared a series of basic features—patterns of economic activity; representation of social and occupational groups; a tendency of institutions, economic enterprises, and prominent people to concentrate principally in one urban center; and institutional and other forms of interaction between Spaniards, Africans, and indigenous peoples. Most of the significant distinctions seem to have resulted from differences in specific local circumstances, rather than, for example, different governmental policies or different personnel. Certainly the very considerable analogies between Spanish society in Peru and Mexico through much of the colonial period are by now familiar.

At the same time, however, we must recall that at the outset substantial differences existed between the two situations. Spaniards reached central Mexico and appropriated the Mexica capital of Tenochtitlán a full decade before Pizarro and his followers captured and executed the Inca emperor at Cajamarca. That event, while doubtless signalling the end of Inca dominance and the beginnings of Spanish control of Peru, did not complete military conquest nearly so definitively as did Cortés's occupation of Tenochtitlán. But if the events at Cajamarca were more ambiguous, the immediate payoff in wealth was spectacularly greater than anything Spaniards had experienced elsewhere, including Mexico. This wealth engendered the deadly factional strife so notable in early Peru but virtually absent in Mexico.

Because of the relative lack of immediate wealth in Mexico, and the historical and geographical connections between the first generation of Spaniards there and Spanish society in the islands, it is useful to consider early Mexico in light of its ties and similarities to the islands as well as to Peru. The limitations of the records for the early Caribbean make extensive comparisons difficult, although the most direct sorts of ties naturally did exist.[104] The conquest of Mexico was virtually a Cuban undertaking, even if many of the men from Cuba also had spent time elsewhere. One of the oidores of the first Mexican audiencia, Licenciado Matienzo, previously served as oidor in Santo Domingo. But beyond such connections other similarities suggest themselves. Neither the islands nor Mexico offered a great windfall of treasure. The lack of wealth probably underlay the ephemeral existence of many of the early towns founded mainly in connection with mining activity in the islands and New Spain. Most of these towns rapidly lost ground to a dominant urban center (Santo Domingo on Hispaniola, Mexico City in New Spain). The initial prolifera-

---

104. Some studies of the early Spanish Caribbean are Sauer, *Early Spanish Main*; Enrique Otte, *Las perlas del caribe: Nueva Cádiz de Cubagua* (Caracas, 1977); Floyd, *The Columbus Dynasty*; Frank Moya Pons, *Después de Colón. Trabajo, sociedad y política en la economía de oro* (Madrid, 1987); Emilio Rodríguez Demorizi, *Los dominicos y las encomiendas de indios de la Isla Española* (Santo Domingo, 1971); Eugenio Fernández Méndez, *Proceso histórico de la conquista de Puerto Rico (1508–1640)* (San Juan, 1970).

SPANISH SOCIETY IN MEXICO CITY   445

tion of towns and active participation of Spaniards in local politics would
suggest, however, that the emergence of a dominant city was not necessarily a foregone conclusion. This was not the contemporary Spanish
pattern; Castile in many senses still was an aggregate of cities and their
subregions. But the nature of the economy and levels of Spanish emigration could not support a fully developed network of Spanish cities and
towns in the early years.

Early Spanish society in the islands might well have been more diverse
in its socioeconomic composition and more demographically balanced than
generally has been thought. Even given the notable mobility of Spaniards
in the islands, towns there rather quickly developed a stable core of vecinos who held offices and repartimientos and engaged in a mix of economic
pursuits (mining and stockraising and later sugar cultivation), using black
slaves in supervisory and skilled capacities and an Indian labor force whose
status (whether encomienda, slave, or naboría) probably varied more in
theory than in fact, all much as in early Mexico. This fairly stable society
in the islands soon attracted Castilian women. According to the repartimiento of 1514, 180 vecinos of the total of 371 on Hispaniola who received
Indians were married to Castilian women and only 62 to Indian women.[105]
Squabbles between local and crown officials and the extensive involvement of all of them in the local economy (including trade in Indian slaves)
and encomiendas, ties based on kinship and common point of origin, and
the claims and presumptions of the Colóns and first conquerors all played
a prominent part in ordering society in the Caribbean, as would similar
factors in early Mexico and Peru.

In thinking about the relationships among the different centers of early
Spanish activity in America, then, it might be helpful not only to point
out similarities but also to question how it was that Europeans were able
to establish such seemingly identical economic enterprises and social and
political forms and institutions in the Caribbean, Mexico, and Peru—
locales that at the time of contact, conquest, and early settlement were
so strikingly different in their geography, accessibility, indigenous populations, resources, and numbers of Spaniards present. That they managed
to do so is, of course, testimony to the Spaniards' single-mindedness of
purpose and relative imperviousness to much of the richness and complexity of the indigenous world of the Americas. This imperviousness in
turn helps to explain how, with the tragic exception of the islands (where
within a generation the native population began to disappear), the real
changes wrought by the Spaniards' advent often were far more limited
and superficial than perhaps they ever realized.

105. Moya Pons, *Después de Colón*, 109.

19
Women and Society in Colonial Brazil
A.J.R. Russell-Wood

Introduction

No aspect of Brazilian history has received so stereotyped a treatment as the position of the female and her contribution to the society and economy of the colony. The white *donzela* and the lady of the 'big house' have been depicted as leading a secluded existence, be it in the innermost recesses of their homes or in conventual cells, immune to harsh realities and safe from brash overtures by pretenders. Of the white woman, it was said, during her lifetime she left her home on only three occasions: to be baptized, to be married, and to be buried. The role of the white woman was seen as essentially passive, victim of the demands of an over-bearing and frequently unfaithful older husband to whom she would bear children, or of a martinet of a father. As for the Amerindian woman, whose beauty led the discoverers to initial raptures of platonic appreciation and then sexual overindulgence, she has rarely been depicted in any role other than that of concubine or lover. The black and mulatto woman, slave or free, became a symbol of sensual arousal and sexual fulfillment. Her power over the white male settler was lauded in popular mythology, verse, and prose. Her domestic duties were irrevocably tied to her sexual role as the plaything of adolescent sons, the butt for the cruelty and sadism of jealous white wives, or the object of the affections of the master of the house.

That there is some truth in each of these stereotypes is undeniable. But uncritical acceptance and repetition by scholars have ignored the basic fact that the female formed part of a larger society. Her role and her contribution were determined, in part, by factors totally unrelated to the nature of her sex, but which formed guidelines for society as a whole in the colony. The position of the woman was established by a code of ethics, by theological and

The following abbreviations have been used: ACDB, Archives of the Convent of the Poor Clares, Salvador; AMB, Municipal Archives, Salvador; APBOR, Public Archives of the State of Bahia, registers of royal orders; APMCMOP, Public Archives of the State of Minas Gerais, registers of the municipal council of Vila Rica; APMSG, Public Archives of the State of Minas Gerais, registers of the Secretaria do Govêrno; ASCMB, Archives of the Santa Casa da Misericórdia, Salvador; BNRJ, National Library, Rio de Janeiro.

2 *A. J. R. Russell-Wood*

legal decrees, and by social and religious attitudes which had comprised the cultural heritage of the Christian countries of Western Europe, and had been transferred to the New World, there to be preserved, strengthened, or modified to meet the needs of colonizing societies. Social mores and the economic situation in this tropical environment were to affect the female no less than the male colonist. In short, it would be as impossible as it would be unrealistic to dissociate the position of the woman from the general economic and social developments in Brazilian history. No less than the male, she was to experience the stresses and strains within society, and those regional variations and economic imbalances which characterized Portuguese America. This essay will argue that the female played a significantly more important role in the social, economic and ideological development of the colony than has been appreciated. Although, in the case of the white woman, the demands of society required that she be out of sight, this should not be interpreted as suggesting that she was out of mind. The roles of Amerindian and black women have received extensive treatment elsewhere. Thus my discussion will deal with the white female, digressing to describe the position of the black or mulatto woman only when this would establish a point of comparison, heighten the contrasting role between females of different colors in the colony, or serve to reinforce the argument.

Two *caveats* must be entered at the outset. Evidence on the role of the white woman in colonial Brazil is not readily available. Memoirs, diaries, or chronicles written by females in Portuguese America have not survived the ravages of time, if they existed at all. Registers of royal orders, gubernatorial correspondence, and legislation are rarely informative in this regard. Thus I have relied on sources in private and public archives such as wills, inventories, municipal licensing ledgers, brotherhood and conventual records, and fiscal registers. Such evidence was gleaned from Rio de Janeiro, São Paulo, Salvador, and Minas Gerais. But it is well to bear in mind that such was the human and ecological heterogeneity of Portuguese America that regional variations may well be found to differ from the picture here depicted. The second *caveat* is prompted by the latter-day adulation of Clio. The welter of recent publications on family history, especially those based on a quantitative approach, has yet to embrace colonial Brazil. Whereas selected cities and regions of Spanish America have provided case studies for scholars, only in São Paulo and Salvador have steps been taken for the collection of demographic data for the colonial period. At the present stage, it would be misleading to adduce conclusions based on partial evidence and tentative findings. Something so basic to our understanding as a documented estimate as to the numbers of migrants to Brazil from Portugal and the Atlantic Islands prior

Women and Society in Colonial Brazil 3

to 1822 has yet to be made.[1] A historian of the role of women must contend with the dearth of data on such fundamentals as the number of female migrants to the colony, or what proportion of the overall population was composed of females. Inadequate conventual, baptismal, and marriage registers make impossible any determination of percentages of women marrying, entering convents, or remaining unmarried. Hopefully the evidence here presented will throw new light on attitudes toward women and inspire a reassessment of their contribution to the building of Portuguese society in the tropics.

Ideologies, Values, Attitudes and the Legal Position of Women

The attitudes of male colonists in Brazil towards women did not differ markedly from their counterparts in Portugal. Male-oriented, male-dominated, patriarchal, and patrilineal societies, the role ascribed to the female was marginal, isolating her from the main stream of developments in the colony. At first sight, such attitudes might appear negative, humiliating the female by relegating her to an inferior position. In fact, closer scrutiny shows that the converse was the case, and the female was held in high regard. Ideals and precepts which in our age would be regarded as restrictive and male chauvinist were regarded as the normal outcome of theological teaching and unreservedly accepted as such by Catholics of colonial Brazil. In a profoundly religious society, even the most foul-mouthed and domineering slave owner was deeply conscious of right and wrong and faced death with fear and trepidation. In practice his attitudes towards women depended on their social position and color. He did not look on a white woman with those same eyes with which he looked on black or Amerindian women. However, rather than a double standard of values, there was a double standard of expectations and of enforcement. Expectation of deviation from behavioral ideals demanded of the white woman increased in inverse proportion to the decreasing degree of whiteness and financial means of the woman. While it was accepted that the white woman was sexually unassailable and sexual promis-

---

[1] Pioneering studies on the family are Emilio Willems, ' The Structure of the Brazilian Family ', *Social Forces*, xxxi, No. 4 (May 1953), pp. 339–45 and ' On Portuguese Family Structure ', *International Journal of Comparative Sociology*, iii, No. 1 (Sept. 1962), pp. 65–79; Donald Ramos, ' Marriage and the Family in Colonial Vila Rica ', *Hispanic American Historical Review*, lv, No. 2 (May 1975), pp. 200–25. Dauril Alden details demographic problems in ' The Population of Brazil in the Late Eighteenth Century: A Preliminary Survey ', *Hispanic American Historical Review*, xliii, No. 2 (May 1963), pp. 173–205. On migration see, Carlos B. Ott, *Formação e evolução étnica da Cidade do Salvador* (2 vols, Salvador, 1955, 1957) i, 46–53; ii, 77–89. Gilberto Freyre's *The Masters and the Slaves* (2nd Eng. lang.ed., New York, 1966) contains a wealth of information on the mores of colonial Brazil.

4   *A. J. R. Russell-Wood*

cuity on her part could result in death at the hand of her husband or father, for the colored woman it was conceded that she was in no position to repel sexual advances by her master and that she might resort to prostitution to buy her freedom. Such was the sexual mystique enshrouding the colored woman that infidelity and promiscuity on her part were regarded as almost inevitable.

European travelers to colonial Brazil commented on the seclusion of the white woman, be she daughter or wife. This was the ideal state for womanhood in the eyes of the colonists, not from any desire to attribute an inferior position to the woman but rather to isolate her from the realities of everyday life. Possibly this attitude was mingled with yet another cultural legacy from the Old World to the New: Marianism. The large number of brotherhoods dedicated to the Virgin was evidence enough of the veneration in which she was held by the colonists.[2] Some of this veneration may have been transferred into everyday attitudes toward lay women. In colonial Brazil the female was a possession to be cherished and protected against coarseness, sexual advances, or any act which might tarnish her purity. This explains in part why colonial fathers were so willing for their daughters to enter convents. If the girl were to choose marriage, no effort was spared to ensure that the transition to her new role should be as painless and effortless as possible. Rare was the girl who came to the altar without being endowed within the financial means of her parents who tried to ensure that the groom should be his bride's social equal. Against this ideological context, the closing of certain avenues to the white woman in Brazil – be they sexual, social, or economic – may be viewed as a positive aspect of colonial society in Portuguese America.

The most explicit contemporaneous commentary on the position of the white female in colonial Brazil and her relations to her family is contained in a tract written by Nuno Marques Pereira and entitled *A Narrative Compendium of the Pilgrim in America* (Lisbon, 1728). A journey to Minas Gerais provided the pretext for a moralistic tract on the evils of the colony. At each stop on his journey, the 'pilgrim' took the opportunity to moralize and to gloss that commandment most relevant to his host's situation. His observations doubtless reflected the attitudes of Pereira's contemporaries and merit close attention.[3]

The 'pilgrim' advocated that, ideally, marriages should be between partners of similar social and economic standing and of about the same age. Once

---

[2] A. J. R. Russell-Wood, ' Aspectos da vida social das irmandades leigas da Bahia no século XVIII ', *Universitas*, No. 6–7 (1970), pp. 189–204 and ' Black and Mulatto Brotherhoods in Colonial Brazil: A Study in Collective Behavior ', *Hispanic American Historical Review*, LIV, No. 4 (Nov. 1974), pp. 567–602.

[3] Nuno Marques Pereira, *Compendio Narrativo do Peregrino da America*. My account is based on Chaps. 13, 14, 19.

married, the wife was to shun the company of ecclesiastics and women of questionable repute because of their propensity for sexual alliances and malicious gossip. The ideal wife should dress modestly, should not covet anything beyond her financial means or social station, and on no occasion speak disparagingly of her husband. In short: 'And thus married women must be strong, discreet, and prudent. Within their homes, they should be diligent. Outside their homes they should be retiring. And at all times they should be exemplary in their conduct and mien and be reputed as long suffering rather than spendthrifts.' Pereira noted that women in Portugal were less tolerant towards their colored domestics than were their Brazilian counterparts, who would go so far as to condone misbehavior or conceal criminal offences committed by a slave girl.

The ' pilgrim ', while describing the obligations of a wife to her husband, emphasised the responsibilities of a husband toward his wife. Pereira noted that many wives were *mal cazadas* (lit: ' badly married ') and had wearied of the married state because of their husband's inconsiderate behavior. In such cases it was the Christian duty of the husband to mend his ways and accord to his wife the attention and respect she deserved. He was not to take concubines, whom the ' pilgrim ' compared to turtles who emerged from the water, deposited their eggs on the beach, and then returned to immerse themselves in an ocean of sin. Nor was the husband to place temptation in the way of his wife. He should not take young men to his home, nor exhibit his wife to male friends as he would a sample of cloth. He was to be vigilant over the company she kept, forbidding her from visiting female friends whose composure or conversation might be injurious. In sexual matters he was to be moderate and not overly demanding.

As *paterfamilias*, the father was responsible for the physical, spiritual, and economic wellbeing of his household which embraced wife, children, and servants. By his example and by maintaining constant vigilance over his children, whom he should not hesitate to chastise, the father should always be conscious of his duties. This vigilance was especially applicable to daughters. The ' pilgrim ' counselled:

Know, Sir, I said to him, there is no force on this earth against which a battle must be so relentlessly waged as woman. The first duty of a father is to bring up his daughters in the faith of the Lord and ensure that they are married at the appropriate time. When the vine matures it must be given shelter and special care. Likewise, a girl on reaching womanhood needs protection, a home, and a husband.

A girl's innocence could only be guaranteed if the father ' were to be as vigilant as Argus by day and by night.' On no occasion should the father allow a daughter from his sight. She should not keep the company of slave girls of dubious morals. Her teachers should be rigorously screened. Pereira quoted the dictum of one mother that she preferred her daughters to be less knowledgeable and more secluded. The conscientious father would 'count and measure', be it the regularity of music or the spacing of a daughter's words or footsteps whenever she was out of his sight. Selection and final approval of a marriage partner were the final responsibilities of a father to his daughter. Pereira cited the adage that 'a father need not lose a moment's rest in marrying off ten sons, but the marriage of a virtuous daughter is the labor of a decade', and gave a final warning against fathers who married off daughters against their will.

The dearth of documentary evidence on female reaction toward such attitudes and the manner in which the white female perceived her own role in colonial society makes assessment difficult. From testaments made by females and occasional letters it appears that white females did not challenge the position ascribed to them by society. In fact, even if a girl or woman had wished to kick against the pricks it would have been difficult for her to find adequate channels for self-expression. Wills made by females comprise only a small number of those dating from the colonial period and which are extant in private archives; nevertheless, these are sufficient to illustrate attitudes of white women on certain issues. Five such themes, basic to an understanding of colonial society, may be singled out for further study: attitude to manual labor; treatment of slaves; religiosity; marriage; vanity.

The dependence of the white female on slaves for the running of her household was unquestioned. That delegation of responsibility to female slaves was allied to scorn for manual labor by white females was only documented when they faced the possibility of being deprived of slave labor. Two examples, both taken from institutions, will illustrate this. The Retirement House of the Most Holy Name of Jesus in Salvador (opened 1716) provided a haven for girls of middle-class families who were of marriageable age and whose honor was endangered by the loss of one or both parents. When the issue of menial labor was first raised, Dom Pedro II had ordered that the inmates should care for themselves and cited the precedent set by convents in Lisbon where even noble recluses had no servants. In 1721 the inmates revolted, alleging that the female warden 'treated them as if they were slaves . . . ordering them to wash crockery and scale fishes and dealing with them harshly despite the fact that they were white women and wards [of the Misericórdia]'. The inmates presented their case to the all-male governing body. The warden was dismissed and the number of slaves increased to such excess as to be the subject of a royal inquiry in 1754.[4] Slaves were also employed for general duties in the Convent of the Poor Clares in Salvador (founded 1677). Nuns were also permitted to have personal servants, but only after petitioning for an apostolic brief. The petition had to be supported by a document signed in secret by the members of the conventual community favoring such an addition and by a letter from the family saying it would meet the additional costs. This directly contravened the papal brief of Clement IX (May 13, 1669) which had authorized 15 servants for general duties, but had expressly stated that no nun should have a slave for her particular needs. Many nuns came to have not only one, but two servants.[5] Some petitions were made less from necessity than from social considerations. In 1701 the two daughters of Manuel Alvares Pereira urged their father to meet a man who had two black female slaves to sell at the bargain price of 150$000 *reis* for the two. The daughters recognized that not only would the slaves satisfy their domestic needs, but their possession would enhance the daughters' standing in the conventual community.[6] In 1883 the Archbishop of Salvador ordered the abbess to reduce the number of servants. At that time 37 servants were serving 13 nuns and 10 resident lay women.[7]

In the attitudes by white females towards slave girls, distinctions of class, color, and civil standing precluded any feeling of common cause. In the early nineteenth century Henry Koster was to write that 'It is said that women are usually less lenient to their slaves than men.' This echoed the advice of the Count of Assumar to an over-zealous official in Minas Gerais about to prosecute the slave of a captain-major. The governor advised restraint 'because these Americans venerate their black slaves as they would demigods'. In their treatment of female slaves, white women ran the gamut from Christian charity to sadistic cruelty. Many left legacies of dowries for slave girls to be married, together with household linen and even furniture. Such legacies often included a clause granting a slave girl her freedom. At the other extreme were white women who prostituted their slave girls for their own gain or were spurred by jealousy to acts of cruelty.[8]

---

[4] King to governor-general, 6 Apr. 1702, APBOR, 7 doc. 15; ASCMB, 14, f. 129; BNRJ, 11, 33, 24, 45, Chap. 29.

[5] ' e nenhuma Freyra possa ter Escrava que a ella particularmente sirva ', ACDB, caixa 1, pasta 1 (i). Exceptions to this brief were Sister Antonia da Piedade (*idem*, caixa 1, pasta 4) and Sister Florencia Maria do Sacramento (*idem*, caixa 1, pasta 18 (ii), *inter alia*.

[6] ACDB, caixa 3, pasta U. Further details on this family and the daughters, one of whom became abbess in 1753, are in A. J. R. Russell-Wood, ' Educação universitária no império português : Relato de um caso luso-brasileiro do século dezassete ', *Studia*, 36 (July 1973), pp. 7–38.

[7] Archbishop to abbess, 25 Oct. 1883, ACDB, caixa 1, pasta 39.

[8] Henry Koster, *Travels in Brazil* (London, 1816), p. 388 : ' . . porq ' estes Americanos

8 *A. J. R. Russell-Wood*

In their attitudes towards marriage, white women followed the precepts of colonial society. White female testators recognized their responsibility to assist unmarried nieces, more distant relations, or the daughters of friends, to make a suitable marriage. Clauses in wills specifically allocated substantial sums of money for dowries. Many followed the example of Joana Fernandes and Maria de Leão, Bahian ladies of the seventeenth century, who provided the capital for trust funds to be established to provide orphan girls of the city and the Recôncavo with dowries to enable them to marry.[9] By such generosity the white female not only recognized her obligations to society, but was also moved by a profound feeling of Christian charity.

Works of social philanthropy were but one aspect of religious conviction. Equally indicative of colonial attitudes were testamentary provisions for funerals and the saying of masses. In this respect the wills of female testators differ only in minor points from those of their male counterparts. Pomp and piety melded to ensure that the funeral would be worthy of the social standing of the deceased and that her soul would be provided for by the saying of masses. Catharina da Silva, twice widowed, who died in São Paulo in 1694, ordered that her body should be buried in the church of St Francis. Her cortège was to be accompanied by the brothers of the Misericórdia and by representatives of other brotherhoods. Masses were to be said for her soul. In Salvador in the early seventeenth century, Maria Salgada left a two-storied house to the Misericórdia with the obligation of saying masses in the brotherhood's chapel for her soul.[10]

In such provisions there was not a little of that vanity and nobilomania which pervaded colonial society. Easily documented for males in their petitions to the crown for the concession of knighthoods in the military-religious orders, evidence of similar aspirations on the part of the white female is more difficult to document. Colonelcies in militia regiments were highly coveted. In 1725 Dom João V warned the Governor of Minas Gerais to scrutinize the social background and capabilities of candidates because it had come to the royal notice that unsuitable people were obtaining such posts, 'dazzled by the honor which such positions bestow on the incumbent, to which their wives are no less susceptible '.[11]

The legal position of the female in the colony depended largely on color

---

reputão os seus negros por semiDeoses ', Assumar to Crown Judge of Rio das Velhas, 1 Jan. 1721, APMSG, 13, f. 13. Cf. Gilberto Freyre, *op. cit.*, for examples of both attitudes.

[9] ASCMB, *Livro 1 do Tombo*, ff. 167–8; *Livro 2 do Tombo*, ff. 46–7.

[10] *Inventários e testamentos. Documentos da secção do arquivo histórico* (Departamento do Arquivo do Estado de São Paulo), No. 23 (1921), pp. 227–307; ASCMB, *Livro 1 do Tombo*, ff. 44–5.

[11] King to Dom Lourenço de Almeida, 9 July 1725, APMSG, 20, doc. 113.

Women and Society in Colonial Brazil 9

and social standing. Because political activity, even at the local level, was regarded as an exclusively male preserve, females were excluded from the lists of the ' good folk of the Republic ', permitted to vote in municipal elections. In other respects the white female enjoyed due process of law and, if this failed, she could appeal directly to the Crown. She could serve as an executrix of a will, inherit and possess land and properties, and could and did frequently hold the legal position of head of household. She could conduct trade and commerce in her own name and could bring legal charges against others. It was not unknown for a daughter to prosecute her father, if he were reticent in furthering her hopes of marriage, and demand payment of her dowry.[12] However, whereas proven adultery was sufficient cause for a man to divorce his wife, for her part the wife was often required to prove a second cause such as cruelty, desertion, or forced prostitution to obtain a divorce. In such cases a lien was placed on all possessions of the defendant, who was responsible for making financial arrangements for the upkeep of the estranged wife and children. During the period of legal separation the estranged wife was placed in the home of a respectable citizen on the order of the vicar-general. After 6 months she could file for divorce and final judgment would be made by the vicar-general. In some cases the ecclesiastical authorities were overzealous. In the 1750s one such divorced woman, Thereza de Jesus Maria, alleged that she was being held against her will in the Retirement House of the Misericórdia in Salvador on the personal orders of the archbishop while her good-for-nothing bookkeeper husband fled to Portugal with her wealth. The crown judge in Salvador, influenced by archiepiscopal pressure, refused to accept her appeals and order her release. Courts looked leniently on crimes of passion where a husband had beaten or killed an adulterous wife, or a wife merely suspected of infidelity.[13]

The colored woman possessed certain legal rights but these were less likely to be respected and courts were reluctant to hand down a judgment in her favor if the defendant were a white person. Slave girls appealed to local authorities and even to the Crown, alleging physical cruelty by masters. Where a master refused all reasonable offers by a slave girl to buy her ' certificate of freedom ', she could prosecute and force him to accept a sum arbitrated by an independent third party. Few slave girls followed this course, either because they were unable to meet the costs of a protracted legal suit or because of fear of reprisal by former masters.[14] Appeals to the Crown were usually successful, although governors warned that charges often lacked substance and that

[12] Nuno Marques Pereira, *op. cit.*, p. 180.

[13] APBOR, 58, ff. 315–440; Luiz Edmundo, *Rio in the Time of the Viceroys* (translated from the Portuguese, Rio de Janeiro, 1936), pp. 319–21.

[14] APMSG, 14, ff. 9, 11v, 13, 54v–5; 59, ff. 143v–4.

slave girls accumulated money for manumission by resorting to prostitution with the full knowledge of their masters.[15] Only in 1871, as the result of the Rio Branco law, were the off-spring of slave mothers born free. Previously such children merely became welcome additions to the slave holdings of a master. Marriage to a slave girl by a free colored reduced him likewise to bondage, and marriage by a male slave to a free black woman did not absolve him from bondage.[16]

Although Amerindians were protected by law from enslavement, bureaucratic negligence in registering royal decrees, pressures by colonists, and their own inability to appeal made Amerindian women susceptible to many of those abuses experienced by black slave women. In 1719 the Count of Assumar told the King about Amerindian girls being sold publicly, left in legacies, given as dowries, and set to work without pay. Such women petitioned district judges and governors for their freedom. Maria Moreira and her three children gained their freedom in 1765 by gubernatorial decree. A Carijó, she had resorted to direct appeal because defective baptismal records made it impossible to obtain documentary evidence and she was too poor to prove her origins through the judicial process. As in other cases concerning Amerindians, she was subjected to ' visual inspection ', and perception played a large part in determining the outcome of such appeals.[17]

Not all Amerindian women were victims of ill-treatment. Catharina Florença, a native of the island of Itamaracá, had been sold in Rio de Janeiro and brought to Minas Gerais with her children. When granted her freedom, she waived charges against her master because he had clothed, housed, and fed her and her family.[18] When Amerindian women were married to black slaves, they were especially susceptible to enslavement, if they were to accompany their husbands. However, their offspring remained free.[19] Although blacks and mulattos were regarded with suspicion, the Crown saw Amerindians as possible means of increasing the population of the colony and as stabilizing factors. A decree of 1755 encouraged Amerindian-white marriages and ordered that the use of such injurious epithets as *caboclo* or *negro* to describe the Amerindians should cease.[20] In the 1740s the Crown approved

---

[15] APBOR, 7, docs. 288, 289, 299, 300; 54, ff. 97–9.

[16] ASCMB, *Livro 2 do Tombo*, f. 31; APMSG, 14, f. 66v.

[17] Assumar to King, 4 Oct. 1719, APMSG, 62 ff. 55–6; APMSG, 59, f. 101v–2 and 60, ff. 88v–91.

[18] She gained her freedom in 1767, APMSG, 89, ff. 37v–8v.

[19] APMSG, 14, ff. 36v–7, 54; 21, ff. 31v–2; 59, ff. 103–4v; 60, f. 122.

[20] *Alvará* of 4 Apr. 1755, APBOR, 55, ff. 129–30. The Directorate (1758) for the administration of Amerindian villages listed among abuses suffered by Indians ' a injusta, e escandalosa introducção de lhes chamarem *Negros;* querendo talvez com a infamia, e vileza deste nome,

suggestions by town councils in Minas Gerais that as many as 200 Amerindian couples be moved from São Paulo to Minas Gerais at royal expense.[21]

Social Role of the White Woman

(a) The Single Girl

The role accorded to the single white girl was no other than that of preparing herself to *tomar estado* (lit: ' to take state '), which meant either entering a convent or marriage. In either case, until the final documents had been signed, the parents lived on tenterhooks of doubts and fears to the point of obsession. The girl's childhood and adolescence were passed in seclusion to remove any possibility of doubt as to her virtue. In some instances family pressures were exerted on the girl either to marry or to enter a convent. But for the most part the concern of the parents was no more than that the girl should ' take state '. Testators left legacies to daughters, nieces, and the female offspring of friends for this, without specifying marriage or convent. Although in 1732 Dom Lourenço de Almeida was to comment caustically that ' it was very fitting for people of low birth to have their daughters take the veil ', there is nothing to suggest that this practice was more prevalent in any one class of colonial society.[22] Even if the final outcome were in defiance of the parents' wishes, a rare event, nevertheless there was a feeling of relief once the decision on the girl's future had been taken.

Should the girl choose to enter a convent, the question arose as to whether this should be in Portugal or Brazil. The outcome was decided by three factors: the proximity of a convent, the color of the intending nuns and the financial resources of the parents. By 1750 most cities in Portuguese America counted at least one convent. Such foundations were the fruits of public and civic pressures, but could not meet the demand for places. Colored girls were not admitted to convents in Brazil, and were compelled to go to Portugal or the Atlantic Islands where they were accepted.[23] Finally, the cost of sending

---

persuadirlhes, que a natureza os tinha destinado para escravos dos Brancos ' APBOR, 61, ff. 199–218v (cl. 10).

[21] APMSG, 86, docs. 25, 27.

[22] ' . . . e como se achão as cabeças de familias com dinhro pa dotes de suas filhas, não cuidão em outra couza senão em as mandarem pa freyras, ou pa as Ilhas, ou pa Portugal e por nenhum cazo as querem cazar, porq' he mto proprio da gente de baxo nascimto o fazer as filhas freiras', Almeida to King, 5 June 1731, APMSG, 32, ff. 105.

[23] APBOR, 53, ff. 167–72; 64, ff. 48–9. In 1699 the archbishop of Salvador ordered an inquiry as to the ' purity of blood ' of an applicant to the convent of the Poor Clares. She had been refused admission because it was rumored that she was the illegitimate daughter of a mulatto woman and Lt. João Luís Ferreira. Despite the additional hardship, the lieutenant commended the nuns for their caution and considered their action wholly justified (ACDB, caixa 1, pasta 27).

a girl to Portugal, paying the fees for her to enter a convent, and the costs of her upkeep were substantial. Such considerations led the ' native citizens and good men ' of the city of São Paulo to remind the Crown in 1736 of a royal favor permitting the Retirement House of Santa Thereza de Jesus to become a convent under the initial supervision of an abbess and nuns from Portugal. The petition informed the King that 13 potential nuns from that city alone had raised 56,000 *cruzados* for such a foundation. A further fourteen people from Minas Gerais had expressed interest. The 33 signatories included the wife of the Paulista pioneer, Pedro Taques de Almeida Paes.[24]

Judging by the number of petitions to the King asking for permission to send or accompany girls to Portugal to enter convents, there was no shortage of fathers willing to meet such costs. Some fathers were prominent figures in the colony. In 1725 the agent in Lisbon of Manuel Nunes Viana gained royal approval for the infamous *poderoso do sertão* to come to Portugal ' to make nuns of his daughters '. In 1726 he placed his six daughters in the convent of São Domingos das Donas in Santarém and returned to Bahia. Nunes Viana deposited 16,000 *cruzados* with the friars of São Vicente de fora in Lisbon, the annual interest to meet the costs of upkeep and maintenance of his daughters. In the 1750s the nuns brought legal action against their brother, Dr Miguel Nunes Viana, charging him with fraud and embezzlement of this capital. This was the subject of a royal enquiry, culminating in a ruling upholding the nuns' claim.[25] Other fathers had aspirations beyond their financial means. In 1729 the viceroy supported the appeal to the King by secretary of state Domingos Luís Moreira, asking Dom João V to intervene on behalf of three daughters whom he wished to place in the Convent of the Poor Clares in Oporto. After twenty years of loyal service, Moreira was too poor to pay the entry fees of his daughters to the convent but had embarked the girls, trusting in the royal favor.[26]

Many colonists were unable or unwilling to meet such financial costs. In Salvador they could choose between the Convent of the Poor Clares or the Lapa Convent. The demand for places in the former was such as to lead the city council in 1717 to petition the King for an increase in the number of places to 100 from the original 50 authorized in 1665.[27] Some fathers entered their daughters as ' pupils ' (*educandas*) in the hope that as such they would be favored when a vacancy occurred among the stipulated quota of nuns. Other hopeful but frustrated fathers followed the examples of Manuel de

[24] Petition of 4 Aug. 1736, APMSG, 63, docs. 20 and 21.
[25] APBOR, 19, docs. 159, 159a; 22, doc. 29; 54, ff. 225–32v; 57, f. 342; 75, f. 188.
[26] APBOR, 25, doc. 44.
[27] Council to King, 25 Aug. 1717, AMB, 176, ff. 119v–20.

Women and Society in Colonial Brazil 13

Almeida Mar who asked the King to intervene so that his niece could be admitted to the convent, or of another prominent Bahian, Domingos Pires de Carvalho, who made a similar appeal on behalf of his daughters. In fact, the granting of such favors fell outside the royal jurisdiction, and places were not reserved for royal nominees. Those who were successful in gaining admission often placed all their daughters in the convent. The secretary to the city council, João de Couros Carneiro, gained the abbess's permission for entry of his three daughters in 1686. The guarantee of protection and seclusion was not cheaply bought. In 1684 master of the field, Pedro Gomes, paid 600$000 *reis* and fees for each of his two daughters to be admitted as novices. Such ' dowries ' were not refundable should the girls not take their final vows. In 1751 the ' dowry ' for a girl wishing to take her vows as a nun was 1600$000 *reis*. Nevertheless, for their own peace of mind the citizens of Bahia did not balk at such expenditures.[28]

Marriage was the more commonly-chosen option open to the single girl. At no time in her life was the female to be the object of so much attention. The choice of groom was made from a small circle of possible pretenders, selected and approved by the girl's parents. For the rural aristocracy of Pernambuco and Bahia, marriage served the double purpose of strengthening family ties among this elitist group and improving their economic position and land holdings. As plantation families fell on hard times, potential suitors from the rising and prosperous urban merchant class were courted to bolster the family position by the infusion of new capital.

The female was aided in her quest for marriage by the institution of the dowry. So important was the dowry that it served as a microcosm for attitudes and ideals and illustrated the interplay of social and economic pressures in colonial Brazil. A dowry was both a symbol of social status and a palliative. On the one hand, the social and economic standing of a doting father could only be enhanced if it were to become common knowledge that his daughter was well-endowed. On the other hand, a substantial dowry could offset lack of charm or beauty on the part of the girl. Such an institution was open to abuse. Many a man married a dowry rather than a bride. So prevalent was this mercenary practice that one petitioner for a royal favor cited in support of his appeal that he had married his wife for love and not for her dowry. Some women fell victims to the wiles of unworthy opportunists. The example of the bookkeeper of low birth who married a rich Bahian widow, Thereza de Jesus Maria, and then absconded to Portugal with her wealth was by no means unique.[29] Whatever the evils of the tradition, for the daughter of a

[28] APBOR, 46, docs. 1, 1a, 1b; ACDB, caixa 1, pastas 4, 32, 36.
[29] The marriage had taken place in the archbishop's palace in Salvador on 7 Mar. 1750, APBOR, 58, ff. 330–40.

14   *A. J. R. Russell-Wood*

wealthy family it was never doubted but that she would be endowed. For the daughter of a middle class or poorer family, a dowry was no less a prerequisite for marriage. For the daughter of poor parents or an orphan, a dowry could mean the difference between an honorable marriage and prostitution.

Dowries made by fathers and mothers to their daughters frequently took the form of possessions, rather than outright cash payments. Several factors may have contributed to this practice: first, the shortage of currency in some regions at different periods; secondly, the desire to preserve the overall estate intact albeit under different ownership; thirdly, the fact that in certain areas an economy prevailed which was based on barter rather than coin. The variety of such possessions is well illustrated by the following case taken from São Paulo in the seventeenth century. Messia Rodrigues, the widow of João Pires to whom she had borne nine daughters and one son, endowed her youngest daughter, Margarida, especially generously. Her husband, Captain António do Canto, received 268$000 *reis* in cash, and possessions valued at 450$000 *reis*. The breakdown of these was as follows (values in brackets): reinforced mud houses (100$000 *reis*); house with a tiled roof (20$000 *reis*); 8 dining room chairs and a sideboard (18$000 *reis*); clothes 44$000 *reis*) one bed, covered with a cotton panoply and bed linen (16$000 *reis*); 6 silver spoons, table pieces, and cotton towels (8$000 *reis*); 100 cows (200$000 *reis*); 40 calves (16$000 *reis*); 8 mares and 1 colt (17$000 *reis*); 6 sheep and 1 lamb (7$000 *reis*); tools and equipment (4$000 *reis*). The dowries of the other daughters included Amerindians, pigs, roofing tiles, and bales of cotton. The practice of giving Amerindians as dowries was especially prevalent in São Paulo, where enslavement persisted despite royal decrees forbidding this practice.[30]

The preservation, or if possible, enhancement of social standing by marriage was never far from the minds of the prestige-conscious colonists. Legacies of dowries to daughters and relatives reveal the strength of this preoccupation. The last instructions of the Paulista Pedro Vaz de Barros to his widow were that she should marry off their two daughters ' as quickly as possible with worthy men who have the ability to follow an honorable career '. Jorge Ferreira, a wealthy property owner, who died in Salvador in 1641, bequeathed the fruits of his labors to his niece, Jerónima Ferreira, as a dowry ' so that the husband whom she marries may be the more ennobled thereby '. Similar sentiments filled Francisco Zorilla and Affonso do Pôrto Poderoso. The former had seen military service and held minor posts including that of procurator of the Indians (*procurador dos Indios*). In 1620 he exacted from

[30] *Inventários*, 17, pp. 115–58.

the King the royal favor (*mercé*) that this post should be granted to his widow in trust for the man who married their only daughter. In 1673 Pôrto Poderoso was granted royal permission to retire from his post as clerk to the High Court of Bahia, which he had held for some thirty years. This post, at his discretion, was to pass to his oldest son or to the man who took his daughter in marriage.[31]

Other dowries were given in recognition of the fact that without them daughters or female relatives would stand little chance of getting married. This was recognized by Marcelino Vieira Machado, captain of Monserrate fortress in the Bay of All Saints. In 1809 he petitioned the Crown for promotion to the rank of sergeant-major, citing thirty-eight years in the royal service. He had been moved to make this request because on an annual salary of 10$000 *reis* it was impossible for him to endow his three daughters. The requested promotion would almost double his salary and permit him to provide dowries for his girls, thereby enabling them to find suitable husbands.[32] That it was essential to bring a dowry to marriage was recognized not only by anxious fathers who made special bequests to daughters. Colonists, many of whom had no children of their own, made testamentary provisions for dowries to be given to nieces, godchildren, the daughters of their executors, or simply to the unmarried female offspring of friends. In an age when personal legacies were comparatively few, and testators preferred to leave their fortunes for the saying of masses or charity, legacies for dowries afforded a notable exception.

Orphan girls were perhaps the most in need of dowries. Loss of a father or of both parents placed the girl's virtue and future in jeopardy. Concern for a girl's moral wellbeing provoked a response on the part of colonists which was nothing short of magnificent. Foundlings left on doorsteps were adopted and provided with dowries. This generosity extended to dowries for slave girls and even for their female offspring. Many testators preferred that the Misericórdia should administer such dowries for orphan girls. These fell into two categories. Specific sums were left to the Misericórdia for immediate allocation to deserving cases, or legacies were made to the Misericórdia for the capital to be placed on loan and a number of dowries financed each year from the interest.[33]

---

[31] *Inventários*, 24, pp. 13–67; ASCMB, *Livro 1 do Tombo*, ff. 143v–53; *Documentos historicos da Bibliotheca Nacional do Rio de Janeiro*, Vol. 16, pp. 142–8; 26, pp. 451–3.

[32] APBOR, 107, ff. 312–15.

[33] A. J. R. Russell-Wood, *Fidalgos and Philanthropists. The Santa Casa da Misericórdia of Bahia, 1550–1755* (London, Berkeley and Los Angeles, 1968), pp. 173–200.

16 *A. J. R. Russell-Wood*

(b) The Married Woman

To separate the position of the white woman in colonial Brazil from her role in marriage would be to ignore the social, ideological and religious context of an age and country. It was unquestioned that her *raison d'être* was to be virtuous as a girl, honorable as a bride, loyal as a wife, and loving towards her children. It was in marriage, with its multiplicity of demands and responsibilities, that the white woman made her major contribution to society. Moreover, only through marriage would a girl become a woman in her own right and in the eyes of others. Attitudes towards the institution of marriage have already been discussed and we may now turn to the more physical aspects of the life of the married woman. The demographic history of colonial Brazil is fraught with difficulties, but certain sources have not been fully exploited in providing data on marriage patterns. One such source comprises testaments dating from the colonial period. In no way can these conclusions be considered definitive, but it is hoped that they may stimulate further detailed research on the part of scholars.

The age at which a girl was regarded as being 'marriageable' depended in part on her parents' financial position and social background. Some girls may have married at only twelve years of age, but such early marriages were the exception rather than the rule. Fourteen was a generally accepted age for a first marriage, and daughters were encouraged by parents to marry early. The relief expressed by Catharina de Araújo 'who rejoices greatly at seeing her daughter protected and made mistress of her own household as she desires', on the occasion of the marriage of her 14-year old daughter, Bernarda, to a Bahian goldsmith, was symptomatic of the reaction of many parents.[34] To judge by conditions imposed by the Misericórdia for the granting of dowries, the age span for first marriages was considered to be between 14 and 30 years of age. That girls matured earlier than boys was recognized by the census of 1776. Males from 7 to 15 years were classified as boys (*rapazes*), whereas the upper age for girls (*raparigas*) was 14. Furthermore, whereas for a woman old age was considered to start at 40, the male only qualified for such a classification on reaching his sixtieth year.[35]

Possibly marriages were contracted against the girl's will, but less frequently than popular mythology and 'cord' literature would suggest. The custom existed of orphan girls in convents and retirement houses being provided for by wealthy benefactors until they came of an age when their elderly protectors

---

[34] ASCMB, *Livro 4 de Acórdãos*, ff. 30v–1r.

[35] Resolution by governing body of Misericórdia, 1 Nov. 1653, ASCMB, *Livro 1 de Acórdãos*, f. 42. On this census see APMSG, 38, ff. 13–14; Dauril Alden, *op. cit.*, and revised figures for Minas Gerais in Kenneth Maxwell, *Conflicts and Conspiracies. Brazil and Portugal, 1750–1808* (Cambridge University Press, 1973).

would claim them in marriage. This practice met with the consent and approval of the authorities. That young girls should marry much older men was commonplace. Parents viewed with approval the suit of a man old enough to be the girl's father or even grandfather, because of the financial security and social position such a marriage would provide. Some child-wives may have accepted such a fate with resignation, but horrifying pictures have been painted of young girls being forced into marriages with tuberculous septuagenarians.

The question of fertility of white women in the tropics is controversial. At the present state of research conclusions must be tentative. There is evidence to support the hypothesis that many white women in colonial Brazil did not bear children. Whether this was due to physiological, psychological or environmental factors is unclear. The answer may well lie in a combination of all three influences. Repeatedly the testaments of white property-owners in the colony asserted the absence of offspring and, in default of these, bequests were made to the Church or to religious orders.

There is no reason to believe that such a situation was restricted to testators whose wills have survived, or who were careful enough to make a will, not a widely-practiced custom in the colony. However, this is not the whole story, and the figures presented (Figure 1) may give a more representative picture of family composition in Portuguese America. This chart was prepared from data obtained from a sample of 142 married couples in São Paulo in the seventeenth century. Much information is lacking, but membership of the Misericórdia or Third Orders suggests that such couples were white and of middle- or upper-class background. Children registered are the offspring of first marriages only. All told, there were 731 legitimate children, which, divided among the 142 families, gives an arithmetic mean of 5.14 children per family. But to assert that the average household (*fogo*) was composed of parents and five children is misleading, because of the asymmetrical distribution of the data. Some families counted as many as sixteen children, but the most frequent value, or mode, is one to two children.

The white woman of colonial Brazil has been depicted as a matronly figure at 20 worn out by successive pregnancies and lack of exercise. Evidence on frequency of childbirth is scanty. Testators often failed to mention the ages of deceased children or of married offspring no longer living under the parental roof. Some few examples tend to bear out the view of repeated pregnancies. Isabel Gomes, who died in 1628 in São Paulo, bore her husband 10 children of the following ages: 23, 20, 18, 12, 10, 8, 6, 3, and 1 year and one not listed. The offspring of another Paulista mother were aged 19, 17, 15, 12, 10, 9, 4, and 2 years. Although one married child of Ignez da Costa was not listed by age,

18 *A. J. R. Russell-Wood*

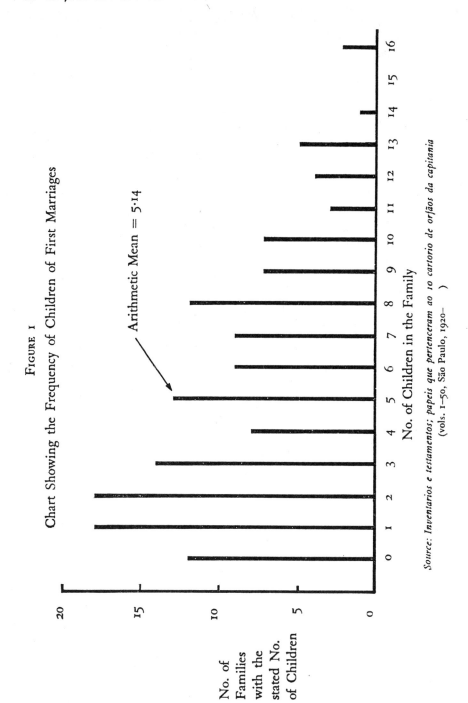

FIGURE 1

Chart Showing the Frequency of Children of First Marriages

Arithmetic Mean = 5·14

No. of Children in the Family

No. of Families with the stated No. of Children

Source: Inventarios e testamentos; papeis que pertenceram ao 1o cartorio de orfãos da capitania (vols. 1–50, São Paulo, 1920–)

Women and Society in Colonial Brazil 19

the recorded ages of the remainder of the family were 20, 19, 18, 16, 15, 10, 8, 7, and 2 years.[36] Infant mortality among whites was high, but not as high as among offspring of black families. The belief that higher colored infant mortality was offset by larger numbers of offspring was challenged in 1821 by the German mining engineer, von Eschwege. Based on observations made in Minas Gerais, his conclusion was that white women were more fertile than mulatto women, and that the fertility of a black woman depended on whether she were free or slave. A survey for the Passo parish of Salvador in 1799 suggests a mortality coefficient of 172.4/1000 for ' innocents ' of white parentage. Although wills rarely specified the age of a child at death, there is no doubt that, be it as a result of infant mortality or later sickness, many white children failed to survive their parents.[37] Such productivity was not without its risk to the health of the mother. Several wills mention that the wife was pregnant at the time of making her last dispositions, ' sick in bed and in fear of death '. The inference is irresistible that her death resulted from complications during pregnancy, or in childbirth.

Of greater interest to students of family history are data concerning generational differences within a family. The age span between eldest and youngest was sometimes as much as 20 years. Of the 7 children of the Paulista Agostinha Rodrigues, her eldest son was 30, whereas her youngest was only 5. The sixteen children of another Paulista family ranged from 34 to 8, spanning 26 years.[38] Such large families provided a form of security, especially in agricultural areas, against the death of a breadwinner. Then, as now in Brazil, children joined the labor force at a tender age, and many a dying father could take solace in the fact that his widow would be helped by their already adult offspring.

A survey of 165 testaments made in São Paulo in the seventeenth century provides information on first and multiple marriages (Figure 2).

Number of Marriages	Male	Female
0	2 (2%)	— —
1	99 (87%)	43 (84%)
2	12 (10%)	7 (14%)
3	1 (1%)	1 (2%)
	—	—
	114	51

FIGURE 2: INCIDENCE OF MARRIAGE AND REMARRIAGE

[36] *Inventários*, 7, pp. 376–8; 10, pp. 99–134; 17, pp. 93–111.
[37] Thales de Azevedo, *Povoamento da Cidade do Salvador* (Bahia, 1955), pp. 204–6.
[38] *Inventários*, 9, pp. 89–105; 24, pp. 245–93.

20   *A. J. R. Russell-Wood*

Conclusions based on such partial evidence must be treated with caution, but are not necessarily unrepresentative of marriage patterns in the colony. It was unlikely that a white woman of marriageable age would remain single in the colony. Those alternatives open to her male counterpart – cohabitation or promiscuity – were barred to her. It also appears that the white woman was more likely to contract a second, or even third, marriage than her male counterpart. The shortage of white women in the colony placed a premium on the eligible widow. Furthermore, the custom of early first marriages by females often resulted in widowhood at a comparatively young age. Finally, the woman's own search for the financial security and social position guaranteed by marriage may have contributed to the greater incidence of remarriage among white females than white males.

The Woman as Head of Household: Social Aspects

The white woman in colonial Brazil frequently occupied the position of head of household. As such she made her most important contribution to the life and economy of the colony. Factors contributing to her assuming such a position were divorce, desertion, and widowhood. Judging by the paucity of references, rarely did estranged couples go to the lengths of formally filing for divorce. In those few recorded cases, the property of the couple was divided by the legal authorities and the female received half of the value at which the property and possessions had been assessed. Custody of children was invariably granted to the mother. In such cases the father was liable for maintenance of the mother and children. The only exception to this rule was when the wife was found to be the guilty party. In 1782, Manuel Nicolau, a native of Crete living in Salvador, was granted permission to return to Portugal with his three young daughters. Custody of the children had been granted to him after his wife had been found guilty of adultery and had been jailed together with her lover.[39]

Far more frequently, the wife was thrown into the position of effective head of household as the result of desertion. Sometimes, she was the victim of circumstances, on other occasions such desertion was intentional. In a highly mobile and essentially opportunist society, the woman not only exerted a stabilizing influence on the family but also had to shoulder the responsibility of bringing up children during their father's absence.

Conditions in the colony were not conducive to a secure family life. Heads of household, with their wives' consent, left families in Portugal or in a Brazilian coastal city rather than endanger their lives in the interior. Few

[39] ASCMB, *Livro 2 do Tombo*, ff. 108v–9v; APBOR, 17, docs. 14, 14a, 14b; APBOR, 75, ff. 281–6.

followed the example of one doughty character who traveled from the hinterland of Pernambuco to Minas Gerais in the 1730s, accompanied by his wife and eight children.[40] Wives and families were often the victims of vengeance born of jealousies and rivalries. In Pitangui in the early eighteenth century, the four young daughters of a prominent Bahian, Manuel de Figueiredo Mascarenhas, were orphaned. Domingos Rodrigues do Prado, ' a rabble rouser, criminal and well known instinctive killer ' had killed their father, the *juiz ordinário,* because he suspected Mascarenhas of informing the governor of Prado's criminal deeds. On another occasion in Minas Gerais, when Martinho Affonso de Mello threw his support behind the local Crown Judge in attempts to establish a village in Papagaio, his life was threatened by the furious local populace, his house and property fired, and his wife compelled to leave the area.[41] Threats of attack by Amerindians or groups of runaway slaves were constant. White settlers were the frequent victims of rape, pillage, mutilation, and murder. To such hazards could be added unsanitary living conditions and the usual gamut of tropical diseases and inadequate medical attention.

Against such a background, breadwinners could scarcely be criticized for not wishing to expose families to such hazards. Many a father left wife and family in Portugal with promises to return. Some died in the colony. Others committed bigamy, or took a concubine. Others simply lost contact with relatives. Soldiers in the dragoons often served terms of 10 years in Minas Gerais before petitioning the Crown for leave of absence of one year to return to their families in Portugal. Royal approval for such leaves and increased family allowances failed to prevent the disintegration of family ties. Petitions by widows for the discharge of soldier sons were invariably granted.[42] Appeals by deserted widows and offspring to the Crown and to the Misericórdia, seeking assistance in tracing husbands and fathers, were commonplace. In 1747 Dom João V asked Gomes Freire de Andrada to verify the whereabouts of one João Pereira Borges. Some 20 years previously he had gone to Minas Gerais, leaving wife and child in Lisbon. His wife complained that 17 years had passed without news of her husband. Thanks to the charity of neighbors and to her skill with her needle, she was supporting herself and their 22-year-old daughter. But such was their indigence that she could not ' give state ' to her daughter. The husband was traced to Brumado in Catas Altas where he had a smithy. The King ordered his return to Portugal to support his family.[43]

[40] APMSG, 54, ff. 129.
[41] APMSG, 11, ff. 200–1v; 12, f. 78.
[42] APMSG, 46, docs. 42, 43, 44, 45; 10, f. 28; APBOR, 22, docs. 24, 24a.
[43] APMSG, 86, doc. 76.

Cases of desertion were not limited to wives and family in Portugal. In Brazil, men left home for long periods while on expeditions to the *sertão*. In default of any news of their whereabouts, they were presumed dead. Soldiers who had married in the colony, and whose tour of duty was over, preferred to desert their wives rather than return with them to Portugal. Colored wives were frequent victims of such neglect.[44]

The emphasis placed by colonial mores on single girls and marriage tended to conceal the inescapable fact that the majority of marriages would end in widowhood. It was more usual for the white female to outlive her spouse than *vice versa*. For the woman who chose not to remarry, the alternative was a struggle not only for her own survival but also as guardian of her children and frequently as owner of property. In such a role the widow was a true head of household with extensive responsibilities. Although relatives and older married children rallied round at times of need, success or failure for the widow and her family lay in her hands. The difficult role into which the widow was cast was acknowledged by husbands who made special clauses in their wills to support their widows.

The first hurdle to be faced by the widow was bureaucratic. This was especially the case if the husband had died intestate, or if the offspring were below 25 years of age. The local ' *provedor* of the dead and absent' not only made an inventory of the possessions of the deceased but also placed a lien on them and all currency holdings. Given the mobility of colonial society, it was not unusual for a person's possessions to be distributed throughout Brazil. Delays were inevitable, severely prejudicing heirs because of devaluation of plantations and death of cattle as the result of neglect. Heirs in Brazil often lost their inheritances because of the ruling that no *provedor* should release the possessions of the deceased without written authorization obtainable only in Lisbon. This absurd ruling was relaxed in 1719, but three years later the town council of Vila Rica informed the King that because of restrictions placed by *provedores* many rich men were buried as paupers and many a young widow was made destitute. Despite reforms and Crown intervention in specific cases, delays and abuses were endemic.[45] Heirs in Portugal making claims in Brazil were passed over by local *provedores*. Delays of 20–30 years were not infrequent. Euzebia Maria da Assumpção, widow of the businessman, Alexandre Manzoni, who had died in Salvador in 1773, asked the Crown for assistance in settling her husband's estate. From Lisbon it was impossible for the widow to enforce payment of debts due to her husband in

---

[44] *Inventários*, 19, pp. 245–55; Russell-Wood, *Fidalgos*, pp. 309–10.
[45] APMSG, 4, ff. 222v–4; APMCMOP, 9, ff. 5v–6v, 9v–10v, 57–62; *idem*, 37, ff. 2–3, 46, 59–60, 81, 82, 99–100v.

Bahia, Minas Gerais, and Goiás. In 1788 the Queen ordered a judge of the High Court in Salvador to be appointed to oversee the collection of these debts.[46] In 1813 the populace of Xique Xique asked for the status of township (*vila*) to be conceded to their village. This appeal was based on the grounds that only thus could a remedy be found to the present situation whereby widows and orphans were left destitute, lost properties, and were unable to collect debts because their nearest legal recourse was 50 leagues distant.[47]

Arrangements made by the deceased for his widow and family varied. The simplest arrangement derived from the time of marriage when a ' division of properties ' was made, enabling the wife to maintain legal possession of her half. Where this was not stated in so many words, the customary practice was for an inventory to be made of the possessions of the deceased. The wife received half of the proceeds derived from the sale of such possessions. Debts and legacies were made from the husband's portion and the residue subdivided. In some cases the deceased had set aside one-third of his portion for the saying of masses for his soul. In other instances this was left to a favorite niece or daughter, or even to his wife. The remaining two-thirds were usually divided among his sons and heirs. Matters could become complicated when, for example, a testator ordered that his ' third ' (*terça*) should be divided equally between legitimate and illegitimate children, and then that the respective halves should be further subdivided so that each child would be a beneficiary.

In some instances the legacies made to the widow were substantial enough to guarantee her security and enable her to bring up children without undue financial strain. But all too many testators left their survivors with no more than their blessing, ' heirs to the poverty I possess.' Sometimes the sum realized by the sale of the deceased's properties and possessions was insufficient even to meet the liabilities and debts he had incurred during his life. Rather than being the beneficiaries of his will, the heirs and widow had to realize their own capital investments to pay these debts. Such straits led the archbishop of Bahia to grant licenses to widows and *donzelas* to ask for alms in public.[48]

The widow was often the executrix of the terms of her husband's will. In this she was usually assisted by a male relative or friend of the deceased. Should the widow die soon after her husband, such a relative became the guardian of the orphaned children. Certain testators placed limitations on

---

[46] APBOR, 78, f. 50; APMSG, 20, doc. 82. On 19 June 1793 the Crown sharply reprimanded the provedor of the dead and absent of Sabará for unjustifiable delays in settling estates, APMSG, 19, doc. 149.

[47] APBOR, 115, ff. 97–107v.

[48] APBOR, 3, doc. 81.

the role of the mother as guardian, should she remarry. One Paulista in the seventeenth century made his wife the guardian (*curadora*) of their children only for as long as she did not remarry. Francisco Pedroso Xavier left his widow Maria Cardoso his ' third ' in addition to the half of his property she had received as his widow. But this supplementary legacy was conditional ' only for as long as she does not remarry because I trust that she will behave honorably towards our children and when and if she should remarry then my " third " is to be divided among my sons and daughters.' [49]

The widow was helped in her task by two factors: first, those benefits derived from larger families; secondly, specific funeral bequests made to her by the deceased for this purpose. Older offspring were exhorted by a dying father to help their widowed mother. One Paulista, Manuel da Cunha Gago, went so far as specially to ask the second son of his first marriage to be generous to his stepmother, Maria Rodriguez, the widow of his father's second marriage. Bequests to provide the widow with the means of fulfilling such responsibilities included the placing of sums of money in trust for dowries to female offspring, supplementary legacies to the widow, and a home or a small-holding to provide a source of income and sustenance.

This assistance could not detract from the awesome responsibility to be shouldered by the widow. Many widows faced the task of bringing up younger children and then providing boys with basic skills or ensuring that girls were suitably married. Maria Rodriguez, the widow of Manuel da Cunha Gago to whom she had borne 12 children and by whom she was pregnant at the time of his death, confronted a household of children aged from 20 to 1. The duties of the widowed mother were not merely directed to supporting herself and her family. Her prime obligation was toward the physical and spiritual welfare of her children. To her fell those tasks as guardian and protector which the ' pilgrim ' had seen as the necessary duties of the *paterfamilias*. Hers was the responsibility of teaching the children Christian doctrine and ' ensuring that they are taught good habits and behavior, the girls to sew and perform domestic tasks and the boys to read, write and count.'

For boys several options were open to the widowed mother. A son could take over the estate or small-holding when he came of age. Other male offspring were induced to sign up for military service or were apprenticed to a trade. Few widows were able to meet the costs of a university education, but some still entertained the hope of most parents in the colony that at least one of their sons might enter the Church. It was not uncommon for fathers or relatives to make legacies specifically for boys wishing to follow such a vocation. The expenditure was substantial, involving travel to Europe and study

[49] *Inventários*, 7, p. 427; 19, p. 293.

there over a period of years. Thus the dedication and sacrifices demanded of one Paulista widow, Euphemia da Costa, cannot be under-estimated. Four of her sons took holy orders. For daughters the hopes of the widow were centered on marriage, and fathers made bequests for the realization of such hopes.[50]

The responsibilities of the widow were not limited to her immediate family and offspring. The taking of concubines and extra-marital relationships were prominent features of colonial life. If a mistress were to be discarded or die, it was customary for the man to bring the children home to his legitimate wife to be cared for, reared, and educated alongside their legitimate children. Foreign travelers to Brazil never ceased to comment on the presence of such children, often of darker hues than the legitimate offspring, at the family table and treated on a basis of equality with children born within wedlock. The attitudes by fathers to such illegitimate offspring were ambivalent. Many simply deserted mother and child and there may have been grounds for the Crown's insistence on a correlation between concubinage and the number of foundling children whose upkeep was a financial drain on town councils in Brazil.

But this was only one side of the story. Other fathers acted most responsibly toward offspring born on the wrong side of the sheet. For the most part the fathers followed the example of Aleixo Leme de Alvarenga who, while acknowledging paternity of children by slave girls, refused to allow bastards to be his heirs. But he made allowances for such children. Aleixo Leme left to his illegitimate daughter, Paula, her mother, who was still in bondage, and two more slaves. Should Paula die, then the mother would become the property of the other illegitimate children she had borne Aleixo. Diogo de Cubas, a *Madrileño* living in São Paulo, exhorted his wife and daughter to look after his illegitimate daughter by a slave. Not only were they to care for her well-being but were to 'indoctrinate her, teach her good customs and make her pray'.[51] This generosity extended in most cases to the mother of the child if she were known. Slave girls not only received their freedom but also household linen, domestic utensils and even, on some occasions, a dowry.

The Woman as Head of Household: Economic Aspects

The vital contribution made by the white woman to the formation of Brazilian society could not be matched by her role in the country's economy. Social mores and the institution of slavery stifled any initiative which the white woman might have been spurred to make. Even at the domestic level

[50] *Inventários*, 16, p. 370; 19, pp. 231–41, 262.
[51] *Inventários*, 19, pp. 5–39; 20, p. 354; Russell-Wood, *Fidalgos*, 182–4.

slaves were charged with the day-to-day provisioning and maintaining of the household. Those few ' cottage industries ' which there may have been were performed by blacks or Amerindians. The contribution which the white female made to the colonial economy was less by dint of her own efforts than as the result of circumstances which she could not avoid. As the widow was forced to assume the position of head of household, so too was death to be instrumental in placing the white woman in positions where she was compelled to take decisions on financial matters and the management of estates. In this regard she belied her traditional image of being divorced from the commercial life of the colony.

Some white women dodged this responsibility, and were content to delegate the administration of estates or inherited properties to sons or more distant relatives. Not infrequently such trust was abused, bringing financial downfall to the woman. Luzia Freire, a widow living in Bahia, refused to make any legacy to her sons-in-law in her will of 1685. Both had cheated her in the management of a sugar plantation and cattle corrals, had misappropriated animals, and had stolen her slaves. Other widows followed the example of Magdalena da Silva, the widow of Manuel Thomé da Cunha, and a native of Mathoím in Bahia. On her husband's death, she rented out her cane plantation for a guaranteed yearly income of 25$000 *reis*. Other widows or daughters who had inherited estates assumed full responsibility for their management. Catharina Paes, after the death of her husband, André Lopes, continued to manage their estate, divided between two major areas in São Paulo. Total holdings comprised 224 cows, 4 oxen, 31 heifers, and 97 bullocks.[52] That such examples were not merely a few entrepreneurial merry widows was shown by a seventeenth-century description of Pernambuco and Alagoas which listed 24 women as cane-growers. They comprised 17 per cent of the total number of sharecroppers in that area.[53]

On rare occasions the white woman did take the initiative. In 1726 one league of land near the ' new road ' was granted to Izabel de Sousa at her request. Recently widowed and with children, her financial resources were slight and she intended to establish herself and support her family by raising cattle. Others maintained small-holdings, small stores, and may even have engaged in black market activities. In the 1760s Dona Ana Maria Barboza de Penha de França, a widow in Minas Gerais, revealed in a petition to the governor a thorough understanding of the economics of operating a gold mining *lavra*, employing some 70 slaves. She asked that restraints be placed

[52] ASCMB, *Livro 2 do Tombo*, ff. 85v–7v, 248–51; *Inventários*, 24, pp. 245–93.
[53] Stuart B. Schwartz, ' Free Labor in a Slave Economy; The lavradores de cana of Colonial Bahia ', in Dauril Alden (ed.), *Colonial Roots of Modern Brazil* (Berkeley and Los Angeles, 1973), pp. 178–9.

on trespassers cutting wood in her lands on the banks of the Rio das Velhas. She needed wood for boxes, wheels, and axles as well as for working the placer mines in the river and for reconstruction of aqueducts bringing water from as far as four leagues away.[54]

Economic interests and landholdings involved their female owners in such topical issues as land grants, division of judicial districts, and taxation. During the 1730s there was hostility throughout Minas Gerais at the collection of the royal ' fifths ' (*quintos*) by means of a capitation tax. In Papagaio in the hinterland of the Rio das Velhas, this culminated in a revolt and attack on the local judge. The evidence indicated that the revolt was the outcome of a conspiracy by powerful landowners and leading *Paulista* families with business interests in that area, rather than a truly popular uprising. Cited as conspirators in the official enquiry were Dona Maria da Cruz and her son Pedro Cardozo, the nephew of Domingos do Prado. In 1737 she and her son were arrested by the Intendant of the royal treasury in Sabará, Dr Manuel Dias Tôrres, who had journeyed into the *sertão*, accompanied by 30 dragoons. Family connexions involved the leading families of Vila Rica and São Paulo, and one conspirator fled to the ranch in Jacobina of Dona Joanna Cavalcante, member of a prominent family, and who was sympathetic to the cause.[55]

This role of the white woman in the colonial economy contrasted markedly with that of the black woman, both slave and free. Subsistence crops, their marketing, and sale on the streets was largely controlled by such women. The repetitive nature of local legislation, forbidding sales of drinks and foodstuffs in mining areas, is testimony enough to the extent of such activities. Free and slave colored women, either on their own behalf or working for a master or mistress, successfully dominated the black market in foodstuffs, produce, fruits and fowls. As owners of shops, taverns and slaughter houses, they played a vital role in community life. Although few, if any, practiced artisan trades, such paramedical professions as midwives and foundling mothers were the virtual prerogative of black females. In this respect there was little occupational distinction between slaves and free coloreds.[56]

The White Woman and Brazilian Colonial Society

In the absence of literary sources, diaries, chronicles, or personal correspondence, it is difficult to assess the value systems of a society. Colonial Brazil is no exception to this rule and has been categorized as male-dominated

[54] APMSG, 28, f. 150; 60, ff. 59–60v.

[55] APMSG, 44, ff. 126–7v, 149, 151–6v; 57, ff. 52v–3; 61, f. 13.

[56] A. J. R. Russell-Wood, ' Colonial Brazil ', in *Neither Slave nor Free. The Freedmen of African Descent in the Slave Societies of the New World*, ed. by D. Cohen and J. P. Greene (The Johns Hopkins University Press, 1972), pp. 98–108.

and patrilineal. New evidence suggests that in this mobile and precarious society the woman was regarded as a stabilizing factor and as the guardian of values which had originated in Europe but had undergone modification in the tropics.

In their wills male testators gave prominence to female survivors, be they widows, daughters, or nieces. Many such testators were not legally married or, if so, had no offspring. Frequently they had lost contact with wives and children, to say nothing of more distant relatives. When the time came to make their wills, 'in fear of death', they were acutely conscious of two factors: the possibility of scurrilous claims being made against their wills; an abhorrence of the possibility (very real in a multi-racial society) that a son or heir might have bastard children by a slave woman and that these should inherit. In preambles and dispositions of their wills, many testators responded first to ideological precepts derived from Europe concerning 'purity of blood', and, secondly, to a realistic assessment of the prevalent social mores in the colony. Even where there was a legitimate son to inherit, a testator would insist that inheritance of his possessions should be restricted to female descendants only. This favoring of the distaff side of a family casts the role of the woman in colonial Brazilian society in a wholly new dimension, as will be seen from the following examples. Diogo Fernandes (died 1621), a tertiary of Saint Francis and brother of the Misericórdia of Salvador, insisted in his will that only descendants on the distaff side should inherit his wealth or possessions. Another Bahian of the early seventeenth century, the bachelor Francisco Dias Baião, also disqualified the sons of his descendants from benefiting from his will and stipulated that only the daughters of such descendants could inherit. Another Bahian bachelor, also of the seventeenth century, António Dias de Ottões, allocated his considerable wealth for a variety of charitable purposes and for the saying of masses. While making legacies of 200$000 *reis* to each of his three sisters, and allocating 200$000 *reis* for his nieces if they were legitimate and alive, he specifically ruled that no legacy should be made to his nephews. Felippe Correia, owner of a sugar plantation in Pituba, ruled in his will of 1650 that a trust be established so that dowries of 400$000 *reis* be available for the female offspring of his sisters. Beneficiaries were limited to female offspring of the distaff side only. Fear that a male descendant might dishonor the family was well expressed in the will of Jerónimo de Burgos and his wife, who instituted a charitable trust in 1664. Any sums left from such a trust were to go to their son, the Crown Judge, Cristóvão de Burgos, and his descendants on the male side and, failing such, the female side. However, this legacy was made on the express condition that they should ' not marry anybody tainted by the blood of the prohibited races '.

Such clauses suggest that the female was seen as the guardian, not only of the social prestige of the family but also as the preserver of ideals of purity of blood deeply rooted in white colonial society.[57]

Such considerations may in large part explain the enthusiasm shown by white colonists for the building of convents and retirement houses. That such convents housed sanctity, piety and devotion is indubitable. But the justification for such expenditures and the impetus leading to their construction were wholly secular. In a petition requesting royal approval for the foundation of the Convent of the Poor Clares, the 'councillors, nobility and people' of Salvador emphasized how fitting would be such consent as a reward for the many services rendered by the citizens to the Crown in the building of the capital of Brazil and the opening up of the hinterland.[58] The townfolk of São Paulo followed a similar tack in their request of 1736 that the Retirement House of Santa Thereza de Jesus be given conventual standing. In 1738, the governor and city council of Rio de Janeiro emphasized how important it was that the city should have a convent. Completion of the Convent of N. Sra da Ajuda had been delayed because the royal consent had contained a clause ruling that intending nuns would have to secure the approval of the Overseas Council in Lisbon. The local worthies had seen this as an insuperable barrier to gaining admittance for their daughters, and enthusiasm had waned. In 1736, two Cupuchin friars had asked the King to allow them to occupy the empty and uncompleted shell. This spurred the city council to ask Dom João V to reject this request and throw his royal support behind the early completion of the building and its occupancy by Capuchin nuns. On his visit to Minas Gerais in 1743, the Bishop of Rio de Janeiro collected alms for this purpose.[59]

Equal enthusiasm was shown in the founding of retirement houses. Although wholly secular, such foundations were motivated by Christian sentiments and an awareness of the need for social charity. Best known was the Retirement House of the Most Holy Name of Jesus, opened in Salvador in 1716 under the auspices of the Misericórdia, and made possible by an endowment of 80,000 *cruzados* by the local philanthropist, João de Mattos de Aguiar, in 1700. This was exceptional, and most retirement houses were more modest. After the death of her husband, Sebastiana Pereira da Conceição lived with her sister and two nieces in cloistral seclusion in a house in the parish of Sto. António Além do Carmo in Salvador. Encouraged by promises, she petitioned the King for permission to establish a retirement house with

[57] ASCMB, *Livro 1 do Tombo*, ff. 23v–8v, 28v–33v; *Livro 2 do Tombo*, ff. 24–9, 97v–8v; *Livro 3 de Acórdãos*, ff. 243v–5.

[58] Royal *provisão* dated 6 July 1665, ACDB, *Livro da Fundação*, f. 2.

[59] APMSG, 63, docs. 20, 21; 66, ff. 159–62v; 82, ff. 162–3.

30   *A. J. R. Russell-Wood*

15 girls. In 1757, the viceroy dampened such hopes in a report to the effect that the promised financial aid would never be forthcoming. He asked the King to refuse permission 'especially because this city already has a great abundance of convents and retirement houses '.[60] Finance was not the problem of the Italian Jesuit, Gabriel de Malagrida, who founded a retirement house for poor women, prostitutes, and girls whose honor was endangered, next to the Soledade church in Salvador. With entry fees ranging up to 3,000 *cruzados*, by 1739 the financial resources of the enterprise topped 90,000 *cruzados*. Granted conventual status, this institution was thereafter known as the Convent of the Ursulines. Wealthy colonists endowed such foundations. In 1787, the queen accepted a proposal by the miner, António de Abreu Guimarães, to set up a trust fund in the district of Sabará: this was destined for the building of three charitable institutions – a leprosarium, a seminary to bring up poor children, and a retirement house for needy girls.[61]

Both convents and retirement houses admitted paying residents for varying periods of time under the names of *educandas*, *recolhidas*, and *porcionistas*. Young girls of good parentage were placed in convents until they married or decided to take the vows. Retirement houses catered more for orphan girls of middle-class parentage whose honor might otherwise be jeopardized. Husbands also placed their wives in retirement houses while journeying to Portugal or on an expedition to the interior. Finally, many widows or divorced women adopted such institutions as more or less permanent homes. Abuse could lead to royal intervention. Laymen were forbidden to meddle in the administration of convents. Nevertheless, such intervention was almost inevitable, given the importance of convents to urban society. The 'rigging' of elections of abbesses by outsiders was not unknown and convents did not escape charges of harboring amorous intrigues.[62] Benefactors of retirement houses invariably ruled that the occupants should be ' white, honorable, poor, and Old Christians '. This also applied to convents. This makes all the more significant the request to Queen Maria by Anna Joaquina do Coração de Jesus, a mulatto (*parda*) native of Bahia, asking for royal approval to establish a Convent of the Immaculate Conception of the Mother of Christ for colored girls. The queen ordered an enquiry in 1797, but there are no records to indicate the outcome of this petition.[63]

Convents and retirement houses afford an instance of collective female behavior, both in domestic affairs and in business management. For their

[60] Viceroy to King, 20 Oct. 1757, APBOR, 58, ff. 563–5. On the Misericórdia see Russell-Wood, *Fidalgos*, pp. 320–36.
[61] APBOR, 48, ff. 184–5; 54, ff. 14, 46–7; 78, ff. 36–43.
[62] APBOR, 20, docs. 91, 91a, 135; 34, docs. 97, 119.
[63] APBOR, 83, f. 272v, correspondence Queen to governor, 8 Nov. 1797.

Women and Society in Colonial Brazil 31

patrimony such institutions depended largely on legacies or fees paid by the incoming incumbents. This capital enabled them to engage in business operations. No banks existed in the colony. It was to such convents that businessmen would come, cap-in-hand, to request loans to finance their commercial ventures. One such was José Ricardo Gomes, a Bahian businessman, who secured a loan of 7,000 *cruzados* from the Convent of the Poor Clares in 1793. By making such capital available, the convents played a vital role in the economy of the colony. Some convents traded in tobacco, sugar, and other commodities.[64] Frequently these were the produce of plantations acquired as legacies or as the result of foreclosure for debts due to the conventual community. Retirement houses did not usually have so secure a financial base, but the Retirement House of Our Lady of the Conception of Macaúbas near Sabará had cultivated so diligently a land grant on the banks of the Rio das Velhas, granted by governor Dom Bras Balthazar da Silveira, that by 1725 the 20 recluses asked for a further six leagues of land so that they could expand their cattle ranching interests.[65]

The lay brotherhoods afforded another example of collective female action. Although women were not permitted to join such brotherhoods, governing bodies looked more favorably on applications by males when they were married. Barred from holding office, wives performed charitable works and helped in the decoration of the brotherhood's church on the occasion of major festivals. Some brotherhoods followed the example of Nossa Senhora da Boa Morte in Salvador and reserved the title of 'judge' (*juiza*) for female benefactors or ladies of noble birth.[66] In all cases brotherhoods assisted, to the best of their financial ability, the widow and offspring of a brother. A wife or widow was also entitled to the privilege of a funeral accompanied by the members of the brotherhood and the saying of masses for her soul in the brotherhood's church.

It may well have been that it was in such convents that the white women of the colony received an education and cultural upbringing otherwise denied to them. Opportunities in the colony to gain an education were minimal even for the male, let alone the female. The female offspring of the wealthier families received private tuition in music and learnt to read and write. But even at the highest levels of white society illiteracy among white women was not unusual. Henry Koster, who visited Brazil in the early nineteenth century attributed this situation to the

---

[64] ACDB, caixa 1, pasta 37. See also Susan Soeiro, 'The Social and Economic Role of the Convent: Women and Nuns in Colonial Bahia, 1677–1800', *Hispanic American Historical Review*, 54, No. 2 (May, 1974), pp. 209–32.   [65] APMSG, 28, ff. 142–3; 59, ff. 22v–3.
[66] Fr. Agostinho de Santa Maria, *Santuario Mariano* ... (Lisbon, 1922), vol. 9, livro 1, título 13, pp. 38–9.

ignorant state in which they are brought up; they scarcely receive any education, and have not the advantages of obtaining instruction from communication with persons who are unconnected with their own way of life, of imbibing new ideas from general conversation. . . . Bring these women forwards, educate them, treat them as rational, as equal beings; and they will be in no aspect inferior to their countrymen; the fault is not with the sex, but in the state of the human being.

In this respect Portuguese women contrasted greatly with Dutch women who were less secluded, drank in public, and whose intelligence was such as for it to be common practice for a Dutch husband to talk business with his wife. However, Dutch soldiers posted to the northeast of Brazil in the seventeenth century preferred the Portuguese as wives rather than their own nationals and co-religionaries. Allegedly, the Portuguese women were not so prone to drink and to neglect their husbands, and they made better wives.[67]

The stifling of intellectual curiosity and lack of interest in cultural matters was matched by a similar indifference to personal appearance on the part of the white woman. From Johan Maurits onwards, European visitors commented unfavorably on the sedentary life of the white woman in Brazil. On those rare occasions when she did leave her home, she was carried by slaves in an enclosed *palanquim*. Nor did the average white woman show any flair for fashion or in dressing herself. Social and financial standing could lead to reservations concerning this generalization, as, too, could the standpoint of an individual. But no researcher can fail to be impressed by the small amount of personal clothing recorded in inventories of deceased females of good birth and of financial means. Apart from every-day wear of an embroidered chemise or smock, items listed in inventories might include a taffeta cloak, a burlap skirt, a loose or a sleeveless jacket, and cheap silk and satin petticoats. Any judgement must take into account two factors. The first was climate. Tropical heat, humidity, and the fact that the white woman was usually secluded in her home were inducements enough to wear the minimum of formal clothing. Furthermore, limitations were imposed by sumptuary laws (1749) intended to reduce expenditure on luxury items and to protect the Portuguese textile industry.[68]

Conclusions

The role of the white woman in colonial Brazil and her contribution to the life of the colony were circumscribed, and to some extent preordained, by tradition, law, and religious beliefs. But, at no time was she divorced from the mainflow of colonial existence and reduced to mere marginality. Every

[67] Koster, *Travels*, p. 388; C. R. Boxer, *The Dutch in Brazil, 1624–1654* (Oxford, 1957), pp. 125–7, 130.
[68] APBOR, 50, ff. 28v–34.

aspect of colonial life was pervaded by a consciousness of her presence. Secluded she may have been in physical terms, and unable to realize her potential in the intellectual or political life of the colony, but she contributed to the building of Portuguese America despite such limitations.

The King, ecclesiastical authorities, viceroys, governors, town councillors and colonists were perpetually concerned for the wellbeing of the white female. To each she held a particular importance. The Crown saw her presence as a stabilizing factor, the preserver of Lusitanian traditions and language, and a catalyst to curb the wanderings of restless and opportunistic males. Moreover, the white woman was seen as the instrument for populating the vast expanses of Portuguese America, offsetting to some extent countless numbers of slaves and free blacks. For the colonist, the white woman was wife and mother of his children, guaranteeing him a certain respectability within colonial society by the mere fact of being married. Moreover, marriage made him eligible for certain official positions denied to bachelors. To every Portuguese, be he King or colonist, the white woman was an object to be cherished and protected.

The idealism surrounding the white woman did not render her impotent and incapable of action on her own accord. As head of household she took up the reins of authority, raising and educating children, and finally ensuring that they had a trade, vocation, or respectable position when the time came for them to leave the homestead. Women managed estates and properties, involving themselves in the day-to-day workings of gold mines, cattle ranches, and sugar plantations. Thus did the white woman make significant contributions to the society and economy of the colony.

The position of the white woman in Portuguese America differed from that of her counterparts in Spanish and English America. This was partly the result of different patterns of migration. Although there was a numerical predominance of males migrating from Spain to the New World, even during the first decade of the sixteenth century, some 10 per cent of all licenses granted were to women and wives accompanying their husbands.[69] Although extensive miscegenation did occur, Spanish America possessed a larger proportion of white women than did Portuguese America for much of the colonial period. In the case of the English colonies in North America, and once allowances have been made for differing migration patterns between New England and Virginia or the Carolinas, the customary form of colonization was the family unit. It would appear that in Spanish and English America the larger number of white women guaranteed a cultural continuity

[69] Magnus Mörner, *Race Mixture in the History of Latin America* (Boston, 1967), pp. 15–16; James Lockhart, *Spanish Peru, 1532–1560. A Colonial Society* (Madison, 1968), p. 163 *et seq*.

34 *A. J. R. Russell-Wood*

absent in Portuguese America. Spanish and English were more widely spoken in the home and the custom of handing over a child to a black nanny for rearing was less prevalent than in Brazil. It is also possible that, because of a less absolute degree of dependence on slave labor, the Spanish or English-born wife was more likely to champion the continuation of European customs, albeit in a New World environment. Finally, it would appear that there was a lesser tendency by English and Spanish to 'go native', or to permit the fusion of their cultural and linguistic heritage with African and Amerindian lifestyles and languages. In short, as the pattern of colonization and the development of Portuguese America were to differ from other European colonies in the Americas, so, too, was the role and contribution of the white woman in Portuguese America to be unique and distinctive. The embodiment of much of the tradition and ideology of the Old World, she showed a remarkable capacity for adaptation to meet the challenge of the New World.

20
Sexual Witchcraft, Colonialism, and Women's Powers: Views from the Mexican Inquisition
Ruth Behar

In 1774 José de Ugalde, a white (*español*) muleteer from a town near Querétaro, appeared before the Mexican Inquisition to lodge an accusation against his mestiza wife, who he claimed had used witchcraft to make him "stupid" (*atontado*) throughout the seventeen years of their marriage.[1] He had recently threatened to kill her if she did not admit what she had done to put him in this state; his wife then told him about the yellow, green, and black herbs which her sister had given her, advising that she serve them to him in water, the corn drink of atole, or food, "so that he would never forget her, or watch over her, or get back too early from his trips." He had learned that she was having an affair, and she shocked him when she went to confess and took communion as though nothing had happened. This so angered him that he tied her to a mesquite tree in order to beat her, reproaching her for having confessed and taken communion sacrilegiously, but "she had gotten loose without his knowing how." When he bound her to the tree a second time, she "called for help to all the saints in the heaven's court and he was not even able to give her a single beating." When for a third time he took her out to the countryside with the intention of beating her, he had no sooner accused her than "they made up and returned home together."

For José de Ugalde, the fact that his wife was misbehaving and that he could not give her the beating she properly deserved was only explainable as the effect of witchcraft. That she, rather than he, was shamelessly having an extramarital affair and that he could do nothing about it showed the extent of her supernatural powers. In bringing his case to the Inquisition he did not worry about admitting his intentions to beat his wife, because it was considered perfectly legitimate for a husband to physically punish his wife when she infringed upon the norms of proper female behavior in marriage. What made him believe the Inquisition would take an interest in his case was his wife's use of food magic to stupefy him, and the larger threat to a patriarchal social structure that was implicit in this act: turning the world upside down by making husbands submissive to their wives.[2]

This brief but tantalizing narrative contains, in compact form, the major themes that animated women's magical power in colonial Mexico, a discourse that had roots in sixteenth-century Spain. This essay will focus on the different meanings given to this discourse by men and women, highlighting the particular characteristics of the Inquisition and of witchcraft in Spain and Mexico. I will concentrate on the specific genre of sexual witchcraft, epitomized in Spain by the literary image of the witch-procuress or Celestina; in Mexico it took on a further cultural elaboration, with uncanny power being ascribed to women of the marginal Indian and mixed castes. Three major themes from the example of José de Ugalde's bewitchment will orient this discussion of women's power. One theme is the image of the world in reverse; the aim of women in these cases, according both to the women themselves and to the men who accused them, was to reverse their subordination to men and gain some degree of control over their husbands or lovers. There was a local language in which this search for control was expressed: in Mexico, a man could be atontado or *asimplado* "stupefied" or "dummied," as happened to José de Ugalde; an especially abusive and violent husband might be subject to his wife's attempts to *amansar*, to "tame" or "domesticate," him; a man who dropped his mistress would perhaps find himself *ligado*, "tied" in such a way that he was rendered impotent; and finally, unnatural illnesses caused by *hechizo* or *maleficio*, sorcery or malefice could make a man waste away.

A second theme in these cases is the efficacy of women's witchcraft. As we see in José de Ugalde's reaction to his wife's use of herbs, the witchcraft powers of women were clearly not ones that women simply ascribed to themselves but were culturally viewed as inherent in their nature. These powers, however, usually needed to be awakened, and thus we find networks of women from all the castes and classes of colonial Mexico passing on stories about various "remedies" (*remedios*) that could be employed when a man was recalcitrant, violent, or unfaithful. José de Ugalde's wife, for example, claimed to have obtained the three magical herbs from her sister. Both in Mexico and in Spain, women who were professional healers and often midwives as well were also consulted for advice and cures.

Typically, women made men "eat" their witchcraft, using their power over the domain of food preparation for subversive ends, a practice that was common in pre-Hispanic times as well as in sixteenth and seventeenth-century Castile.[3] From the number of cases in which food was the medium for witchcraft, it appears that ingestion was thought to be one of the most effective ways of passing on the polluting substances of witchcraft; in eating, the pollution was introduced directly and effectively into the body. Women frequently used menstrual blood or the water that had cleansed their "intimate parts" to make up the ensorcelled food or drink that they served to their husbands. The logic behind this was clearly that of the "metaphorical extension," by which the ingestion of a woman's bodily essences worked, by means of analogy, to subdue, tame, or attract the man who consumed them.[4] The belief that food could be used to harm rather than to nurture gave women a very specific and real power that could serve as an important defense against abusive male dominance. And perhaps, too, women's serving of ensorcelled food to men was another kind of reversal, sexual rather than social: a way for women to penetrate men's bodies.

A last, and crucial, theme of all these Inquisition cases is the mediating role of the church in domestic and sexual matters. Whether the discourse of sexual magic and witchcraft took place among women passing on "remedies" or between bewitched and bewitcher, the church was there to listen in. The church solicited such discourses by requiring confession and by making public the Edicts of Faith in which superstition, witchcraft, and magic were denounced as sins.[5] The church had also insinuated itself into the domain of the family and sexuality, by controlling the rites of marriage and by defining sexual and domestic sins.[6] So, it was natural for men and women to bring their confessions and their denunciations about these matters to the church, and especially to the Inquisition, translating their domestic conflicts and sexual ambivalence into a religious discourse. Thus, José de Ugalde thought that the Inquisition would be interested in his marriage and the fact that it had, in his view, gotten mysteriously out of control.

Gender, Power, and Religion: From Spain to Mexico

What these three themes point to is an intersection of gender, power, and religion. I will consider this intersection from the various points of view of the actors involved in women's witchcraft: that of the religious élite, who in large part set the terms of the discourse; that of the men who felt themselves bewitched; and that of the women who attempted to gain power through witchcraft.

As Michelle Rosaldo and other feminist anthropologists have pointed out, in most societies women are denied culturally legitimate authority in the public sphere.[7] Thus, whatever power women do have is thought to be illegitimate, negative, and disruptive. Beliefs about women as pollutors are one widespread example of the negative powers attributed to women, as in parts of New Guinea, where men will carry out their wives' wishes for fear that if a woman is angered she may pollute her husband by serving him food while she is menstruating.[8] This analogy is significant given the frequent use of menstrual blood by colonial Mexican women in preparing ensorcelled food for their husbands, a practice that has persisted in various parts to this day.[9] Beliefs about the witchcraft powers of women likewise attribute to women a negative, polluting influence. In viewing women's power as illegitimate, we have to ask a key question: in whose eyes is this power illegitimate? Clearly, in a male-dominated society, it is from the male point of view that women's power becomes defined as negative, as an inversion of the social/ sexual order. Even from the female point of view, this power appears illegitimate to the degree that women internalize the values of the male-dominated symbolic order.

In northern Europe the illegitimacy of women's power was dealt with, in the sixteenth and seventeenth centuries, by carrying out witch-hunts, in which women were the main targets of persecution and extermination.[10] Women's witchcraft was taken seriously by the religious élite of northern Europe, but in the process of the hunt their powers were magnified and transformed from a simple power to heal or to harm on a one-to-one basis into a demonic conspiracy that threatened both God and the state. As Christina Larner has pointed out in her study of witch-hunting in Scotland, an essential prerequisite for a witch-hunt was the existence of an élite with the zeal and the bureaucratic machinery to carry out the investigations, arrests, and punishments of those accused of witchcraft.[11] The presence of an élite convinced of the fact that witches did exist and did have dangerous powers is, in large part, what fueled witch-hunts, as opposed to witchcraft beliefs, in northern Europe.

Spain was different. Spain had true heretics to contend with: the *conversos* (converts) from Judaism and Islam, whose supposed insincere conversion threatened the purity of the faith. The Inquisition, after all, was instituted to deal with them.[12] Yet Spain was not completely devoid of small-scale witch panics; these involved only the local authorities and took place during the sixteenth and early seventeenth centuries in the northern regions of Galicia, Cataluña, and the Basque Country, with the most famous being the witch panic of Zagarramurdi in Navarra.[13] By the 1620s these panics were mostly over, however, because they were put down by the Suprema, the Supreme Council of the Inquisition in Madrid, which took a decidedly skeptical attitude towards witchcraft. Epitomizing this attitude was the work of the inquisitor Alonso de Salazar Frías, whose close, legalistic examination of the confessions concerning sabbats and intercourse with devils in the Zagarramurdi witch panic led him to conclude that "I have not found the slightest evidence from which to infer that a single act of witchcraft has really occurred . . . I deduce the importance of silence and reserve from the experience that there were neither witches nor bewitched until they were talked and written about."[14]

The general view of the Spanish religious élite was that witchcraft was a sign of ignorance rather than heresy and could be dealt with through such religious means as Christian instruction, confession, and absolution.[15] Witches flying through the air and meeting in sabbats were delusions and fantasies, beyond the legal province of cause and effect and the rules of evidence. It is significant that the word for the witches' sabbat used in Spain is *aquelarre*, a Basque word. The idea of the sabbat apparently never really took hold in Castile and southern Spain, either on the popular or élite level. Instead, the kind of witchcraft one finds in Castile and southern Spain involved love magic and sexual bewitchment. Julio Caro Baroja has suggested that the witchcraft which flourished in northern Spanish communities was of a distinctly rural order, concerned with community tensions—like, I would add, the witchcraft that existed in northern Europe. On the other hand, the love magic and sexual witchcraft common in Castile and southern Spain (as well as in much of Italy) was decidedly urban, and more concerned, in the tra-

Sexual Witchcraft, Colonialism, and Women's Powers 183

dition of the Celestina, with dyadic domestic and erotic relationships.[16] Unlike the northern European image of the witch as an old,
ugly, and poor woman, the women involved with witchcraft in Castile were usually young unmarried women, widows, wives abandoned by their husbands, or women living in casual unions with
men; they were maids and servants, sometimes prostitutes, and in
southern Spain often *moriscas*, women of mixed Spanish and Moor-
ish blood.[17]

To give a few examples of the discourse of sexual witchcraft employed by Spanish women, we can mention the sixteenth-century
case of Catalina Gómez, who claimed to have used witchcraft to im-
prove her relationship with her husband, who mistreated and beat
her.[18] Leonor de Barzana, a conversa of Jewish descent from Toledo,
claimed that many of her female neighbors had approached her for
remedies to increase their husbands' love for them. Similarly, Juana
Hernández, apparently a prostitute, claimed to have used techniques of divination "at the request of many women, who wanted to
know the goings-on of their lovers and husbands, whether they took
on other women." Significantly, she had learned about divination
from a morisca. Isabel de la Higuera, from Daimiel, explained to a
man that he had been rendered impotent by means of a magical ligature that had worked its way into his body through an orange, given
to him by a woman, that was filled with "certain dirty things."[19]
This Castilian tradition of sexual magic and witchcraft crossed the
Atlantic and took hold in Mexico, flourishing in urban centers like
Mexico City, as well as in the more open, racially mixed, and economically fluid mining, ranching, and hacienda areas farther orth.

The confessions and accusations of love magic and sexual witchcraft that people brought to the Inquisition, both in Spain and Mexico, were placed in the category of "superstition" and dealt with leniently, for the most part. The Spanish Inquisition and its colonial
Mexican tribunal shared a common inquisitorial style, seeking to
understand the motives of a person's beliefs or acts rather than being
concerned with establishing legal responsibility for the deeds of
witchcraft or magic, as were secular judges in northern Europe. Thus
the outcome of a case hinged less on the question of whether a person was guilty or not guilty than on subtler distinctions between
"repentant and unrepentant sinners, between accidental and deliberate sinners, between knaves and fools."[20] What mattered most to
the inquisitors was that penitents have a sense of guilt and shame,

and display a willingness to confess all and be reintegrated into the church. And if the confessions touched on sex, all the better, since the lusts of the body, both in thought and in deed, were especially singled out for close inspection and castigation.[21]

While men like José de Ugalde in central Mexico went to the Inquisition with sincere complaints about the magical powers women wielded, the inquisitors tended not to take these accusations seriously. Unlike the secular judges of northern Europe, who viewed women's power as illegitimate in the sense that it threatened the state and society through the conspiracy of the "coven," the inquisitors of Spain and Mexico viewed women's power as illegitimate in the sense that it was a delusion and therefore not really a form of power at all.[22] By thus devaluing the discourse of women's magical power, not taking it altogether seriously, the Hispanic religious élite trivialized and denied what on the local level was viewed as a source of power for women.

Sin, Guilt, and Confession: Women's Ambivalence

The attitude of the Inquisition had two contradictory effects on women in colonial Mexico. On the one hand, the leniency of the inquisitors made it possible for networks of women to pass the word on about magical alternatives to the church's mediation in domestic affairs; in some cases, women were even able to construct an alternative religious ideology, centering on devil pacts, that challenged the dominant religion. On the other hand, those women who internalized inquisitorial ideas about the delusion of believing in witchcraft found themselves devaluing their own efforts to gain magical power and becoming angry and disgusted with themselves for seeking to subvert the established order.

As an example from colonial Mexico of how women could internalize inquisitorial ideas, we have the case of Magdalena de la Mata, a woman over fifty years of age who appeared before the tribunal of San Juan del Rio in 1715.[23] She began her confession by recalling an incident of domestic violence: on one occasion, her husband, a mestizo like her and the owner of a drove of beasts of burden, had beaten her so badly that he had made her bleed. Seeing herself treated so wretchedly by her husband, upset and angry, Magdalena went to Beatris, an Indian woman, and asked her to give her an herb she could use on her husband so he would cease treating her so badly.

Beatris, admonishing her to keep the remedy a secret, explained to Magdalena how to go about producing a magical ligature or "tying" that would make her husband impotent. The remedy was to take an egg, pierce it with a straw, and in it place a few of her husband's hairs; then she was to bury the egg in the ground where her husband urinated. Following these steps, Beatris claimed, Magdalena's husband would be "tied."

Ligatures caused by witchcraft were the usual explanation for male impotence both in popular and learned European belief. Heinrich Kramer and James Sprenger, the German inquisitor-authors of the witch-hunting treatise known as "The Hammer of Witches," went so far as to suggest that witches collected the male organs of the men they made impotent, putting them in a "bird's nest, or shutting them up in a box, where they move themselves like living members, and eat oats and corn."[24] Or, at least, the devil made such illusions possible. From the Spanish Inquisition, a case is preserved from Puebla de Montalbán, stating that in 1758 the townspeople believed that Aunt Fruncida had a little pail in which she kept the members of men who had suffered magical ligatures; in Lillo, in 1780, rumor had it that La Gorrinera kept male members hung up on a clothesline.[25]

In Mexico, women both confessed to having attempted ligatures and were accused by men of having carried out ligatures—but this ultimate effort to strike at the central symbol and reality of male dominance by rendering the phallus powerless was for some women so radical that they often ended up censoring and repressing their own desires. Thus, Magdalena pierced the egg, filled it with her husband's hairs, and buried it, pouring some of his urine over the ground. But one day later, she confessed to the inquisitor and ran back to the site and unburied the egg, overcome with repentance for having carried out such a ludicrous act. Throwing the egg away, she exclaimed, " 'Away from me, devil!' And she had been crying ever since, begging God to have mercy on her, as she also begged of this Holy Tribunal."

Her local parish confessor, she said, had refused to absolve her until she confessed to the Inquisition. She admitted, she had been on the verge of keeping quiet about this sin altogether, but looking into her soul she had seen that she had to confess it. She cried as she spoke, and the inquisitor, "seeing her tears, and her repentance, and her demonstration of faith . . . told her to attend to the fact that she is

Christian, and that she should never be afraid to confess her sins to her confessor and that she should always confess what is most particular, and that which seemed the most shameful to her." So long as she confessed and truly repented, the inquisitor assured her, she would always be pardoned by the Holy Tribunal. With this, and a caution about not paying heed to superstitions and criticizing them whenever she came across them, she was absolved.

The notions propounded by the church about sin, guilt, and devotion, which women were taught to take especially seriously, often made it impossible for them to use the magical resources at their disposal for retaliating against husbands who exceeded the bounds of proper conjugal dominance.[26] What political and economic control lower-class women, especially married women, had was negligible, and they were frequently victims of a husband's aggression both in the countryside and in towns.[27]

Since women were left with few domains in which to assert themselves, they developed, in Mexico and elsewhere in Latin America, a rich symbolic language of beliefs and acts for resisting, punishing, and even controlling the men who dominated them. This was a language saturated with violence: just as men hit their wives, women retaliated with a more subtle form of violence. And because the Mexican Inquisition treated offenders in a lenient, paternal fashion, it participated in the dialogue about male/female conflict and sexual witchcraft. The details of that dialogue were of little interest to the inquisitors; what mattered most to them was that what was confessed be "that which seemed the most shameful" and that the confession be accompanied by the sinner's requisite "tears of contrition," so important to early modern Spanish religious devotion.[28]

The Inquisition did little to hinder the diffusion of sexual witchcraft among women of the various caste strata of colonial Mexico. Yet the position of women remained equivocal. Women, unable to reconcile the contradictions between the proper behavior expected of them as Catholics and the witchcraft they knew for taming and tying men, ended up by expressing disgust and self-hatred. They threw away the remedies they had used, became angry with themselves for the violent emotions they had given vent to, and ran tearfully to confess to the parish priest and the inquisitors, seeking absolution. It was as if an internalized Inquisition, an alternate discourse, sounded inside their heads, muting the discourse of women's magical power.

13. Representation of the devil in an inquisitorial investigation for heretical activities. Source: Archivo General de la Nación, Mexico City, Inquisición, vol. 1281, fol. 61 (1790).

188   *Ruth Behar*

14. Collage of dolls imitating religious images, found in a suit against a woman (Rosalia López) for witchcraft. Writing suggests favors received after intercession. Source: Archivo General de la Nación, Mexico City, Inquisición, vol. 1533, exp. 1 (1767).

Entertaining thoughts of cutting off their husband's sexual powers (a quite literal emasculation in the cases of "tying") was for many women a sinful fantasy, associated with the devil. When Magdalena de la Mata threw away the egg she had tried to use to tie her husband, she exclaimed, "Away from me, devil!" Other cases like this abound. Marcelina Gertrudis, the 25-year-old wife of a free mulatto, confessed that, five years before, she had been upset and in tears because her husband was having an affair with another woman. She lamented her condition to her neighbor, María, a mulatta, and María responded, "Don't worry, sister, once when my husband was lost like yours is now, and I was suffering like you are now. An uncle of mine named Juan de Bargas, seeing my suffering, for pity of me made up a remedy with which my husband came to despise the other woman." This remedy, something her uncle gave her to place in her husband's food, had worked extremely well, María said, and she had begged her uncle to tell her of what it had consisted. When her uncle at last began to tell her that part of the remedy included placing peyote in water, she appeared so shocked that he refused to divulge any more information to her. Marcelina, hearing just this incomplete account of the "remedy," was quick to respond to María with the following: "May God not let me think of such a thing. That can't be good, that seems like devil's stuff. Let my husband do what he wants, for there is a God who is our remedy."[29]

Similarly, 20-year-old María Guadalupe Dávalos, who lived on an hacienda in Querétaro, recounted in 1792 how, seeing her in tears because her husband had just given her a beating soon after she had brought his food to him in the fields, a woman neighbor said to her: "Don't be stupid, we have a remedy, and you will see how your husband will die. Put a bucket of water under your bed when your husband is sleeping, and place a lit candle in it, and when [the candle] has gone out, your husband, too, will be gone and dead." To this María Guadalupe replied, "I won't do it. Let God, who can, kill him."[30]

Some women, hearing of this discourse, responded with a suspicious skepticism. Francisca de los Angeles, a mulatta who was married to a mestizo shoemaker in Querétaro, appeared before the Inquisition in 1692 to make a confession about "a few things that had made her apprehensive because they seemed suspicious" that she had seen while living for two years in the house of Clara de Miranda, a mestiza and an aunt of her husband.[31] Francisca noted that

190   *Ruth Behar*

life with her husband was difficult, that hers was a *mala vida*. Seeing what Francisca suffered at close range, Clara de Miranda had told her that if she wanted "to change her husband's behavior and turn him into a simpleton, she should take a few of the fat worms that drag themselves along the ground on their backs, that can be found under the earth, and once dried and turned into powder serve them to him in food and drink." On two occasions Clara de Miranda went to the trouble to bring these worms to Francisca, but she refused to take them.

Another time, Francisca's husband had just combed his hair when Clara de Miranda entered the room, saying, "Your husband is a fool. Why does he leave those fallen hairs lying around? They can do him harm." Francisca asked her how such a thing was possible. And Clara de Miranda told her, "If you take a frog and tie one of those hairs around its neck and take a thorn and run it from its head to its feet, your husband will waste away." Yet another time, she offered Francisca a different remedy to pacify her husband's behavior, telling her to place a swallow in a hole in the wall above their bed, saying the words, "Here I place you, Cristóbal" (*Aqui te meto, Cristóbal*). Clara de Miranda had told another woman that to make her husband care for her she should let a leech suck blood from her thigh and, after drying and grinding it, give it to him to drink; or she could prepare his chocolate with the water she had used to cleanse herself after having intercourse with him. Ana, an Indian woman who had been a friend of Clara's, also told Francisca that "to stupefy men and to tame them it was good to give them to drink the custom of women (*la costumbre de las mujeres*)." While Francisca had never seen Clara or Ana serve these things to men, just the mention of them in everyday conversation had made her sufficiently suspicious to go confess to a local priest who, in turn, sent her to the Inquisition for absolution.

For Marcelina, María Guadalupe, and Francisca, as for other colonial Mexican women, the discourse about the magical control of men, with its reversal of the social/sexual order and strange metaphoric practices and "cuisines," was simply diabolical, inspiring shock, fear, suspicion, and disgust. Such women seemed to think that if they had to choose between two evils—a mala vida with their husbands or doing devil's stuff—it was their obligation, as proper Christians, to choose the first.[32] Well Christianized by a church that taught the female sex to take its precepts especially seriously, these women seemed to think it was better to have the clear conscience that came from the holy martyrdom of knowing that they were on the side of God than to provoke the devil by flirting with "his stuff." In confessing to their local priests and later to the inquisitors, they betrayed themselves as well as their female friends, neighbors, and relatives, thereby giving in to the structure of male domination and turning in those women who posed a threat to that structure. Such women were their own best inquisitors.

While some women internalized the Inquisition's devaluation of female supernatural power, thereby devaluing their own and other women's efforts at resisting male hegemony, many women also openly rejected Catholic ideology and embraced the devil. Viewing themselves as beyond salvation, these women purposely chose to be connected with the Evil One. They made pacts with the devil, who, by their own accounts, acted as a kinder, more loyal, and more interested companion than their true-life husbands. Thus, María Rosa, an Afro-Indian (or *loba*) in a Zacatecan hacienda, claimed in 1747 that she had a 20-year pact with the devil, which she had entered into after her husband had run off with another woman.[33] The devil appeared to her "in the figure of a dog that hung around her skirts and cajoled her and talked to her; it would affectionately scratch her if she didn't pay attention to him." Or, Juana de los Santos, a young creole (of Spanish descent) woman from Nayarit, claimed in 1736 that she had made a pact with the devil seven years before to be able to follow the goings-on of her mulatto husband in his affairs and to take vengeance on his mistresses.[34] For her, the devil was a handsome young mulatto, a kind and loving alter-ego of her husband, who would visit her every day and ask how she was doing and who, indeed, helped her catch her husband with a mistress. Both these women made their pacts with the devil on the advice of other women, who initiated them into the counterreligious world of evil—in María Rosa's case, by being led into a room where a little dog, whose posterior she kissed, promised "to help her in any way he could," and in Juana de los Santos' case, by being given a picture of the devil by another white woman who had, like herself, had a bad marriage with a mulatto.

Interethnic Networks of Cures and Suspicions

One common feature of all of these cases involving women's use of sexual witchcraft and devil pacts is the existence of a network of women exchanging remedies and advice about marital and sexual relationships. This network was not only an interethnic one, but also an interclass one, and it included women of both the upper and lower social strata of colonial Mexico. Most typically, well-off white women, who were addressed as "doña" and lived comfortably with servants and coaches, had close contacts, even friendships, with Indian women, often cast in the role of magical specialists in the colony. The latter provided them with a cornucopia of indigenous powders and roots, as well as hummingbirds for use in love magic. In some cases, such élite white women would get Indian women to carry out sorcery for them.

Thus, in Guanajuato in 1725, doña Francisca de Parada, who lived in the house of an uncle who was a priest, asked Mathiana, an Indian woman, for help in "playing a joke" on a man who had betrayed her in a promise of marriage.[35] Mathiana was a healer who frequented the Parada household, both to provide cures and "to get something to eat of what they cooked." Out of the love she had for Francisca de Parada, Mathiana claimed that she had called upon the devil, with whose aid she would fly to the side of Francisca's ex-suitor; then she would carry him off to a deserted spot where she and another Indian woman would torture him and make him dance and kiss the devil-goat's posterior. This interesting relationship between Francisca de Parada and Mathiana, rooted in a mundane domestic reality in which an Indian woman exchanged her magical medical wares for her daily sustenance, points also to the exchange of mystical notions, so widespread in the colony, an exchange that forged a complex and hybrid religious culture. Indian women, as in this example, not only provided the paraphernalia for cures, but in the course of exchanging remedies with women of other caste and class groups acquired European ideas about the witches' sabbat and the powers of the devil. The exchanges moved in more than one direction, with creoles assimilating Indian remedies for carrying out love magic and sexual witchcraft.

Officially, the Mexican Inquisition was forbidden to prosecute Indians after its establishment in 1571, when it was decided that In-

Sexual Witchcraft, Colonialism, and Women's Powers 193

dians, as neophytes, were too new to the faith to be responsible for inquisitions of their consciences.[36] Only Spanish creoles, mestizos, African slaves, and their mixed offspring were to be subject to the strictures of the Inquisition. Yet, Indians who were Hispanicized, or at least integrated into the larger community, often figured in the background of many cases and occasionally even provided testimony. When such Indians did appear, strong magical powers were attributed to them, in the general way in which those at the margins elsewhere in Spanish America were thought to hold dangerous powers.[37] Likewise, magical powers were attributed to mulatto healers in Mexico, and in southern Spain magical powers were ascribed to morisco healers.[38] Thus, women from the marginal groups in colonial society—Indians, mulattas, mestizas—who were involved in cases of sexual witchcraft had, from the point of view of men, a kind of double power: that inherent to their sex and that inherent to their caste, as the following example will show.

In 1740, Francisco Bibanco, a resident of an hacienda near Mexico City, wrote the Inquisition a letter in which he accused María Antonia de Caiseros, a mestiza, of having caused him to go blind suddenly because he had failed to marry her as he had promised.[39] Remarking "how widespread sorcery and its teachers are," especially among Indians, "who fear one another for their cunning," he explained that he had broken off with María Antonia because he had heard of her "evil deeds." Although he had provided her with a dowry, she had still taunted him, saying, "You can still see, blind one? Soon you won't." Then one day she spread flowers on the path ahead of him and immediately afterwards he went blind. Doctors could not cure him and the priest's exorcism had no effect, a clear sign that he was bewitched. He pleaded with the inquisitors to take his case seriously, because otherwise "more such evil works will be committed against our holy Catholic faith, for they have many vengeances and would bewitch whomever they want to, making a display of it, with little fear of God."

As in the opening example involving José de Ugalde, we find a man sufficiently convinced of a woman's witchcraft powers to accuse her before the Inquisition. Like José de Ugalde, who wanted to beat this uncanny power out of his wife, Francisco Bibanco, too, considered this more direct means of undoing the spell María Antonia had placed on him. When a male friend suggested to him that he sim-

194   Ruth Behar

ply "give that evil woman a good round of lashes," he replied that he had not done so for fear that she would go to the priest and convince him that he had made her pregnant.

Francisco Bibanco's suspicion of María Antonia, a mestiza, had to do with his perception of her as "Indian"; she was, it seems, bicultural, speaking to him in Spanish and to her mother and neighbors in Nahuatl. Bibanco viewed her as linked to an Indian world of vengeance and witchcraft that threatened, in his own words, "our holy Catholic faith." Her power, for Francisco Bibanco, seemed to reside equally in her gender and in her cultural foreignness.

Accusations by creole Spanish men against women of Indian and mixed castes come up frequently in the Mexican Inquisition records, suggesting that the discourse of women's witchcraft power became enmeshed in the colonial ideology of caste hierarchy.[40] Similarly, in southern Spain, the apparent predominance of moriscos and gypsies in the commerce of magic points to a general pattern linking magic and power to peripheral groups. Paradoxically, the powerless and the conquered, whether Indians or Moors, were viewed as having dangerous occult powers. Thus, to the intersection of gender, power, and religion we must also add caste, so that inevitably we must go beyond an analysis of women to get at the sources of women's power.

The Inscription of Sexual Witchcraft into Colonial Power

The effectiveness of sexual witchcraft, in part, grew out of a distinction between natural and unnatural illness that had roots both in pre-Hispanic and contemporaneous Castilian beliefs. This distinction was widely accepted by the general populace, as well as by priests, inquisitors, and the medical doctors of the period. Those illnesses that neither exorcism nor medicine could cure were the illnesses of evil (*maleficio*) and of witchcraft (*hechicería*). In such cases, only the person who had worked the harm could undo it. We have considered a few examples involving men who perceived that they had been made to suffer such unnatural illnesses at the hands of a woman, whether wife, rejected wife-to-be, or mistress. I have suggested that the efficacy of women's magical powers resided in the "otherness" of their sex and their race. Now, in my last example, I would like to bring together the diverse strands of gender, power, religion, race, and illness, to place sexual witchcraft in the widest possible social context—that of colonial relations of power and subordination.

In 1733 Fray Diego Núñez, prior of the monastery of Our Lady of the Assumption in Amecameca, not far from Mexico City, wrote a long letter of accusation to the Inquisition detailing how Manuela de Bocanegra, his mulatta slave, had bewitched him.[41] Manuela, he claimed, had without a doubt ensorcelled him with the help of the devil, and he had medical proof of various sorts to prove it. With this assertion he proceeded to tell the inquisitors in minute detail about the illnesses his slave had placed on him through her witchcraft.

At first his arms hurt so much that he could barely move them and no medicine could cure him, until by chance he was healed by the incense of the Agnus Dei candle. This was followed by an inability to urinate for eleven days, from which he finally recovered after another slave, a brother of Manuela, gave him a print of Saint Salvador Horta. Then he slept for six hours and upon waking expelled about "twenty or more normal measures." The worst of the illness was yet to come: the horrid aches in "the most humid and painful parts of the body" that had besieged him for eight months and made him expel more than two hundred stones in a single fortnight. Both urination and defecation had become horrendously painful, and the things his body expelled were strangely unnatural. His was not a natural illness affecting the humors of the body, Fray Diego felt certain, because his pain was continuous and vehement, and was especially awful on Sundays. What is more, with proper scientific style he had carried out experiments on the bizarre things that his body expelled and had deduced that his slave, Manuela, was at the root of them.

The stones, he explained, were all different: some were spongy, others porous, and while most were smooth and solid, they varied in color, such that they looked as if they had come not from his own body but from an anthole. And he asked: Is it natural to engender "from one and the other end: eyebrows, eyelashes, and every type of hair from my own body?" Extracted from his urine and excrement "and extremely carefully cleaned and examined they appear to be blond, thin, wavy, and a few of them greying, each of them mine according to their size, style, and arrangement as compared with those that at present are still attached to my body." Nor can the body produce, he went on, pieces of wool, a paintbrush such as those used in the art of painting, and the hair of cats, dogs, deer, and pigs com-

196 *Ruth Behar*

monly used to make the brushes employed for painting. Also unnatural was the shifting appearance of his excrement: at times it looked like tiny emeralds; at other times like the exact shape and style of foods he had once consumed voraciously and now hated; at times like olives from Seville; and still at other times like goat excrement that when heated would smoke and burst, giving all those present a nasty headache. These careful examinations and experiments with the products of his own body confirmed the fact that according to "medical knowledge this was diabolic maleficio." The very things expelled by his body, as Fray Diego put it, were "signs" that when read properly pointed to the person responsible for his illness: namely, his mulatta slave.

The signs inevitably pointed back, as well, to his slave's sexuality. Fray Diego was certain that the reason Manuela de Bocanegra had ensorcelled him was that he had caught her once in the sexual act, "in flagranti delicto," with a young painter who lived in the room next to hers in the monastery. At the time he scolded both of them severely, and this scolding provoked in his slave the desire for vengeance. What better way to take revenge on him than by diabolically introducing into his body the tools of her lover's craft! Thus, she had made him consume her lover's paintbrushes and the hair of which brushes were made. Since it was only from her hands that he received food and drink and had his clothes tended to, she had the advantage of being in control of the whole of his domestic life. With great cunning she had used this intimacy to gather his own hair and other of his bodily substances in order to reintroduce them into his body and thereby make him "engender" them again in wretched pain. In a later addition to his testimony Fray Diego noted that Manuela de Bocanegra had once induced her brother, also his slave, to sprinkle love powders (*polvos de buen querer*) in his chocolate, so that he would "come to love said mulatto and mulatta."

This accusation may appear to be nothing more than the ravings of a gravely ill and solipsistic priest. But placed within the context of our earlier discussion of sexual witchcraft, it becomes both comprehensible and illuminating. Indeed, Fray Diego was not the first to see an implicit parallel between the attempts of women to attract, tame, and harm men through sexual witchcraft and the magical or, in his terms, diabolical efforts of slaves to control their masters. As early as 1614 a slave owner, Leonor de Hinojosa, reported to the Inquisition that her black slave, Agustina, had in her possession a root named

Sexual Witchcraft, Colonialism, and Women's Powers 197

puyomate, which was used both to attract and repel members of the opposite sex.[42] The slaveholder had made this discovery while beating her slave, who admitted that she had acquired the root, interestingly, from a Spanish healer, who told her to serve it to her master in cocoa in order to "tame" her (again, we see that the networks of magical exchange flowed in various directions). The word *amansar*, meaning to tame or domesticate, was used here as in the cases of sexual witchcraft, suggesting an explicit metaphorical connection between both the oppressive condition of being a woman and a slave and the desire to soften and "culture" the natural brutality of their husbands and masters, in what was a key reversal of the ethos linking "woman," "nature," and "slave" as wild and in need of conquest.

The relation between Fray Diego and his slave Manuela was a domestic relation, almost like that of husband and wife. She prepared his food and his clothes, and all would have been well except that her master caught her in the act of "adultery." Fray Diego's accusation against Manuela de Bocanegra is reminiscent of those accusations we encountered earlier involving men who felt they had been bewitched by women with whom they had had an intimate relationship. As in those cases, the unnatural illness Fray Diego suffered was clearly seen by him as resulting from witchcraft, and particularly from witchcraft transmitted through the medium of food. His excessively elaborated discourse about his illness, a thick Rabelaisian description of his ingestion and digestion, takes us back to our earlier discussion of how women made men "eat" their witchcraft. He highlighted not only the process of eating but also that of expelling the ensorcelled objects from the body, which became a kind of "evidence" in Fray Diego's case against his slave.

For Fray Diego, Manuela de Bocanegra's powers seemed to reside not just in her sex and in her caste but also in her position as a slave. Their relationship was made up of a series of dyads of domination: man and woman, priest and lay person, white and mulatta, and master and slave. It was as a woman, a mulatta, and especially as a slave, the most marginal and oppressed position in colonial society, that Manuela threatened Fray Diego. Hers was a supreme example of the power of the powerless, and she threatened him—as did the women who used sexual witchcraft menaced their victims—by inverting the social order and putting the dominated on top. Significantly, Fray Diego even claimed in his testimony that his slave had radically feminized his body, for in the course of his illness a wound had sud-

198   *Ruth Behar*

denly appeared along the length of his bottom, in the form of piles that had "transmuted the lower posterior to look like that of the female sex." His slave's witchcraft had declassed him, turning him into a kind of slave; it had re-gendered him as a woman.

Clearly for Fray Diego to have been able to fashion this accusation against his slave he had to have been familiar with the discourse of sexual witchcraft, as he most certainly was, for he explicitly said that Manuela de Bocanegra had even tried to put love powders in his cocoa. His participation in the popular beliefs of his time went further than the witchcraft accusation against his slave, however. Believing himself to be bewitched, he had taken the advice of a female neighbor, doña Josefa de Acosta, and sought out the services of a *curandera*, or healer (who was also a midwife), a mulatta by the name of Gertrudis.[43]

Gertrudis gave him an herb to drink in water and had him immerse himself in a *temascal*, or hot bath. This produced a wound in his backside that later healed with the application of a pink oil. Later she gave him two different mixtures to drink that increased his pains, and when he complained to her she told him that he would have to be patient about seeking a cure because what he had was hechizo, ensorcellment. Gertrudis then told him that Manuela was the one who had him that way, that she had in her possession a doll of him, and that she had known that he was the one who had ordered that she be beaten and sent to work in a sweatshop (*obraje*), where she had vowed to take revenge on him. Indeed, Fray Diego had sent Manuela away after becoming ill and deducing that she was at the root of his illness. The beating he ordered she be given was as routine a part of master/slave relations as it was of husband/wife relations; interestingly, Fray Diego recovered somewhat when his slave was away in the sweatshop—in her proper, subjugated position in the social structure, in other words—and he became seriously ill again when she was released. So desperate was he, in fact, that he begged Gertrudis to get the doll from Manuela, to whom he promised her liberty in exchange.

But his dealings with Gertrudis came suddenly to a halt when he discovered that she was not simply a healer and a midwife but also a sorceress and a dealer in sexual witchcraft. He made this discovery, interestingly enough, when a young Spanish woman, María Rodríguez, went to him for confession and disclosed that Gertrudis had offered her green, yellow, and white powders as well as a green porcelain "little head with little horns" so that she would have "lots of money and men would run after her." During the few days she carried around these powders and the little head, María Rodríguez said that men who had previously treated her "honestly" wanted suddenly "by force to engage in dishonest acts" and offered her lots of money; so she threw it all away and things went back to normal immediately. Hearing this, Fray Diego realized that Gertrudis was more than just a healer and that rather than curing him she was harming him further, possibly in agreement with his slave Manuela. He had found a hole in one of his shirts, as if someone had taken scissors and cut into the cloth, and ever since Gertrudis had given him the last mixture to drink he had been expelling rags and rotten hairs through his urine. Thus, Fray Diego ended up suspecting that this mulatta healer, together with his mulatta slave, were at the root of his strangely unnatural illness.

The records provide no clue as to what became of Fray Diego, or how the Inquisition reacted to his case. While Fray Diego's case is somewhat extraordinary because of the degree of his involvement in witchcraft, it does show that members of the religious élite shared in this popular discourse and could themselves participate actively in using it when illness and other misfortunes required explanation. Like the men who accused the women they had been in relationships with, Fray Diego ended up accusing his mulatta slave of having brought about his strange illness because he could find no other interpretation for his loss of control over his own body. In other words, like the French peasants who claim not to believe in witchcraft today until a series of misfortunes comes along to make them lose all sense of control, he was "caught."[44] Once "caught," only his slave's witchcraft could account for his utter powerlessness, in the same way that José de Ugalde could accuse his wife of having turned him into a fool. And again, only the church, through the Holy Office, seemed to offer the proper solace, cure, and interlocutor in these cases in which women of the marginal social classes dangerously overturned the social/sexual order.

Conclusions: The Paradox of Women's Witchcraft Powers

It is well known that women tend to exercise power in the private rather than the public domain, and in this essay we have seen how female power operated on the most private level of all, that of sexual

200   Ruth Behar

relationships. While we tend to think of power as having to do with the control of material resources or the activities and movements of large groups of people, women's power is usually of a different, more muted, less obviously recognizable sort. As this material on women's witchcraft powers shows, control within the symbolic domain is also a form of power. While placing herbs and powders in the food they served to their husbands, or burying eggs to carry out a ligature, may seem to be trivial means of exercising power, in fact the real stakes were political, given that women's ultimate aim was to control and change the behavior of the men who dominated them. Even beyond anything women actually attempted to carry out, the cultural assignment of mystic powers to women served as a check on the excesses of male dominance.[45] Yet what was given with one hand was taken away with the other: the church's interpretation of witchcraft as superstition at once trivialized women's power and turned it into a shameful, if minor, sin.

These cases involving sexual witchcraft, which formed part of a larger corpus of "superstitions" regarded as trivial by the late colonial Inquisition because they involved the marginal social classes, were part of the everyday stuff of Inquisition proceedings.[46] The inquisitors tended to dismiss them lightly, concentrating instead, until the midseventeenth century, on the more serious religious crimes of heresy and blasphemy and, in the late colonial period, on antiroyalist clerics and other intellectual dissenters of the colonial regime. Historians, too, have tended to dismiss these cases, the inquisitorial minutiae, as not being spectacular enough to warrant investigation.

In comparing aspects of women's supernatural powers first between northern Europe and Spain, then between northern Spain and Castile, and finally between Castile and central Mexico, I have sought to shed some light on the various ways in which witchcraft was treated by the religious élite and how this affected the exercise of female power. In particular, I tried to give a sense of how an urban Spanish understanding of female power, focusing on love magic and ligature, got transfered to the New World and there became linked to the caste system and to, apparently, very violent domestic relations between men and women of different racial backgrounds.

In conclusion I want to point out the paradox of women's supernatural power, a paradox that exists in any power exercised by women. While women's witchcraft powers were thought effective on

Sexual·Witchcraft, Colonialism, and Women's Powers   201

the local level, especially by men who feared they had lost the upper hand in sexual relationships, it is clear that women exercised these powers within a male-dominated system, and thus their resistance was at best limited and piecemeal, as women's own devaluation of their power showed. Even allowing for this paradox, the discourse of women's magical power made it possible for them to put into question and challenge, if unsuccessfully, the structures of inequality— the very structures that made it necessary for them to use symbolic weapons to combat real domination and oppression.

Acknowledgments

This paper is based on field and archival research carried out with the aid of a Fulbright Senior Research Award and a grant from the Organization of American States. It forms part of a larger project on witchcraft in colonial and contemporary Mexico, for which I have received generous support from the Program in Atlantic History, Culture and Society at Johns Hopkins University through a Rockefeller Residence Fellowship, the Harry Frank Guggenheim Foundation, and the Society of Fellows at the University of Michigan. To all these institutions I extend my sincere thanks. Earlier versions of this paper were presented to the Department of Anthropology at the University of Chicago, the Department of Anthropology at the University of Texas, Austin, and the Western Societies Program at Cornell University. Special thanks go to Asunción Lavrin for her comments and encouragement and to David Frye, my husband, for listening to this paper on several different occasions.

Notes

1. Archivo General de la Nación, Mexico City, Ramo Inquisición (hereafter cited as AGN, Inquisición), 894:53–54v.

2. Here I will be elaborating on ideas concerning the potential subversion of order in gender relations that appear in Natalie Z. Davis, "Women on Top," in her *Society and Culture in Early Modern France* (Stanford: Stanford University Press, 1975), pp. 124–51; Steven Ozment, *When Fathers Ruled: Family Life in Reformation Europe* (Cambridge: Harvard University Press, 1983), pp. 52–53, 71, 76–77.

202   *Ruth Behar*

3. On food magic, see Bernadino de Sahagún, *Historia general de las cosas de Nueva España*, 4 vols., ed. Angel M. Garibay K. (Mexico City: Editorial Porrúa, 1981), 2:150–51. A survey of indigenous "superstitions," incantations, and witchcraft practices in seventeenth-century New Spain is available in Hernando Ruiz de Alarcón, *Treatise on the Heathen Superstitions That Today Live among the Indians Native to this New Spain, 1629,* trans. and ed. J. Richard Andrews and Ross Hassig (Norman: University of Oklahoma Press, 1984); Noemí Quezada, *Amor y magia amorosa entre los aztecas* (Mexico City: Universidad Nacional Autónoma de México, 1975); Sebastián Cirac Estopañán, *Los procesos de hechicerías en la Inquisición de Castilla la Nueva (Tribunales de Toledo y Cuenca)* (Madrid: CSIC, 1942), pp. 81–83. For a study of a witchcraft process among the Chichimecs, see, Ruth Behar, "The Visions of a Guachichil Witch in 1599: A Window on the Subjugation of Mexico's Hunter-Gatherers," *Ethnohistory* 34:2 (Spring 1987), 115–38.

4. On metaphor theory, see James W. Fernández, *Persuasions and Performances: The Play of Tropes in Culture* (Bloomington: Indiana University Press, 1986), pp. 28–70.

5. On the ways in which the Edicts of Faith inspired confessions, see Patricia Aufderheide, "True Confessions: The Inquisition and Social Attitudes in Brazil at the Turn of the XVII Century," *Luso-Brazilian Review* 10 (1973): 208–40.

6. On the role of the church in setting rules for domestic and sexual behavior, see Lavrin's essay in this volume.

7. Michelle Zimbalist Rosaldo, "Woman, Culture, and Society: A Theoretical Overview," in *Woman, Culture, and Society*, ed. Michelle Zimbalist Rosaldo and Louise Lamphere (Stanford: Stanford University Press, 1974), pp. 17–42; Sherry B. Ortner, "Is Female to Male as Nature Is to Culture?" in *Woman, Culture, and Society*, ed. Rosaldo and Lamphere, pp. 67–87; Sherry B. Ortner and Harriet Whitehead, "Introduction: Accounting for Sexual Meanings," in *Sexual Meanings: The Cultural Construction of Gender and Sexuality*, ed. Sherry B. Ortner and Harriet Whitehead (Cambridge: Cambridge University Press, 1981), pp. 1–27; Jill Dubisch, "Introduction," in *Gender and Power in Rural Greece*, ed. Jill Dubisch (Princeton: Princeton University Press, 1986), pp. 3–41.

8. On pollution beliefs and the dangerous powers of women's sexuality, see Mary Douglas, *Purity and Danger: An Analysis of the Concepts of Pollution and Taboo* (London: Routledge and Kegan Paul, 1966). On pollution beliefs in New Guinea, see Shirley Lindenbaum, "A Wife is the Hand of Man," in *Man and Woman in the New Guinea Highlands*, ed. Paula Brown and

Sexual Witchcraft, Colonialism, and Women's Powers 203

Georgeda Buchbinder (Washington, D.C.: American Anthropological Association, 1976), pp. 54–62; Raymond C. Kelly, "Witchcraft and Sexual Relations," in *Man and Woman*, ed. Brown and Buchbinder, pp. 36–53; Elizabeth Faithorn, "The Concept of Pollution among the Kafe of the Papua New Guinea Highlands," in *Toward an Anthropology of Women*, ed. Rayna R. Reiter (New York: Monthly Review Press, 1975), pp. 127–40.

9. On contemporary cases of food magic involving the use of menstrual blood and pubic hair (likewise part of a woman's bodily essences), see Lois Paul, "The Mastery of Work and the Mystery of Sex in a Guatemalan Village," in *Woman, Culture, and Society*, ed. Rosaldo and Lamphere, pp. 281–99. On page 198, she notes that "women know that menstrual blood is one of their own ultimate weapons against intractable husbands," citing the following informant remark: "Many men have eaten their beans with the blood of their wives and didn't know it." See also Anna Rubbo, "The Spread of Capitalism in Rural Colombia: Effects on Poor Women," in *Toward an Anthropology of Women*, ed. Rayna R. Reiter, pp. 333–57.

10. On the European witch-hunt, see E. William Monter, *Witchcraft in France and Switzerland: The Borderlands during the Reformation* (Ithaca: Cornell University Press, 1976); H. C. Erik Midelfort, *Witch-Hunting in Southwestern Germany, 1562–1684: The Social and Intellectual Foundations* (Stanford: Stanford University Press, 1972); Keith Thomas, *Religion and the Decline of Magic* (New York: Charles Scribner's Sons, 1971); Joseph Klaitz, *Servants of Satan: The Age of the Witch-Hunts* (Bloomington: Indiana University Press, 1985).

11. Christina Larner, *Enemies of God: The Witch-Hunt in Scotland* (Baltimore: Johns Hopkins University Press, 1981).

12. See Henry Kamen, *Inquisition and Society in Spain in the Sixteenth and Seventeenth Centuries* (Bloomington: Indiana University Press, 1985).

13. On the Zagarramurdi witch panic, see Gustav Hennigsen, *The Witches' Advocate: Basque Witchcraft and the Spanish Inquisition (1609–1614)* (Reno: University of Nevada Press, 1980). For a good discussion of the small-scale witch panics in northern Spain, see Carmelo Lisón Tolosana, *Brujería, estructura social y simbolismo en Galicia* (Madrid: Akal Editor, 1979), pp. 9–51.

14. Kamen, *Inquisition*, pp. 212–13.

15. Henry Kamen, "Notas sobre brujería y sexualidad y la Inquisición," in *Inquisición española Mentalidad: inquisitorial*, ed. Angel Alcalá (Barcelona: Editorial Ariel, 1984), pp. 226–36; E. William Monter, *Ritual, Myth and Magic in Early Modern Europe* (Athens: Ohio University Press, 1983), p. 102.

204   *Ruth Behar*

16. On the contrast between northern Spanish witchcraft and southern Spanish urban witchcraft, see Julio Caro Baroja, *Las brujas y su mundo* (Madrid: Alianza Editorial, 1966). For urban love magic in Italy, see Mary O'Neil, "Magical Healing, Love Magic and the Inquisition in Late Sixteenth-Century Modena," in *Inquisition and Society in Early Modern Europe*, ed. Stephen Haliczer (London: Croom Helm, 1987), pp. 88–114.

17. On the type of women involved in Spanish cases of love magic, see Cirac Estopañán, *Los procesos*, p. 215.

18. Information on Leonor de Barzana, Juana Hernández, and Catalina Gómez are found in Cirac Estopañán, *Los procesos*, pp. 210–11.

19. Cirac Estopañán, *Los procesos*, p. 81.

20. Monter, *Ritual, Myth and Magic*, p. 72.

21. On confession and sexuality, see Gruzinski's essay in this volume; Michel Foucault, *The History of Sexuality*, vol. 1: *Introduction* (New York: Vintage Books, 1980).

22. On the devaluation of women's powers by the Spanish Inquisition, see Claire Guilhem, "La Inquisición y la devaluación del verbo femenino," in *Inquisición española: Poder político y control social*, ed. Bartolomé Bennassar (Barcelona: Editorial Crítica, 1981), pp. 171–207. On the Mexican Inquisition, see Richard D.Greenleaf, *The Mexican Inquisition of the Sixteenth Century* (Albuquerque: University of New Mexico Press, 1969), and "The Inquisition in Eighteenth-Century New Mexico," *New Mexico Historical Review* 60, no.1 (Spring 1985): 29–60; Gonzalo Aguirre Beltrán, *Medicina y magia: El proceso de aculturación en la estructura colonial* (Mexico City: Instituto Nacional Indigenista, 1980); Solange Behocaray Alberro, *La actividad del Santo Oficio de la Inquisición en Nueva España, 1571–1700* (Mexico City: Instituto Nacional de Antropología e Historia, 1981).

23. The account of Magdalena de la Mata is taken from AGN Inquisición, 878:314–16.

24. Heinrich Kramer and James Sprenger, *The Malleus Maleficarum of Heinrich Kramer and James Sprenger*, trans. Montague Summers (New York: Dover, 1971 [1486]), p. 121.

25. Cirac Estopañán, *Los procesos*, p. 81.

26. Asunción Lavrin, "Women and Religion in Spanish America," in *Women and Religion in America*, vol.2: *The Colonial and Revolutionary Periods*, ed. Rosemary Radford Ruether and Rosemary Skinner Keller (San Francisco: Harper & Row, 1983), p. 45.

27. William B. Taylor, *Drinking, Homicide and Rebellion in Colonial Mexican Villages* (Stanford: Stanford University Press, 1979), p. 95; Silvia M.

Arrom, *The Women of Mexico City, 1790–1857* (Stanford: Stanford University Press, 1985), p. 232.

28. William A. Christian, Jr., "Provoked Religious Weeping in Early Modern Spain, in *Religious Organization and Religious Experience*, ed. J. Davis (London: Academic Press, 1982), p. 107.

29. AGN, Inquisición, 878:389. In this case the role of the mulatto uncle, who was clearly a healer, is significant. Like Indian men and women, mulatto men and women frequently appear in the late-colonial Inquisition cases as providers of cures and remedies for healing, magic, and sexual witchcraft.

30. AGN, Inquisición, 998, exp. 5.

31. The account of Francisca de los Angeles is taken from AGN, Inquisición, 685, exp. 10.

32. For the concept of marriage and mala vida sce Boyer's essay in this volume.

33. AGN, Inquisición, 911:334–76.

34. AGN, Inquisición, 812, exp. 19. Both this and the previous case involving women's devil pacts are treated in more detail in Ruth Behar, "Sex and Sin, Witchcraft and the Devil in Late Colonial Mexico," *American Ethnologist* 14 (1987): 35–55.

35. AGN, Inquisición, 1029, exp. 9.

36. Richard D. Greenleaf, "The Inquisition and the Indians of New Spain: A Study in Jurisdictional Confusion," *The Americas* 22 (October 1965): 138–66.

37. On the shamanic power of those at the margins, see Michael Taussig, "Folk Healing and the Structure of Conquest in Southwest Colombia," *Journal of Latin American Lore* 6 (1980): 217–78; Frank Salomon, "Shamanism and Politics in Late Colonial Ecuador," *American Ethnologist* 10 (1983), pp. 413–28.

38. Richard L. Kagan, "Eleno-Elena: Annals of Androgyny in Sixteenth-Century Spain," manuscript, p. 23, notes that many popular healers were moriscos.

39. The account of Francisco Bibanco is taken from AGN, Inquisición, 929, exp. 10.

40. Examples of such denunciations abound in the records of the Mexican Inquisition. See, for instance, the case of José de Ugalde, above, and the denunciation by Lorenzo Martínez, a white farrier, against his former mistress, a mestiza, in 1709 (AGN, Inq., vol. 765, exp. 9). See also, AGN, Inquisición, 953, exp. 25 (1748). Here, a white baker from Querétaro accused his mulatta mistress of having served him ensorcelled milk that had left a ball of lead in his

stomach, the doctors who treated him could offer no cure, and one of them told him that "it didn't appear to be a natural illness but rather something they had been placed on him." Even before the mulatta ensorcelled him, however, one particular incident had made him suspicious. She had once entered the room when he had been sleeping. Having lifted her on top of him, he told her to be quiet; she had said to him, "You be quiet, because with that pig jaw of yours I could strangle you." These words, he said, had made him suspect what he later found out: that she was, indeed, a witch, because only a witch would have dared utter words as harsh as those to a man. A proper Christian woman—a proper Christian white woman?—it appears, would not have been so disobedient, so bold, or so utterly disrespectful of the order of social/sexual relations.

41. The account of Fr. Diego Muñoz is taken from AGN, Inquisición, 765, exp. 15.

42. This case is cited in Solange Alberro, "Inquisición y proceso de cambio social: Delitos de hechicería en Celaya, 1614," *Revista de dialectología y tradiciones populares* 30 (1974): 346–47. For the use of puyumate in colonial Mexico, see Aguirre Beltrán, *Medicina y Magia*, p. 17; Noemi Quezada, *Amor y magia amorosa entre los aztecas*, p. 96.

43. AGN, Inquisición, 765, exp. 19.

44. On the notion of how people get "caught" in witchcraft beliefs, see Jeanne Favret-Saada, *Deadly Words: Witchcraft in the Bocage* (Cambridge: Cambridge University Press, 1980).

45. For an elaboration of this idea in a contemporary account of sexual witchcraft, see Lois Paul, "Mastery of Work," pp. 281–99.

46. On the development of class ideas among the late colonial inquisitors, see Behar, "Sex and Sin," pp. 48–51.

21

The *Signares* of Saint-Louis and Gorée: Women Entrepreneurs in Eighteenth-Century Senegal

George E. Brooks, Jr.

FROM THE FIFTEENTH century on, Europeans traded along the coast of West Africa—the westernmost perimeter of a vast African commercial complex of whose extent even the most astute Europeans were only vaguely aware.* The earliest mariners along the coast were the Portuguese, who initially carried on a shipboard commerce. Soon, however, adventurers from Portugal and the Cape Verde Islands began to settle among coastal and riverine societies in order to benefit from increased proximity to the sources of this African commerce. Termed *lançados* because they "threw themselves" among Africans, these men established relationships with the most influential women who would accept them in order to obtain commercial privileges. In pursuit of their objectives, *lançados* adopted many of the customs and practices of the African societies; indeed, many shed so much of their Portuguese culture as to be characterized as *tangomaos*, "renegades." Descendants of their alliances with African women were called *filhos da terra*, "children of the soil," and, with their dual cultural background (and sometimes their mothers' social rank and prerogatives as well), were in an advantageous position to serve as brokers manipulating African and European trading networks.†

* I am indebted to the volume editors and to Jan Phillips Bianchi, Charles S. Bird, William B. Cohen, John Hargreaves, M. Jeanne Peterson, and Margaret Strobel for contributions and suggestions. Viviane Cochran and Ethel Richardson typed the penultimate draft.

† For background see Rodney 1970, chap. 3; António Carreira, *Cabo Verde; Formação e Extinção de uma Sociedade Escravocrata, 1460–1878* (Lisbon, 1972),

GEORGE E. BROOKS, JR.

That African women in the Senegambia and Upper Guinea
Coast regions did enjoy social rank and prerogatives seems clear.
Malinke oral traditions relating to pre-European times make vague
mention of Bainounka "queens" living along the upper Gambia
River. There is more reliable evidence that women with outstanding qualities of leadership and with wealth acquired through trade
ruled West African villages in traditional times (Galloway 1974,
chap. 2). But further research is needed to fill the large gaps in our
knowledge of the status and socioeconomic roles of women in
West Africa before the arrival of the Europeans. What is certain
is that African and Eurafrican women who were wealthy traders
or possessed property and influence were treated with marked
respect by Africans, Eurafricans, and Europeans alike. In the eighteenth and nineteenth centuries, such women were customarily
addressed by the titles *nhara* (in Portuguese Guinea), *senora* (in
the Gambia), or *signare* (in Senegal)—titles derived from the Portuguese *senhora*.* They often possessed numerous domestic slaves,
trading craft, and houses, as well as quantities of gold and silver
jewelry and splendid clothing. Indisputably they knew how to
acquire wealth, how to employ it profitably, and how to enjoy it
as well.

To date very little has been published on the *nharas* of Guinea-
Bissau, and only slightly more on *senoras* in The Gambia. Though

chap. 2; and Jean Boulègue, *Les Luso-Africains de Sénégambie, XVI–XIX siècle*
(Dakar, 1972), pp. 11–21.

* Women wielded considerable social and economic influence already in the
seventeenth century in the Senegambia region and along the Upper Guinea
Coast. Rufisque, on the Senegal coast, was one of the earliest Portuguese trading
centers and had several women residents of note: a Senhora Philippa, described
as a "dame Portugaise" by Boulègue (*Les Luso-Africains*, pp. 54–55), controlled
European access to trade there in 1634; an unnamed "Portugaise" held the
same power in 1669; and a Senhora Catti, the African widow of a Portuguese
trader, served as commercial agent for the Damel (ruler) of the Wolof state of
Cayor in 1685 (p. 71). A Eurafrican woman known as Marie Mar was renowned
during this period for her aid to shipwrecked seamen (*Les Luso-Africains*,
pp. 61–62, 72). But most famous of all was the formidable Bibiana Vaz, a Eurafrican who built up an extensive trading empire between the Gambia and
Sierra Leone rivers in the 1670's and 1680's and who held captive the captain-
major of Cacheu for fourteen months in 1684–85 and instigated a short-lived
Eurafrican "republic" (Rodney 1970: 209–10).

The Signares of Saint-Louis and Gorée 21

both primary and secondary sources exist on the *signares* of Senegal, much of the literature is highly romanticized, biased, or distorted, based as it is on data collected by, or information available from, European men. In the course of this paper I attempt to point out many of the problems associated with these sources and to present a balanced assessment of the women traders of Senegal.

Senegal: Saint-Louis and Gorée

Although there were many influential trading women in the Senegambia and Upper Guinea Coast regions in the eighteenth and early nineteenth centuries, the largest number was concentrated in Senegal, and it was there that the greatest development and elaboration of what may be termed "signareship" occurred. This is not surprising, since during that period many more Europeans lived at Saint-Louis and Gorée than anywhere else in West Africa. Indeed, the number of Europeans at those two settlements at times probably exceeded the number at all the other forts, settlements, and factories in West Africa combined.

The island of N'Dar in the Senegal River—on which the French founded the settlement of Saint-Louis in 1659—is only a mile and a half long and an eighth of a mile wide. Gorée is an even smaller island—a half-mile long and a few hundred yards wide—cradled by the Cape Verde peninsula. A settlement there was established originally by the Portuguese, who were later ousted by the Dutch, who in turn were displaced by the French in 1677. The population of both islands increased steadily during the eighteenth century: Saint-Louis had an estimated population of some 3,000 by 1764, and more than 6,000 by 1785; Gorée had some 1,000 inhabitants in 1767, and some 1,800 by 1785.* European residents included the employees of successive French trading companies and the officers and troops of the garrisons. Some who sought their fortunes in

* See Dodwell 1916: 274; and Cariou n.d.: 35. I am grateful to Dr. Cariou for making his manuscript available to me in 1966; my interest in *signares* owes much to his scholarship. See also Silvain Meinrad Xavier Golberry, *Fragmens d'un voyage en Afrique, fait pendant les années 1785, 1786, 1787* (Paris, 1802), vol. 1, pp. 154–55; vol. 2, pp. 60–61.

Senegal were men with outstanding qualities, but many were of mediocre ability and character. Oftentimes the soldiers represented the dregs of European society—men with criminal records, debauched, and diseased—and were more likely to acquire "civilizing" influences from Africans than to impart them.

The role of African women (primarily of the Wolof and Lebou peoples) was a factor of great influence on the special developments that occurred in Senegal. These women had considerable independence of action in their own societies, and were strongly attracted by the economic opportunities that arose with the coming of the Europeans. And European men were no less attracted to them for their beauty and commercial enterprise. Given the circumstances, cohabitation and economic collaboration for mutual advantage were virtually inevitable.

Social and demographic data are sparse for the first half of the eighteenth century, but available evidence indicates that the principal characteristics of "signareship" must have evolved during the long period of uninterrupted French occupation of Saint-Louis and Gorée prior to 1758. Details recorded in André Delcourt's study of this period provide hints of the developments in progress. The regulations of the Senegal Company* forbade its employees to traffic with African women, but successive governors in Saint-Louis, confronted with local realities and needs, sought to obtain authorization for Company employees to marry local women. Governor Dubellay (1722–25) argued that such a policy would encourage long-term service and reduce the turnover of Company employees. But since there were only five young Eurafricans aged from twelve to fifteen in Saint-Louis suitable for marriage, Dubellay also suggested that the Company undertake to send out six to eight *parisiennes* aged fifteen to sixteen each year so that Company employees might marry them. The Company directors rejected both propositions, again expressly forbidding marriages between whites and women of color (Delcourt 1952: 95,123).

* The "Senegal Company" refers to La Compagnie Française des Indes et la Concession du Sénégal, which functioned until 1767.

The Signares of Saint-Louis and Gorée 23

A decade later, another governor, Devaulx (1733–34), together with his advisory council, reopened the issue on the grounds that Company regulations had not prevented sexual and commercial arrangements and that sanctioning marriages might make clandestine commerce easier to control. They also invoked Christian precepts, adding that Eurafrican women and girls would be freed from the necessity of living in sin, as was currently the case, since circumstances in Senegal made Eurafricans dependent on whites for their existence. That Eurafricans were alleged to be dependent on whites suggests that they—and their mothers—were held apart from Wolof society. Their position was made marginal by the Company's practice of not permitting a woman's children to inherit property acquired by a Company employee—a reprehensible policy productive of much injustice and ill-will. Delcourt (1952: 124ff.) reports this policy in effect in the 1730's, but it seems to have been abandoned a few years later. What happened is that Europeans living in Senegal came to adopt Wolof and Lebou marriage and inheritance practices, with the responsibilities and obligations they entailed.

By mid-century, *signares* had attained considerable economic consequence and had contributed to creating a Senegalese life-style so attractive to Europeans that they refused to obey Company directives against cohabitation and commerce with African women. Pruneau de Pommegorge's account (1789: 2–7), distilled from 22 years' experience in West Africa ending in 1765, would serve with few modifications until well into the nineteenth century.*

The women on the island [Saint-Louis] are, in general, closely associated with white men, and care for them when they are sick in a manner that could not be bettered. The majority live in considerable affluence, and many African women own thirty to forty slaves which they hire to the Company. Each year the domestic slaves make the voyage to Galam engaged as sailors; they bring back to their mistresses fifteen, twenty, even up to thirty weight of gold for the sale of two hogsheads of salt which

---

* For a more detailed description dating from a generation or so later, see Lamiral 1789: 44–59. Among the minor changes that had occurred since Pruneau de Pommegorge's time, *signares* were now shielded from the sun on their promenades by parasols borne by young girls.

they are permitted to embark duty-free. The women have some of this gold made into jewelry, and the rest is used to purchase clothing, because they adore, as do women everywhere else, fashionable clothing. Their mode of dress, characteristically very elegant, suits them very well. They wear a very artistically arranged white handkerchief on the head, over which they affix a small narrow black ribbon, or a colored one, around their head. A shift à la française, ornamented; a bodice of taffeta or muslin; a skirt of the same and similar to the bodice; gold earrings; anklets of gold or silver, for they will wear no others; red morocco slippers on the feet; underneath their bodice a piece of two ells of muslin, the ends of which dangle beneath the left shoulder—thus appareled when they go out in public, they are followed by one or two young girls who serve as their chambermaids, likewise well dressed, but somewhat more lightly and a little less modestly than is our own custom. One becomes accustomed very quickly, however, to viewing these almost nude women without becoming embarrassed. Their customs are different from ours, and when one becomes accustomed to their nudity it ceases to make any more impression than if they were covered up.

The women being thus escorted when they go out, they frequently encounter a *griot* (a type of man who sings someone's praises in return for money); in such instances he does not lose the opportunity to precede them declaiming their praises with all the exaggerations he can think of, and some immodesties which they know, the women being so flattered that in the rapture excited by this adulation they often fling some of their garments to the singer when they have nothing left in their pockets to give him.

Next to finery, the greatest passion of these women is their dances, or *folgars*, which they sometimes hold until daybreak, and during which one drinks a great deal of palm wine, *pitot* (a type of beer), and also wines from France, when they are able to procure them. The usual way to praise those who have excelled in dancing is to fling a cloth or a handkerchief over them, which they return to the person who has thrown it, making a deep bow to thank him.

Some of these women are married in church, others à la mode du pays, which in general consists of the consent of both parties and the relatives. It is remarked that the latter marriages are always more successful than the former; the women are more faithful to their husbands than otherwise is the case. The ceremony which follows the latter form of marriage is not in fact as becoming as is the good behavior of the women.

The morning following the consummation of the marriage, the relatives of the bride come at daybreak and carry off the white cloth on which the couple have spent the night. Do they find the proof they search for? They affix the cloth at the end of a long pole, waving like a flag; they parade this all day long in the village, singing and praising the new bride and her chastity; but when the relatives have not in fact found such proof the morning after, they take care to substitute for it as quickly as possible.

Many aspects of Pruneau de Pommegorge's account continue to be relevant in modern-day Senegal. Senegalese women still possess an unrivaled flair for displaying clothing, jewelry, and other finery. *Or de Galam* (gold from Galam) is still the byword for quality and purity. The single white handkerchief headpiece described by Pruneau de Pommegorge soon evolved into the striking cone-shaped turban, artfully constructed with as many as nine colored handkerchiefs, that became the hallmark of *signares* in Senegal and The Gambia. *Folgar* is a Portuguese word that passed into West African languages to describe a carefree frolic or general rejoicing. The rites and reciprocities associated with marriage *à la mode du pays* are discussed in a later section.* *Griots* belong to a special endogamous social class, or "caste," associated with many societies living on the coast and in the interior of West Africa. They were (and are) professional entertainers, musicians, singers, and dancers (Gamble 1967: 45), and their role is analogous to that of the bards or troubadours of medieval Europe: they were attached to the leading families as praise-singers, keepers of family histories and genealogies, counselors to rulers, and educators of the young (see Bird 1971: 16–18). Traditionally, *griots* had the privilege of mocking people or using abusive language with impunity, with the result that they were generally well rewarded to ensure their favor. Female *griots* were often hairdressers, an occupation that gave them a matchless opportunity to learn and pass on gossip. They also had a reputation for lascivious dancing and for otherwise having an immoral influence on young women (Gamble 1967: 45).

In another section of his account, Pruneau de Pommegorge (1789: 28–29) testifies to the beauty, intelligence, and remarkable adaptability of Wolof women, which made them much sought after as slaves by French colonists in the West Indies. They were reputed to be so adept that within a few months of their arrival in the Antilles they knew how to sew, speak French, and perform

* For definitions of these and other terms, see R. Mauny, *Glossaire des expressions et termes locaux employés dans l'Ouest Africain* (Dakar, 1952), pp. 37, 48.

GEORGE E. BROOKS, JR.

other duties as well as European servants, with the consequence that they were especially sought after for service as chambermaids. This Wolof "adaptability" is a theme discussed by numerous observers.

The Reverend John Lindsay, chaplain aboard one of the British vessels that captured Gorée in December 1758, and a subsequent visitor to Saint-Louis, also praised Senegalese women (1759: 77–78).

> As to their women, and in particular the ladies (for so I must call many of those in Senegal) they are in a surprising degree handsome, have very fine features, are wonderfully tractable, remarkably polite both in conversation and manners; and in the point of keeping themselves neat and clean (of which we have generally strange ideas, formed to us by the beastly laziness of slaves), they far surpass the Europeans in every respect. They bathe twice a day, ... and in this particular have a hearty contempt for all white people, who they imagine must be disagreeable, our women especially. Nor can even their men, from this very notion, be brought to look upon the prettiest of our women, but with the coldest indifference, some of whom there are here, officers' ladies, who dress very showy, and who even in England would be thought handsome. You may, perhaps, smile at all this; but I assure you 'tis a truth. Negroes to me are no novelty; but the accounts I received of them, and in particular the appearance of the females on this occasion, were to me a novelty most pleasing. They were not only pretty, but in the dress in which they appeared, were even desirable. Nor can I give you any drapery more nearly resembling theirs, than the loose, light, easy robe, and sandal, in which we see the female Grecian statues attired; most of which were of exceeding white cotton, spun, wove into narrow slips of six or seven inches, and sewn together by themselves. Their hair, for it differs a little from wool, very neat and curiously plaited; and their persons otherways adorned, by earrings, necklaces, and bracelets, of the purest gold.
> And indeed I cannot help thinking, that it was to the benefit of the African company in general, and the happiness of those they sent abroad in particular; that, with such promising inhabitants, the French suffered no white women to be sent thither.

There was, however, no easy fraternization, to the dismay of the British seamen, and Reverend Lindsay was at pains to describe (p. 79) the women's high reputation for chastity and respectable behavior, a theme that will be discussed below.

Who the women described by Pruneau de Pommegorge and Reverend Lindsay were, and what classes of society they belonged

The Signares of Saint-Louis and Gorée 27

to, are frustrating historical questions, since few sources mention either the names or the status of women discussed. And where the names of women are given, those of Eurafricans have no European surnames. The hierarchy of Wolof and Lebou social classes is as follows: freeborn (*jambor*); persons of slave descent (*jam*); blacksmiths and leatherworkers (*tega* and *ude*); persons descended from slaves of the above (*jam i tega* and *jam i ude*); griots (*gewel*); and persons descended from their slaves (*jam i gewel*). In traditional times, marriage across class lines was extremely rare. An exception was when a wealthy freeborn man, after marriage to several freeborn wives, married a *jam* woman (called a *tara*) for her beauty. In such cases, the *tara* and her children were accorded freeborn status (Ames 1956: 156–57). Sources suggest that many of the women associated with Europeans were *jam*. Probably a number, too, were from the *griot* class. Only one specific reference to a freeborn woman was found, that of a Walo [?] "princess" married to the French commandant of Gorée in 1758 (Lindsay 1759: 80, 89–90).

Also living at Saint-Louis, Gorée, and other West African commercial centers were numerous Africans known as *grumetes*, who were associated with European and Eurafrican trading activities. *Grumete* (Crioulo), *gourmet* (French), and *grumetta* (English) all derived from the word for ship's boy or cabin boy in various European languages, and *grumete* was the name given to Africans hired aboard European vessels as pilots and seamen from the fifteenth century on. *Grumetes* were recruited from West African seafaring peoples for a variety of tasks afloat and ashore: they served as boatbuilders, longshoremen, and guards for slave barracoons, but they were chiefly employed as sailors and their maritime skills made them invaluable to European and Eurafrican traders. They generally spoke *Crioulo*, "Black French," or "Black English," wore European-style clothing, and adopted some Christian practices. Almost no information has been recorded concerning *grumete* women; in some communities they seem to have belonged to the same African society as their men, in others they likely were local women taken to wife, and in still others they were perhaps a combination of the two (Rodney 1970: 77, 79; Nardin 1966). Evidence is lacking, but it is likely that the *grumete* communities at Saint-Louis and Gorée together with the *jam* social grouping were the principal sources of the women who associated with European males.

Where Pruneau de Pommegorge and Reverend Lindsay dwelled on the positive attributes of Senegalese women, the noted French botanist Michel Adanson subjected them and the leading administrators in Senegal to a searching critique. Adanson, who had spent the years from 1749 to 1753 in Senegal collecting and studying specimens, prepared a *mémoire* for the Minister for Foreign Affairs in 1763 on the occasion of the return of Gorée to French control following the Seven Years War. (Both Gorée and Saint-Louis had been captured by British forces in 1758; Gorée was returned to France in 1763, but Saint-Louis remained under British control until 1779.) He was highly critical of a number of corrupt practices associated with *signares* that interfered with the proper administration of the Senegal Company and were grossly unfair to its lower-ranked French employees. He charged that *signares* were accorded double or triple rations—whatever they wanted—from the Company's stores, and that as a general practice their domestic slaves were fed with meat and millet at the Company's expense. The slaves of *signares* hired in the Company's service carried on trade on behalf of their mistresses and those high-ranking Company officials in collusion with them, with the result that the *signares* obtained the choicest merchandise, including commodities not available to the lower-ranked French employees. Adanson asserted that these latter—Frenchmen who were workers, soldiers, sailors, and even officers of the lower grades—went without, while the "bloodsuckers" and their male associates banqueted upon provisions diverted from their use. He blamed such practices on the Company's regulations forbidding its employees to marry and bring out women from France; the consequences were that men lavished upon African women housing and amenities that would have befitted European women. He acknowledged that such behavior was not surprising, suggesting that in a hot climate men are especially sensible to women's charms—not the least Frenchmen, who are always attracted to "a sex as dangerous as it is attractive."*

Adanson's *mémoire* is informative on other practices. Regarding the offspring of such unions, he states that boys were employed in the Company service as hired laborers and sailors (*grumetes*). They were not categorized as slaves, even in cases where the mother had been a slave. Girls were accorded the same privileges as their mothers, and made alliances with Company officials in furtherance of their own interests. The growing numbers of domestic slaves possessed by them, together with those owned by their mothers, were an increasing drain on the Company's resources.†

Whether as a result of Adanson's indictment of past administrative corruption or not, the French government introduced significant changes in West African commerce in 1763. Gorée was placed under royal administration with an appointed governor, and freedom of commerce was proclaimed. However, independent traders soon learned that free trade was little more than a declaration of principle insofar as West Africa was concerned. Collusion between commercial interests associated with the new Senegal Company (the Compagnie de Guyane) and royal officials made the measure a dead letter. The royal governors proved to be readily corruptible and preoccupied with lining their own pockets (Knight-Baylac 1970a: 58–60). *Signares* must have welcomed the advent of the royal administration, inasmuch as the new royal officials posted to Senegal, like the military officers, had little to occupy their time. Seemingly most followed the example of their superiors and associated with *signares* in illicit trading ventures.

The Abbé Demanet, who accompanied the French expedition

---

* Cited in Cariou n.d.: 18–19. Adanson is the earliest source located to date mentioning the title *signare*. According to him, the women so termed themselves. Poncet de la Rivière, the commandant of Gorée in 1764, related that women were called *signares* more for their "Portuguese appearance" than for their origins, since they were of French-African descent. De la Rivière's comment is cited in Madeleine Saulnier, "Une réception royale à l'île de Gorée en 1831," *Revue de l'Histoire des Colonies Françaises*, 6 (1918), p. 344, n. 1.

† Again I draw on Dr. Cariou's "Promenade à Gorée" (n.d.: 19). That children of a woman slave were accorded freeborn status following their mother's marriage to a freeborn man accords with traditional Wolof practice.

dispatched to reoccupy Gorée in 1763, criticized the lack of initiative European traders there and at other trading communities displayed while the women associated with them were becoming wealthy in commerce (1767: 116–17): "Each and every one had become absorbed in his own diversions and was debilitated by indolence. Simple clerks, ordinary employees with low-level appointments, reached expenses of 10,000 francs a year. One sees today on Gorée, at Senegal, and in the Gambia some of their concubines who have fortunes of 100,000 livres, even though prior to this business, so pernicious in different respects, they owned nothing whatever." Like other sources, Demanet is uninformative on the names of the women or the means by which they carried on their commercial affairs. Besides using their domestic slaves, *signares* presumably employed relatives and took advantage of ties with African traders and rulers on the mainland, but details on such matters are not recorded in contemporary European accounts.

The revelations of Adanson and the Abbé Demanet concerning conditions in Senegal are borne out by the research of Dr. Cariou and Mme. Knight-Baylac on the history of Gorée. In 1749, ten of the thirteen private properties on the island belonged to Eurafricans, nine of whom were women. In 1767, the richest woman on Gorée, Caty Louette, then associated with a Captain Aussenac, owned 25 male and 43 female domestic slaves. A plan of Gorée prepared in 1779 by Evrard Duparel shows that of eighteen compounds belonging to the French government, eleven were occupied by *signares* (Knight-Baylác 1970b: 402–3). Many of Adanson's and Demanet's charges are repeated in letters cited in a volume compiled by J. Machat. *Signares* living on Gorée were castigated for spending their days in idleness, for dressing in a manner calculated to arouse violent passions, for inciting whites to debauchery, and for sowing disunity and sickness among them. Royal administrators were accused of collaborating with the *signares* in illicit commerce in order to gain the wealth necessary to attract and support them and indulge their taste for luxuries; in the meantime they prevented other Frenchmen from doing the same (Machat 1906: 88–89).

The dearth of information concerning the British administration of Saint-Louis from 1758 to 1779 makes it impossible to compare events there with those on Gorée (held by Britain 1758–63 and 1779–83; French-ruled for the remainder of the century). John Barnes, who arrived in Saint-Louis in December 1763 to take charge of the post for the African Company described the fort as a "dismal heap of ruins" and characterized the British garrison as "a set of the most mutinous, drunken, abandoned fellows I ever met with," which says as much about their officers. According to Barnes, Saint-Louis had about 3,000 inhabitants, including a considerable number of nonindigenous Africans. Soldiers and sailors, together with Africans, drank and brawled in the numerous taverns on the island (Dodwell 1916: 274–75).

In contrast to France, which had allowed Saint-Louis to be administered by monopolistic trading companies, Britain established an ill-conceived "Province of Senegambia" (1765–83) that linked Saint-Louis with James Fort in the Gambia River—the two separated, though, by French-ruled Gorée. Moreover, Parliament decreed free and open commerce for all British subjects and instituted a governor's council composed of nine local inhabitants together with four ex officio members (Martin 1927: 66–71). These and other measures accorded Senegalese privileges and opportunities long denied them under French rule. One important consequence was that Eurafrican men asserted themselves as never before.

Economic and social developments at Saint-Louis are difficult to trace for the period of British rule; unfortunately for historians, Colonel Charles O'Hara, the governor of Senegambia from 1766 to 1775, was notorious for his negligence of official correspondence and record-keeping. However, some idea of what went on during O'Hara's administration emerges from the complaints made against him. The rise of Eurafrican men in the colony's affairs is evident from a petition of grievances drawn up in 1776: it was signed by fifteen inhabitants, all males, including one Eurafrican who had become unofficially recognized as the "mayor" representing the population of Saint-Louis. O'Hara was accused of numerous arbitrary and despotic acts taken without consulting the governor's council or following judicial process. The evidence collected for an official inquiry reports other corrupt practices. Military officers were charged with openly engaging in commerce, contrary to regulations, with, one may safely assume, the collaboration of *signares*. One of the allegations against O'Hara himself was that materials allocated for the repair of the fort's walls and storehouses were used instead on the homes of his "concubines" (Martin 1927: 76, 88–90; Dodwell 1916: 296–98; Hargreaves 1969: 76–84). By the time France recaptured Saint-Louis in 1779, Eurafricans had acquired notable wealth and influence in the community, which French authorities were constrained to come to terms with in the years following.

War broke out between France and Britain in 1778. The following January a French squadron captured Saint-Louis to end more than two decades of British rule. Four months later, in May 1779, British forces captured Gorée, which they held until 1783, when by the terms of the peace treaty both Saint-Louis and Gorée were designated French possessions.

The decade between 1783 and the renewal of warfare between France and Britain in 1792 represents a period of considerable French commercial expansion in the Senegambia and along the Upper Guinea Coast. Profits from trade trickled down to all elements of society in Senegal. This, together with government disbursements on forts and public buildings and expenditures by the trading community on trading craft and a number of comfortable private residences, contributed to a period of unprecedented affluence for the inhabitants of Saint-Louis and Gorée. The period takes on a special romantic aura in popular literature and historical studies alike from its association with the name of the Chevalier de Boufflers, the last royal governor of Senegal. Boufflers forsook the sun-baked sands of Saint-Louis for the milder airs of Gorée, where he shared companionship and a commercial partnership with Anne Pépin, one of the island's beautiful *signares*.* The

---

* Evocative descriptions of this golden age of Goréen history can be found in Pierre Cariou, "La Rivale inconnue de Madame de Sabran dans l'Ile de Gorée," *Notes Africaines*, 45 (Jan. 1950), pp. 13–15; and *idem*, "Costumes d'autrefois à Gorée, *France Outre-Mer*, 270 (April 1952), pp. 38–41. The Chevalier de Boufflers was a *litterateur* of some note, in part owing to a correspondence ex-

The Signares of Saint-Louis and Gorée **33**

Boufflers era is noteworthy, too, for the number of Frenchmen who published accounts of their experiences in West Africa prior to the French Revolution. Most of these accounts were written to promote schemes for French commercial expansion, but they include much descriptive material on West African peoples. Although they are very uneven in quality and insight, and marred in some instances by flagrant plagiarization, these sources contribute to the description and analysis of some of the most important features of "signareship" in Senegal.

Eurafrican Society in the 1780's

By the mid-1780's, Saint-Louis and Gorée had large populations of Eurafricans and free Africans who owned numerous domestic slaves. According to Golberry's estimates cited earlier (p. 21, fn.), Saint-Louis's population of more than 6,000 included some 2,400 Eurafricans and free blacks and about the same number of domestic slaves, besides 600 French soldiers, government officials, and members of the trading community, and about 60 permanent white residents. (There were, in addition, roughly 1,000 trade slaves held in the fort and in the cellars of houses on the island.) The population of Gorée was similar, but on a smaller scale: of an estimated total population of 1,840, there were 116 Eurafrican and free black property-holders and their families; 522 free blacks without property; 1,044 domestic slaves; 70 to 80 Europeans, including government administrators, officers, soldiers, and employees of the Senegal Company; and 200 or so trade slaves held for shipment.

It is impossible to estimate the number of *signares* among the Eurafrican and free black population cited above. Whatever their numbers, *signares* clearly were the chief element in creating a way of life on Saint-Louis and Gorée that combined features of Wolof and European society, and that was highly attractive and beneficial to European men who came to Senegal. That *signares* directed affairs for their own purposes is likewise evident.

---

changed with Mme. de Sabran, to whom he was secretly married. A poem from that wise and gifted Frenchwoman to the chevalier includes the memorable couplet "Sois constant tout au moins si tu ne m'es fidèle;/Penses à moi souvent dans les bras de ta belle."

Marriage "à la mode du pays"

One of the informative sources on *signares'* marriage patterns is Geoffroy de Villeneuve, who made two voyages to Senegal in 1785–88 and learned Wolof during the two years he lived at Saint-Louis and Gorée. He summarizes the prevailing practices (1814: 1, 68): "The women of color and the wealthy free black women take the Portuguese title *signare* or *nhara*: They freely contract a type of limited marriage with Europeans, regarding themselves as legitimate wives, remaining faithful, and giving the father's name to the children who result from the union. The departure of the white for Europe, with no expectation of returning, breaks the ties of matrimony, and she soon after enters a new contract. The ceremonies observed at the time of this union are the same as those of the Africans' marriages." Prélong, director of the hospital on Gorée from January 1787 to mid-May 1789, asserted that in most cases a woman's parents considered it a "great honor" for their daughter to marry a white man, and their consent constituted the only formality. The European arranged a large banquet to which all the woman's relatives were invited, and feasting and dancing continued for several days accompanied by the music of *griots*. The morning following the nuptials, the sheet stained with the evidence of the bride's virginity was paraded in triumph; this, Prélong noted, was the "sole dowry" that the woman brought the man. The practice was at the point of falling into disuse, he claimed, because Frenchmen found it repugnant, and because it was known often to be a hoax.

If the woman was a slave, the husband purchased her freedom as a wedding present. He also provided her with a place to live—depending on his means, a small house or an African-style dwelling. Following the marriage, the women were reputed to be very faithful, were assiduous in household duties, lavished tender care on their husbands, and contributed significantly to their careers by imparting their knowledge of the customs of the country. The husband purchased a slave for each child to provide for its support. Prélong reports that most of the children were baptized, but

The Signares of Saint-Louis and Gorée 35

he offers convincing evidence that Catholicism was not firmly rooted among Gorée's inhabitants (Prélong 1793: 298–300; cf. Lamiral 1789: 53–54; and Labarthe 1802: 163–65).

The marriage arrangements described by Prélong and other French observers do not differ significantly from traditional Wolof marriage practices. According to Wolof custom (and Muslim law), the father had the right to arrange for his daughter's marriage without her consent. The prospective groom was expected to make generous presents to the bride and her parents whenever he visited them prior to the marriage, and he sealed the engagement with a special payment to the mother and father, *ndah i far*, "to drive off rivals." However, once the marriage payment was settled with the parents and the wedding took place, the husband could take his bride home immediately. This was a change from traditional practice, where consummation did not usually occur until a month or more following the wedding, which neither party might actually attend (Gamble 1967: 65–68; Ames 1956).

It is evident that the women considered themselves properly married, adhered to accepted norms of married behavior, and expected the same of their partners. The parade of the sheet attesting to the bride's virginity—so discomfiting to Europeans' sensibilities—was an integral part of the ceremonies, for virgins commanded higher bridewealth, and a girl's lapse from chastity prior to her marriage was an embarrassment to the family and grounds for immediate divorce. Following the marriage, a Wolof woman guarded her reputation by maintaining chaste behavior and by demanding the same of her husband as well. Whatever European men may have thought of their responsibilities and of restraints on their actions in contracting such marriages, it would seem that the women were quite successful in enforcing appropriate behavior. To be sure, Saint-Louis and Gorée were so small that it would have been virtually impossible to keep extramarital liaisons secret. But wives defended their rights with fearsome weapons: Reverend Landsay reported with shock that many women on Gorée kept sawfish blades in their houses ready to shred the flesh of rivals in any quarrel (1759: 80); and Prélong reported firsthand an instance of

an African woman poisoning her former lover and the Eurafrican
he left her for with a solanum (a plant of the nightshade family)
that grew on Gorée (1793: 275–76). One may suppose that *signares*
held no less potent a sanction over their husbands from their role
in shared commercial enterprises.

When a European left Senegal, according to Labarthe (1802:
164–65), the custom on Gorée was for his wife to accompany him
to the water's edge, where she scooped sand from his final foot-
print into a handkerchief, which she tied to the foot of her bed.
She remained faithful to him unless she learned that he would
not return, in which case she was released from the marriage and
free to marry again. All the sources are curiously silent on the emo-
tional aspects of the farewells. Probably some men found themselves too imbued with Senegalese ways ever to leave, and some of
these must be counted among the permanent European residents
recorded in the censuses.

When a woman remarried, she raised her new children along
with those from her former marriage (or marriages), each child
keeping its father's name. Information is lacking on a *signare*'s
second and subsequent marriages, notably what role her parents
had and whether they received bridewealth. At Gorée, a *signare*'s
children inherited her wealth, following Lebou practice, which
was for children to inherit from their mother without interference
from their father. But practices may have differed at Saint-Louis,
since the Wolof traditionally practiced double descent before the
acceptance of Islam.(Gamble 1967: 60–61, 94; Angrand 1946: 33).

There is every reason to suppose that *signares* or aspiring *signares*, rich or poor, were careful to ally themselves with worthy
partners. Clearly the older, more experienced *signares* who had
acquired households of domestic slaves and established commercial networks were a "catch" for European men. It is noteworthy,
for example, that the impecunious Chevalier de Boufflers chose a
woman nearly thirty years of age, one who had at least one child
from one or more previous marriages, was already well-off from
trade, and was the sister of Nicholas Pépin, the spokesman for

Gorée's inhabitants. Other high-ranking European officials must likewise have sought and negotiated partnerships with the wealthiest and most enterprising *signares* (Cariou 1950: 15).

Signares receive such disproportionate attention in European sources that it is difficult to assess what the circumstances may have been for women whose mothers were not *signares* and who were thus not provided with the contacts to attract a European administrator, Company official, or military officer. Such women, whether born at Saint-Louis or Gorée, African migrants from the adjoining mainland, or members of Eurafrican families located elsewhere on the Upper Guinea Coast, must have settled for the less eligible Europeans. They would be the persons mentioned as cohabiting with European soldiers, sailors, and lower-ranked Company employees, whose pay could not support the permanent relationships the *signares* demanded. Such liaisons doubtless ranged from casual affairs to relationships as long-term as those of the *signares*. Women likely took "calculated risks" with newly arrived Europeans, especially junior Company employees and young army officers, in hopes of eventually parlaying a liaison into a marriage. Some aspirant *signares* must have succeeded; at the least they acquired increased language ability and knowledge of European practices, and they probably augmented their store of wealth as well, thereby increasing the possibility that they might be more successful in the future.* Others, whether deficient in trading acumen or adaptability, may have returned to their societies or, in some cases, lapsed into casual prostitution. This would explain references to "excessive debauchery" and the spread of venereal disease.† Casual affairs

---

* Prélong 1793 contains a revealing anecdote about a young Eurafrican who, upon marrying a soldier, gave him her only valuable possessions—her gold jewelry—so he could enter trade (pp. 299–300). Launched by this "grubstake," the man succeeded to the enrichment of them both. It should be evident from the material in this paper, however, that *they* entered trade, and that her assistance was necessary for his success.

† On these matters see Knight-Baylac 1970b: 398–400; and Prélong 1793: 275. Prélong relates that marabouts living on the mainland opposite Gorée could cure venereal diseases with a treatment of sudorific herbs and milk in five to six weeks. African women requiring treatment crossed to the continent stating their intention to go "prendre le lait à la grande terre."

with whites outside marriage were not sanctioned by the Lebou community on Cape Verde, for de Villeneuve reported that illegitimate babies fathered by whites or Eurafricans on the mainland opposite Gorée were killed, and that their mothers were enslaved (1814: 4, 115–16).

Signares' Households

Signares who were successful in commerce and marriage presided over large households and compounds inhabited by numerous domestic slaves. From the 1760's on, many of the houses in Saint-Louis and Gorée were constructed of brick and stone by domestic slaves who were trained to be expert masons and carpenters. Such houses were surrounded by walls of the same material or by palisades of reeds. The ground floors of the houses contained kitchens, pantries, storerooms, and cells for securing trade slaves held for sale. The *signare* and her family lived on the upper floor, which had high-ceilinged, airy rooms with large windows opening onto balconies. The windows were kept shuttered against sunlight during the day and were opened to sea breezes in the cool of the late afternoon before sunset. Indicative of both the expansion of commerce and the increasing affluence of the inhabitants of Saint-Louis and Gorée in the 1770's and 1780's are the growing number of such dwellings: on Gorée, an increase from fewer than six in 1772 to more than 50 by 1789, all constructed of slabs of basalt and lime mortar made from seashells (Prélong 1793: 285).

An American shipmaster who traded at Saint-Louis in 1815 described the households and compounds and remarked on the many economic activities that went on there (Bennett & Brooks 1965: 65–66).*

The houses are mostly built of stone and brick; they are large and convenient. The lower floor is appropriated to the servants, storerooms, stables or any other purpose. The second floor is divided into a hall, a sitting room, and several small bed apartments. One or more sides are

---

* For a description of the Eurafrican life-style on Gorée in 1815, see J. A. Carnes, *Journal of a Voyage from Boston to the West Coast of Africa* (Boston, 1852), pp. 40–41, 47–48.

The Signares of Saint-Louis and Gorée 39

generally furnished with a piazza running the whole length, which affords a pleasant walk. The whole is surrounded by a high brick wall, the solitary gate to which is constantly guarded by one or two slaves who let no one or no thing out but with their master's order. These houses and walls are plastered and whitewashed and at a distance have a very elegant appearance. A closer view, however, so connects the idea of a Prison with thick walls, grated windows, and guarded gates as to destroy the lively interest excited in a stranger's mind on viewing them from shipboard. Each house may in fact be considered a fortress where the master on his sofa views and directs from the piazza his numerous slaves below. These all have their huts ranged round the wall within the yard, and it is not uncommon to see carpenters, coopers, blacksmiths, weavers, tailors, etc., all in operation at once at their respective works belonging to the same yard. For every man of any note makes it a point to have one or more families of his slaves brought up to each kind of work either of use or ornament.

Fortunate indeed was the European who could associate with a *signare* possessed of such a household and skilled labor force.

Domestic slaves were treated indulgently—indeed, almost like members of the family—by their owners. This was especially true in the cases of the women who were responsible for household work and child-rearing, and of their children, who were brought up together with those of the *signare*. Domestic slaves were never sold into the trade except in extraordinary circumstances—for threatening the life of a free person or exhibiting incorrigible antisocial behavior. Their value as sailors, boatbuilders, carpenters, blacksmiths, coopers, masons, and weavers was well appreciated by their owners, who recognized the shortsightedness of according them bad treatment (Lamiral 1789: 338–40; Pelletan 1800: 99–100). The increasing number of domestic slaves on Gorée is another measure of the growing commerce and wealth of the island's traders in the second half of the eighteenth century. Estimates of 131 in 1749, 710 in 1767, more than 1,200 in 1774–76, and 1,044 in 1785–86 generally represent between two-thirds and three-fourths of the entire population of the island at each date.*

Signares' residences were the centers of entertainment and recre-

* Knight-Baylac 1970b: 401–2. It appears that some of the domestic slaves had their own slaves (p. 405).

ation at Saint-Louis and Gorée, inasmuch as both communities lacked cafés, theaters, opera houses, and other diversions popular with Europeans of the time. The *folgars*, or "balls," featured European-style dancing by mixed couples and provided *signares* with opportunities for displaying their beauty, richest costumes, jewelry, dancing ability, and social graces. Though the principal purpose of the *folgars* was social and recreational, it seems certain that they had other functions as well. What better opportunity for an unattached or newly arrived European to meet a potential partner, perhaps through the introduction and manipulation of a *signare* who was married to one of the most influential men in the government, Company, or military garrison, and who was also acting as matchmaker, preceptor, and confidant for female relatives and friends? To be sure, such matchmaking would be concerned with important commercial opportunities, especially when the man had privileged access to trade goods, shipping, or other resources largely controlled by the Europeans in the community.

Folgars must likewise have served as occasions to acculturate members of the community to elite social mores. If the *signares* and Europeans held center stage, there were also *griot* musicians, domestic slaves serving refreshments, and numerous onlookers taking it all in. Girls and young women, especially, would have observed the *signares* and European men closely, memorizing the dance steps, listening to their conversations, and learning their mannerisms. Slave or free, they would have watched in anticipation of opportunities to come.* The *folgars* and other recreations arranged by the *signares* thus represented an admirable combination of pleasure and business, with a style and character far removed from the debaucheries associated with European recreations in forts, factories, and settlements elsewhere on the coast—excesses of all sorts precipitated by boredom, homesickness, poor health, and depression, all of which contributed to a mean and short-lived existence in West Africa. Marriage to *signares* provided Europeans

* For the heterogeneous assemblage attending a *folgar* at Saint-Louis in 1841, see the watercolor by Edward Auguste Nousveaux reproduced in Henri Nicholas Frey, *Côte Occidentale d'Afrique* (Paris, 1890), pp. 12–13.

The Signares of Saint-Louis and Gorée   41

with a life-style, a regimen, that contributed much to their survival and well-being in tropical Africa.

Certain realities, sometimes forgotten, concerning Europeans living in eighteenth- and early-nineteenth-century West Africa need to be appreciated. Europeans generally suffered from chronic poor health as a result of infection by malaria, dysenteries, and other tropical ailments imperfectly diagnosed and treated. Prélong, who examined the hospital records on Gorée, reported that between one-sixth and one-fifth of the Europeans there died each year; for Saint-Louis, he asserted, the rate was three in ten. Nearly all the deaths occurred during the rainy season, from July to October.* Under the circumstances, a European living in a *signare's* household enjoyed the best possible conditions: a companion who spoke his language and was familiar with European ways, a stable home life, regular and well-prepared meals, and sensible recreational outlets, all of which were conducive to good health, both physical and psychological. And during periods of illness, he could rely on nursing and attentive care from the *signare* and her female domestics.

Senegambia and the Upper Guinea Coast in Changing Times

The 1780's may well represent the high point of "signareship" in Senegal. The generation of European conflicts following the French Revolution caused considerable disruption of West African commerce. Gorée was captured by a British squadron in 1800, retaken by French forces in January 1804, and captured again by the British later the same year and held by them until the end of the Napoleonic wars. Following the French surrender of Saint-Louis in July 1809, the trade of the Senegambia stabilized somewhat; but the suppression of the slave trade contributed to years

---

* Prélong 1793: 264. Medical theories and treatments of the time are interestingly described in Philip D. Curtin, *The Image of Africa; British Ideas and Action, 1780–1850* (Madison, Wisc., 1964), pp. 71–87. Curtin calculates that "somewhere between 25 and 75 percent of any group of Europeans newly arrived on the Coast died within the first year. Thereafter, the death rate was much less, perhaps on the order of 10 percent per annum, but still substantial" (p. 71).

of commercial disorganization in the Senegambia and Upper Guinea Coast, until the commercialization of peanuts in the 1830's and 1840's provided a new economic base for the region.

The peace treaty ending the Napoleonic wars returned Saint-Louis and Gorée to France. As a consequence, many of the British traders who had settled in Senegal during the war years moved to the Gambia, where a detachment of British troops founded a new settlement, Bathurst, on Banjul Island at the mouth of the Gambia River in March 1816. The British traders often were accompanied by *signares,* who brought their families and domestic slaves. The latter, together with additional artisans engaged from Saint-Louis and Gorée, constructed residences and business establishments along the lines of those in Senegal. The number of Wolofs who settled in Bathurst was so considerable that "Jollof Town" became the settlement's most populous section. The business section was known as "Portuguese Town," since many Luso-Africans from along the Gambia River, Cacheu, Bissau, and the Cape Verde Islands moved to Bathurst. Thus the settlement of Bathurst owes much to "overlapping" Eurafrican traditions.*

The *signares* (termed *senoras* in the Gambia) lent a distinctive character to Bathurst in the early years of the settlement. The families that came from Senegal seem to have remained together, and there was considerable visiting back and forth with relatives in Saint-Louis and Gorée, which would have served to reinforce the social patterns derived from there. Yet for reasons that need to be elucidated, the institution of "signareship" did not take roots in the Gambia or continue beyond the first generation. Seemingly it was stifled by the influx of new arrivals from Britain, few of whom—whether traders, government officials, or military officers —deviated from "proper" British behavior to live openly with Eurafrican or African women, whatever they might do clandestinely. British authors are discreet about such matters, but it can

---

* For the early years of Bathurst and the contributions of the British traders and *signares* from Senegal, see J. M. Gray, *A History of the Gambia* (London, 1966), chap. 21; and F. Mahoney, "Notes on Mulattoes of the Gambia Before the Mid-Nineteenth Century," *Transactions of the Historical Society of Ghana,* 8 (1965), pp. 120–29.

The Signares of Saint-Louis and Gorée **43**

be discerned that, in contrast to the family lives of the traders and their *signares*, there developed at Bathurst a rootless bachelor community of a type found elsewhere in British areas of West Africa. Open and unrepentant racism was one characteristic of this community; two others were reckless gambling and alcohol= ism.*

South of the Gambia, in the long-established Portuguese settlements at Cacheu and Bissau, circumstances were similar to those in Senegal. Some *nharas* wielded influence unmatched elsewhere in West Africa. The redoubtable Rosa de Carvalho Alvarenga was the dominant personality in the Cacheu area in the 1820's and 1830's: she was called upon to mediate differences between Portuguese authorities and local Africans as a court of last resort. Much of the authority exercised by her famous son, Honório Pereira Barreto, who became governor of Portuguese Guinea, derived from her preeminent influence in the area. Another illustrious *nhara* was Mae Aurelia Correia, whose influence with the Bijago people contributed to the fact that she and her husband, Caetano José Nozolini, dominated the commerce of the Geba and Grande rivers in the 1830's and 1840's. Along the Nunez, Pongo, and other rivers to the south where Eurafrican families operated as intermediaries, incoming European and Eurafrican traders who wanted to establish factories found it expedient to marry local Eurafrican women, some of whom were leading traders. A list of such notable women from the 1830's to the 1850's would include Eliza Proctor, Mary Faber, and Isabella Lightburn.†

* European debauchery is a neglected theme in West African history. British authors are generally very discreet, but for insightful accounts relating to The Gambia and Sierra Leone, see Thomas Eyre Poole, *Life, Scenery, and Customs in Sierra Leone and the Gambia* (London, 1850), vol. 1, pp. 159–61, 290–98; W. Winwood Reade, *Savage Africa* (New York, 1864), pp. 63–65, 323–24; and George Thompson, *The Palm Land or West Africa, Illustrated* (London, 1858; new ed., 1969), pp. 356–57.

† Little has been published concerning women traders in these areas. See the present author's "Enoch Richmond Ware, African Trader: 1839–1850, Years of Apprenticeship," *The American Neptune*, 30, no. 3 (July 1970), pp. 178–85, and no. 4 (Oct. 1970), pp. 232–33; Christopher Fyfe, *A History of Sierra Leone* (London, 1962), pp. 220, 226–27, 254–55; and Bruce L. Mouser, "History of Trade and Politics in the Guinea Rivers, 1790–1865" (unpublished Ph.D. dissertation, Indiana University, 1971), chaps. 5 and 6.

44   GEORGE E. BROOKS, JR.

Perspectives on "Signareship"

If the development of signareship in Senegal has yet to be fully explored—especially with regard to the question of the social origins of the women concerned—the main lines of development seem clear. Signareship represented an economic nexus between European men pursuing personal gain (usually illegally) and African and Eurafrican women determined to acquire European merchandise. It was the women who provided access to African commercial networks, furnished households with skilled domestic slaves, and proved indispensable as interpreters of African languages and cultures: in short, *signares* skillfully manipulated two trading complexes and cultures to further their own ends. Yet signareship represented a social nexus, too, and *signares* helped create a way of life, an *ambiance*, that went far beyond the economic relationship. Once the process was well begun, it was so advantageous and attractive to all involved, at least in Senegal, that it became self-perpetuating. The two societies, Senegalese and French, partially blending, largely coexisting, created a complex cultural relationship that transcends facile explanation or analysis.

22

Iroquois Women, European Women

Natalie Zemon Davis

In the opening years of the seventeenth century in the Montagnais country, Pierre Pastedechouan's grandmother loved to tell him how astonished she had been at the first sight of a French ship. With its large sails and many people gathered on the deck, she had thought the wooden boat a floating island. She and the other women in her band immediately set up cabins to welcome the guests.[1] The people on a floating island appeared also to a young Micmac woman of the Saint Lawrence Gulf in a dream which she recounted to the shaman and elders of her community and which came true a few days later when a European ship arrived.[2]

Across the Atlantic, Mother Marie Guyart de l'Incarnation also first saw the Amerindian lands in a dream-vision, a vast space of mountains, valleys, and fog to which the Virgin Mary and Jesus beckoned her and. which her spiritual director then identified as Canada. By the time she had boarded the boat in 1639, she hoped to "taste the delights of Paradise in the beautiful and large crosses of New France." Once at Québec, she and her sister Ursulines kissed the soil, Marie finding the landscape just like her dream except not so foggy. The Christianized Algonquin, Montagnais, and Huron girls, "freshly washed in the blood of the lamb, seem[ed] to carry Paradise with them."[3]

The similarities and differences in the situation and views of these women in the sixteenth and first half of the seventeenth centuries is my subject in this essay. I want to look at the Amerindian women of the eastern woodlands in terms of historical change – and not just change generated by contact with Europeans, but by processes central to their own societies. I want to insist on the absolute simultaneity of the Amerindian and European worlds, rather than viewing the former as an earlier version of the latter, and make comparisons less polarized than the differences between "simple" and "complex" societies. I want to suggest interactions to look for in the colonial encounter other than the necessary but overpolarized twosome of "domination" and "resistance," and attribute the capacity for choice to Indians as to Europeans. The

NATALIE ZEMON DAVIS

Amerindian case may also be a source of alternative examples and metaphors to illumine the European case. Indeed, an ideal sequel to this essay would be an inquiry about the history of European women that made use of Iroquois tropes and frames.

The term "Iroquois women" in my title is a shorthand for both the Hurons and the Iroquois among the nations speaking the Iroquoian languages, from whom many of my examples will be drawn, and in some instances for women of the groups speaking Algonquian languages, peoples from primarily hunting, fishing, and gathering communities such as the Montagnais, Algonquins, Abenakis, and Micmacs. On the whole, I will stay within the region penetrated by the French, though the woodlands Indians themselves ranged well beyond its reach. My sources are the classic travel accounts and the Jesuit and other religious relations from the eastern woodlands (including the writings of Marie de l'Incarnation and the women Hospitalers of Québec); ethnographic studies, including those based on archeological research and material culture; and collections of Amerindian tales and legends and customs made over the last 150 years and more.[4]

The Hurons and Iroquois alike lived from a digging-stick agriculture, gathering, fishing, and hunting.[5] The men opened the fields for cultivation, but the women were the farmers, growing maize, beans, squash, and in some places tobacco. The women also were the gatherers, picking fruits and other edible food and bringing in all the firewood. When villages changed their base, as they did every several years, it was sometimes in fear of their enemies, but ordinarily because the women declared the fields infertile and the suitable wood exhausted for miles around. The men were in charge of hunting, fishing, and intertribal trading, but the active women might well accompany their husbands or fathers on these expeditions when not held back by farming or cabin tasks. Along the way the women were expected to do much of the carrying, although if there were male prisoners with the band, their masters would have them help the women.[6] Warfare was in the hands of the men.

Responsibility for the crafts and arts was similarly divided. Men made weapons and tools of stone, wood, and sometimes bits of copper, carved the pipes, built the cabins, and constructed frames for canoes and snowshoes. Women were in charge of anything that had to do with sewing, stringing and weaving, preparing thread and laces by hand-spinning and winding, stringing snowshoes, and making baskets, birchbark kettles, nets, and rush mats. Once the men had made a kill at the hunt, the animal was the women's domain, from skinning and preparing the hide, softening and greasing the furs, to making garments and moccasins. The women were the potters, and also made all the decorative objects of porcupine quills, shells (including wampum necklaces and

IROQUOIS WOMEN, EUROPEAN WOMEN

belts), beads, and birchbark. They painted the faces and bodies of their husbands and sons so that they would look impressive when they went visiting, and decorated each other for dances and feasts. As for the meals, the women took care of them all, pounding the corn into flour and cooking much of the food in a single kettle. (Similar work patterns were found among the Algonquian-speaking peoples, where horticulture was only occasionally practiced and where the women were thus on the move much of the time with the men.)

This division of labor looked very lopsided to the French men who first reported it, presumably contrasting it with European agriculture, where men did the ploughing, where women did the weeding and gardening, and where both did wooding and carrying, and with European crafts like leather and pottery, where men had a predominant role. "The women work without comparison more than the men," said Jacques Cartier of the Iroquois whom he had met along the Saint Lawrence in 1536; "the women do all the servile tasks, work[ing] ordinarily harder than the men, though they are neither forced or constrained to do it," said the Recollet Gabriel Sagard of the Huron women in 1623. "Real pack-mules," a Jesuit echoed a few years later.[7] Marie de l'Incarnation, in contrast, took the women's heavy work for granted, perhaps because she heard about it from the Huron and Algonquin women in a matter-of-fact way in the convent yard rather than seeing it, perhaps because she herself had spent her young womanhood in a wagoner's household, doing everything from grooming horses and cleaning slops to keeping the accounts.[8] In any case, Sagard noted that the Huron women still had time for gaming, dancing, and feasts, and "to chat and pass the time together."[9]

The differences that even Marie de l'Incarnation could not fail to recognize between her life in France and that of Huron and Iroquois women concerned property, kinship structures, marriage, and sexual practice. Whereas in France private or at least family property was increasingly freeing itself from the competing claims of distant kin and feudal lords, among both the Iroquois and the Hurons collective property arrangements – village, clan, band, or tribal – prevailed in regard to hunting and gathering areas and to farming plots. Matrilineality and matrilocality seem to have been more consistently practiced among the Iroquois than among the Hurons,[10] but for both societies the living unit was a long-house of several related families, in which the senior women had a major say about what went on. (The Algonquian-speaking peoples counted descent patrilineally and dwelt in smaller wigwams and summer lodges.)

Parents often suggested potential marriage partners to their children (among the Iroquois, it was the mothers who took the initiative), but then the younger generation had to act. A Huron youth would ask the

NATALIE ZEMON DAVIS

permission of the parents of a young woman and give her a substantial present of a wampum collar or beaver robe; if, after a sexual encounter for a few nights, she gave her consent, the wedding feast took place.[11] As there was no dowry and dower but only a bride gift, so there was no property in the way of inheritance: the deceased took some of his or her mats and furs and other goods away to the other world, while the bereaved kin were given extensive gifts "to dry their tears" by the other members of their village and clan.[12]

Without property inheritance and without firm notions about the father's qualities being carried through sexual intercourse or the blood,[13] sexual relations between men and women were conducted without concern about "illegitimate" offspring. There could be several trial encounters and temporary unions before a marriage was decided on, and openly acknowledged intercourse with other partners was possible for both husband and wife. When a Huron father was questioned one day by a Jesuit about how, with such practices, a man could know who his son was, the man answered, "You French love only your own children; we love all the children of our people." When Hurons and Algonquins first saw the Québec Hospital nuns in 1639 – three women all in their twenties – they were astonished (so one of the sisters reported) "when they were told that we had no men at all and that we were virgins."[14]

Clearly there was room in the Iroquoian long-house and Algonquian wigwam for many quarrels: among wives at their different long-house fires, among daughters and parents about consent to a suitor,[15] among husbands and wives about competing lovers.[16] One Jesuit even claimed in 1657 that some married women revenged themselves on their husbands for "bad treatment" by eating a poisonous root and leaving the men with "the reproach of their death."[17] Much more often, an unsatisfactory marriage simply ended in divorce, with both man and woman free to remarry and the woman usually having custody of the children.[18]

In such a situation the debate about authority had a different content from that in Renaissance and early seventeenth-century Europe, where a hierarchical model of the father-dominated family was at best moderated by the image of companionate marriage or reversed by the husband-beating virago. Among the Amerindians, physical coercion was not supposed to be used against anyone within the family, and decisions about crops, food consumption, and many of the crafts were rightfully the women's. If a man wanted a courteous excuse not to do something, he could say without fear of embarrassment "that his wife did not wish it."[19]

When we leave the long-house fire and kettle for the religious feast or dance and council meeting, we have a different picture again. Religious belief among both the Algonquian- and Iroquoian-speaking peoples

246

IROQUOIS WOMEN, EUROPEAN WOMEN

was diverse and wide-ranging, their high divinities, sacred manitous, and omnipresent lesser spirits remembered, pondered over, and argued about through decentralized storytelling. Recollets and Jesuits, hearing such accounts, would challenge the speakers: "How can the creator Yoscaha have a grandmother Aataentsic if Yoscaha is the first god?" they would ask a Huron. "And how could Aataentsic's daughter get pregnant with Yoscaha and his evil twin Tawiscaron if men had not yet been created?" "Was Atahocan definitely the first creator?" they would ask a Montagnais. Huron or Montagnais would then reply that he did not know for sure: "Perhaps it was Atahocan; one speaks of Atahocan as one speaks of a thing so far distant that nothing sure can be known about it." Or that he had the account from someone who had visited Yoscaha and Aataentsic or had seen it in a dream. Or, politely, that the French beliefs about "God" were fine for Europe but not for the woodlands. Or, defiantly, that he would believe in the Jesuits' God when he saw him with his own eyes.[20]

The Recollets and Jesuits reported such exchanges only with men, Father Lejeune even adding, "there are among them mysteries so hidden that only the old men, who can speak with credit and authority about them, are believed."[21] Marie de l'Incarnation, always attentive to women's roles and pleased that Abenaki belief included the virgin birth of the world-saver Messou, said only that traditional accounts of the "Sauvages" were passed on "from fathers to children, from the old to the young."[22] Women were certainly among the listeners to Amerindian creation accounts, for the "ancient tales" were told, for instance, at gatherings after funerals,[23] but were they among the tellers of sacred narratives? Speculation from the existing evidence suggests the following picture: during the sixteenth and early seventeenth centuries, men, especially older men, were the tellers of creation stories at male assemblies (as for the election of a chief)[24] and at mixed gatherings, but women recounted Aataentsic's doings along with many other kinds of narrative to each other and to their children.[25] If this be the case, then the situation of women in the eastern woodlands was rather like that of their Catholic contemporaries in Europe. There, for the most part, Catholic belief systems were formally taught by doctors of theology and male preachers and catechizers, and women reflected on such doctrine among themselves in convents and told Christian stories to their children.

To the all-important realm of dreams, however, Amerindian women and men had equal access. Huron and Iroquois notions of "the soul" and "the self" were more inflected, articulated, or pluralistic than Christian notions of the living person, where a single soul animated the body and where reason, will, and appetite were functions warring or collaborating within. Huron and Iroquois saw "the soul" as "divisible" (to use Father Brébeuf's term about the Huron), giving different names and some

NATALIE ZEMON DAVIS

independence to different soul-actions: animation, reason, deliberation, and desire. The desiring soul especially spoke to one in dreams – "this is what my heart tells me, this is what my appetite desires" (*ondayee ikaton onennoncwat*); sometimes the desiring soul was counseled by a familiar *oki* or spirit who appeared in a dream in some form and told it what it needed or wanted, its *ondinoc*, its secret desire.[26] In France, dreams and the time between sleeping and waking were the occasion for extraordinary visits from Christ, the saints, the devil, or the ghosts of one's dead kin. In the American woodlands, dreams were a visit from part of oneself and one's *oki*, and their prescriptions had wider effect, forestalling or curing illness and predicting, sanctioning, or warning against future events of all kinds.

Amerindian women and men thus took their dreams very seriously, describing, evaluating, and interpreting them to each other, and then acting on them with intensity and determination. For a person of some standing, the village council might decide to mobilize every cabin to help fulfill a dream. So a woman of Angoutenc in the Huron country went outside one night with her little daughter and was greeted by the Moon deity, swooping down from the sky as a beautiful tall woman with a little daughter of her own. The Moon ordered that the woman be given many presents of garments and tobacco from surrounding peoples and that henceforth she dress herself in red, like the fiery moon. Back in her long-house, the woman immediately fell ill with dizziness and weak muscles, and learned from her dreams that only a curing feast and certain presents would restore her. The council of her birth-village of Ossassané agreed to provide all she needed. Three days of ritual action followed, with the many prescribed gifts assembled, the woman in her red garments walking through fires that did not burn her limbs, and everyone discussing their dream desires through riddles.[27] She was cured in an episode that illustrates to us how an individual woman could set in motion a whole sequence of collective religious action.[28]

Women also had important roles in dances intended to placate the *oki* spirits or to drive out evil spirits from the sick. Among the Hurons, a few women who had received a dream sign might be initiated along with men into a society whose curative dance was considered "very powerful against the demons"; among the Iroquois, women were received in several healing and propitiary societies.[29] To be sure, women were accused of witchcraft – that is, of causing someone's death by poisoning or charms – but no more than Huron and Iroquois men, and *okis* or *manitous* in mischievous action were not gendered female more than male.[30]

The major asymmetry in religious life in the sixteenth and seventeenth centuries concerned the shamans. The Arendiwane, as the Hurons called them ("sorcerers" or "jugglers" in the language of the

IROQUOIS WOMEN, EUROPEAN WOMEN

Jesuits), comprised the master shamans, who diagnosed and cured illness by dealing with the spirit world, and the lesser religious leaders, who commanded winds and rains, predicted the future, or found lost objects. The Jesuits scarcely ever described women in these roles among either the Algonquian-speaking or Iroquoian-speaking peoples, and Marie de l'Incarnation mentioned none at all. An Algonquin woman was known "to be involved in sorcery, succeeding at it better than the men"; a woman "famous" among the Hurons for her "sorcery" sought messages from the *Manitou* about what kinds of feasts or gifts would cure an illness; a Montagnais woman entered the cabin where the male shamans consulted the spirits of the air and through shaking the tent-posts and loud singing was able to diagnose an illness and foresee an Iroquois attack.[31] Indeed, soothsaying seems to have been the one shamanic function in which women were welcome, as with the old woman of Teanaostaiaë village in the Huron country, who saw events in distant battles with the Iroquois by looking into fires, and the Abenaki "Pythonesses" who could see absent things and foretell the future.[32]

Most of the time, however, a woman was simply an aide, marking on a "triangular stick" the songs for the dead being sung by a Montagnais medicine man so their order would be remembered; walking around the shaman and his male performers at a prescribed moment in a ritual to kill a far-away witch.[33] Surely the herbal remedies known to be used by later Amerindian women must have had their antecedents in the female lore of the sixteenth and early seventeenth centuries,[34] and it is hard to imagine that there were no religious specialists associated with the menstrual cabins of the Iroquian communities and the Montagnais. It may have been precisely the beliefs about defilement that barred women from handling the sacred shamanic objects and rattle used in spirit cures. Across the Atlantic, the powers and dangers of menstruation kept European *religieuses* from touching altars and chalices too directly and kept Catholic laywomen away from the mass during their periods. Among the Hurons, the presence of a pregnant woman made a sick person worse, but was required for the extraction of an arrow; among the French Catholics, the glance of a post-partum woman brought trouble to people in streets and roadways. Among the Amerindians, medicine men were to abstain from sexual intercourse before their ceremonies; among the Europeans, Catholic priests were to abstain from sexual intercourse all the time.[35]

The most important asymmetry among Indian men and women was political. In the female world of crops, cooking, and crafts, women made the decisions; in lodge and long-house, their voice often carried the day. Village and tribal governance, however, was in the hands of male chiefs and councils, and, apart from the Iroquois, women's influence on it was informal. (Only among the Algonquian peoples of southern New

NATALIE ZEMON DAVIS

England and the mid-Atlantic coast do we hear of women sometimes holding authority as sunksquaws along with the more numerous male sachems.)[36] Huron villages and Algonquin and Montagnais settlements often had two or more chiefs, their access to this honor partly hereditary but even more based on assessments of their eloquence, wisdom, generosity, or past prowess. The chiefs presided over frequent local council meetings, where women and young warriors were rarely present and where pipe-smoking men gave their views, the eldest among them being accorded particular respect. At larger assemblies of several clans and villages, the young men were invited as well, and sometimes the women.[37] When council or assembly decisions required embassies to other villages or nations – to seek support in war or to resolve disputes – the envoys were chiefs and other men.

In Iroquois communities, women had more formal roles in political decisions than elsewhere. Here, to women's advantage, succession to chieftancies was more strictly hereditary, passing matrilineally to a sister's son or another male relative named by the woman. Here among the Onondagas – so we learn from the pen of Marie de l'Incarnation – there were "women of quality" or "Capitainesses" who could affect decisions at local council meetings and select ambassadors for peace initiatives.[38] At least by the eighteenth century important women could attend treaty councils of the Iroquois nations, and perhaps they did so earlier.[39]

Now it is precisely in regard to this political life that major historical changes had occurred in the American/Canadian woodlands and villages from the fourteenth through sixteenth centuries. The evidence for these changes comes in part from archeologists: tobacco-pipes become more elaborate, pottery and sea shells are found further from their place of origin, and human bones in ossuaries show signs of being "cut, cooked and split open to extract the marrow."[40] The evidence comes also from the collective memory of Hurons and Iroquois after European contact and from Indian stories and legends.

A double picture emerges. First, warfare became more prevalent and intense, with the seizure of women as wives[41] and the adoption of some male captives and the torture and cannibalization of others. European contact then added to the complicated history of enmity and exchange between Iroquois and Hurons. As a Huron chief recalled to some Onondagas in 1652,

> Have you forgotten the mutual promises our Ancestors made when they first took up arms against each other, that if a simple woman should take it on herself to uncover the Sweat-house and pull up the stakes that support it, that the victors would put down their arms and show mercy to the vanquished?[42]

The two roles assigned to women by intensified warfare – the woman-

250

IROQUOIS WOMEN, EUROPEAN WOMEN

adoptor of an enemy and the woman-enemy incorporated as wife – must have had important consequences for consciousness. Let us consider here only the enemy wife, a position in which women living in Europe rarely found themselves (even though the foreign queens of Spain and France might have felt divided loyalties when their husbands went to war in 1635, the marriages had been made as peaceful alliance).[43] In the eastern American woodlands, Algonquin and Huron captives became Iroquois wives; Iroquois captives became Huron wives. Nor was their origin forgotten: Pierre Esprit Radisson among the Mohawks in 1652 discovered that his adoptive mother had been taken from the Huron country in her youth; Father Le Moyne among the Onondagas the next year was approached by a Huron wife who "wanted to pour out her heart to him."[44] This suggests that to the Amerindian habit of self-discovery through dream analysis was added for the enemy wife another source for self-definition: the experience of being forcibly transplanted, alone or with only a few of her kin, to a people who had a different language and burial ground from her ancestors. When the enemy wife was also a Christian in a non-Christian village, the impulse toward self-definition might be all the stronger, but the process predated conversion.

This setting for self-consciousness is rather different from those in which Renaissance historians usually locate the discovery of "the individual" or of a renewed sense of self among European Christians. There we stress how persons set themselves off against those whom they resembled, against their own kind and kin: some of Montaigne's best self-discovery occurred when he played himself off against his friend La Boétie and against his own father. The Amerindian enemy wife (and the adopted male enemy as well) represent a contrasting historical trajectory. Still, they should make us more attentive to European situations where the experience of "foreignness" and "strangeness" could prompt consciousness of self as well as of group. The emergence of Jewish autobiography by the early seventeenth century is a case in point.[45]

Along with intensified warfare, a second associated change took place in the eastern American woodlands in the fifteenth, sixteenth, and early seventeenth centuries: intertribal political federations appeared along with a new peacemaking diplomacy. The Huron League, or League of the Ouendats as they called themselves, was made up of four nations or tribes, two of them establishing themselves as "brother" and "sister" with a grand council in the fifteenth century, the other two being adopted, one in the last decades of the sixteenth century and the other in the early seventeenth century.[46] The Iroquois League of the Five Nations, the Houdénosaunee – three Elder Brothers and two Younger Brothers – was probably founded around 1500.[47] Its origin was memorialized in the Deganawidah Epic about a divine Iroquois seer, Deganawidah, who

251

NATALIE ZEMON DAVIS

preached peace, converted a Mohawk chief Hiawatha away from canni-
balism, and then together with him transformed the wicked and obstruc-
tive Onondaga chief Thadodaho into a willing collaborator. (Women
enter the epic through Deganawidah's grandmother, who foresaw his
peace-bringing role in a dream; his mother, who received divine guidance in hidden seclusion and then gave birth to Deganawidah as a virgin;
and the daughter of Hiawatha, who died sacrificially in the encounter
with Thadodaho.)[48]

Among the many fruits of the League formation was the development
of a language of politics and diplomacy: a set of rules and styles of
communication that operated around the local council fire, on embassies
to rouse for war or make amends for a murder, at large assemblies, and
at general councils of the federation. At council meetings, where many
opinions were given, matters opened with the leader's appreciative
words about the men's safe arrival, no one lost in the woods or fallen in
the stream or slain by an enemy. A special tone of voice was used for all
the comments and opinions – the Hurons called it *acouentonch* – "a
raising and lowering of the voice like the tone of a Predicant à l'antique,
an old style Preacher," said a Jesuit in 1636.[49] Always the men spoke
slowly, calmly, and distinctly, each person reviewing the issues before
giving his opinion. No one ever interrupted anyone else, the rhythm of
taking turns aided by the smoking of pipes. No matter how bitter the
disagreement – as when some Huron villages wanted to rebury their
ancestors' bones in a separate grave – courteous and gentle language
was sought. The Hurons said of a good council, *Endionraondaoné*,
"even and easy, like level and reaped fields."[50]

In more elaborate public speeches, for example, as an envoy or at a
large assembly or to make a treaty, still another tone of voice was used –
"a Captain's tone," said a Jesuit, who tried to imitate it among the
Iroquois in 1654. Mnemonic devices were used "to prop up the mind,"
such as marked sticks and, for a major event, the ordered shells on a
wampum necklace or belt. Arm gestures and dramatic movements
accompanied the argument, and the speaker walked back and forth,
seeming "marvelous" to Jacques Cartier in 1535, and to the later Jesuits
"like an actor on a stage."[51] At the 1645 treaty between the Iroquois, the
French, the Algonquins, and the Montagnais, the tall Mohawk chief
Kiotseaeton arose, looked at the sun and then at all the company and
said (as taken from a rough French translation):

"Onotonio [the French governor], lend me ear. I am the whole of
my country; thou listenest to all the Iroquois in hearing my words.
There is no evil in my heart; I have only good songs in my mouth.
We have a multitude of war songs in our country; we have cast
them all on the ground; we have no longer anything but songs of

IROQUOIS WOMEN, EUROPEAN WOMEN

rejoicing." Thereupon he began to sing; his countrymen responded; he walked about that great space as if on the stage of a theatre; he made a thousand gestures; he looked up to Heaven; he gazed at the Sun; he rubbed his arms as if he wished to draw from them the strength that moved them in war.[52]

Throughout, in all political speech, many metaphors and circumlocutions were used, which made it difficult to follow for anyone who had not learned the system. "Kettle" could denote hospitality ("to hang the kettle"), hostility or killing ("to break the kettle," "to put into the kettle"), and ritual reburial of ancestors ("Master of the Kettle," the officer for the Feast of the Dead).[53]

Meanwhile, the persons who were literally in charge of the kettle and who literally reaped the cornfields so that they were easy and even were not deliverers of this oratory. Women strung the shells for the wampum necklaces and belts used in all diplomacy, but they did not provide the public interpretations of their meaning. (Even the Algonquian sunksquaws of the central Atlantic coast are not known for their speeches, and it is significant that Mary Rowlandson, captive of the sunksquaw Weetamoo in 1676, said of her mistress only that "when she had dressed herself, her work was to make Girdles of Wampom and Beads.)"[54] To be sure, councils had to accede to the request of any woman to adopt a prisoner who would replace her slain or dead male relative, but this desire could be discovered by a word or gesture. Only one occasion has come down to us where a Huron woman gave a speech at an assembly: during the smallpox epidemic of 1640 at a large and tumultuous gathering of Ataronchronons, an older woman denounced the Jesuit Black Robes as devils spreading disease.[55] Even in the most favored case of the Iroquois, where the chiefs had been enjoined by Hiawatha to seek the advice of their wisest women about resolving disputes and where captains' wives might accompany an embassy, women never orated as ambassadors – the Five Nations never "spoke through their mouths" – and their opinion at treaty councils was given by a male Speaker for the Women.[56]

Indian men trained their sons in oratory: "I know enough to instruct my son," said an Algonquin captain in refusing to give his son to the Jesuits. "I'll teach him to give speeches." Huron men teased each other if they made a slip of the tongue or mistake, and accorded the eloquent speaker praise and honor. When the Mohawk chief Kiotseaeton wanted to persuade the Hurons to take part in a peace treaty with the Iroquois, he presented a wampum necklace "to urge the Hurons to hasten forth to speak. Let them not be bashful [*honteux*] like women." The Hurons "call us Frenchmen women," said the Recollet Sagard, "because too impulsive

253

and carried away [*trop précipités et bouillants*] in our actions, [we] talk all at the same time and interrupt each other."[57]

It seems to me that connections between political change, eloquence, and gender can be similarly constructed in the North American villages and woodlands and in Western Europe in the fifteenth, sixteenth, and early seventeenth centuries. Renaissance political oratory, emerging in both republics and monarchies, and the art of formal diplomacy were part of a masculine political culture. As Leonardo Bruni said, "Rhetoric in all its forms – public discussion, forensic argument, logical fencing and the like – lies absolutely outside the province of women." The privileged few with a right to public pronouncement – the queens or queen regents and a rare learned woman – required exceptional strategies if their voice were to have an authoritative ring.[58]

Some European women sought the chance to speak publicly (or semi-publicly) in religion instead: members of radical and prophetic sects from the first Anabaptists to the Quakers; Protestants in the early days of the new religion, before Paul's dictum that women should not speak in church was strictly enforced; Catholics in the new religious orders, like Marie de l'Incarnation's Ursulines and the Visitation of Jeanne de Chantal, where women preached to and taught each other.[59]

Can we find evidence for a similar process in the eastern American woodlands, that is, did Amerindian women try to expand their voice in religious culture while Amerindian men were expanding political oratory? Conceivably, the role of women in dream analysis (which, as we have seen, involved describing one's dreams publicly and playing riddle games about them at festive fires) may have increased in the course of the sixteenth century. In 1656 an Onondaga woman used her dream-swoon to unmask the Christian Paradise to her fellow Iroquois: she had visited "Heaven," she announced to them, and had seen the French burning Iroquois.[60] Conceivably, the women soothsayers whom the Jesuits met were not simply filling a timeless function open to women, but were recent shamanic innovators. Conceivably, the Iroquois Ogiweoano society of Chanters for the Dead, described in nineteenth-century sources as composed of all or predominantly women, was not a timeless institution, but a development of the sixteenth and seventeenth centuries.[61]

The evidence we do have concerns Amerindian women who converted to Christianity. Some of them used the new religion to find a voice beyond that of a shaman's silent assistant, even while Jesuits were teaching them that wives were supposed to obey their husbands. Khionrea the Huron was one such woman, her portrait drawn for seventeenth-century readers by Marie de l'Incarnation. Brought to the Ursuline convent by her parents in 1640, when she was about twelve, Khionrea had been given the name Thérèse, Marie de l'Incarnation's

IROQUOIS WOMEN, EUROPEAN WOMEN

favorite saint, and had learned to speak both French and Algonquin and to read and write. Two Huron men from her village came to the convent two years later and she preached to them through the grill:

> They listened to this young woman with unrivalled attention, and one day, when they were on the point of being baptized, one of them pretended no longer to believe in God and so she need no longer speak to him of faith or baptism. Our fervent Thérèse . . . became disturbed and said, "What are you talking about? I see the Devil has overturned all your thoughts so that you will be lost. Know you well that if you died today, you would go to Hell where you would burn with Devils, who would make you suffer terrible torments!" The good man laughed at everything she said, which made her think that he spoke with a spirit of contempt. She redoubled her exhortations to combat him, but failing, she came to us in tears. "Ah," she said, "he is lost; he's left the faith; he will not be baptized. It hurt me so to see him speak against God that if there had not been a grill between us, I would have thrown myself on him to beat him." We went to find out the truth . . . and the man affirmed that he had done this only to test her faith and zeal.[62]

Several months afterward Khionrea's parents came to take her back to her village to marry, expecting her to be "the example of their Nation and the Teacher (Maîtresse) of the Huron girls and women." Instead her party was captured by Iroquois, a number were slain, and Thérèse was married to a Mohawk. A decade later, in 1653, she was the mistress of the several families of her Iroquois long-house, still praying to her Christian God and leading others publicly in prayer.[63] Khionrea may have been placating *oki* spirits as well – though Marie de l'Incarnation would have hated to think so – and inspired non-Christian women in her village to experimental religious action. One thinks especially of how Christian forms and phrases could have been appropriated to elaborate and lengthen Indian propitiary prayer.

Cécile Gannendaris is another example of a Huron woman who found an authoritative voice through a new religious mix. Her biography was left by the Sisters of the Québec Hospital where she died at an advanced age in 1669, her Christian "virtue" being demonstrated not only by her fighting off "seducers" in her youth with smoldering logs and spanking her children "when they deserved it," but by giving spiritual guidance to her first and second husbands. Especially she taught and preached, "converting numerous Savages and encouraging them to live more perfectly."

> She was so solidly instructed in our mysteries and so eloquent in explaining them that she was sent new arrivals among the Savages

NATALIE ZEMON DAVIS

who were asking to embrace the faith. In a few days she had them ready for baptism, and had reduced the opinionated ones beyond defense by her good reasoning.

The French were impressed with her as well, the Jesuits learning the Huron language from her lips, the newly established Bishop of Québec coming to visit her in her cabin, and the Frenchwomen sending her gifts of food. The Hospital Sisters thought that Gannendaris's clarity of expression and discernment were a break with her Huron past, or, as they put it, "had nothing of the savage [*rien de sauvage*] about them." We would interpret these talents differently, as drawing on a Huron tradition of lucid male discussion around the council fire and on a long-house practice of women's teaching, here transformed by Christian learning and opportunity into a new realm of speech.[64]

When Iroquois women became interested in Christianity, the oratori-cal force of young converts struck them right away. In the fall of 1655, an Onondaga embassy came to Québec to confirm peace with the Hurons and their French allies and to invite the Black Robes to their villages. A chief's wife ("*une Capitainesse*," in the words of Marie de l'Incarnation) visited the Ursulines with other Onondagas several times and listened to the Huron Marie Aouentohons, not yet fifteen and able to read and write in French, Latin, and Huron. Aouentohons catechized her sister seminarians before the company and made a speech (*une harangue*) both to the chief and his wife:

> Send me as many of my Iroquois sisters as you can. I will be their older sister. I will teach them. I will show them how to pray and to worship the Supreme Parent of All. I will pass on to them what my teachers have taught me.

She then sang hymns in Huron, French, and Latin. The Capitainesse asked the Ursulines how long it would take their daughters to acquire such accomplishments.[65]

Religious eloquence was not, of course, the only kind of expressive-ness that attracted some Indian women to Christianity.[66] The spirituality of the "Servant of God" Katherine Tekakwitha, daughter of a Mohawk chief and an enemy-wife Algonquin, was marked by heroic asceticism, intense female companionship, and absorption in mental prayer. Her holy death in 1680 at age 24 was followed by shining apparitions of her and by miracles at her tomb near Caughnawaga. But even Tekakwitha's life involved teaching, as she spoke to the women while they did their cabin tasks of the lives of the saints and other sacred themes and as, toward the end of her life, she instructed those drawn by her reputation on the virtues of virginity and chastity. As her confessor reported it, "At these times her tongue spoke from the depths of her heart."[67]

256

IROQUOIS WOMEN, EUROPEAN WOMEN

In one striking way, then, Iroquois and Huron women faced what European historians could call a "Renaissance" challenge in regard to voice and some of them made use of religious tools and the "Catholic Reformation" to meet it. But neither rebirth nor a return to a privileged past would be an image of change that came readily to them. In the thought of the Algonquian- and Iroquoian-speaking peoples of Marie de l'Incarnation's day, sacred time turned around on itself, but there was no historical golden age from which humankind had declined and to which it might hope to return. When people died, their souls divided into two, one part gradually moving toward the setting sun to the Village of the Dead, the other part remaining with the body "unless someone bears it again as a child."[68] There was no fully developed theory of reincarnation among the Hurons, however. Gaps were filled not so much by rebirth as by adoption: the adoption of the dead person's name, which otherwise could not be mentioned; the adoption of a captured enemy to replace a slain son. Things could be created anew, like wampum, which came from the feathers of a fierce and huge wampum bird, slain to win the hand of an Iroquois chief's daughter and then put to the new uses of peacemaking.[69] Institutions could be created anew by joint divine and human enterprise, as with Deganawidah and Hiawatha and the confederating of the Five Iroquois Nations.

Models for abrupt change were also available. One was metamorphosis, the sudden and repeatable change from bear to man to bear, from trickster to benefactor to trickster – changes emerging from the double possibilities in life, the ever-present destabilizing potentiality for twinning[70] (a potentiality that makes interesting comparison with the sixteenth-century fascination with Ovidian metamorphosis). A second model was the sudden fall to a totally different world. The first fall was at creation, when the pregnant woman Aataentsic plunged from the sky through the hole under the roots of a great tree (according to one version recounted to the Jesuit Brébeuf), landed on the back of a great turtle in the waters of this world, and after dry land had been created, gave birth to the deity Yoscaha and his twin brother. Falls through holes, especially holes under trees, are the birth canals to experiences in alternative worlds in many an Indian narrative.[71] A seventeenth-century Huron woman, describing Marie de l'Incarnation's life, might say that she tried to fulfill the promptings of a dream, as a person must always do, but what she thought would only be a boat trip turned out to be a fall down a hole. What that alternative world would become remained to be seen.

I hope that one of the Amerindian women in Marie's convent yard told her a seventeenth-century version of the Seneca tale of the origin of stories. We know it from the version told by the Seneca Henry Jacob to Jeremiah Curtin in 1883, where a hunting boy is its protagonist;[72] perhaps a woman's version 230 years before would have used a wooding

NATALIE ZEMON DAVIS

girl instead. Set in the forest, the tale called to my mind Marguerite de Navarre's rather different storytelling field in the Pyrenees – a conjoining of alternative worlds. An Orphan Boy was sent each day into the woods by his adoptive mother to hunt for birds. One day he came upon a flat round stone in the midst of a clearing. When he sat upon it he heard a voice asking, "Shall I tell you stories?" "What does it mean – to tell stories?" the boy asked. "It is telling what happened a long time ago. If you will give me your birds, I'll tell you stories."

So each day the Orphan sat on the stone, heard stories, and left birds, bringing home to his mother only what he could catch on the way back. His mother sent other boys from the long-house and even men to follow him to find out why his catch had diminished, but they too were captivated by the stories and would say "haa, haa" with approval now and again. Finally, the stone told the Orphan Boy that he should clear a larger space and bring everyone in the village to it, each of them with something to eat. The boy told the chief, and for two days at sunrise all the men and women of the village came, put food on the stone, and listened to stories till the sun was almost down. At the end of the second day the stone said,

> I have finished! You must keep these stories as long as the world lasts. Tell them to your children and your grandchildren. One person will remember them better than another. When you go to a man or a woman to ask for one of these stories, bring a gift of game or fish or whatever you have. I know all that happened in the world before this; I have told it to you. When you visit one another, you must tell these things. You must remember them always. I have finished.

NOTES

14 IROQUOIS WOMEN, EUROPEAN WOMEN
Natalie Zemon Davis

An initial version of this essay was given on May 2, 1992, at the University of Chicago Centennial Colloquium "Do We Need 'The Renaissance'?" A somewhat different version will appear in the papers of the conference, edited by Philippe Desan, Richard Strier, and Elissa Weaver.

1 Paul Le Jeune, *Relation de ce qui s'est passé en la Nouvelle France en l'année 1633* (Paris, 1634) in Reuben Gold Thwaites, *The Jesuit Relations and Allied Documents* (henceforth *JR*), 73 vols (Cleveland, Ohio: Burrows Brothers, 1896–1901), 5: 118–21, 283 n. 33. Pierre Pastedechouan was born about 1605 and taken to France around 1618 by the Recollet brothers, then returned to Canada in 1625, living sometimes with the Jesuits and much of the time with the Montagnais. See also Gabriel Sagard, *Le Grand Voyage du pays des Hurons* (1632), ed. Réal Ouellet (Quebec: Bibliothèque québécoise, 1990), 58.

2 "The Dream of the White Robe and the floating island/Micmac," in Ella Elizabeth Clark, *Indian Legends of Canada* (Toronto: McClelland & Stewart, 1991), 151–2; also Silas Rand, *Legends of the Micmac* (New York: Longmans Green, 1894). For another Amerindian telling of the floating island and the coming of Europeans, see the excerpt from William Wood (1634) in William S. Simmons, *Spirit of the New England Tribes. Indian History and Folklore* (Hanover, NH: University Press of New England, 1986), 66. For a use of the floating island to describe origins of the Amerindians from a race of white giants, see "The Beginning and the End of the World (Okanogan of the Salishan Languages)," in Paula Gunn Allen, ed., *Spider Woman's Granddaughters. Traditional Tales and Contemporary Writing by Native American Women* (Boston: Beacon Press, 1989), 106–7. For references to the motif-type "Island canoe," see Stith Thompson, ed., *Tales of North American Indians* (Cambridge, Mass.: Harvard University Press, 1929), 275 n. 14.

3 Marie de l'Incarnation and Claude Martin, *La Vie de la vénérable Mère Marie de l'Incarnation première supérieure des Ursulines de la Nouvelle France* (Paris: Louis Billaine, 1677; facsimile ed. Solesmes: Abbaye Saint-Pierre, 1981), 228–30, 400, 408. Marie de l'Incarnation, *Correspondance*, ed. Dom Guy Oury (Solesmes: Abbaye Saint-Pierre, 1971), no. 28, 64–5, no. 41, 91.

4 General bibliographical orientation can be found in Dean R. Snow, *Native American Prehistory. A Critical Bibliography* (Bloomington: Indiana University Press for the Newberry Library, 1979); Neal Salisbury, *The Indians of New England. A Critical Bibliography* (Bloomington: Indiana University Press for the Newberry Library, 1982); James P. Ronda and James Axtell, *Indian Missions. A Critical Bibliography* (Bloomington: Indiana University Press for the Newberry Library, 1978). The writings of James Axtell have been pioneering in the study of the American Indians in their encounter with Europeans: *The European and the Indian: Essays in the Ethnohistory of Colonial North America* (Oxford and New York: Oxford University Press, 1981); *The Invasion Within. The Contest of Cultures in Colonial North America* (New York and Oxford: Oxford University Press, 1985); *After Columbus. Essays in the Ethnohistory of Colonial North America* (New York and Oxford: Oxford University Press, 1988); *Beyond 1492. Encounters in Colonial North America* (New York and Oxford: Oxford University Press, 1992). A general historical and ethnographical orientation to the Amerindian peoples of Canada is R. Bruce Morrison and C. Roderick Wilson, eds, *Native Peoples. The Canadian*

NOTES

Experience (Toronto: McClelland & Stewart, 1986). Bruce G. Trigger's *Natives and Newcomers. Canada's "Heroic Age" Reconsidered* (Kingston and Montréal: McGill-Queen's University Press, 1985) is an excellent presentation of both archeological and historical evidence. Important studies of Iroquoian-speaking peoples include Elisabeth Tooker, *An Ethnography of the Huron Indians, 1615–1649* (Washington, DC: Smithsonian Institution for the Huronia Historical Development Council, 1964); Conrad Heidenreich, *Huronia. A History and Geography of the Huron Indians* (Toronto: McClelland & Stewart, 1971); Bruce G. Trigger, *The Children of Aataentsic. A History of the Huron People to 1660*, new edn (Kingston and Montréal: McGill-Queen's University Press, 1987) [with much archeological material from before the seventeenth century]; Lucien Campeau, *La mission des Jésuites chez les Hurons, 1634–1650* (Montreal: Editions Bellarmin, 1987), especially 1–113 on the pre-contact Hurons; Francis Jennings, *The Ambiguous Iroquois Empire. The Covenant Chain Confederation of Indian Tribes with English Colonies from Its Beginnings to the Lancaster Treaty of 1744* (New York: W. W. Norton, 1984); Francis Jennings, William Fenton, Mary Druke, and David R. Miller, eds, *The History and Culture of Iroquois Diplomacy. An Interdisciplinary Guide to the Treaties of the Six Nations and Their League* (Syracuse: Syracuse University Press, 1985); and Daniel K. Richter, *The Ordeal of the Longhouse. The Peoples of the Iroquois League in the Era of European Colonization* (Chapel Hill: University of North Carolina Press for the Institute of Early American History and Culture, 1992). Important studies of Algonquian-speaking peoples include Alfred Goldsworthy Bailey, *The Conflict of European and Eastern Algonkian Cultures, 1504–1700*, 2nd edn (Toronto: University of Toronto Press, 1969); Simmons, *Spirit of the New England Tribes*; Colin G. Calloway, ed., *Dawnland Encounters. Indians and Europeans in Northern New England* (Hanover, NH and London: University Press of New England, 1991); W. Vernon Kinietz, *The Indians of the Western Great Lakes, 1615–1760* (Ann Arbor: University of Michigan Press, 1965); Richard White, *Indians, Empires, and Republics in the Great Lakes Region, 1650–1815* (Cambridge: Cambridge University Press, 1991). Penny Petrone provides an introduction to Amerindian literary genres in *Native Literature in Canada. From the Oral Tradition to the Present* (Toronto: Oxford University Press, 1990). A major study of the art and material culture of Amerindian peoples, with much early historical evidence, is *The Spirit Sings. Artistic Traditions of Canada's First Peoples. A Catalogue of the Exhibition* (Toronto: McClelland & Stewart for the Glenbow-Alberta Institute, 1988). Special studies of Iroquois women have a long history behind them: a collection of essays from 1884 to 1989 is W. G. Spittal, ed., *Iroquois Women. An Anthology* (Ohsweken: Iroqrafts, 1990). Marxist and feminist approaches opened a new chapter in the study of Indian women of northeastern America in the work of Judith K. Brown, "Economic Organization and the Position of Women among the Iroquois," initially published in *Ethnohistory*, 17 (1970) and reprinted in *Iroquois Women*, 182–98, and Eleanor Leacock, "Montagnais Women and the Jesuit Program for Colonization," in Mona Etienne and Eleanor Leacock, eds, *Women and Colonization. Anthropological Perspectives* (New York: Praeger, 1980), 25–42. Karen Anderson's recent *Chain Her by One Foot. The Subjugation of Women in Seventeenth-Century France* (London and New York: Routledge, 1991) does not carry the conceptual argument beyond Leacock's pioneering essay. A new historical and ethnographical study of Iroquois women is under way by Carol Karlsen. An introduction to the history of Amerindian women of many regions is Carolyn Niethammer, *Daughters of the Earth. The Lives and Legends of American Indian*

NOTES

Women (New York: Macmillan, 1977). Paula Gunn Allen has published several works that draw on a mix of historical examples, legends, and women's values and lore in her own Lakota family in order (as she says in the subtitle to *The Sacred Hoop*) "to recover the feminine in American Indian traditions": *The Sacred Hoop: Recovering the Feminine in American Indian Traditions*, 2nd edn (Boston: Beacon Press, 1992); *Spider Woman's Granddaughters*; and *Grandmothers of the Light. A Medicine Woman's Sourcebook* (Boston: Beacon Press, 1991).

5 Among many primary sources for this information on the division of labor: Sagard, *Grand Voyage*, Part 1, ch. 7 and passim, and *JR*, 5: 132–3.

6 On women being assisted in carrying tasks by male prisoners, see Marc Lescarbot, *The History of New France*, trans. W. L. Grant, 3 vols (Toronto: Champlain Society, 1907–1914), Book 6, ch. 17, 3: 200, 412.

7 Jacques Cartier, "Deuxième voyage de Jacques Cartier (1535–1536)," ed. Théodore Beauchesne in Charles A. Julien, ed., *Les Français en Amérique pendant la première moitié du 16e siècle* (Paris: Press Universitaires de France, 1946), 159. Sagard, *Grand Voyage*, 172. Sagard applied to the Huron women what Lescarbot had said in his *Histoire de la Nouvelle France* (1609), about women of the Micmacs and other Algonquian-speaking groups:

> J'ay dit au chapitre de la Tabagie [on banquets] qu'entre les Sauvages les femmes ne sont point en si bonne condition qu'anciennement entre les Gaullois et Allemans. Car (au rapport même de Iacques Quartier) "elles travaillent plus que les hommes," dit-il, "soit en la pecherie, soit au labour, ou autre chose." Et neantmoins elles ne sont point forcées, ne tourmentées, mais elles ne sont ni en leurs Tabagies [at their banquets], ni en leurs conseils, et font les oeuvres serviles, à faute de serviteurs.

Lescarbot, *New France* 3: 411. *JR*, 4: 204–5 ("ces pauvres femmes sont de vrais mulets de charge").

8 Marie de l'Incarnation, *Correspondance*, no. 97, 286; no. 244, 828–9. Marie de l'Incarnation and Claude Martin, *Vie*, 41–3, 54–5.

9 Sagard, *Grand Voyage*, Part 1, ch. 7, 172.

10 Heidenreich (*Huronia*, 77) gives two sources for Huron matrilineality. First, a single sentence from Samuel Champlain where, after noting that Hurons are not always sure of the father of a child because of permitted sexual promiscuity in marriage, he goes on,

> in view of this danger, they have a custom which is this, namely that the children never succeed to the property and honors of their fathers, being in doubt, as I said, of their begetter, but indeed they make their successors and heirs the children of their sisters, from whom these are certain to be sprung and issued

(*The Works of Samuel Champlain*, trans. H. P. Biggar, 6 vols [Toronto: Champlain Society, 1922–1936], 3: 140). Second, an unclear description of cross-cousin marriage by Sagard (*Grand Voyage*, Part 1, ch. 11, 199) that could apply to either a patrilineal or matrilineal situation. Elsewhere Sagard, said that after divorce Huron children usually stayed with ther father (201). Heidenreich concluded that matrilocality was sometimes practiced, sometimes not (77). In *Children of Aataentsic*, Trigger talks of a "matrilineal" preference among the Iroquoians more generally, but adds that their "kinship terminology and incest prohibitions seem to reflect a bilateral ideal of social organization." He suggests that Huron boys in the lineages of chiefs

NOTES

lived with their mother's brother, and that when they married their wives came to live with them rather than following the matrilocal principle (55, 100–2). See also Trigger's *Natives and Newcomers*, 117, 208 and Richter, *Ordeal of the Longhouse*, 20. Lucien Campeau shows from evidence about specific Huron families described in the *Jesuit Relations* that the Hurons were not consistent in matrilocal living arrangements nor in the matrilineal passing of chiefly honors (*Mission des Jésuites*, 54–8). Karen Anderson takes Huron matrilineality and matrilocality for granted, but does not review the Jesuit evidence or mention Campeau's book (*Chain Her by One Foot*, 107, 193). A mixed practice in regard to lineage and dwellings creates an interesting and variegated situation for Huron women.

11 Sagard, *Grand Voyage*, Part 1, ch. 11, 198–9; *JR*, 14: 18–19; 27: 30–1; 30: 36–7; Claude Chauchetière, *The Life of the Good Katharine Tegakoüita, Now Known as the Holy Savage* (1695) in Catholic Church, Sacred Congregation of Rites, *Positio . . . on the Introduction of the Cause for Beatification and Canonization and on the Virtues of the Servant of God Katharine Tekakwitha, the Lily of the Mohawks* (New York: Fordham University Press, 1940), 123–5; Pierre Cholenec, *The Life of Katharine Tegakoüita, First Iroquois Virgin* (1696) in Catholic Church Sacred Congregation of Rites, *Cause fir Beatification*, 273–5. Tooker, *Ethnography*, 126–7; Trigger, *Children of Aataentsic*, 49.

12 Sagard, *Grand Voyage*, Part 1, ch. 1, 291–2. *JR*, 10: 264–71. The remaining goods of the deceased were not given to his or her family, but after the burial were given to "recognize the liberality of those who had made the most gifts of consolation" at the funeral (*JR*, 43: 270–1).

13 Intercourse itself as the sole source of conception was problematized in folktales in which females get pregnant from passing near male urination or scratching themselves with an object used by a male (Claude Lévi-Strauss, *Histoire de lynx* [Paris: Plon, 1991], 21–2). Among some Amerindian peoples today, pregnancy is believed to occur only through many occasions of intercourse (Niethammer, *Daughters of the Earth*, 2). Among the Hurons in the seventeenth century, it was believed that the body-soul of a deceased person might sometimes enter the womb of a woman and be born again as her child (*JR*, 10: 285–7). When an adult male died, and especially an important male, such as a chief, his name was given to another person, not necessarily kin to the bereaved, and he then took up the deceased person's role and attributes (*JR*: 10: 274–7, 23: 164–9; Alexander von Gernet, "Saving the Souls: Reincarnation Beliefs of the Seventeenth-Century Huron," in Antonia Mills and Richard Slobodin, *Amerindian Rebirth: Reincarnation Belief among North American Indians and Inuit* [forthcoming Toronto: University of Toronto Press, 1993]). These adoptive practices carry with them a very different sense of the succesion of qualities from that current in sixteenth- and seventeenth-century Europe, where lineage and stock were so important.

14 *JR*, 6: 254–5. Jeanne-Françoise Juchereau de St Ignace and Marie Andrée Duplessis de Ste Hélène, *Les Annales de l'Hôtel-Dieu de Québec, 1636–1716*, ed. Albert Jamet (Québec: Hôtel-Dieu, 1939), 20.

15 Sagard reported a "grande querelle" between a daughter and a father who refused to give his consent to the suitor she desired, so the latter seized her (*Grand Voyage*, Part 1, ch. 11, 199–201; this story was already recounted by Lescarbot, ibid., 203 n. 4). Marie de l'Incarnation, *Correspondance*, no. 65, p. 163.

16 In addition to occasional reports in the *Jesuit Relations* of jealousy among spouses are the legends about a wife who goes off with a bear lover and the husband's efforts at retrieval or revenge. Lévi-Strauss, *Histoire de lynx*, 146;

NOTES

"The Bear Walker (Mohawk)," in Herbert T. Schwarz, ed., *Tales from the Smokehouse* (Edmonton, Al.: Hurtig Publishers, 1974), 31–5, 101. A similar theme with a buffalo lover in "Apache Chief Punishes His Wife (Tiwa)," in Richard Erdoes and Alfonso Ortiz, eds, *American Indian Myths and Legends* (New York: Pantheon Books, 1984), 291–4.

17 *JR*, 43: 270–1.

18 *JR*, 8: 151–2; 23: 186–7; 28: 50–3 ("en leurs mariages les plus fermes, et qu'ils estiment les plus conformes à la raison, la foy qu'ils se donnent n'a rien de plus qu'une promesse conditionelle de demeurer ensemble, tandis qu'un chacun continuera à rendre les services qu'ils attendent mutuellement les uns des autres, et n'offensera point l'amitié qu'ils se doivent; cela manquant on iuge le divorce estre raisonnable du costé de celuy qui se voit offensé, quoy qu'on blasme l'autre party qui y a donné occasion"). On women ordinarily having custody of the children, *JR*, 5: 136–9; Marie de l'Incarnation, *Correspondance*, no. 52, 123 ("c'est la coûtume du païs que quand les personnes mariées se séparent, la femme emmène les enfans").

19 *JR*, 5: 172–3, 180–1. For an example of a wife using the need for her husband's assent to allow her infant to be baptized (possibly an excuse to cover her own reluctance), see *JR*, 5: 226–9.

20 Sagard, *Grand Voyage*, Part 1, ch. 18, 253–7; *JR*, 5: 152–7, 6: 156–63, 7: 100–3, 8: 118–21, 10: 128–39, 144–8. Marie de l'Incarnation, *Correspondance*, no. 270, 916–17. Tooker, *Ethnography*, 145–8 and Appendix 2; Elisabeth Tooker, ed., *Native North American Spirituality of the Eastern Woodlands. Sacred Myths, Dreams, Visions, Speeches, Healing Formulas, Rituals and Ceremonials* (New York: Paulist Press, 1979); Campeau, *Mission des Jésuites*, ch. 7; Axtell, *Invasion Within*, 13–19.

21 *JR*, 8: 117–19. *JR*, 30: 60–1, for an evidently all-male gathering to elect a new captain among the Hurons:

> Ils ont coustume en semblables rencontres de raconter les histoires qu'ils ont appris de leurs ancestres et les plus éloignées, afin que les ieunes gens qui sont presens et les entendent, en puissent conserver la memoire et les raconter à leur tour, lors qu'ils seront devenus vieux.

Creation accounts were among the tales told at the gathering.

22 Marie de l'Incarnation, *Correspondance*, no. 270, 917–18. Also, Jean de Brébeuf on the Hurons: "Or cette fausse creance qu'ils ont des ames s'entretient parmy-eux, par le moyen de certaines histoires que les peres racontent à leurs enfans" (*JR*, 10: 148–9).

23 *JR*, 43: 286–7.

24 *JR*, 30: 58–61: Paul Ragueneau describes the telling of creation stories by men at meeting for the election of a chief, where "les anciens du païs" were assembled.

25 Women storytellers are documented among the Amerindians in the early nineteenth century (Clark, *Indian Legends of Canada*, x–xi; Jeremiah Curtin, ed., *Seneca Indian Myths* [New York: E. P. Dutton, 1922], 243, 351; Marius Barbeau, ed., *Huron-Wyandot Traditional Narratives in Translations and Native Texts* [Ottawa: National Museum of Canada, 1960], 2–3), and individual women can be traced back to the eighteenth century (e.g., the Seneca grandmother of Johnny John, who told her grandson "A Man Pursued by his Uncle and by His Wife" and whom John described in 1883 as having lived "to be one hundred and thirty years old" [Curtin, *Seneca Indian Myths*, 307]; the Huron-Wyandot Nendusha, who lived to a hundred and told the traditional tales to her grandson, an elderly man in 1911 [Barbeau, *Huron-Wyandot*

Narratives, 2]). According to Penny Petrone, herself an honorary chief of the Gulf Lake Ojibway and specialist on Amerindian tales, some oral narratives were the "private property" of certain tribes, societies within tribes, or of particular persons and families. These could be told and heard only by certain persons (*Native Literature in Canada*, 11). Petrone does not mention gender as a factor in these exclusions and has herself collected sacred tales from Tlingit women; but the cultural habit of restricting the pool of tellers for certain narratives might account for the fact that formal recitals of creation accounts were attributed by the Jesuits and even by Marie de l'Incarnation to men. On the other hand, these sacred stories could not have been successfully passed on if the women with good memories and narrative skills had not also told them on many occasions. (For a woman with evident storytelling skills, see *JR*, 22: 292–5: the blind woman's story about how her grandfather got a new eye.) Petrone thinks my speculation about different settings in which men and women told the sacred stories in the early period is plausible (phone conversation of January 18, 1993). Paula Gunn Allen maintains that Amerindian stories about "women's matters" were for the most part told by women to other women (Allen, ed., *Spider Woman's Granddaughters*, 16–17).

26 *JR*, 8: 22–3; 10: 140–1, 168–73; 17: 152–5; 33: 188–91. Tooker, *Ethnography*, 86–91 and Iroquois evidence, 86, n. 62, 87, n. 63. Dreams could also involve the departure of the rational soul from the body to observe distant events or places.

27 *JR*, 17: 164–87.

28 *JR*, 43: 272–3 for an Iroquois woman who came to Québec to get a French dog of which her nephew had dreamed, and discovering the dog had been taken elsewhere, took a voyage of over four hundred miles through snow, ice, and difficult roads to find the animal.

29 *JR*, 30: 22–3. On the Huron "confraternities," Campeau, *Mission des Jésuites*, 105. Brébeuf's description of a special dance group for curing a man of madness had 80 persons in it, 6 of whom were women (*JR*, 10: 206–7). Games of lacrosse were also ordered for healing purposes (10: 184–7), but this would be only for men. Shafer, "The Status of Iroquois Women," (1941) in Spittal, ed., *Iroquois Women*, 88–9. For an early eighteenth-century picture of Iroquois women and men doing a curing dance together, see the illustration to *Aventures du Sr. C. Le Beau* reproduced by Ruth Phillips, "Art in Woodlands Life: the Early Pioneer Period," in *The Spirit Sings*, 66.

30 *JR*, 10: 222–3, for the Amerindian definition of *sorciers*: "ceux qui se meslent d'empoisonner et faire mourir par sort," who, once declared as such, can have their skulls smashed by anyone who comes upon them without the usual amends for a murder (compensatory gifts to the bereaved kin). For old men accused and punished as sorcerers: *JR*, 13: 154–7, 15: 52–3. Tooker, *Ethnography*, 117–20. The Jesuits also use the word "sorcerer" as one of several perjorative terms for all the various medicine men and shamans among the Amerindians, though there was some uncertainty among the fathers about whether they were actually assisted by Satan (*JR*, 6: 198–201; 10: 194–5, Brébeuf: "Il ya donc quelque apparence que le Diable leur tient la main par fois").

31 *JR*, 14: 182–3; 8: 26–61; 9: 112–15. A Montagnais *sorcière* recieved messages from the Manitou (*JR*, 31: 242–3). Huron women were prepared to blow on a sick person when no medicine man was around to do it (*JR*, 24: 30–1).

32 *JR*, 8: 124–7; 38: 36–7. The Huron soothsayer is the only reference given to women shamans in Tooker, *Huron Indians*, 91–101. Leacock's statement that

NOTES

"Seventeenth-century accounts . . . referred to female shamans who might become powerful" ("Montagnais Women," 41) gives as supporting evidence *JR*, 6: 61, which includes no reference whatsoever to this topic, and 14:183, the woman "involved in sorcery," mentioned in my text. Robert Steven Grumet gives seventeenth-century evidence for women "powwows" or "pawwaws" among the central coast Algonquians of southern New England ("Sunksquaws, Shamans, and Tradeswomen: Middle Atlantic Coastal Algonkian Women during the 17th and 18th Centuries," in Etienne and Leacock, eds, *Women and Colonization*, 53).

33 *JR*, 6: 204–7. On sticks as mnemonic devices, see William N. Fenton, "Structure, Continuity, and Change in the Process of Iroquois Treaty Making," in Jennings, ed., *Iroquois Diplomacy*, 17. *JR*, 6: 194–9: at this ceremony, intended to make a distant enemy die, all the women were sent from the cabin but one, who sat next to the shaman and moved around the backs of all the men once during a specified point in the ceremonies. A similar ceremonial role in the sacrifice of the corpse of a person dead by drowning or freezing (*JR*, 10: 162–5). To appease the sky's anger, the body is cut up by young men and thrown into the fire. Women walk around the men several times and encourage them by putting wampum beads in their mouths. Among the Hurons, if a pregnant woman entered the cabin of a sick person, he or she would grow sicker (*JR*, 15: 180–1). By the presence of a pregnant woman and the application of a certain root, an arrow could be extracted from a man's body. In all of these examples, it is the female body, pregnant or not-pregnant, which is the source of power or danger.

34 Niethammer, *Daughters of the Earth*, 146–63 on herbal medicine and medicine women. Her examples of women shamans come from a later period and, except for the Menominee story about Hunting Medicine (collected 1913), are all from regions other than those of the Algonquian- and Iroquoian-speaking peoples. In *Grandmothers of the Light* and *The Sacred Hoop*, Paula Gunn Allen develops a modern medicine woman's culture based on Amerindian values and tales of goddesses. Her examples of women shamans are all from the late nineteenth and twentieth centuries (*Sacred Hoop*, 203–8). On the earlier period: "Pre-contact American Indian women valued their role as vitalizers because they understood that bearing, like bleeding, was a transformative ritual act" (ibid., 28).

35 Champlain, *Works*, 3: 97–8; Sagard, *Grand Voyage*, Part 1, ch. 4, 132–3. The critical issue may be the menstrual taboos, which would allow women to deal with certain matters, but, as Niethammer points out, would prevent women from handling "the sacred bundle" of the shaman (*Daughters of the Earth*, xii). Pregnant women: *JR*, 15: 180–1; 17: 212–13. Sexual restraint for men before shamanic ceremonial: *JR*, 15: 180–1. Menstrual separation and the power of the glance of the menstruating woman: *JR*, 29: 108–9; 9: 122–3. Separation of post-partum women among Algonquian peoples: Nicholas Perrot, *Memoir on the Manners, Customs, and Religion of the Savages of North America* (c. 1680), in Emma Helen Blair, ed. and trans., *The Indian Tribes or the Upper Missippi Valley and Region of the Great Lakes*, 2 vols (Cleveland, Ohio: Arthur Clark, 1911; New York:Klaus Reprint, 1969), 1: 48.

36 The best study is Grumet, "Sunksquaws, Shamans, and Tradeswomen," 46–53. See also Niethammer, *Daughters of the Earth*, 139–41; Carolyn Thomas Foreman, *Indian Women Chiefs* (Muskogee: Hoffman Printing Co., 1966); Samuel G. Drake, *The Aboriginal Races of North America*, 15th edn (Philadelphia: Charles Desilver, 1860), Book III, chs 1, 4 on the Wampanoag sunksquaws Weetamoo and Awashonks.

37 Descriptions of government and councils from Champlain, *Works*, 3: 157–9; Sagard, *Grand Voyage*, Part 1, ch. 17, 229–32; Brébeuf in *JR*, 10: 229–63; Bailey, *Algonkian Cultures*, 91–2; Heidenreich, *Huronia*, 79–81; Campeau, *Mission des Jésuites*, ch. 5; Fenton, "Iroquois Treaty Making," 12–14. Evidence in regard to women: Champlain on men's conduct on council meetings: "ils usent bien souvent de ceste façon de faire parmy leurs harangues au conseil, où il n'y a que les plus principaux, qui sont les antiens: Les femmes et enfans n'y assistent point" (1: 110); Sagard, 230–1, talking about local council meetings: "Les femmes, filles et jeunes hommes n'y assistent point, si ce n'est en un conseil général, où les jeunes hommes de vingt-cinq à trente ans peuvent assister, ce qu'il connaissent par un cri particulier qui en est fait" 230–1); Brébeuf, on the council chamber:

> la Chambre de Conseil est quelque fois la Cabane du Capitaine, parée de nattes, ou ionchées de branches de Sapin, avec divers feux, suivant la saison de l'année. Autrefois chacun y apportoit sa busche pour mettre au feu; maintenant cela ne se pratique plus, les femmes de la Cabane supportent cette dépense, elles font les feux, et ne s'y chauffent pas, sortant dehors pour ceder la place à Messieurs le Conseillers. Quelquefois l'assemblée se fait au milieu du Village, si c'est en Esté [this may have been the time when women could most easily attend and listen, NZD], et quelquefois aussi en l'obscurité des forests à l'ecart, quand les affaires demandent le secret.
>
> (*JR*, 10: 250);

Paul Le Jeune on the Huron community of both "pagans" and Christians at Saint Joseph (Silléry): The Christian elders decided

> d'assembler les femmes pour les presser de se faire instruire et de recevoir le sainct Baptesme. On les fit donc venir, et les ieunes gens aussi. Le bon fut qu'on les prescha si bien que le iour suivant une partie de ces pauvres femmes, rencontrant le Pere de Quen, luy dirent, "Où est un tel Pere, nous le venons prier de nous baptiser, *hier les hommes nous appellerent en Conseil, c'est la premiere fois que iamais les femmes y sont entrées*"
>
> (italics mine; *JR*, 18: 104).

Drawing from a general description of Huron civility, in which Brébeuf talks of marriages, feasting, and other kinds of sociability and comments

> Ce qui les forme encor dans le discours sont les conseils qui se tiennent quasi tous les iours dans les Villages en toutes occurrences: et quoy que les anciens y tiennent le haut bout, et que ce soit de leur iugement qui dépende la decision des affaires; neantmoins s'y trouve qui veut et chacun a droit d'y dire son advis
>
> (*JR*, 10: 212),

Karen Anderson assumes that women could be present at any Huron council meeting and speak whenever they wanted (*Chain Her by One Foot*, 124). But this is in contradiction to other evidence, including more specific evidence given some pages later by Brébeuf himself. Brébeuf was following the usual practice in men's writing in the sixteenth and seventeenth centuries and using "chacun" (and other general nouns and pronouns) to refer to men; the paragraph in question is describing male civility.

38 Marie de l'Incarnation, *Correspondance*, no. 161, 546, September 24, 1654 ("Ces capitainesses sont des femmes de qualité parmi les Sauvages qui ont

NOTES

voix delibérative dans les Conseils, et qui en tirent des conclusions comme les hommes, et même ce furent elles qui déléguèrent les premiers Ambassadeurs pour traiter de la paix"); no. 191, 671. In 1671, Father Claude Dablon said of Iroquois women of high rank that they

> are much respected; they hold councils, and the Elders decide no important affair without their advice. It was one of these women of quality who, some time ago, took the lead in persuading the Iroquois of Onnontagué, and afterward the other nations, to make peace with the French.
>
> (*JR*, 54: 280–1).

This is surely the same Onodaga "capitainesse" who visited the Ursuline convent during the embassy of 1654. In contrast, in the early eighteenth century Pierre-François-Xavier de Charlevoix claimed of the Iroquois that "the men never tell the women anything they would have to be kept secret, and rarely any affair of consequence is communicated to them, though all is done in their name" (quoted in W. M. Beauchamp, "Iroquois Women," *Journal of American Folklore*, 13 [1900], reprinted in Spittal, ed., *Iroquois Women*, 42–3). Carol Karlsen, currently engaged in a study of Iroquois women, says she has found considerable variation from period to period and nation to nation: in some instances, women attend council, in some they have meetings of their own and their views are communicated to the council (Lecture at Princeton University, March 25, 1993). Daniel Richter, in his important recent study *The Ordeal of the Longhouse*, describes women's roles in naming which man in a hereditary chiefly family would assume the role of leadership, and concludes that there "appears to have been a form of gender division of political labor corresponding to the economic and social categories that made women dominant within the village and its surrounding fields while men dealt with the outside world (43)."

39 Jennings, ed., *Iroquois Dipolomacy*, 124.
40 Trigger, *Natives and Newcomers*, 94–108. An example of the archeological work that allows one to historicize the Amerindian past is James F. Pendergast and Bruce G. Trigger, *Cartier's Hochelaga and the Dawson Site* (Montréal and London: McGill University Press, 1972), see especially 155–6, 158–61.
41 Sagard mentions women and girls kept by Hurons from war as wives or to be used as gifts, *Grand Voyage*, Part 1, ch. 17, 239. *JR*, 9: 254–5: Le Jeune, talking of some Iroquois prisoners seized by Algonquins, comments more generally: "Il est vray que les Barbares ne font point ordinairement de mal aux femmes, non plus qu'aux enfans, sinon dans leurs surprises, voire mesme quelque ieune homme ne fera point de difficulté d'épouser une prisonniere, si elle travaille bien, et par apres elle passe pour une femme du pays."
42 *JR*, 40: 180–1.
43 Elizabeth of France, sister of Louis XIII, was the wife of Philip IV of Spain; Anne of Austria, sister of Philip IV, was the wife of Louis XIII. John Elliott, *Richelieu and Olivares* (Cambridge: Cambridge University Press, 1984), 12, 113.
44 Pierre Esprit Radisson, *The Explorations of Pierre Esprit Radisson*, ed. Arthur T. Adams (Minneapolis: Ross & Haines, 1961), 26. *JR*, 41: 102–3.
45 I treat and give further bibliography on the issues in this paragraph in "Boundaries and the Sense of Self in Sixteenth-Century France," in Thomas Heller, Morton Sosna, and David Wellbery, eds, *Reconstructing Individualism*.

NOTES

Autonomy, Individuality, and the Self in Western Thought (Stanford: Stanford University Press, 1986), 53–63, 332–5 and "Fame and Secrecy: Leon Modena's *Life* as an Early Modern Autobiography," in Mark Cohen, trans., *The Autobiography of a Seventeenth-Cenury Venetian Rabbi: Leon Modena's "Life of Judah"* (Princeton: Princeton University Press, 1988), 50–70.

46 *JR*, 16: 226–9; Trigger, *Children of Aataentsic*, 58–9, *Natives and Newcomers*, 104; Campeau, *Mission des Jésuites*, 22–6.

47 Fenton, "Structure, Continuity, and Change," in Jennings, ed., *Iroquois Diplomacy*, 16; Jennings, *Iroquois Empire*, 34–40; Trigger, *Children of Aataentsic*, 162–3, and Richter, *Ordeal of the Longhouse*, ch. 2. Grumet talks of "Coastal Algonkian confederacies" in the "early historic contact period" ("Sunksquaws," 47), but he may be referring to alliances rather than federations. White, *The Middle Ground* does not give evidence for Algonquin confederations in the Great Lakes region until the late eighteenth century. Of course, these alliances must also have stimulated diplomatic and oratorical skills.

48 Horatio Hale, ed., *The Iroquois Book of Rites* (Philadelphia: D.G. Brinton, 1883), ch. 2: a historical telling of the founding work of Deganiwidah and Hiawatha, collected during Hale's visits to the Reserve of the Iroquois nations in the 1870s; 180–3: the stories he collected about the death of Hiawatha's daughter. J. N. B. Hewitt, "Legend of the Founding of the Iroquois League," *American Anthropologist*, 5 (April 1892): 131–48 (the legend of Deganiwidah, Hiawatha, and Thadodaho, collected by Hewitt in 1888). Clark, *Indian Legends*, 138–45; Erdoes and Ortiz, *American Indian Myths and Legends*, 193–9. Fenton, "Structure, Continuity, and Change," 14–15; J. N. B. Hewitt, "The Status of Woman in Iroquois Polity before 1784," in *Iroquois Women*, 61–3.

49 Brébeuf in *JR*, 10: 256–7. "Ils haussent et flechissent la voix comme d'un ton de Predicateur à l'antique." "Raise and lower the voice" would seem a better translation than "raise and quiver the voice," the translation given on 257.

50 Champlain, *Works*, 1: 110; Sagard, *Grand Voyage*, Part 1, ch. 15, 220; and especially Brébeuf in *JR*, 10: 254–63. Le Jeune on the Montagnais, *JR*, 5: 24–5: "They do not all talk at once, but one after the other, listening patiently."

51 On mnemonic devices and wampum belts strung by women, see Fenton, "Structure, Continuity, and Change," 17–18, and Michael K. Foster, "Another Look at the Function of Wampum in Iroquois-White Councils," in Jennings, ed., *Iroquois Diplomacy*, 99–114. Captain's tone and walking back and forth: *JR*, 41: 112–13. Cartier, "Deuxième voyage," 132: "Et commença ledict agouhanna . . . à faire une prédication et preschement à leur modde, en démenant son corps et membres d'une merveilleuse sorte, qui est une sérymonye de joye et asseurance."

52 Barthélemy Vimont in *JR*, 27: 252–3. Vimont himself was depending on an interpreter for the words, and admitted that he was getting only "some disconnected fragments" (264–5).

53 Brébeuf in *JR*, 10: 256–9, 278–9. Fenton, "Structure, Continuity, and Change," 16 and "Glossary of Figures of Speech in Iroquois Political Rhetoric," in Jennings, ed., *Iroquois Diplomacy*, 115–24; Petrone, *Native Literature*, 27–8.

54 "Narrative of the Captivity of Mrs. Mary Rowlandson, 1682," in Charles H. Lincoln, ed., *Narratives of the Indian Wars, 1675–1699* (New York: Charles Scribner's Sons, 1913), 150. It would be interesting to know what speech strategies Weetamoo used when she negotiated her support for King Philip in his war against the English in the 1670s. When a Wyattanon woman spoke

NOTES

to President Washington together with other delegates from Prairie Indian communities in 1793, she did so only because her uncle, Great Joseph, had died and she was representing him. In the transcription made by Thomas Jefferson, she said "He who was to have spoken to you is dead, Great Joseph. If he had lived you would have heard a good man, and good words flowing from his mouth. He was my uncle, and it has fallen to me to speak for him. But I am ignorant. Excuse, then, these words, it is but a woman who speaks." Thomas Jefferson, *The Writings of Thomas Jefferson*, ed. Andrew A. Lipscomb, 20 vols (Washington, DC: Thomas Jefferson Memorial Association, 1903), 16: 386–7.

55 Marie de l'Incarnation to Mother Ursule de Ste Catherine, September 13, 1640, *Correspondance*, no. 50, 117–18. This is the only account we have of the woman's speech; Marie must have heard about it from one of the Jesuits on the Huron mission, and with her characteristic sensitivity to women's words and actions, included it in her letter to the Mother Superior at her former convent at Tours. In the *Relation* of 1640, the Jesuit Superior Jerome Lallemant talks about the conflict about the Jesuits at this same "conseil general," but does not mention a woman speaker (*JR*, 19: 176–9).

56 "Hiawatha the Unifier," in Erdoes and Ortiz, *American Indian Myths*, 198; Marie de l'Incarnation, *Correspondance*, no. 168, p. 565. Jennings, ed., *Iroquois Diplomacy*, 13, 124, 249. "Speaking through my mouth" is the phrase used by envoys and ambassadors: "Escoute, Ondessonk, Cinq Nations entieres te parlent par ma bouche" (*JR*, 41: 116).

57 *JR*, 5: 180–1; 10: 258–9; 27: 262–3; Sagard, *Grand Voyage*, Part 1, ch. 15, 220. Le Jeune also comments on Montagnais reaction to the French talking all at the same time: "A Sagamore, or Captain, dining in our room one day, wished to say something; and not finding an opportunity, because [we] were all talking at the same time, at last prayed the company to give him a little time to talk in his turn, and all alone, as he did" (*JR*, 5: 24–5).

58 Leonardo Bruni, "Concerning the Study of Literature, A Letter to . . . Baptista Malatesta," in W. H. Woodward, *Vittorino da Feltre and other Humanist Educators* (Cambridge: Cambridge University Press, 1897; reprinted New York: Teachers College of Columbia University, 1963), 126. Margaret L. King, *Women of the Renaissance* (Chicago: University of Chicago Press, 1991), 194. For a few well-born Italian women with training in good letters who managed to give orations, see Margaret L. King and Albert Rabil, Jr, *Her Immaculate Hand. Selected Works by and about the Women Humanists of Quattrocento Italy* (Binghamton: Medieval & Renaissance Texts & Studies, 1983), nos. 2, 4, 6, 7. For an overview of queenly strategies, see N. Z. Davis, "Women in Politics," in Natalie Zemon Davis and Arlette Farge, eds, *A History of Women in the West*, 3: *Renaissance and Enlightenment Paradoxes*, (Cambridge, Mass.: Harvard University Press, 1993), ch. 6.

59 Phyllis Mack, *Visionary Women: Ecstatic Prophecy in Seventeenth-Century England* (Berkeley: University of California Press, 1992). [Margaret Fell Fox], *Womens Speaking Justified, Proved and Allowed of by the Scriptures* (London, 1666 and 1667). Natalie Zemon Davis, "City Women and Religious Change," *Society and Culture in Early Modern France* (Stanford: Stanford University Press, 1975), ch. 3. Elizabeth Rapley, *The Dévotes. Women and Church in Seventeenth-Century France* (Montréal and Kingston: McGill-Queen's University Press, 1990). Linda Lierheimer, "Female Eloquence and Maternal Ministry: The Apostolate of Ursuline Nuns in Seventeenth-Century France" (Ph.D. diss., Princeton University, 1994).

60 *JR*, 43: 288–91.

NOTES

61 Ann Eastlack Shafer, "The Status of Iroquois Women," in Spittal, ed., *Iroquois Women*, 108; Tooker, *Ethnography*, 91, n. 75. It has been suggested that the False Face society was created among the Iroquois during the 1630s (Trigger, *Natives and Newcomers*, 117) and that the Midewiwin society of shamans developed in the central Great Lakes region in the course of the eighteenth century (Phillips, "Art in Woodlands Life," 64–5). Could one find archeological, visual, or other evidence that would allow one to historicize the relation of Amerindian women to religious action in the healing and other shamanic societies?

62 Marie de l'Incarnation, *Correspondance*, no. 65, 165–6.

63 Marie de l'Incarnation, *Correspondance*, no. 65, 165–9; no. 73, 201; no. 97, 281; Appendix, no. 9, 975; no. 11, 977 (letter from Thérèse); no. 18, 988, (letter from an Ursuline, almost certainly Marie, to Paul Le Jeune, 1653: "Nous avons appris que nostre Séminariste Huronne, qui fut prise il y a environ dix ans par les Iroquois, estoit mariée en leur pays; qu'elle estoit la maistresse dans sa cabane, composée de plusieurs familles; qu'elle priot Dieu tous les jours et qu'elle le faisoit prier par d'autres." Campeau provides the name Khionrea (*La Mission des Jésuites*, 86).

64 Juchereau and Duplessis, *Hôtel-Dieu de Québec*, 161–3.

65 Marie de l'Incarnation to Claude Martin, 12 October 1655 in *Correspondance*, no. 168, 565–6. François du Creux, *The History of Canada or New France*, trans. Percy J. Robinson, 2 vols (Toronto: The Champlain Society, 1951–2), 2: 698–700. Du Creux's report was based on the letters sent to him by Marie de l'Incarnation (referred to in her *Correspondance*, 642, 719), which he simply incorporated into his *Historia canadensis* (Paris: Sébastien Cramoisy, 1664).

66 See the fine discussion of Jacqueline Peterson in her essay "Women Dreaming: The Religiopsychology of Indian White Marriages and the Rise of Metis Culture," in Lillian Schlissel, Vicki Ruiz, and Janice Monk, eds, *Western Women. Their Land, Their Lives* (Albuquerque: University of New Mexico Press, 1988), 49–68. I am treating the relation of Amerindian women to Christianity from other points of view in my chapter on Marie de l'Incarnation in *Women on the Margins* (forthcoming Harvard University Press).

67 Cholenec, *Life of Katharine Tegakoüita* in *The Cause for Beatification and Canonization . . . of the Servant of God Katharine Tekakwitha*, 257, 299.

68 *JR*, 10: 286–7. Alexander von Gernet analyzes the evidence for Huron beliefs regarding souls after death and the various ways in which the qualities of the dead could be saved for the living in a remarkable essay, "Saving the Souls," in Mills and Slobodin, eds, *Amerindian Rebirth*.

69 "The first wampum (Iroquois and Huron-Wyandot)," in Clark, *Indian Legends*, 55–6 from a story collected by Erminnie A. Smith, in 1883 (170, 176). Another Iroquois version of the origin of wampum, which also connects it indirectly with feathers and directly with treaty use, in "Hiawatha and the Wizard (Onondaga)," ibid., 138–41, from a story collected by J. N. B. Hewitt in 1892 (172, 174). See Hewitt, "Legend of the Iroquois," 134–5.

70 The twin motif is widely discussed in regard to Indian stories (for example, Erdoes and Ortiz, eds, *American Indian Myths and Legends*, 73ff.) and is the central theme of Lévi-Strauss, *Histoire de lynx*.

71 Brébeuf, *JR*, 19: 126–9. Erdoes and Ortiz discuss the "fall through a hole" as a motif in *American Indian Myths and Legends*, 75, and there are several examples analyzed in Lévi-Strauss, *Histoire de lynx*.

72 Curtin, ed., *Seneca Indian Myths*, 70–5. Curtin collected myths in the Seneca reservation in Versailles, NY in 1883 as an agent of the Bureau of Ethnology of the Smithsonian Institute (v). Curtin's version given in Clark, ed., *Indian*

NOTES

Legends, 37–40, and in Susan Feldmann, ed., *The Story-Telling Stone. Traditional Native American Myths and Tales* (New York: Dell, 1991), 161–6.

23

Blue and Brown: Contraband Indigo and the Rise of a Free Colored Planter Class in French Saint Domingue

John Garrigus

In 1791 the French Caribbean colony of Saint-Domingue became the site of the only successful slave uprising in the history of the New World. As the French Revolution reshaped the political and social institutions of the mother country, Saint-Domingue's free people of color, led by an indigo planter from the island's southern peninsula, began a campaign for civil reform that helped destabilize colonial slave society. Despite their pivotal role in what would become the Haitian Revolution, relatively little is known about this important population. Widely acknowledged to be the largest and wealthiest group of its kind in the New World, this class comprised a remarkable 47 percent of the colony's free inhabitants in 1788. While elsewhere in the eighteenth-century Caribbean free coloreds tended to be urban based, most of Saint-Domingue's *gens de couleur* dwelt in the countryside and a number were successful planters.[1] By 1790 members of this class owned enough slaves and plantations that they were said to possess one-third of the colony.[2]

While this was an exaggeration, it was a believable one. That very year, for example, Julien Raimond, a free *quarteron* (one-quarter African de-

* I would like to thank Paul Lachance, Joan Scott, and Michel-Rolph Trouillot for their comments on an earlier version of this article.

[1] Herbert S. Klein, *African Slavery in Latin America and the Caribbean* (New York, 1986), pp. 237-38; Robert Stein, "The Free Men of Color and the Revolution in Saint-Domingue, 1789-1792," *Histoire Sociale-Social History*, 14 (1981), 7-28; John D. Garrigus, "A Struggle for Respect: The Free Coloreds of Saint-Domingue, 1760-69" (Ph.D. diss., The Johns Hopkins University, 1988).

[2] Abbé Grégoire, "Lettre aux philanthropes sur les malheurs, les droits et les réclamations des gens de couleur de Saint Domingue" (Paris, 1790), p. 3; this is perhaps Grégoire's misreading of a pamphlet by the Abbé de Cournand, who maintained that free coloreds "formed a third of the free population of the colony, a considerable number of whom are proprietors" and "the proprietors of this interesting class, form at least a third of what are called *habitans* in the colony." See de Cournand's "Requête présentée à nosseigneurs de l'assemblée nationale, en faveur des gens de couleur" [S.l.n.d.], pp. 1, 4.

scent), and his wife, a free *mulâtresse* (one-half African ancestry), sold three plantations and over 100 slaves in the parish of Aquin in Saint-Domingue for 320,000 livres.[3] Raimond lived in a style that was more than comfortable by the standards of most colonial planters. Between 1767 and 1784 he spent at least 2,213 livres on jewelry and, with his brothers, paid over 4,000 livres to a local tailor. He acquired silver and crystal table service and gave more than double the price of a field worker for a slave pastry chef and confectioner. In four purchases between 1773 and 1781 he spent over 1,500 livres on books, music papers, and pamphlets.[4]

In 1783 the free colored planter Michel Depas-Medina died, leaving an estate at Aquin whose inventory covered some 60 pages and cost his heirs 1,200 livres in notarial fees, the price of a field slave. Depas-Medina's main plantation had 67 slaves, 27 slave huts, an animal pen, and seven different outbuildings; another smaller farm remained uninventoried. In his dining room the notaries found fourteen silver place settings and assorted silver table service, while in his study they discovered an "optical box" and prints for viewing with this device.[5]

Pierre Casamajor was another wealthy free man of color at Aquin. When he died in 1773 he left property worth nearly 134,000 livres to be divided among his large family, including a plantation with 57 slaves. His estate included silver place settings for twelve, a silver tea service, mahogany furniture, Indian cotton bed clothing, and a slave valet and cook.[6]

How did this prosperous free colored class emerge in a colony best known for its enormous sugar plantations and massive slave population? One explanation links the wealth of Saint-Domingue's free people of color on the eve of the French and Haitian Revolutions to the dramatic increase in coffee exports from the colony in the second half of the eighteenth century.[7] Due in part to social and economic changes in Europe, the value of coffee exports rose to rival that of sugar from 1767 to 1789. According to this explanation, profits from coffee provided a "definitive impetus" for the socially mar-

---

[3] Archives Nationales de France [hereafter cited as AN], Minutier Centrale, 30 August 1790, Rouen register 99, vente. In 1780 a French day laborer could expect to earn, at most, one livre a day; 10,000 livres would be a comfortable annual income in provincial France. See Robert Forster, *Merchants, Landlords, Magistrates: The Depont Family in Eighteenth-Century France* (Baltimore, 1980), p. 234.

[4] Archives Nationales de France, Section Outremer [hereafter cited as ANSOM], 5 April 1785, Paillou reg. 1452, dépôt des papiers, Aquin. For more on Raimond, see John D. Garrigus, "Julien Raimond," in *Brown Power in the Caribbean*, Gad Heuman and David Barry Gaspar, eds. (forthcoming).

[5] ANSOM, 15 October 1783, Paillou reg. 1451, inventaire, Aquin.

[6] ANSOM, 29 April 1773, Belin Duressort reg. 105, inventaire, Aquin.

[7] Michel-Rolph Trouillot, "Motion in the System: Coffee, Color, and Slavery in Eighteenth-Century Saint-Domingue," *Review*, 5 (1982), 331-88.

TABLE 1

POPULATION OF SAINT-DOMINGUE ACCORDING TO GENERAL CENSUSES[8]

Census Year	Whites	Free Coloreds	Slaves	Total
1713	5,689	1,189	24,156	31,034
1740	11,540	2,525	108,854	120,394
1754	14,258	4,861	172,548	191,667
1771	18,418	6,180	219,698	244,296
1775	20,438	5,897	261,471	287,806
1780	20,543	10,427	251,806	282,776
1786	25,000	15,000	340,000	380,000
1788	30,826	27,548	465,429	523,803

ginal free people of color, relegated to hitherto unprofitable hillside farms. Coffee earnings from such properties increased the wealth and the size of Saint-Domingue's free population of color, thereby straining definitions of this class that stressed its subordination to white colonists. The coffee "boom" therefore helped prepare these people of African descent for the Haitian Revolution, which by 1804 had rejected not only racial slavery but French colonial rule as well.[9]

There is much to substantiate this thesis. The rise of coffee exports from the late 1760s does coincide with substantial increases in Saint-Domingue's free colored population as measured by general colonial censuses. The late 1760s and early 1770s also witnessed the introduction of colonial legislation restricting the economic and social mobility of free coloreds vis-à-vis whites. And coffee planters did play a significant role in the Revolution at Saint-Domingue. The coffee planter Vincent Ogé launched an abortive but important free colored revolt in 1790 and Toussaint Louverture, the black general of Saint-Domingue's slave armies after 1793, has recently been revealed to have been a free man and coffee planter before the slave upris-ing.[10] Perhaps the most appealing aspect of this thesis is that it asserts the connections between economic change in Europe, at the "center" of the

[8] Ibid., pp. 354, 358-60.
[9] ANSOM, G^{1}509, N°s 12, 21, 28, 30, 31, 32, 36, and 38.
[10] Gabriel Debien, Jean Fouchard, and Marie-Antoinette Menier, "Toussaint Louverture avant 1789: Legendes et réalités," Conjonction, 134 (1977), 66-80; David P. Geggus, "Toussaint Louverture and the Slaves of the Bréda Plantations," The Journal of Caribbean History, 20 (1985-86), 31-35. For a detailed analysis of the growth of discriminatory legislation in Saint-Domingue, see Yvan Debbasch, Couleur et liberté: Le jeu du critère ethnique dans un ordre juridique esclavagiste (Paris, 1967).

236   BLUE AND BROWN

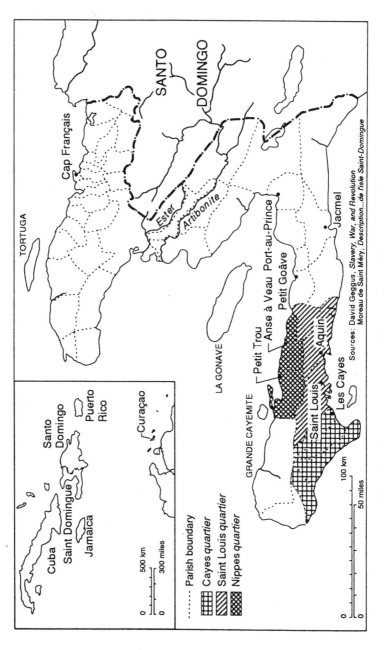

MAP 1. THE *QUARTIERS* OF CAYES, SAINT LOUIS, AND NIPPES

Atlantic trade system, and social and political change in Saint-Domingue, on the "periphery" of that system. The rise of a new commodity, increasingly consumed by Europeans of the middle and laboring classes, "operated to loosen France's grip" on the Caribbean island that produced this product. At least a decade before the great slave revolt on Saint-Domingue's sugar plantations, the rise of coffee estates on the geographic–and social–margins of France's most lucrative colony undermined colonial racism and weakened imperial control.[11]

Yet, as this paper will demonstrate, the wealth of Saint-Domingue's most vocal free colored planters, Julien Raimond and his neighbors in Aquin parish, was not based on coffee, but on another crop–indigo.[12] Throughout the eighteenth century indigo brought an international smuggling network to Saint-Domingue's southern coast. Although coffee may have increased the value of free colored property at the end of the eighteenth century, at Aquin members of this class overcame their geographical and social marginality by growing indigo and taking part in an illegal but lucrative commerce. In this parish along Saint-Domingue's southern coast [see Map 1] the first generation of a prosperous free colored class was already in place by 1760, and its members were probably described as "white" in official census reports. Succeeding generations in this part of the colony relied on astute investments and far-flung kin networks to forge an even greater wealth by the 1780s. Regardless of reports of a late eighteenth-century boom in coffee and in the free population of color, Saint-Domingue's most prominent free families of color traced their European and African ancestors in the colony, and the roots of their prosperity, back to the early 1700s. Aquin and the surrounding parishes were not demonstrably "typical," but social and economic developments there suggest the powerful influence of the Atlantic world on French Saint-Domingue.

* * *

The territory the French called Saint-Domingue in the eighteenth century was aptly renamed Haiti or "land of mountains." The name is especially appropriate along Haiti's southern peninsula, whose mountains are the highest in the Caribbean.[13] Forbidding terrain was but one reason this region was

---

[11] Trouillot, "Motion in the System," pp. 332-33.

[12] Trouillot acknowledges that Aquin does not fit his thesis. *Ibid.*, p. 355 n.58.

[13] Paul Moral, *Le paysan haïtien: étude sur la vie rurale en Haïti* (Port au Prince, 1978), pp. 73, 78, 87, 92, 111.

238   BLUE AND BROWN

the last to be fully settled by the French. Isolation from Atlantic shipping lanes shut the southern coast off from the metropolitan commerce that nurtured plantations and settlements elsewhere in the colony. Without a steady supply of African slaves or a reliable flow of trade with the mother country, the southern peninsula remained economically undeveloped in comparison with the wealthy plantation districts and bustling ports of Cap Français and Port-au-Prince.[14]

According to official export statistics, sugar and coffee were by far Saint-Domingue's two most important products. In 1765 they comprised over 95 percent of the colony's commodity exports to France by weight. In 1788 the total tonnage of all exports had more than doubled while that of coffee had increased nearly six times; together sugar and coffee accounted for nearly 97 percent of the total.[15] None of the other export crops listed in these statistics–cotton, indigo, and cacao–has received the attention given to sugar and coffee in accounts of Saint-Domingue's plantation economy. Of these three only cotton exports grew from 1765 to 1788, nearly tripling in total official shipping weight. French West Indian growers were an important supplier of Britain's early textile industry, and by the 1780s dozens of ships ferried Saint-Domingue cotton to London and Liverpool. Even so it remained less than three percent of the colony's official exports by weight.[16] Indigo occupied an even smaller share in these exports.

Such sources have led historians of Saint-Domingue to describe indigo as a transitional crop.[17] When the colony was first settled by the French in the mid-seventeenth century, tobacco was its primary export, but a severe drop in prices forced many colonists to adopt alternative cultures after 1680. Smaller landowners and those who could not afford additional labor or installations turned to cotton and cacao, which could be grown with a minimum of investment. But as one colonist complained in 1690, "only rich planters can make a living, since they have the means to grow indigo." This

---

[14] Among the many contemporaries who noted this fact, see the "Observations" of Count Dautichamp, dated 1782, in AN, Col. F³190, pp. 97-99.

[15] Jean Tarrade, *Le commerce colonial de la France à la fin de l'Ancien Régime*, 2 vols. (Paris, 1972), I, p. 34.

[16] Seymour Drescher, *Econocide: British Slavery in the Era of Abolition* (Pittsburgh, 1977), p. 57 table 12; Paul Butel, "L'essor antillais au XVIIIᵉ siècle," in *Histoire des Antilles et de la Guyane*, Pierre Pluchon, ed. (Toulouse, 1982), pp. 117-18.

[17] See, for example, Butel, "L'essor antillais," p. 117; or Gabriel Debien, *Le plan et les débuts d'une caféière à Saint-Domingue: La Plantation la Merveillere* (Port-au-Prince, 1943), p. 10. Even Père Labat, visiting the southern coast in 1701, lumped indigo with tobacco as a crop that helped planters acquire the wealth to build sugar works. Jean-Baptiste Labat, *Nouveau voyage aux isles de l'Amérique*, 8 vols. [repr.; Fort-de-France, Martinique, 1972 (Paris, 1742)], VII, pp. 91-92.

delicate low-growing plant required intensive labor, at least two workers per *carreau* (2.8 acres) to plant, weed, and harvest. According to Père Labat, who visited the southern coast in 1701, "The ground where one wants to plant the indigo seed is hoed and cleaned five times. . . . Sometimes cleanliness is taken so far that the ground is swept as one would sweep a room." Once harvested the indigo grass was soaked and drained in a series of large masonry basins and stirred to increase its exposure to oxygen. The resulting precipitate was packed into small canvas sacks to dry. Despite its expense relative to tobacco, by 1713 over a thousand indigo works were reported in the colony, making the dye Saint-Domingue's leading export product.[18]

Yet, like tobacco, indigo's market price dropped as supplies increased. Colonial officials complained that dye prices had fallen 40 percent with Saint-Domingue's entry into production, and in 1698 some planters were already experimenting with sugar, which now dominated the economies of older French colonies like Martinique and Guadeloupe.[19] Throughout the late eighteenth century, indigo was apparently in both absolute and relative decline in Saint-Domingue, its official export tonnage falling by more than half from 1765 to 1788 while that of other crops doubled. By 1788 its share of the colony's official commodity exports by weight had dropped from 2 percent to 0.39 percent. From the perspective of many French merchants after 1765 "indigo gradually became of secondary importance in colonial trade."[20] Closer examination of the southern peninsula, however, proves how misleading such a statement is for this region, at least.

While disadvantaged by its location *vis-à-vis* France, Saint-Domingue's southern coast was within easy reach of the Central American isthmus and the eastern Caribbean. The peninsula was an ideal site for smuggling into Spain's mainland colonies and the first official French attempt at colonization there was undertaken for precisely that reason. In 1699 a royal company was given exclusive rights over the southern coast, where it hoped to build a contraband center to penetrate Spanish America. In 1720 the company collapsed. Not only did English and Dutch interlopers surpass the French in dealings with the Spanish, but they smuggled goods in and out of the

---

[18] Jacob Price, *France and the Chesapeake* (Ann Arbor, MI, 1973), pp. 74-91; AN, Col. F³133, pp. 275-77; AN, Col. C⁹ᴮ18; Labat, *Nouveau voyage*, IV, pp. 4, 141, 144; letter of October 6, 1690, cited in Charles Frostin, *Les révoltes blanches à Saint-Domingue aux XVII et XVIIIᵉ siècles* (Paris, 1975), pp. 125-26; Rita J. Adrosko, *Natural Dyes and Home Dyeing* (New York, 1971), pp. 15-17.

[19] Price, *France and the Chesapeake*, p. 99.

[20] John G. Clark, *La Rochelle and the Atlantic Economy During the Eighteenth Century* (Baltimore, 1981), pp. 163-64.

company's own lands. The region was now opened to settlement like the rest of the colony, although direct trade with France was only re-established in 1740, according to some contemporaries.[21]

Much of the scholarship on the southern peninsula stresses its commercial salvation through the rising fortunes of coffee after 1760. Indeed by the middle of the nineteenth century the region was the coffee-growing capital of independent Haiti.[22] At the same time, general census totals for Saint-Domingue suggest that the number of indigo plantations peaked in 1739, while the cultivation of sugar and coffee was just beginning to expand.[23] But when general census figures for indigo, sugar, coffee, and cotton in the three *quartiers* of Cayes, Saint Louis, and Nippes are graphed as a percentage of the totals reported for Saint-Domingue, a different picture emerges of the relation between indigo and coffee in the southern peninsula. While registering an increasing share of the colony's indigo works, Cayes, Nippes, and Saint Louis clearly lagged behind the colony as a whole in coffee production [see Charts 1-4].

This is corroborated by a document entitled "Increase and Decrease in the Population of Cayes . . . from 1750 to and including 1787" [see Chart 5]. Cayes, west of Aquin, was by far the southern peninsula's leading plantation district, but this contemporary analysis of the plantations there over a thirty-year period suggests that not even coffee, cotton, or sugar could match the expansion of indigo. Why then the sharp decline in Saint-Domingue's official indigo exports?

Elsewhere in the Caribbean basin during this period indigo production was rising, not falling. Guatemala had produced the first New World indigo for export in the sixteenth century and this trade continued strongly through the end of the eighteenth century with many small farmers switching to indigo from beans, rice, or corn. An increasing demand for dyes in Europe

---

[21] Hilliard d'Auberteuil, *Considerations sur l'état présent de la colonie française de Saint-Domingue, ouvrage politique et législatif*, 2 vols. (Paris, 1776), I, pp. 58, 67, 279, 281-83; Moreau de Saint Méry, *Description topographique, physique . . . de la partie française de l'isle de Saint-Domingue* [repr.; Paris, 1959 (Philadelphia, 1797)], pp. 1167-69, 1241-42, 1300-01; Pierre de Vassière, *Saint-Domingue (1629-1789): La société et la vie créoles sous l'ancien régime* (Paris, 1909), p. 40; Charles Frostin, *Les révoltes blanches à Saint Domingue* (Paris, 1975), pp. 274-76; Charles Frostin, "Les Pontchartrain et la pénétration commerciale française en Amérique espagnole," *Revue Historique*, 245 (1971), 314.

[22] Paul Moral, "La culture du café en Haïti: Des plantations coloniales aux 'jardins' actuels," *Les cahiers d'outre-mer*, 8 (1955), 252.

[23] It is difficult to compare the crops directly, because until the middle of the century the census counted coffee bushes, while measuring indigo and sugar by the number of refineries constructed for these products. ANSOM, $G^1 509$ N°s 12, 21, 28, 30, 31, and 32.

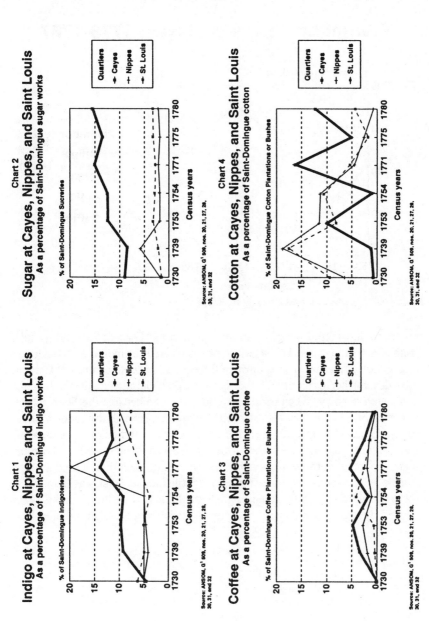

Chart 1

Indigo at Cayes, Nippes, and Saint Louis
As a percentage of Saint-Domingue indigo works

Source: ANSOM, G¹ 509, nos. 20, 21, 27, 28, 30, 31, and 32

Chart 2

Sugar at Cayes, Nippes, and Saint Louis
As a percentage of Saint-Domingue sugar works

Source: ANSOM, G¹ 509, nos. 20, 21, 27, 28, 30, 31, and 32

Chart 3

Coffee at Cayes, Nippes, and Saint Louis
As a percentage of Saint-Domingue coffee

Source: ANSOM, G¹ 509, nos. 20, 21, 27, 28, 30, 31, and 32

Chart 4

Cotton at Cayes, Nippes, and Saint Louis
As a percentage of Saint-Domingue cotton

Source: ANSOM, G¹ 509, nos. 20, 21, 27, 28, 30, 31, and 32

242   BLUE AND BROWN

Chart 5
Plantation Crops at Cayes, 1753-1787

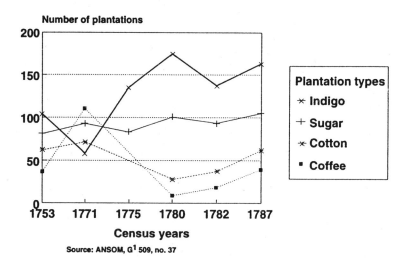

Source: ANSOM, G¹ 509, no. 37

produced substantial increases in official prices at Guatemala's indigo fairs from 1760 through the 1770s, while prices offered for indigo at Amsterdam rose steadily from the 1680s through the early nineteenth century.[24] Caracas provides further evidence of the dye's market viability at the end of the eighteenth century, when newly introduced indigo became the Spanish colony's second major export crop, and one grown primarily by modest planters on rented land. Indeed, French price series show indigo prices increasing 150 percent from 1749 to 1790 while coffee values increased by no more than 30 percent in the same period.[25] About half of the indigo traded through France was re-exported, since the same textile industry that was demanding more and more cotton from the English and French West Indies in the 1780s needed dyestuffs that came mostly from French and Spanish colonies.[26]

[24] Robert S. Smith, "Indigo Production and Trade in Colonial Guatemala," *Hispanic American Historical Review*, 39 (1959), 182, 197, 198, 201, 205; Troy S. Floyd, "The Guatemala Merchants, the Government and the *Provincianos*, 1750-1800," *Hispanic American Historical Review*, 41 (1961), 105.

[25] Smith, "Indigo Production and Trade in Colonial Guatemala," p. 203; P. Michael McKinley, *Pre-Revolutionary Caracas: Politics, Economy, and Society, 1777-1811* (Cambridge, 1985), pp. 48, 52; Jean Tarrade, *Commerce colonial*, II, pp. 771-72 Table 12.

[26] "Between 80 and 90 percent of indigo receipts at La Rochelle entered the entrepôt for reexport to foreigners," Clark, *La Rochelle and the Atlantic Economy*, p. 163. Tarrade claims that between 40 and 65 percent of French indigo was reexported, *Commerce colonial*, II, p. 753 Table 7; Smith, "Indigo Production and Trade," p. 209 n.91.

If coffee had marked advantages over sugar as a crop, indigo offered as many or more. Like coffee it did not require large numbers of slaves to be grown profitably. An official report before a notary in the Nippes *quartier* in January 1774 estimated that in a single year an adult slave on a fully equipped plantation could produce 40 pounds of indigo worth 1,000 livres, or roughly one-half that slave's purchase price. Roseline Siguret's study of indigo and coffee plantations in the southern peninsula from 1757 to 1791 found two indigo plantations with over 100 slaves but others had as few as 35. While irrigation was necessary to grow sugar cane in many regions, indigo grew best in the dry and sandy conditions found in the southern peninsula.[27]

As price information reveals, indigo was in high demand not only early but also late in the eighteenth century. It was exceptionally easy to store and transport, a valuable characteristic in a region where French traders called so intermittently. During the many wartime blockades of Saint-Domingue, as shipping prices reached record heights, indigo, of all the plantation goods, was in greatest demand, even before refined white sugar. Cotton was third in order of desirability, then coffee, and finally brown sugar. Unlike coffee, moreover, indigo was not a new crop with a five to seven year start-up time, but one that had been cultivated for at least two generations in the southern peninsula. The most daunting aspect of indigo planting was the complex process of refining the dye, and until the 1770s such knowledge was only available through long apprenticeship. By the end of the eighteenth century, sizeable indigo planters were investing more and more in animal-driven machines and other technical improvements on their estates and new "scientific" methods of indigo manufacture were being published. At the same time, colonial officials and planters were working secretly to bring cochineal, another highly profitable dye originally produced in Spanish America, to Saint-Domingue.[28]

Strong foreign demand, declining official export statistics, and exceptional ease of transport all suggest that the indigo grown on the southern peninsula entered the European market through illegal channels. Indeed,

---

[27] AN, Col. F³133, p. 188; the assumed market price of indigo in this estimation was 12 and one half livres per pound. See Roseline Siguret, "Esclaves d'indigoteries et de caféières au quartier de Jacmel (1757-1791)," *Revue française d'histoire d'outre-mer*, 55 (1968), 193, 201. On the soil, water, and equipment necessary for indigo growing, see the article on "indigo" in the 1777 *Supplément à l'Encyclopédie*, 21 vols. [repr.; Stuttgart-Bad Cannstatt, 1966-67 (Amsterdam, 1776)], XX, pp. 585-92.

[28] Richard Pares, *War and Trade in the West Indies, 1739-63* (London, 1963), p. 330; "Indigo," *Supplément à l'Encyclopédie*, XX, p. 585; James E. McClellan III, *Colonialism and Science: Saint Domingue in the Old Regime* (Baltimore, 1992), pp. 67, 152-58.

from the very beginning of French settlement this coast had been part of an Atlantic smuggling system. It may be true that one of the major effects of coffee planting in Saint-Domingue was to suggest "the possibility and the rewards of trading permanently outside of French control."[29] However, it was indigo, from the earliest days of formal colonization in the southern peninsula down to the century's end, that was most closely identified with international contraband. In 1732 there was so much contraband in the south that the colonial minister approved the suggestion of Saint-Domingue's governor that either the main harbor on the Ile à Vaches opposite the town of Cayes be filled or its fresh water source diverted into the sea to discourage smugglers based there.[30] Neither of these projects was ever undertaken and Cayes continued to be a major interlope center while Versailles closed at least one eye to this traffic.

Colonial administrators were indecisive in enforcing the national trade monopoly because they were charged both with protecting French commerce from foreign competition and encouraging the growth of colonial agriculture, which clamored for more slaves and cheaper supplies than France could provide. This was especially true in the south, where in 1786 the colonial governor observed that "several [officials] are reluctant to patrol against these smugglers and declare that they cannot help prevent a commerce that sustains and enriches that region."[31] One indication of the volume of contraband traffic along the southern coast comes during times of war, when neutral ships were authorized to supply the colony with food. During the American Revolution, the price of a barrel of flour at the main colonial port of Cap Français, in the north, rose to 180 livres in 1779 from a peacetime price of 60 to 70 livres. On the other side of the colony, however, Dutch merchants from Curaçao brought so much wheat to Cayes that the price of a barrel there was only 66 livres. During the Seven Years' War, Dutch traders kept the price of wheat at Cayes down to 50 livres a barrel in 1760 and 1761.[32]

This Dutch traffic was an important part of commerce along the southern coast. Even during blockades French officials voiced their exasperation with Curaçao merchants who arrived at Saint Louis, not to trade provisions for local brown sugar and coffee as administrators had hoped, but to exchange

[29] Trouillot, "Motion in the System," p. 370.

[30] Léon Vignols, "Land Appropriation in Haiti in the Seventeenth and Eighteenth Centuries," *Journal of Economic and Business History*, 2 (1930), 121.

[31] Tarrade, *Commerce colonial*, II, p. 599 n.31.

[32] Charles Frostin, "Saint-Domingue et la révolution américain," *Bulletin de la société d'histoire de la Guadeloupe*, 22 (1974), 99-101; Pares, *War and Trade*, p. 388.

cloth for indigo.[33] Curaçao's location and its convenient Dutch neutrality gave it easy access to the southern coast of Saint-Domingue, but the products available there, especially the indigo, were so tempting for merchants that even the English were unable to restrain from trade.

In the Seven Years' War English traders profited from the exchange of prisoners with the French to load their ships with products from Saint-Domingue, and indigo was the most popular of these. Jamaica's laws against prejudicial wartime trade only stated that merchants were not to ferry back anything "contrary to the interests of Jamaica," and a merchant defending himself before a British judge against charges of smuggling claimed that "indigo has always been admitted to an entry and that it is notorious that it is not produced in quantities sufficient to supply our manufactures." He went on to claim, with substantiation from Jamaica's receiver general, that over 2,000 livres in duties on French indigo had been collected in the colony in one year of the war.[34]

Evidence of this Jamaican indigo trade with the southern coast exists from the 1740s through the end of the century. According to Richard Pares, "it was likely true" that England's Admiral Knowles attacked and conquered the fort at Saint Louis in 1748 in order to load his warships with French indigo destined for England. Others who proposed wartime raids to destroy French West Indian plantations cited the encouragement of Jamaican indigo cultivation as a positive result of such attacks, suggesting that the commerce in dye from Saint-Domingue was so extensive that Jamaicans had no reason to grow their own. According to the 1758 *Histoire et commerce des Antilles anglaises*, nearly all the indigo that left Jamaica was grown in the French or Spanish colonies.[35] When the British opened four free ports in Jamaica in 1768, they forbade the importation of coffee, sugars, molasses, ginger, and pimento, but said nothing about indigo or cotton.[36] Several decades later colonial writers like Hilliard d'Auberteuil and Venault de Charmilly claimed that two-thirds of the south's indigo production and a higher share of its cotton went illegally to Jamaica, where merchants would pay twenty percent more than French traders. Jamaica was also favored because planters there could exchange their indigo and cotton for slaves. Slave inventories drafted in the 1790s confirm that the English were the source of as many as one-half of the slaves in some parts of the southern peninsula.[37]

[33] Pares, *War and Trade*, p. 383.

[34] *Ibid.*, pp. 357, 417-19.

[35] *Ibid.*, pp. 183, 180, 417 n.3.

[36] Tarrade, *Commerce colonial*, I, p. 298.

[37] Hilliard d'Auberteuil, *Considérations*, I, pp. 58, 279, 281-83; Charles Frostin, *Les révoltes blanches à Saint Domingue* (Paris, 1975), pp. 274-76; B.R. Mitchell and Phyllis Deane, *Abstract of*

246   BLUE AND BROWN

Examples of this illegal international commerce can be found in the contract registers kept by royal notaries who worked along the southern coast, especially at Aquin, in the Saint Louis *quartier*. In May 1780, for example, Jacob Abraham, a merchant peddler (*marchand pacotilleur*) from Curaçao, drafted an affidavit concerning the loss of a note for 310 pounds of indigo given him by a local merchant.[38] In September of that year, Nicholas Danisy, a Dutch captain who normally lived at Curaçao, drafted a public statement at Aquin where he was "in recovery." He asked his debtors to come to his store at the Aquin pier to settle their affairs before his departure for Curaçao. The following July, Danisy was again at Aquin, this time identified as a "former Dutch captain, presently a merchant living at the Aquin pier."[39] The traffic between Curaçao and Aquin also operated in the other direction. In 1767 the widow of a royal notary drafted a blank power of attorney to collect debts owed her in Curaçao where she held one-quarter interest in a ship.[40]

Family and religious contacts were an important ingredient in this illegal trade.[41] In 1784 David Orobio Furtado of Montego Bay, Jamaica, one of the free ports in that island, visited Aquin to collect 6,823 livres in specie that David Henriques had recovered there for him. Four years later Orobio Fourtado [sic] was again at Aquin to give the merchants David Henriques and his brother Jacob power of attorney "to administer all the commerce and other business" he might have in Saint-Domingue.[42] With the Henriques, Orobio Furtado had chosen a Sephardic Jewish family–like his own, presumably–long involved in commerce between France, Jamaica, Barbados, London, Spain, Portugal, and Curaçao.[43] In 1783 David and Jacob Hen-

---

British Historical Statistics (Cambridge, 1962), pp. 285-90, does not list the value of dyestuffs imported into Great Britain until 1805; David P. Geggus, *Slavery, War and Revolution: The British Occupation of Saint-Domingue, 1793-1798* (Oxford, 1982), p. 80 n.12; Geggus, "The Slaves of British-Occupied Saint Domingue: An Analysis of the Workforces of 197 Absentee Plantations, 1796-1797," *Caribbean Studies*, 18 (1978), 19.

[38] ANSOM, 10 March 1780, Monneront reg. 1403, déclaration, Aquin.

[39] ANSOM, 16 September 1780, Monneront reg. 1403, déclaration de depart, Aquin; ANSOM, 31 July 1781, Monneront reg. 1403, vente, Aquin.

[40] ANSOM, 7 July 1787, Belin Duressort reg. 102, procuration, Aquin.

[41] Zvi Loker, "Were There Jewish Communities in Saint-Domingue [Haiti]?," *Jewish Social Studies*, 45 (1983), 135-46.

[42] This could easily have been indigo; the Londoner Isaac Miranda and his Jamaican affiliate John da Costa "were accused of smuggling fifty-two casks of indigo from the French," a cargo worth over 8,800; Stephen Fortune, *Merchants and Jews: The Struggle for British West Indian Commerce, 1650-1750* (Gainesville, FL, 1984), p. 150. ANSOM, 13 October 1784, Monneront reg. 1406, quittance, Aquin; ANSOM, 30 June 1788, Monneront reg. 1414, procuration, Aquin.

[43] According to Fortune, *Merchants and Jews*, p. 34, Jacob Josua Bueno Henriques of Bayonne France had approached the English Crown about opening gold mines in newly conquered Jamaica, at the

riques had formally dissolved a partnership made the previous year at Cap Français with Moises Nunes Moreau to share a boat worth 21,000 livres.[44] Two years later they began the purchase of a sizeable estate at Aquin, buying up the debts of its deceased owner. They signed contracts with masons to tear down the sugar refinery and install an indigo works, including slave huts, a drying shack, an animal-powered machine to draw water for indigo distillation, and another device to stir their indigo basins. At the same time, in 1787, they entered a nine-year partnership with another planter to grow coffee.[45]

* * *

The profitability of the international trade in indigo was closely connected to the rise of a prosperous free colored planting class along the southern coast of Saint-Domingue, especially in the Aquin parish.

Because of its location on Saint-Domingue's economic as well as geographical periphery, the southern peninsula became home to free men and women of African descent early on. In 1702, for example, before the region had been officially opened for settlement, a damp hollow between the Saint Louis and Nippes *quartiers* sheltered a thriving population of free colored cocoa farmers, after whom the spot was named Fond des Nègres.[46] Whether they were former slaves freed for military service against raiding buccaneers or men and women fleeing bondage, these settlers were attracted to the area for its isolation from the rapidly expanding slave plantation economy. When a wave of new European colonists, largely unmarried men, entered the region after 1720, a number of them entered alliances with families of color that were already established there.

same time requesting naturalization for himself and two brothers; Peter Henriques of London in 1688 brought Spanish cocoa into that city by way of Curaçao and Amsterdam, see *Ibid*., pp. 94-95; in 1699 a Philip Henriques was arrested on his way from Jamaica to Cartagena with a cargo of 115 slaves; a Philip Henriques and his brother David Henriques, Sr., lost 17,000 to Spanish privateers when four of their ships were taken in 1703 and 1704, *Ibid*., p. 150.

[44] ANSOM, 7 April 1783, Belin Duressort reg. 108, resilation de société, Aquin.

[45] ANSOM, 12 August 1785, Monneront reg. 1409, vente, Aquin; ANSOM, 8 October 1785, Monneront reg. 1409, transport de créance, Aquin; ANSOM, 24 May 1786, Monneront reg. 1410, depôt, Aquin; ANSOM, 22 June 1786, Monneront reg. 1410, dépôt, Aquin; ANSOM, 10 March 1787, Monneront reg. 1412, marché, Aquin; ANSOM, 23 March 1786, Monneront reg. 1410, marché, Aquin; ANSOM, 1 May, 1786, Monneront reg. 1410, marché, Aquin; ANSOM, 8 November 1787, Monneront reg. 1410, société, Aquin.

[46] Labat, *Nouveau voyage*, VII, pp. 114-15 wrote after his 1701 visit, "These people are extremely fertile . . . . they raise their children with amazing ease." Moreau de Saint Méry, *Description*, pp. 1197-98.

248   BLUE AND BROWN

Pierre Raymond, for example, was a Frenchman who arrived in Saint-Domingue's southern peninsula early in the eighteenth century. In 1726 he married Marie Begasse, a legitimately born free *mulâtresse* whose white father was already a planter in the region. Marie, who could sign her name, brought a dowry of at least 6,000 livres to this union; Pierre, on the other hand, could not sign his name and his financial contribution to the household, if there was one, was not recorded.[47] Marie Begasse's sister also married a French immigrant, a surgeon from Languedoc. Within twenty years, with the help of their slaves, Pierre and Marie Begasse Raymond had built a plantation with a handsome six room house in her native Bainet parish. In the 1750s, however, Bainet suffered increasingly from drought, so the couple transferred their large family along with their slaves to a dilapidated farm in nearby Aquin parish. Although Pierre Raymond was at least 50 years old when the family relocated, the Raymonds had transformed their new home into a valuable estate within another twenty years. At his death in 1772 at the age of 80, Pierre Raymond owned 115 slaves and an indigo plantation with nine major buildings, thirty-five slave cabins, and an expensively furnished residence.[48]

Pierre and Marie Begasse Raymond raised ten children to adulthood, almost all of whom signed their names with a practiced hand. At least two of their five daughters attended convent schools in France and married propertied Frenchmen, one at Bordeaux and the other at Toulouse. A daughter who died unmarried in 1773 left a plantation with thirty-eight slaves, eleven of whom had been gifts from her parents, "wanting to give her the same advantages they had given to their other children."[49]

The five Raimond[50] sons also received parental dowries and/or inheritance portions and began their adult careers managing their father's indigo works, animal pens, and provision grounds. As the Raimonds grew older they followed their father's strategy of buying and rebuilding abandoned properties, often in fraternal partnership. Within six years François and Jean-Baptiste Raimond quadrupled the value of an indigo plantation they

[47] Luc Nemours, "Julien Raimond, le chef des gens de couleur et sa famille," *Annales historique de la révolution française*, 23 (1951), 257.

[48] ANSOM, 17 December 1756, Delinois reg. 478, vente, Saint Louis; Moreau de Saint Méry, Description, 1154, 1238; ANSOM, 1 July 1772, Belin Duressort reg. 1056, inventaire, Aquin.

[49] ANSOM, 19 August 1761, Daudin de Belair reg. 429, donation, Aquin.

[50] Free colored children of white men often spelled their names differently from their fathers, especially after a 1773 law prohibited such persons from using "white" names and ordered them to adopt names of African origin. Pierre Raymond's children used both the spellings of the family name, though "Raimond" was used most frequently. Yvan Debbasch, *Couleur et liberté: Le jeu du critère ethnique dans un ordre esclavagiste* (Paris, 1967), p. 69.

worked together. In 1770 their brother Julien joined this partnership, but three years later he bought an indigo estate of his own nearby. In part by selling property his father had left him, Julien was able to acquire for the significant sum of 75,000 livres a fertile but neglected plantation described as "in total ruin." His younger brother Guillaume joined in this project, lending his slaves and skills to rebuilding the estate. After eight years he received 18,370 livres from Julien in compensation for his efforts. By the 1780s, with the plantation well-established, Julien Raimond hired an artisan to construct an elaborate machine to draw well water for his soaking basins and subscribed 200 livres for the publication of new information about the distillation of indigo dye.[51] In 1782, with a personal wealth estimated by his friends at 202,000 livres, Raimond married the wealthy free mulatto daughter of one of his father's white neighbors. His bride, Françoise Dasmard Challe, was the widow of a French immigrant and she brought a dowry of over 80,000 livres.[52]

Although most children of color, unlike the Raimonds, were born out of wedlock, many of those who became successful planters began with assistance from a white father. Jean Labadie, for example, a white planter at Aquin, made careful arrangements to insure that his five mulatto sons, all illegitimate, would inherit his slaves. In 1761 he formally deeded 24 African workers worth 15,000 livres to his oldest son Guillaume. The senior Labadie died the following year, naming white planters with free colored children of their own as executors of his estate. These men conveyed Labadie's property to his mulatto sons.[53]

Yet such an inheritance did not guarantee future prosperity. In 1791 Julien Raimond, writing in Paris, cited Guillaume Labadie as an example of the wealth and intelligence of Saint-Domingue's free colored planters, emphasizing how this eldest son had transformed his share of the patrimony: "Today Labadie has 150 slaves belonging to him alone and much money

[51] ANSOM, 22 September 1764, Daudin de Belair reg. 431, vente, Aquin; ANSOM, 20 August 1773, Belin Duressort reg. 106, vente, Aquin; ANSOM, 10 July 1769, Belin Duressort reg. 103, vente, Aquin; ANSOM, 1 January 1775, Sibire de Morville reg. 1583, vente, Aquin; ANSOM, 14 December 1774, Belin Duressort reg. 106, déclaration, Aquin; ANSOM, 15 October 1781, Monneront reg. 1403, affranchissement, Aquin; ANSOM, 22 February 1781, Monneront reg. 1403, dissolution, Aquin; ANSOM, 5 April 1785, Paillou reg. 1452, dépôt des papiers, Aquin; ANSOM, 13 October 1781, Monneront reg. 1403, marché, Aquin.

[52] ANSOM, 10 February 1782, Monneront reg. 1404, mariage, Aquin.

[53] ANSOM, 9 August 1760, Casamajor reg. 360, testament, Aquin; ANSOM, 18 August 1761, Daudin de Belair reg. 429, donation entre vifs, Aquin; ANSOM, 18 August 1761, Daudin de Belair reg. 429, donation entre vifs, Aquin; ANSOM, 25 February 1762, Daudin de Belair reg. 430, testament, Aquin.

[*argent comptant*], as well as his plantation. . . . If Labadie's surviving brothers are not as wealthy as he is, it is because they are still stubbornly cultivating those inferior lands [left them by their father]."[54] A drought had forced Guillaume to abandon his father's lands and build his own indigo works on another Aquin plantation he purchased in 1764 for 25,000 livres.[55]

Julien Raimond and Guillaume Labadie were builders and risk-takers, but their fathers' wealth and planting experience were clearly important to their own success in the delicate business of growing and distilling indigo. Family connections were equally important in colonial trade and access to such trans-Atlantic kin networks was another key to the prosperity of Aquin's free families of color. Although he worked with his brothers and married locally, Julien Raimond inhabited a world whose boundaries were much wider than those of the Aquin parish. When an inventory of his commercial papers was deposited with a notary in 1785, 40 percent of these documents [60 of 159] included overseas transactions.[56] Of these, two-thirds were receipts issued by captains from France's main colonial port of Bordeaux, where at least one of his sisters had married and settled. Although Raimond did deal with other French ports, none of them was as prominent among his receipts as the Dutch entrepôt at Curaçao, in the eastern Caribbean. Curaçao played an even greater role in the careers of Aquin's other prosperous free colored planters, as the family history of Michel Depas-Medina illustrates.

When the southern coast opened to colonization in the 1720, Michel Lopez Depas was the royal physician at Saint-Domingue's early capital of Petit Goâve [see Map 1], where he also served on the ruling Superior Council. Although he converted to Christianity in Saint-Domingue, Lopez Depas was born a Jew of Sephardic descent at Bordeaux, where Lopès-Depas [sic] was a prominent name in the Jewish merchant community. Observing Michel's success in the colony, several of his brothers followed him to Saint-Domingue and settled along its southern frontier. A second brother, François Depas, raised nine legitimate children at Aquin. Through commerce and marriage this colonial branch of the Depas clan maintained its ties to the Sephardic merchant families of Bordeaux, most notably the Gradis, who were arguably the most powerful merchants in eighteenth-

---

[54] Julien Raimond, *Observations sur l'origine et les progrès du prejugé des colons blancs contre les hommes de couleur* (Paris, 1791), pp. 31-32.

[55] ANSOM, 1 August 1765, Daudin de Belair reg. 432, donation, Aquin; ANSOM, 25 April 1761, Daudin de Belair reg. 429, vente, Aquin; ANSOM, 29 January 1764, Daudin de Belair reg. 431, Aquin, vente.

[56] ANSOM, 5 April 1785, Paillou reg. 1452, dépôt des papiers, Aquin.

JOHN GARRIGUS   251

century France.[57] They also participated in contraband trade with Curaçao, where Lopez Depas was a common name in the marriage registers of the Jewish community.[58]

In Saint-Domingue the Lopez Depas were not only merchants but planters as well. In 1763 Philippe Lopez Depas, a third brother, owned an estate at Aquin with 63 slaves valued at 200,000 livres.[59] By this time Saint-Domingue's Jewish families, especially those along the southern peninsula, had become so wealthy that the colony's governor Charles d'Estaing tried, unsuccessfully, to levy special taxes on them. Thanks to their ties with the influential Gradis house of Bordeaux, the Lopez Depas escaped d'Estaing's proposed tax on Jews. The family was also permitted to pass its colonial property to a second generation, despite official prohibitions.[60]

A free mulatto named Michel Depas was one member of this second generation. Apparently named after his uncle, the respected doctor and judge, this Michel Depas was the illegitimate son of the indigo planter Philippe Lopez Depas. The social gulf between the original Michel Lopez Depas and his free colored nephew, however, was not one that the uncle cared to breach. In 1762 none of the free colored Depas nephews and nieces were counted among the heirs to the doctor's considerable estate. The social separation of these two sides of the Depas family was further emphasized in

---

[57] Zvi Loker, "Docteur Michel Lopez De Paz: Médecin et savant de Saint-Domingue," *Revue d'histoire de la médicine hébraïque*, 33 (1980), 55-57; Moreau de Saint Méry, *Description*, pp. 1196, 1236, 1251, 1518-19; Pierre Pluchon, *Nègres et Juifs au XVIIIᵉ siècle* (S.l, 1984), p. 59; one of Michel Lopez Depas' nieces married into the Gradis family and another into the Mendès family at Bordeaux; two of François' sons became merchants, first at Aquin and then at Nippes. ANSOM, 3 June 1762, Daudin de Belair reg. 430, vente, Aquin; ANSOM, 16 January 1764, Daudin de Belair reg. 431, affranchissement, Aquin.

[58] In 1775, for example, a Sarah Lopez "dePas" of Bordeaux married into a merchant family at Curaçao. See Isaac S. and Suzanne A. Emmanuel, *History of the Jews of the Netherlands Antilles* (Cincinnati, 1970), pp. 828-30, 964-66; Pluchon, *Nègres et Juifs*, p. 109; ANSOM, 15 November 1768, Belin Duressort reg. 102, procuration, Aquin.

[59] ANSOM, 3 December 1754, Casamajor reg. 360, vente, Aquin; ANSOM, [illegible] February 1763, Daudin de Belair reg. 430, vente, Aquin; the median price for the sale of rural land in the Saint Louis *quartier* of which Aquin formed a part was 6,750 livres in the period 1760-69. The average price was 23,846 livres.

[60] Zvi Loker, *Jews in the Caribbean: Evidence on the History of the Jews in the Caribbean Zone in Colonial Times* (Jerusalem: Misgav Yerushalayim, Institute for Research on the Sephardi and Oriental Jewish Heritage, 1991), p. 230, contains a transcription of AN, Col C9A 120 "IIIème Expedition / Nottes sur les Juifs de St. Louis, et des Cayes qui ont offert par requêtes et pour être tolerés de contribuer au bien publique" by then governor Charles d'Estaing; Loker, *Jews in the Caribbean*, pp. 255, 265, reproduces documents illustrating the major role played by the Gradis in furnishing specie for royal operations in Saint-Domingue in the 1770s and 1780s; *Ibid.*, pp. 238-39, reprints documents from AN Col. E 209 and 210 describing the successful attempt of the Depas and Gradis families in 1781 to insure their inheritance of an estate at Aquin.

1777 when the mulatto Michel Depas became Michel Medina, in compliance with recent regulations against the use of "white" family names by free persons of color.[61] Notarial documents nevertheless continued to identify him as "Michel Medina called Michel Depas" or as "Depas-Medina."[62]

Although unable to use the family name, Michel Depas-Medina, like his white father, uncles, and cousins, worked within the Lopez Depas kin network. He sold his indigo to the local representative of the Gradis family, into which his white cousins had married. By 1765 he had accumulated enough wealth, and perhaps notoriety, to attract the attention of Governor d'Estaing.

> Michel Depas, troublemaker [*mauvais sujet*], against whom there are a multitude of complaints by the planters; free mulatto and bastard [*Batard*]. He owns a very sizeable plantation at the Grande Colline with 120 slaves; moreover he has another plantation at the Colline à Mangon with 30 slaves. He has rebelled several times against commands which have been given to him in the interest of good public order. This man was formerly a courtier of Mr. Gradis.[63]

Although he was not beloved by colonial officials, Michel Depas-Medina was a wealthy man. His death inventory, drafted in 1783, showed that he owned more slaves than his white father Philippe, and that his personal effects included a silver table service and other articles of leisure that marked a successful planter.[64] He was survived by at least seven sons, three of whom married in the spring and summer of 1785 as their father's estate was settled.[65]

---

[61] In July 1773 the Council of Port-au-Prince registered a ruling by the colonial governor and intendant that "To usurp the name of a white family line ['race'] could cast doubt on the status of persons, confuse the succession of estates, and eventually destroy the insurmountable barrier between whites and people of color established by public opinion and maintained by the wisdom of the government." All free people of color were henceforth to adopt "a surname drawn from the African idiom, or from their profession and color, which however can never be that of a white colonial family." Moreau de Saint-Méry, *Lois et constitutions des colonies françaises de l'Amérique sous le vent*, 6 vols. (Paris, 1785-90), V, p. 448.

[62] In 1730 the Medina family, like the Lopès Depas, had figured prominently in the community of Portuguese Jews at Bordeaux. Medina was also a prominent merchant family at Curaçao. Pluchon, *Nègres et Juifs*, p. 59; Emmanuel, *History of the Jews*, pp. 691, 695, 697, 700, 1034; ANSOM, 7 June 1762, Daudin de Belair reg. 430, dépôt d'acte privé, Aquin.

[63] Zvi Loker, *Jews in the Caribbean*, p. 230, cites AN, Col C9A, p. 120.

[64] ANSOM, 15 October 1783, Paillou reg. 1451, inventaire, Aquin.

[65] ANSOM, 10 January 1785, Paillou reg. 1452, mariage, Aquin; ANSOM, 11 April 1785, Paillou reg. 1452, mariage, Aquin; ANSOM, 7 July 1785, Paillou reg. 1452, mariage, Aquin.

Like the Frenchmen Pierre Raymond and Michel Lopez Depas, David Casamajor arrived in the southern peninsula in the 1720s as it officially opened to settlement. A royal notary and planter, Casamajor built Aquin's first pier in 1730, providing himself and his neighbors in these isolated mountains with direct access to the sea–and to smugglers from Curaçao and Jamaica. About 25 years later a royal land grant near this pier was awarded to "Pierre called Casamajor," one of at least three mulatto sons born out of wedlock to David Casamajor and the slave Marie Madeleine. For the next decade Pierre Casamajor was Aquin's public warehouse agent, charged with the safekeeping of indigo and other outgoing cargoes. Although free men of color rarely held even minor positions of public trust, Pierre Casamajor, like Julien Raimond, Guillaume Labadie, and Michel Depas-Medina, was the son of a prosperous local notable. By his death in 1773, he had expanded into planting, leaving an estate whose total value was nearly 134,000 livres, including 57 slaves and an indigo plantation to be divided among his large family.[66]

By the 1750s and 1760s the first wave of French colonists to Aquin had produced an ambitious and capable second generation whose hard work, investment, and utilization of family resources yielded considerable success. This second generation, in turn, laid the foundations for a third. In 1756 Pierre Casamajor's illegitimate daughter Marie Rose Casamajor contracted a marriage with Thomas Ploy. From her father Marie Rose received a dowry valued at 18,800 livres, including provision grounds, household furnishings, six silver place settings, and six slaves, one of them a valet. The warehouser's new son-in-law was living proof of the connections between Aquin and Curaçao, for Thomas Ploy was a mulatto, the illegitimate son of Antoine Ploy and Anne Marie, a free black woman from that Dutch trading center.[67]

At an auction in 1762, five years after his alliance with the Casamajor family, Thomas Ploy purchased an abandoned terrain and buildings adjoining his father-in-law's property at the Aquin pier.[68] He paid 2,155 livres to acquire land that had originally been valued at 12,000 livres, for, like the indigo plantation purchased by Julien Raimond in 1772, Ploy's new grounds had been severely neglected by their former owner. The main warehouse had lost its doors and windows and its straw roof had entirely rotted away, leading the notary to describe it as "uninhabitable, even irreparable."

[66] ANSOM, 29 April 1773, Belin Duressort reg. 105, inventaire, Aquin; ANSOM, 9 February 1768, Depuis de Lavau reg. 582, testament, Nippes; Moreau de Saint Méry, *Description*, pp. 1235, 1462.
[67] ANSOM, 4 June 1756, Delinois reg. 478, mariage, Saint Louis.
[68] ANSOM, 12 December 1761, Daudin de Belair reg. 429, mis en possession, Aquin.

Among the scattered debris was a dovecôte "rotten and ready to fall" and an "entirely unusable" kitchen building, with its oven "fallen totally into ruin." By 1788, however, Ploy's waterfront property had been rebuilt and revalued–at 45,000 livres.[69] He had constructed a house of squared timber and cement and this, like his two new or refurbished warehouses, was "in fairly good condition," with all doors and windows secure and a roof shingled in expensive mahogany.

Ploy's relationship with the Casamajor family was an important part of his success as a warehouser, merchant, and eventually planter. In 1773, for example, he acquired from the Casamajor estate a parcel of land adjoining his wife's dowry property.[70] Ties to the eastern Caribbean were another of Ploy's advantages, allowing him to participate in the same trade that had brought prosperity to the Casamajors and the Depas. In 1783 the family alliances connecting Curaçao and Aquin were strengthened when Ploy's daughter married Jean Louis Garsia [sic], a native of the same Curaçao parish as Ploy's own mother. The Garcia DePas family had been at Curaçao since before 1674 and was allied there with the Lopez dePas. Garsia, who was living at the Aquin pier in 1783, brought 4,000 livres in "furnishings, effects and merchandise" to the marriage. Two years earlier when Julien Raimond paid 49 livres "to the cargo of the Venissien ship La Bonne Concorde for merchandise sold and delivered by Ploy," it was Jean Louis Garsia "acting for the said Ploy" who signed the receipt.[71]

Like Julien Raimond, Thomas Ploy dealt with French merchants as well as those from Curaçao. His stores at the Aquin pier allowed him to hold shipments for captains and other traders.[72] By selling these stored goods Ploy could add a sales commission to his warehousing fee, although this practice did not always endear him to his clients. In February 1765 a white merchant down the coast at Cayes wrote to his associate at Aquin,

Monsieur,
I hope that you will render me an essential service for the twenty hogsheads of wine that Captain Fouque sends to S[ieu]r Ploy, warehouser, which are still unsold by his fault of not having warned me in time; I would have sold them to M[onsieu]r Exaudy, but the greed of this M[onsieu]r Ploy to earn a commission has ruined them [through spoilage in the heat]. Please have him show them . . . I do not think this Mons[ieu]r Ploy bold enough to demand ware-

[69] ANSOM, 29 January 1788, Cartier reg. 341, inventaire, Aquin.
[70] ANSOM, 28 January 1788, Cartier reg. 341, inventaire, Aquin.
[71] Emmanuel, *History of the Jews*, p. 966; ANSOM, 22 February 1783, Paillou reg. 1451, mariage, Aquin; ANSOM, 5 April 1785, Paillou reg. 1451, dépôt des papiers, Aquin,
[72] ANSOM, 19 March 1765, Daudin de Belair reg. 432, inventaire, Aquin.

house fees [but] since these are people who leave nothing to chance, you will abandon [the wine] to him.[73]

From the Aquin pier, Ploy, like his father-in-law Pierre Casamajor before him, expanded into planting. An inventory of the property Ploy held in community with his wife in 1788 listed 32 slaves, most of them working at the cotton estate he had founded on a royal land grant.[74] The property his wife had brought to the marriage was established as a livestock pen, but Ploy's chief residence was still at the Aquin pier, where his belongings included nine silver place settings worth over 600 livres.

If Thomas Ploy himself had not become a planter and slave owner on the scale of Julien Raimond, Michel Depas-Medina, or Pierre Casamajor, his son was poised to attain this status. In January of 1783, one month before his sister married Jean Louis Garsia of Curaçao, Jacques Thomas Ploy leased a dilapidated coffee and cotton plantation belonging to the Depas-Medina estate. This connection between the Ploys and the Depas-Medina was solidified the following November when Jacques Thomas married a free *quarteronne* related to the Depas-Medina clan on her mother's side. In the marriage contract Jacques Thomas Ploy identified himself as a free *quarteron*, like his new spouse, despite the fact that both his parents were labelled "mulâtres" in that same document. The bride's parents were both *quarterons*. Each set of parents contributed 15,000 livres to the new household and in 1788 Thomas Ploy agreed to let his cotton plantation pass under his son's control.[75]

* * *

The growing prosperity of the Ploys, the Depas-Medinas and the Raimonds was shared by many of their free colored neighbors at Aquin. Notarized sales contracts from the parish reveal the expanding economic weight of free people of color vis-à-vis whites. In the years 1760-69 100 sales were drafted at Aquin, and of these 50 involved persons at some time labelled *gens de couleur*. Twenty years later, in the period 1780-89, 244 sales were contracted at Aquin and 140 (58 percent) involved free people of color.[76]

---

[73] Letter annexed to ANSOM, 9 February 1763, Daudin de Belair reg. 430, procès verbal, Aquin.

[74] ANSOM, 29 January 1788, Cartier reg. 341, inventaire, Aquin.

[75] ANSOM, 17 November 1785, Belin Duressort reg. 108, mariage, Aquin.

[76] Note that the general census, over this same period, reported that free coloreds in Aquin's *quartier* jumped from being 16 percent of the free population in 1771 (146 of 888) to 47 percent in 1788 (926 of 1959). The inadequacy of census reporting is discussed below.

256   BLUE AND BROWN

TABLE 2

DECILE RANKINGS OF ALL NOTARIZED SALES IN AQUIN PARISH FROM 1760-1769 SHOWING PARTICIPATION OF FREE PEOPLE OF COLOR[77]

Percentile	Value of Sale in Colonial Livres	% of These Sales Involving Free People of Color	% of All Free Colored Sales
1-10	150-600	90% (9/10)	18%
10-20	600-1,100	80% (8/10)	16%
20-30	1,400-1,800	60% (6/10)	12%
30-40	1,841-3,000	60% (6/10)	12%
40-50	3,000-4,000	90% (9/10)	18%
50-60	4,000-6,000	40% (4/10)	8%
60-70	6,000-8,000	40% (4/10)	8%
70-80	9,000-15,000	20% (2/10)	4%
80-90	17,705-25,232	10% (1/10)	2%
90-100	30,000-476,500	10% (1/10)	2%
		Free coloreds participated in 50% (50/100) of valid cases	100%

These sales contracts illustrate an important change in the economic status of Aquin's free population of color. From the 1760s to the 1780s the average value of free colored sales increased from 3,985 livres to 10,793 livres, while the average value of sales involving only whites sank from 28,754 to 16,293. In the 1760s free colored participation in these transactions was concentrated in the least valuable sales [see Table 2 and Chart 6]. But by the 1780s free people of color were participating at a much higher rate in sales at all levels of value, including the highest [see Table 3 and Chart 6]. In the 1760s only one of the ten sales in the highest decile involved a free person of color; in the 1780s free coloreds participated in twelve of the twenty-four sales at this highest level.

Analysis of sales contracts suggests that Aquin's wealthiest free families of color and their less prosperous neighbors had achieved a new economic visibility by the end of the eighteenth century. But was this prominence due to demographic increases on the order of 200 and 400 percent as recorded

[77] These are taken from a study of the 4,882 notarial records surviving from the *quartiers* of Cayes, Nippes and Saint Louis in the period 1760-69. Of these, 565 were from the parish of Aquin. The sales analyzed in this table include all sales of urban and rural land, slaves, animals, and boats drafted by the notaries of this parish. For a more complete analysis, see Garrigus, "A Struggle for Respect," chap. 5.

JOHN GARRIGUS   257

TABLE 3

DECILE RANKINGS OF ALL NOTARIZED SALES IN AQUIN PARISH,
1780-1789 SHOWING PARTICIPATION OF FREE PEOPLE OF COLOR[78]

Percentile	Value of Sale in Colonial Lives	% of These Sales Involving Free People of Color	% of All Free Colored Sales
1-10	200-1,400	63% (15/24)	11%
10-20	1,500-2,000	75% (18/24)	13%
20-30	2,000-3,000	75% (18/24)	13%
30-40	3,000-4,000	58% (14/24)	10%
40-50	4,000-6,000	63% (15/24)	11%
50-60	6,000-9,000	42% (10/24)	7%
60-70	9,000-12,000	63% (15/24)	11%
70-80	12,000-15,575	48% (12/25)	9%
80-90	16,000-30,000	38% (9/24)	7%
90-100	33,000-300,000	50% (12/24)	9%
		Free coloreds participated in 58% (138/239) of valid cases	101%

in general colonial censuses? [see Table 1]. Evidence from the colony's southern peninsula suggests that the answer to this question is no; Aquin's free population of color did not suddenly double or quadruple. These census categories grew because officials began to pay greater attention to racial distinctions within free colonial society.

As the family histories above demonstrate, sexual contact between men of European descent and women of African ancestry was widespread in colonial society and white paternity of free colored children was frequently recognized. Although interracial marriage was officially condemned, such alliances were common, at least along the southern coast. According to the church registers of Fond des Nègres, Jacmel, and Cayes de Jacmel, located just east of Aquin, roughly seventeen percent of all recorded religious marriages during the eighteenth century in these parishes were interracial.[79]

[78] These are taken from the 1,339 surviving notarial contracts drafted in Aquin, in the period 1780-89. As above, these sales include urban and rural land, slaves, animals and boats.

[79] Yvan Debbasch, Couleur et liberté, p. 47; Moreau de Saint Méry, Description, p. 110; Jacques Houdaille, "Trois paroisses de Saint-Domingue au XVIIIᵉ siècle," Population, 18 (1963), 100.

258   BLUE AND BROWN

Chart 6

Free Colored Participation in Sales at Aquin
In deciles, by value of sale; 1760-69 versus 1780-89

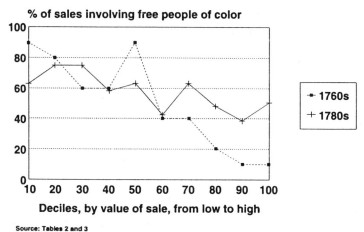

% of sales involving free people of color

Deciles, by value of sale, from low to high

Source: Tables 2 and 3

As a result, by the middle of the eighteenth century the region's free population had become racially integrated to the point that observers were unable to agree about how many inhabitants were of pure European descent and how many had some degree of African ancestry. In 1730, for example, the general colonial census counted only 12 free people of color among the 317 whites in Bainet parish.[80] Yet in 1731 an official inspecting the militia at Bainet–just five years after Julien Raimond's father Pierre had married Marie Begasse there–informed the governor that "there are few whites of pure blood there because all the whites willingly ally themselves by marriage with the blacks, who, by their thrift, acquire property more easily than the whites."[81]

The clearest illustration of these conflicting definitions of race dates from 1753 when the resident militia captain of Cayes compiled a census based on 588 declarations submitted by heads of households in his *quartier*. Although

[80] Moreau de Saint Méry, *Description*, p. 1155.

[81] AN, Col F³91, pp. 96-97. A similar event occurred in the 1860 census of Natchitoches Parish Louisiana, compiled by a non-resident, who "erroneously identified six of the households . . . as being of completely white racial heritage." Gary B. Mills, *The Forgotten People: Cane River's Creoles of Color* (Baton Rouge, 1977), p. 104.

the captain and the general colonial census for 1753 counted close to the same number of slaves, free unmarried women, arms-bearing men, and inhabitants of Cayes overall, the two documents disagreed over how to apply racial labels to nearly 100 free persons. The captain identified 50 percent more of his neighbors as free people of color than the general census did.[82]

Such discrepancies underscore the extent to which the category "free colored" was socially defined and the degree to which that definition varied within the colony and over time. In 1753 both the Cayes captain and the general census used the category "mulâtres et nègres libres" to count free persons of color, and these terms were widely taken to refer to all free persons of some African descent through the 1780s. But strictly speaking this label described only a subset of the free colored population, for colonial society theoretically recognized ten additional racial categories between *blanc* and *nègre*, besides *mulâtre*. By the mid-eighteenth century the southern coast had a number of free inhabitants, like the Raimonds at Aquin, who were acknowledged to be of African descent, but were recognized to be neither black nor mulatto. Depending on the interpretation of a census official through the 1770s, the Raimonds and their neighbors might be counted among local "mulâtres et nègres libres" or might be categorized as "blancs." "Affranchi," or "freedman," was another term frequently used for free people of African parentage, although by mid-century there were many persons like Julien Raimond, Guillaume Labadie, or Thomas Ploy who were not "freed," but had been born into freedom.[83]

In 1782 the category "mulâtres et nègres libres" was replaced on the general census by two classifications, thereby affording a greater specificity.[84] From that date compilers could differentiate between "gens de couleur, mulâtres, etc." and "nègres libres." Prosperous and respected free persons who at one time would not have been considered "mulâtres et nègres libres" were now identified as "gens de couleur." Census figures show the greatest increase for the colony's free colored population beginning in this same period. According to the general census report on the Saint-Louis *quartier*, which included Aquin parish and three others [see Chart 7], between 1780 and 1782 the free population of color grew from 229 to 479, while the white population shrank from 716 to 661. By 1788 the two groups were counted as nearly the same size; reportedly the district's free

[82] ANSOM, G¹509, Nos. 26 and 27.
[83] Moreau de Saint Méry, *Description*, pp. 83, 89.
[84] ANSOM, G¹509, No. 33.

260   BLUE AND BROWN

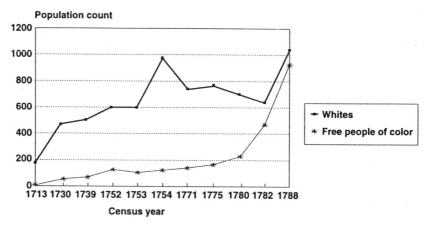

Chart 7
Whites and Free People of Color
In the St. Louis quartier, including Aquin

Aquin was 1 of 4 parishes within St Louis
Source: ANSOM G1 509 Nos 12, 20, 21, 24
27, 28, 30, 31, 32, 33, and 38.

population of color had expanded by a factor of four, from 229 to 926, in eight years.[85] What Saint-Domingue's official censuses portray as a free colored population explosion on the eve of the French Revolution may indeed reflect little more than a redrawing of the line socially separating persons of European parentage from those with both European and African ancestry.[86]

This shift was obvious in the notarial contracts drafted for wealthy free men of color. In Saint-Domingue, as in France early in the eighteenth century, *Sieur*, *Demoiselle*, or *Madame* were titles given in documents to respected members of society; those farther down the social scale were referred to without any appellation, or as *le nommé*. Well into the 1770s Julien Raimond and his brothers were identified as *Sieur* in official documents and no mention was made of their color, despite the fact that other free persons of color in the same transactions were assigned racial labels. In 1775, for example, "Sieurs François Raimond and Guillaume Raimond"

[85] *Ibid.*, Nos. 32, 33, and 38.
[86] *Ibid.*, Nos. 33 and 38; Debbasch, *Couleur et liberté*, p. 101. This was one of the major themes of Julien Raimond, *Observations sur l'origine et les progrès du préjugé des colons blancs contre les hommes de couleur* (Paris, 1791).

signed the marriage contract of "Gabriel *mulâtre libre*," a saddle maker born of a free black woman and an "unknown father." Although critical of Thomas Ploy's greed, a Cayes merchant cited above nevertheless accorded him the respectful titles "Sieur" and "Monsieur" in 1763.[87]

By 1780 such appellations were no longer regularly applied to the Raimonds or to Thomas Ploy and racial labels were attached to their names as to those of other persons of color. For example, in 1787 "Thomas Ploy M.L. [*mulâtre libre*]" sold land near Aquin's pier to David Garcia [sic], probably related to Ploy's son-in-law from Curaçao. Revealing the sensitive and still ill-defined nature of such racial labels, the notary drafting the sales contract originally identified David Garcia also as "M.L.," but crossed out these initials and squeezed the word "Sieur" into the margin.[88] It must be noted that the respect enjoyed by families like the Raimonds and Depas-Medinas did not simply evaporate at century's end. The notaries who drafted official documents still differentiated these wealthy clients from other free coloreds, but in more subtle ways. In March 1783, for instance, a contract of sale was registered between "Julien Raimond, Q.L. [*quarteron libre*], legitimate son of the late Sieur Pierre Raymond," and "*la nommée* Marie Madelaine *griffe libre*."[89] Nevertheless, by the 1780s prosperous free men of color, including Raimond, had lost much of their social standing *vis-à-vis* whites. Pierre Raymond, though illiterate, had served as parish sexton in the 1740s, yet his articulate and wealthy son Julien, as a *quarteron*, was ineligible for even this minor post that many planters refused as too time-consuming.[90]

* * *

This article does not contend that Aquin was a typical parish, nor that the families studied here were widely representative of Saint-Domingue's free population of color. But Aquin was the home of a reform movement that destabilized the slave regime by 1791, inadvertently preparing the way for

[87] ANSOM, 26 September 1775, Belin Duressort reg. 106, mariage, Aquin; ANSOM, 9 February 1763, Daudin de Belair reg. 430, procès verbale, Aquin; see letter cited above.

[88] ANSOM, 5 July 1787, Cartier reg. 341, vente, Aquin.

[89] ANSOM, 9 May 1781, Monneront reg. 1403, transport de créance, Aquin; ANSOM, 8 March 1783, Monneront reg. 1405, vente, Aquin; AN, Col F³91, p. 191. A *griffe* was the female child of a mulatto and a white, according to Moreau de Saint Méry, *Description*, 86.

[90] Moreau de Saint Méry, *Lois et constitutions des colonies françaises de l'Amérique sous le Vent* (Paris, 1784-90), III, p. 382; Debbasch, *Couleur et liberté*, p. 51; Garrigus, "A Struggle for Respect," pp. 319-39.

the slave uprising. When the Declaration of Rights of Man and Citizen was adopted in August 1789, Julien Raimond and his Aquin neighbors had spent five years in correspondence with Louis XVI's colonial ministry and Raimond himself had paid several visits to Versailles. Henceforth he would be the most prominent of the free men of color lobbying for colonial reform at the National Assembly.[91]

Aquin and families like the Raimonds, the Depas, and the Ploys illustrate that the rise of Saint-Domingue's free people of color cannot simply be ascribed to the new profitability of coffee. Evidence from these indigo planters and merchants does, however, demonstrate the impact on colonial society of late eighteenth-century shifts in the Atlantic economy. The weakening of mercantilist policies and the rise of new consumption patterns in Europe–all developments that fostered the rise of coffee–were also vital to the growing prosperity of Aquin's indigo planters. These changes laid the foundation for the political power of Saint-Domingue's free population of color after 1789.

The story of Aquin also demonstrates the deep roots of the colony's wealthiest free planters of color. In the southern peninsula, at least, these families could trace both their European and African founders to the beginning of settlement in the eighteenth century. While newcomers failed at the complexities of producing saleable indigo dye, Julien Raimond and his brothers built on three generations of family expertise. While some planters railed at French merchants for neglecting the southern coast, families like the Depas-Medinas and the Ploys used their geographic marginality to an advantage in a thriving contraband trade. These profits came not just with the growing importance of coffee after 1760, but from the earliest years of the eighteenth century.

Free colored economic success was not launched in the 1780s, only accelerated. Colonial racism, however, was growing just as rapidly. The social identity of many free men and women whose parents or grandparents had been African slaves was ambiguous during the first two-thirds of the eighteenth century. But by the 1780s, though they were planters, merchants, and slaveowners, Julien Raimond, Guillaume Labadie, and Thomas Ploy

---

[91] See Garrigus, "Julien Raimond" (forthcoming); and Mercer Cook, "Julien Raimond, Free Negro of St. Domingo," *Journal of Negro History*, 26 (1941), 139-70. Raimond's numerous publications include *Observations adressées à l'Assemblée Nationale par un deputé des colons américains* (S.l., 1789); *Observations sur l'origine et les progrès du prejugé des colons blancs contre les hommes de couleur* (Paris, 1791); and *Véritable origine des troubles de St.-Domingue, et des différentes causes qui les ont produits* (Paris, 1792).

were officially labelled "men of color" and, therefore, second-class citizens. As these men saw it, racial tensions in the 1780s were not caused by an increase in the free population of color, but by the humiliation directed at erstwhile citizens like themselves. When France began to recast its definition of "citizen" in 1789, Aquin's wealthy free men of color were ready to lay formal claim to a civil status they had once informally enjoyed.

24

The Enigma of Jamaica in the 1790s: New Light on the Causes of Slave Rebellions

David Geggus

THE history of resistance to slavery in the British Caribbean reveals a remarkable paradox. It was precisely during the "Age of Revolution" (1776-1815), when French St. Domingue experienced the most successful slave revolt of all time, that the frequency of slave rebellions and conspiracies reached an all-time low in the British colonies. The case of Jamaica appears especially enigmatic. That island's slaves made an impressive record of violent resistance from the seventeenth century to the 1830s. Yet the slave regime there seems hardly ever to have been so stable as during the 1790s,[1] a decade that brought not only the massive uprising in neighboring St. Domingue but also the epochal abolition of slavery by the French Republic.

At first sight, Jamaica in the 1790s would appear to have been the most vulnerable of all slave societies to the inflammatory example of St. Domingue and attempts of proselytizing agents to spread its message. Although not quite as close to St. Domingue as were its Spanish neighbors, Cuba and Santo Domingo, Jamaica possessed by far the largest concentration of slaves within a day's sail of the scene of revolt. Moreover, while Spain and the French Republic were allies after 1795, the imperial rulers of Jamaica and St. Domingue were at war during almost all the period in view. British planters had additional cause for alarm in the progress of the antislavery campaign in Britain, which was much discussed in Jamaica and in England almost led to parliamentary abolition of the slave trade six months after the uprising began in St. Domingue.[2]

---

[1] The main exception was the 1750s, a period of unusual calm in all the Caribbean.

[2] Though the slave revolt may have assisted the passage of the abolition bill through the House of Commons in Apr. 1792, events in Paris and St. Domingue thereafter turned British opinion against all reforming measures and the bill failed in the House of Lords (David Geggus, "British Opinion and the Emergence of Haiti, 1791-1805," in James Walvin, ed., *Slavery and British Society, 1776-1846* [London, 1982], 124-125). The French Revolution thus furthered the antislavery

As a sugar colony—and after St. Domingue's destruction, suddenly the largest sugar exporter in the world—Jamaica shared the propensity of all such societies to large-scale slave rebellion. More than this, Jamaica's slaves had an exceptionally violent tradition of resistance that was to continue to the end of slavery in the 1830s. In the island's mountainous interior lived five officially recognized communities of Maroons, who were policemen for the slave regime[3] but also permanent symbols of successful revolt for the colony's 250,000-300,000 slaves. In 1795 the biggest of these communities humiliated the plantocracy in a withering guerrilla war, which hit the British at a moment of imperial and military crisis.

Expansion of the Jamaican economy throughout these years helped sustain a huge surge of slave imports. Retained slave imports had averaged 5,662 per annum in 1785-1787; through the 1790s they averaged close to 12,000 per annum, and Kingston received more slaves than any other port in the Americas. In 1793, when over 25,000 Africans were added to the population in that one year alone, famine was feared. Thousands of prisoners of war and refugees from St. Domingue, some with their slaves, also crowded into Jamaica's towns during much of the 1790s. Their presence served to publicize the slave revolt in the neighboring colony, and some were supporters of it. They also helped fuel an unusually high level of epidemic disease, which decimated the European garrison and by 1796 had considerably weakened the local militia.[4]

An expanding sugar economy, food shortages, large numbers of unassimilated Africans, the prospect of foreign invasion, the mountainous terrain and presence of maroons, rumors connected with antislavery campaigns, the distraction or weakening of the forces of control: all these factors commonly contributive to slave insurrections[5] were present in Jamaica in the 1790s, over and above the threat from St. Domingue itself.

In these years, the Spanish and Dutch Caribbean witnessed considerable slave unrest, and in the British Windward Islands uprisings took place with French assistance. From Louisiana to Bahia the St. Domingue Revolution inspired discontented nonwhites to acts of resistance. Even so, and despite their impressive history of resistance, Jamaica's slaves remained quiescent. In Jamaica the "Age of Revolution" coincided with a trough in the history of slave rebellion. Between the Hanover conspiracy

---

cause in France but retarded it in England, although in both countries its early impact was limited.

[3] They captured and returned runaway slaves in exchange for bounty payments. The capitalized form, "Maroons," is used to distinguish members of the five settlements, recognized by treaty in 1739, from subsequent runaways.

[4] David Geggus, "Jamaica and the Saint Domingue Slave Revolt, 1791-1793," *The Americas*, XXXVIII (1981), 219-233.

[5] Orlando Patterson, *The Sociology of Slavery: An Analysis of the Origins, Development and Structure of Negro Slave Society in Jamaica* (London, 1967), 273-283; Eugene D. Genovese, *From Rebellion to Revolution: Afro-American Slave Revolts in the Making of the Modern World* (Baton Rouge, La., 1979), 11-12.

of 1776 and the Ibo plot of 1815, Jamaica's plantations experienced only a few minor disturbances, just as elsewhere in the British Caribbean slave conspiracies and revolts were remarkably few in the forty years preceding the Barbados insurrection of 1816.[6] This is perhaps the more surprising in view of the central role that Eugene Genovese assigns the French Revolution in the history of slave resistance.[7]

The subject of this article is therefore a portion of an enigma. The article will examine five episodes that constituted the main challenges to the Jamaican plantocracy of the 1790s. It will suggest that the impact of the St. Domingue Revolution on Jamaica's slaves was slight, at least as measured by overt response. The final section, setting the subject in context, will attempt to explain why this was so and, drawing on data from a number of American societies, will consider implications for the study of slave resistance in general.

REACTIONS OF THE SLAVES, 1791-1792

At the outset it should be acknowledged that the sources for studying slaves' attitudes and actions are all imperial or plantocratic and rarely firsthand.[8] They are perhaps at their best for the opening months of the St. Domingue crisis, when in a flurry of defensive activity Jamaican planters set up committees of security, which seem to have investigated rumors thoroughly.

The evidence shows that Jamaican slaves were well informed of events in St. Domingue, that they responded positively, and that on the densely populated north coast a rebellion apparently was planned for Christmas 1791.[9] Within a month after the August uprising in St. Domingue, slaves in Jamaica were singing songs about it. By November, whites were

[6] Michael Craton, *Testing the Chains: Resistance to Slavery in the British West Indies* (Ithaca, N.Y., 1982); Anthony Synnott, "Slave Revolts in the Caribbean" (Ph.D. diss., University of London, 1976). Though many slaves participated actively in the insurrections of free coloreds, Caribs, and whites in Grenada and St. Vincent in 1795-1797, and though the aims of these insurrections included the ending of slavery, I do not class these as slave rebellions. My main criteria for defining the nature of a rebellion are the distribution of leadership roles, autonomous action, and above all the degree of participation by different social groups.

[7] Genovese, *Rebellion to Revolution, passim.* For differing views see Craton, *Testing the Chains,* 13-14, 161-171, and David Geggus, *Slave Resistance Studies and the Saint Domingue Slave Revolt: Some Preliminary Considerations,* 2d imp. (Miami, Fla., 1983), 23-26.

[8] The main sources for this study are the governor's correspondence (C.O. 137) and the Journals of the Assembly (C.O. 140), Public Record Office; and the Council Minutes and the letterbooks and minutes of the assembly's Committee of Correspondence, Jamaica Archives, Spanish Town. I also used the *Royal Gazette* (of Jamaica) for 1791-1794 and a small amount of private correspondence in the Slebech Papers, National Library of Wales, Aberystwyth.

[9] The following four paragraphs summarize Geggus, "Jamaica," *Americas,* XXXVIII (1981), 223-225.

complaining of "insolent" behavior and that the slaves had become "so different a people from what they were." "I am convinced," wrote one master, "that the Ideas of Liberty have sunk so deep in the minds of *all* Negroes, that whenever the greatest precautions are not taken they will rise." "Head negroes" were overheard talking of killing whites and dividing up their lands. "Negroes in the French country," they said, "were men."[10] In one plantation forge, lead shot was secretly cast and cutlasses were made. In particular, "Coromantee" slaves (Akan and Ga speakers) were reported to be plotting rebellion. One confessed that an insurrection was planned for Christmas 1791. He had intended to join in, he said, because they were his people. He was astonished, however, to see the Maroons, many of whom had "Coromantee" forebears, join with the whites when the militia was mustered.[11]

One band of runaways did decide at this time to attack whites. Led by Brutus, an escapee from the workhouse, this band, eighteen strong, had been living in symbiosis with the slaves of the Brampton Bryan estate in Trelawny Parish, trading with them, attending their dances, and having wives on the plantation. The slaves on the estate, moreover, now threatened to join Brutus if their absentee master did not return and replace their cruel overseer. Before there was any violence, however, Brutus was captured by the militia, in January 1792.

While the activity of the Coromantee community harks back to the major rebellions of 1760 and 1765, when hundreds of Coromantees revolted, it was the conspiring by skilled slaves, those with some stake in the system, that most worried planters, for this was uncomfortably reminiscent of events in St. Domingue. Yet nothing happened. There is little evidence of panic among whites. Gov. Adam Williamson remained sanguine, at least in his correspondence, which shows him confident that the measures taken would kill any thought of revolt. Apparently he was right. The Christmas holiday was the crucial test. It was precisely then, however, that (for the first time in nine years) the militia turned out—over 8,000 strong including 1,000 cavalry. Together with the garrison, then at unprecedented strength, along with the Maroons and with slaves willing to give evidence of conspiracies, this show of force surely made potential rebels think twice. Their moment passed. An extra regiment arrived in February and three more in the autumn.

As early as January 1792, we find Williamson writing somewhat smugly that the slaves were peaceful and wondering why whites were so busy. Although the situation in St. Domingue steadily worsened, serious doubts were never again entertained as to the safety of Jamaica. The passage of the slave trade abolition bill in April prompted no more than some "insolence" on the part of blacks in Kingston. A large number of slaves brought in by St. Domingue refugees certainly disturbed "people who

[10] Adam Williamson to Henry Dundas, Nov. 6, 1791, C.O. 137/89.
[11] Report of the St. James committee of security, Jan. 13, 1792, and Williamson to Dundas, Nov. 27, 1791, C.O. 137/90.

remembered the years 1760 and 1765," but as most of these slaves spoke no English they had little communication with Jamaican slaves. In any case, the situation in St. Domingue was already well known.[12] As a result, Jamaica's blacks assuredly saw themselves and their masters in a new light. As will be shown below, however, the evidence suggests that the stability of a slave society was determined less by the ideas circulating in the slave quarters than by the strength and unity of the slaveowning class. Otherwise it is difficult to reconcile the slaves' positive response to the news from St. Domingue with their failure to take action.

Mention should also be made of a mysterious secret society discovered in Spanish Town in November 1791. Called the Cat Club, its members "assembled drinking King Wilberforce's health out of a cat's skull . . . but will not divulge the business."[13] The following August, a black described as "the notorious Dagger" and two other obeah men were transported for reasons unknown, and in the spring of 1794 the Baptist preacher George Leile was arrested "for sedition."[14] Though evidence of tensions between white and black, none of these events appear related to the revolution in St. Domingue. Slave imports soared in 1793; famine threatened; slavery was declared abolished in St. Domingue; and much of the Jamaica garrison was soon transferred there[15]—but during the three years following the spring of 1792 no signs of slave unrest were reported in Jamaica.[16]

THE FREE COLORED PETITION OF 1792

Some alarm was generated, however, in late 1792 when a group of Kingston mulattoes, or free coloreds,[17] petitioned the assembly for the repeal of certain discriminatory laws, such as those restricting free coloreds' rights of inheritance and right to testify in court.[18] Occurring just when mulattoes were beginning to dominate affairs in St. Domingue, the petition was considered dangerous (although reasonable) by most whites.[19] Free coloreds constituted about one-third of the Jamaica militia.

[12] This influx continued spasmodically down to 1798 but gave rise to no serious incident. See Gabriel Debien and Philip Wright, "Les colons de Saint-Domingue passés à la Jamaique, 1792-1835," *Bulletin de la Société d'Histoire de la Guadeloupe*, XXVI (1975), 3-216.

[13] Thomas Barritt to Nathaniel Phillips, Dec. 8, 1791, Slebech Papers.

[14] *Royal Gaz.*, 1792, nos. 23, 27, 1794, no. 14.

[15] Profiting from the outbreak of war with France, the British government hoped to annex the valuable colony. Beginning in Sept. 1793, British troops held some districts for as long as five years but overall made little headway.

[16] The statement in Genovese, *Rebellion to Revolution*, 21, that a French landing in Jamaica provoked several slave uprisings in 1793 is without foundation.

[17] As the majority of free nonwhites in the West Indies were of mixed racial descent, contemporaries often used these terms as synonyms and to include the minority of free blacks.

[18] Correspondence for Dec. 1792, C.O. 137/91; Add. MSS 12431, 223-233, British Library, London; Kean Osborn to Phillips, Dec. 5, 1792, Slebech Papers.

[19] See n. 18.

While little is known about the petition's genesis,[20] it is hard not to think that its timing must have owed something to the St. Domingue mulattoes' winning of full equality the previous spring. This was the first time Jamaican free coloreds had taken political action. Nevertheless, the petition's demands were mild. They bore no imprint of universalist ideology (appeal to natural law) but lay rather within the British (even Jamaican) tradition of gradual reform. The petitioners, who were elders of the Methodist church, did not seek confrontation. Their demands were to be partially met in 1796, but only as a reward for services rendered in the Second Maroon War.

THE SECOND MAROON WAR AND THE QUESTION OF FRENCH INFILTRATION

This war of nine months is too well known to need much commentary here.[21] It involved only the largest of the five Maroon communities, Trelawny Town, whose 600 inhabitants lived in the highlands south of Montego Bay on the boundary between St. James and Trelawny parishes. The conflict erupted in July 1795. Fighting continued from August through December, though the last insurgents did not surrender until March 1796. Tying down numerous troops and militia, the Trelawny Maroons inflicted humiliating losses and were defeated only by a combination of artillery, hunting dogs, loyal slave rangers, and the neighboring Maroons of Accompong Town, able guerrilla fighters like themselves, who knew their home terrain. Above all, for half a year the Trelawny rebels kept the colonists on tenterhooks lest the conflict spark a massive uprising of slaves. This the rebels indeed tried to do, but were unable to attract more than 100-250 runaways (and of these it is not clear how many actually joined with them).

Two questions need to be addressed. What did the conflict have to do with the St. Domingue Revolution, and why could the Maroons not garner more support?

The conflict began at what was probably the planters' darkest hour in the Caribbean with revolts breaking out everywhere from Demerara to Cuba. It was also the nadir of the British war effort in the West Indies. The French, led by the Jacobin Victor Hugues with free colored, Carib, and slave support, had retaken Guadeloupe and St. Lucia. Now they seemed poised to recapture St. Domingue and to seize the British colonies of Grenada and St. Vincent as well. French privateers were ruining British commerce and moving freely off Jamaica's north coast. France's new tactic of waging war by liberating the oppressed was seen by the British as "unprecedented" and "unjustifiable and barbarous," and was extremely worrying.[22]

---

[20] Gad J. Heuman, *Between Black and White: Race, Politics, and the Free Coloreds in Jamaica, 1792-1865* (Westport, Conn., 1981), 23-24.

[21] See below, n. 24.

[22] War Minister Henry Dundas, W.O. 1/60, 351-356, W.O. 1/62, 431-435,

Alexander Lindsay, Lord Balcarres, since April 1795 the new governor of Jamaica, was quick to regard the Trelawny Maroons as part of this French-inspired movement and later put forward evidence to justify his opinion, which was accepted in Whitehall. According to the best-known history of the British Caribbean, the Maroon War was "inspired by the example of the French islands and, it was believed, by actual French agents."[23] The Maroons' statements, however, reveal almost no sign of libertarian ideology, and almost everyone who has studied the conflict has maintained that it arose primarily or entirely out of local causes.[24] These were, over the long term, a growing land shortage in Trelawny Town, lax enforcement of laws regarding the Maroons, weakening of forces of control within the town, and dissatisfaction with the town superintendent appointed in 1792. Discontent was abruptly brought to a head in July 1795, when two Maroons guilty of theft were whipped in the public workhouse by a runaway slave they themselves had captured (in their role as slave catchers). Being punished like slaves was perceived by Maroons as deeply insulting, and in addition they were jeered on their journey home by the slaves of Montego Bay and the surrounding plantations.

Despite the provocative and warlike reaction of younger Maroons, scholars have tended to agree that war could have been avoided had the pompous and inexperienced governor responded in a conciliatory fashion, as many local planters wished him to do. Instead Balcarres was aggressively uncompromising and insisted on unconditional surrender, partly because he believed that the Maroons were in league with French agents. As early as October 1793, Léger Sonthonax, the Republican commissioner in St. Domingue, had proclaimed that the Blue Mountain Maroons, in eastern Jamaica, were waiting to rebel at his command and fall on Kingston,[25] but such a public announcement can only have been propa-

---

P.R.O. Although often depicted as a mulatto, Victor Hugues, the civil commissioner, came from a family of white Marseilles tradesmen (Anne Pérotin-Dumon, *Etre patriote sous les Tropiques* [Basse Terre, 1985]).

[23] J. H. Parry and P. M. Sherlock, *A Short History of the West Indies*, 3d ed. (London, 1971), 165.

[24] Robert Charles Dallas, *The History of the Maroons* (London, 1803); Alan E. Furness, "The Maroon War of 1795," *Jamaican Historical Review*, V (1965), 30-49; Edward Brathwaite, *The Development of Creole Society in Jamaica, 1770-1820* (Oxford, 1971); Barbara Klamon Kopytoff, "The Maroons of Jamaica: An Ethnohistorical Study of Incomplete Politics, 1655-1905" (Ph.D. diss., University of Pennsylvania, 1974); Daniel Schafer, "The Maroons of Jamaica: African Slave Rebels in the Caribbean" (Ph.D. diss., University of Minnesota, 1973); Craton, *Testing the Chains;* Richard Hart, *Slaves Who Abolished Slavery* (Kingston, 1980-1985), II.

[25] Nouvelles Acquisitions Françaises, 14878, fol. 125, Bibliothèque Nationale, Paris. This was evidently a response to the recent British invasion of St. Domingue. In later proclamations both Sonthonax and Toussaint Louverture would refer to the past resistance of the Jamaica Maroons as an example of black heroism. On the other hand, the St. Domingue planters, looking more to present

ganda. The following April a black who could speak both French and English was arrested in the parish of St. Thomas in the East apparently carrying a certificate signed by Sonthonax.[26] As the affair is not mentioned in official correspondence, however, it may have been discovered to be a mistake. By early 1795, rumors were circulating that French government representatives in North America were sending secret agents to the Caribbean. The numerous and laxly guarded prisoners of war from St. Domingue in jail or on parole around Kingston were also said to be trying to spread "French principles."[27] Nonetheless, Balcarres's first response (July 19) to the news of the Maroons' hostility was that it was probably a local matter and that he would try to negotiate. Four days later he changed his mind on hearing that French prisoners released from the prison ships had gone to "the Maroon country." The Trelawny Maroons themselves reportedly said that "if the brigands come down they would instantly join them,"[28] but there is no firsthand account of this, and it does not in any case suggest that there had been contact between them.

Clare Taylor has recently written that "there was clear proof that French insurgents were stirring up the Maroons."[29] She refers solely to a letter of September 16 by a plantation attorney expressing fears that "fugitives from Trelawny Town have joined the Maroons of Nanny Town near Bath [in eastern Jamaica], with some of the French Brigands from Hispaniola, which is partly indicated by a letter found in the possession of a Count F—— taken up in Kingston a few days ago as a spy."[30] This is interesting new evidence but scarcely proof of anything, especially concerning the Trelawny Maroons. Why was the count's letter not mentioned by the governor or published by the assembly, as were other relevant papers? One suspects another unsubstantiated rumor.[31]

While Michael Craton presents the war as primarily a product of local causes, he also has suggested that the Maroons may have received encouragement from foreign agents. He cites two pieces of evidence. The first is a statement by a Jamaican slave regarding an envoy who had been sent (apparently by Maroons) "to France . . . [who reported] Things are not there as they are here, there all are Citizens and upon a footing, here we are kept in ignorance. . . . If they [the French] get the better then will

---

reality, asked in 1791 that the Maroons be sent to fight against their slave rebels. As late as 1787, the French minister of marine thought the Maroons might support a French invasion of Jamaica but was informed to the contrary by the governor of St. Domingue (C9A/159, 70, Archives Nationales, Paris).

[26] *Royal Gaz.*, 1794, no. 15.

[27] Committee of Correspondence, Out-letters, Jan. 31, 1795; C.O. 137/94-95.

[28] C.O. 140/85, 21. The British tended to call all their nonwhite opponents in the West Indies "brigands."

[29] Taylor, "Planter Comment on Slave Revolts," *Slavery and Abolition*, III (1982), 249.

[30] Barritt to Phillips, Sept. 16, 1795, Slebech Papers.

[31] See below, n. 35.

be the time for us to come forward."[32] However, the versions of this document that I have seen suggest, first, that it was not, as Craton implies, a direct report of Maroon activity or of the envoy's words, but merely of a conversation between unknown slaves or free coloreds, overheard imperfectly in Montego Bay, and, second, that Craton's interpolations in brackets are incorrect, that the envoy had not returned, and that the speakers who were overheard were waiting to see how the Maroons, not the French, would fare.[33] It was thus simply hearsay reported secondhand and offers no evidence of actual Maroon contact with the French.

The other piece of evidence cited by Craton is a long and detailed deposition, dated August 28, 1795, by a French prisoner, Jean-Joseph Maurenson, who said that the French representative in Philadelphia (Citizen Fauchet) had sent many agents to Jamaica, most of them bilingual free coloreds. One was from the parish of Trelawny; another was the friend of a Maroon chief; others had gone to contact the Maroons, though Maurenson did not actually state that contact was made. In an earlier work, I, like Craton, found the document convincing.[34] Unfortunately, neither of us realized that Maurenson repudiated his statement inside a month; he had invented it, he said, so as to escape incarceration, hoping to be sent instead as a spy to Philadelphia.[35]

If one also considers that during the war foreign agents were never seen among the Maroons, were never arrested anywhere in Jamaica, and were never mentioned by Maroons when trying to win support, then the case for even minimal foreign involvement just about vanishes. Although favorable to Balcarres, planter Bryan Edwards's account of the war makes no reference to foreign emissaries.[36] No doubt, the Maroons hoped to profit from British difficulties in St. Domingue—this they said themselves—and perhaps specifically from the July departure for St. Domingue of the 83rd Regiment. This considerably weakened the garrison just when the onset of the hurricane season cut maritime links with Europe and reduced the number of seamen on the island. More generally, Maroons may have been encouraged by the British army's poor performance against the rebel blacks in St. Domingue and elsewhere during the previous year. But one can scarcely say more; indeed, after the summer of 1795 Governor Balcarres himself had little to say on the subject.

Even so, there is no reason to doubt that the Directory in Paris and Citizen Fauchet in Philadelphia were hoping to repeat in Jamaica Victor Hugues's success in the Windward Islands. Probably much remains to be

[32] Statement of Leah Fletchell, Aug. 27, 1795, cited in Craton, *Testing the Chains*, 213. "France" here no doubt means St. Domingue. The interpolations in brackets are Craton's.
[33] Council Minutes, Sept. 21, 1795; C.O. 140/85, 19-20.
[34] David Patrick Geggus, *Slavery, War, and Revolution: The British Occupation of Saint Domingue, 1793-1798* (Oxford, 1982), 150, 385.
[35] Dallas, *Maroons*, I, 229, 356-357, II, 291-292.
[36] Bryan Edwards, *Historical Survey of the Island of St. Domingo* (London, 1797), 303-353.

discovered about their activities. Yet the evidence suggests that they had difficulty bringing their plans to fruition. Early in 1796 French privateers plumbed bays on the Jamaican coast.[37] Admiral Joseph de Richery's squadron, expected from France all that spring and summer, was under orders to carry an invasion force from St. Domingue, but it went to Newfoundland instead.[38] Commissioner Sonthonax was urged by colleagues on several occasions to intervene in Jamaica, but he appears to have been too hard-pressed to organize anything beyond the defense of St. Domingue. His correspondence of 1796 shows he had little idea of what was happening in Jamaica, and a gauche attempt to gain information under a flag of truce was easily scotched by the Kingston authorities.[39] André Rigaud, the free-colored leader in southern St. Domingue, was better placed geographically and perhaps militarily, but in the summer of 1796 he broke away from the Republicans for over a year. In August Balcarres briefly mentioned suspicions about French links with the Windward Maroons (of eastern Jamaica), but a week later was expressing confidence and sent more troops to St. Domingue.[40]

It is curious therefore that the following summer (1797) Balcarres yielded to a manufactured invasion scare and declared martial law. The cause was a letter by Sonthonax that detailed plans for invading Jamaica with a fleet of privateers and mentioned preparations already made in eastern Jamaica.[41] Having been dropped near British-occupied Port-au-Prince, the letter was fairly obviously a Republican attempt to direct British attention from St. Domingue. Yet with the British position in St. Domingue crumbling and refugees again flooding into Jamaica, Balcarres could not take any chances. Not until 1799, however, can one be sure that French agents actually were sent to Jamaica.[42]

To the question why the Trelawny Maroons gathered so little support, Bryan Edwards's answer was that the colonial garrison was too strong.[43] Slaves realized that rebellion would be hopeless, especially as the 83rd Regiment was recalled only a few days after it had sailed. Though Edwards overestimated the size of the regiment, the point is important. Also significant was the novel presence in Jamaica of several cavalry corps, which could be rapidly deployed. According to Balcarres, they "over-awed" the slaves.[44] Even though the slaves apparently had no desire to help the Maroons achieve their particularist ends, they could still have taken advantage of the war to wage their own struggle. As already noted,

[37] Committee of Correspondence, Out-letters, Feb. 5, 1796.
[38] Nouv. Acq. Fr. 14878, fol. 230.
[39] Sonthonax Correspondence, Vol. I, Bib. Nat.; Geggus, *Slavery, War, and Revolution,* 384.
[40] Balcarres to the duke of Portland, Aug. 14, 20, 1796, C.O. 137/98.
[41] Council Minutes, July 1, 1797.
[42] See below, p. 287.
[43] Edwards, *Survey,* 331-333.
[44] Balcarres to Portland, July 23, 1795, C.O. 137/95.

some were overheard saying: let's wait and see. Others speculated as to what might be achieved if all the Maroon communities acted together.[45]

But the Maroons did not combine. The Accompongs were related to the Trelawnys but were also rivals for hunting grounds and in dispute with them over possession of their copy of the Maroon Treaty of 1739. Rumors circulated about links between the Trelawnys and the Windward Maroons, but these remain unsubstantiated. The latter did prove recalcitrant, failing to obey when summoned to meet the governor, but this is not surprising given Balcarres's oft-displayed duplicity. (He planned to seize the Nanny Town Maroons.)[46] The history of the relations of the Maroon towns was, in general, one of conflict rather than of solidarity, and in this dispute there was no immediate common interest. Even the Trelawnys themselves were much divided.

As to relations between Maroons and slaves, many commentators put great emphasis on their mutual antagonism, some contemporaries speaking of violent hatred. To be sure, slaveowners exaggerated such divisions between nonwhites, but there seems little reason to doubt that Maroon disdain and slave envy were real. The very incident that began the war is vivid testimony to a sharp sense of separate identity. For over fifty years Maroons had had interests not simply separate from those of slaves but (as slave catchers) in direct conflict with them. In every rebellion and alarm since 1740 they had turned out to support the slaveowners.[47] Some were slaveowners themselves. Hence, when the Maroon Edmund Parkinson claimed he was fighting to free all the slaves,[48] he was doubtless regarded with some skepticism. The raiding of slave provision grounds by Maroons (which may or may not have predated the war) was another source of friction.

Dallas noted that the Maroons were already phenotypically distinct from the bulk of the slave population,[49] and there were surely cultural barriers between them as well. In view of the Trelawnys' ethnic affiliation, it is interesting that Balcarres mentioned that they were joined by "Coromantee" runaways.[50] (One thinks of the 1791 evidence cited above.) Although three-quarters of adult Maroons by now bore British names, and most had family names, too, taken from planter patrons,[51] the Trelawnys apparently still spoke something closely resembling Akan, as well as English. After 1750, however, and especially in the 1790s, far more

[45] Barritt to Phillips, Oct. 16, 1795, Slebech Papers.

[46] Balcarres to the attorney general, Dec. 26, 1795, C.O. 137/96.

[47] Synnott, "Slave Revolts," 389.

[48] See Craton, Testing the Chains, 218. This is the only episode I am aware of that suggests universalist ideas among Maroons. Other Maroons said they would eventually kill slaves who did not join them.

[49] Dallas, Maroons, I, 88.

[50] Balcarres to Dundas, Dec. 31, 1795, C.O. 137/95. Dallas claimed that slaves who joined the Maroons came only from abandoned estates in the vicinity (Maroons, I, 217-218).

[51] C.O. 140/88, 11-18.

Ibo and Bantu than "Coromantees" were brought to Jamaica.[52] This may have added to the Maroons' isolation.

THE "REBELLIOUS RUNAWAYS" OF 1798

At the end of the war the Trelawny Maroons were deported to Nova Scotia. This action opened up the fringes of the Cockpit Country to new settlers and bands of runaways. In July 1796, a few months after the conflict ended, small groups of runaways began raiding, even destroying, provision grounds in the Trelawny backcountry and driving off their slave cultivators. By March 1797, local whites were calling for military assistance against them, but the governor and Council refused as long as the raids were limited to provision grounds and the occasional abduction of female slaves. Encouraged perhaps by this official neglect, their numbers increased noticeably toward the end of 1797, when they were said to employ a full-time recruiting party.[53]

Constantly moving between settlements in the forest, the fugitives had few firearms and did not use them against the colonists, but in February 1798 the situation changed abruptly. Cuffee, a recent runaway, leading a dozen men, seized arms and ammunition from Coxheath pen (that is, ranch), whence he and several others had fled at different times. They declared that they were going to kill the owner, James McGhie (then absent), and stop him from harvesting his crop. McGhie's two sugar estates, Dromilly and Hampstead Retreat, had similarly lost several runaways. Now the Council recommended action. In April, when a coffee planter was killed, some small properties were burned, and stock animals were mutilated, settlers abandoned the Trelawny backcountry and Balcarres moved up troops while parties of "blackshot" (free colored and slave rangers) were raised. Acts of arson continued in May, though only two or three colonists seem to have been killed. Increasing in number and confidence, the runaways now issued (bogus) challenges to the whites to do battle, which, however, the former always avoided. The leaders continued to speak of killing McGhie as their aim.

Perhaps the main question here is why these runaways moved to the offensive when they did. As with Brutus's band of six years before, their example shows that an individual maroon band could shift from symbiosis with a slave regime to threatening it (a point worth noting, given the controversy among historians over the nature of *marronage*).[54] Contemporaries acknowledged this ambiguous status with the term "rebellious [or riotous] runaways." Though these early months of 1798 brought the collapse of the British position in St. Domingue and a new flood of refugees into Jamaica, it appears unlikely that the runaways were influ-

[52] Philip D. Curtin, *The Atlantic Slave Trade: A Census* (Madison, Wis., 1969), 160; below, n. 85.

[53] Council Minutes, Aug. 25, 1796, Mar. 11, June 10, Nov. 2, 1797. The main sources for the rest of this section are C.O. 140/89, 106-114; Council Minutes, Feb.-June 1798; and examination of Patty and Juba, C.O. 137/100.

[54] See below, n. 63.

enced by outside events. To some extent, their aggressive campaign was probably a function of increasing numbers and perhaps also related to settler encroachment, but specifically it seems connected with the flight of Cuffee in September 1797.

Cuffee and several others of McGhie's absconded slaves were clearly waging a personal war of revenge. Interestingly, another band active at the same time was led by a young "Congo," a "shipmate"[55] of another McGhie runaway who had been hanged for participating in the Maroon War. Evidence of broader aims than revenge appeared in May 1798, when the insurgents declared that the backcountry provision grounds belonged to them.[56] Presumably, they hoped eventually to enjoy a position in Jamaican society similar to that of the Trelawny Maroons.

Planters feared that Cuffee's band, who, unlike the Trelawnys, had no record of mistreating slaves, would more easily be able to win slave support. In May "disaffected" slaves were said to be joining them daily, though others resisted the band's attacks and put out the fires they lit. At the end of March the five westernmost parishes took censuses of missing slaves. The totals represent barely .5 percent of the parishes' slave populations. In Trelawny Parish, out of 142 fugitives (going back thirty years in some cases) 21 had fled in 1797 and 49 in January-March 1798.[57] Contemporaries thought that the raiders numbered 70 or 100. One band numbered about 30, while Cuffee's was variously described as containing 40 men divided into two parts, or just 19 men and 9 women. Probably it was segmented; even within the smaller group there was an inner core, apparently composed of Coromantees, which ate together. It was also divided between a militant minority who wanted to fight and a majority who preferred to avoid the patrols and whom Cuffee with eight others finally abandoned in July.

Although Monica Schuler describes these events as a "Pan-African revolt," the term does not seem quite justified.[58] Cuffee's band was indeed multiethnic, but apparently the weaker for it, and we have no evidence that it actually cooperated with the "Congos." In April the second driver of the Scarlett family's Peru estate "harangued several of his countrymen and others, Mundingoes and Coromantees," calling on them to join the "rebel runaways" in the neighborhood, but only three are reported to have followed him.[59] Elsewhere, we see flashes of interethnic tension. An armed slave driver who fought off an attack was derided by his assailants: "You damned Chamba cut-face s.o.b. . . . we will do for you." And it was

[55] An African who had shared the Middle Passage. The almost contemporaneous Boca Nigua uprising in Santo Domingo makes an interesting comparison. Led by Africans, it, too, began as an act of personal revenge; see below, n. 115.

[56] C.O. 140/89, 113.

[57] Council Minutes, June 11, 1798.

[58] Schuler, "Afro-American Slave Culture," *Historical Reflections*, VI (1979), 129.

[59] C.O. 140/89, 109.

said that a kidnapped boy would be killed "because he was a creole."[60]

After some months Balcarres was persuaded to mobilize the Accompong Maroons against the runaways, who then rapidly vanished from sight; their fate is unknown. A member of the Scarlett family was shot dead in August, but by October the crisis was considered over.[61] These events of 1798 revealed many fascinating details of life in the forest.[62] Situated on the borderline between *marronage* and revolt, they also are of some theoretical interest,[63] and they illustrate the transition taking place from ethnic to pan-African revolts. Nonetheless, limited in aims and scope, they had nothing to do with the St. Domingue Revolution.

THE FRENCH INVASION PLAN OF 1799

In 1798 the French government and its representatives in St. Domingue again contemplated invading Jamaica. Not until November 1799, however, was the official agent in St. Domingue, Philippe Roume, able to send spies to Kingston to prepare the ground by gaining support among the French community there and also among the Blue Mountain Maroons, with whom one of the spies claimed (apparently falsely) to have links. Soon after arriving in Jamaica the spies were arrested. They had been secretly betrayed by Toussaint Louverture himself. To make St. Domingue autonomous or independent of France, Toussaint needed British assistance or at least acquiescence. The French knew this, and one of their aims in invading Jamaica was to sunder Toussaint's entente with Britain. Toussaint declined to fall into the trap.[64]

Hence, despite the assertions of Roberto Palacios and Jean Fouchard,[65] it is by no means certain that all the fathers of Haitian independence saw the destruction of slavery in the Americas as the best means of preserving their own freedom. Under the typically beguiling title of "Marrons du Grand Vent," Fouchard has recently made a case for viewing the foreign policy of the Emperor Dessalines, the first Haitian head of state (1804-1806), as secretly emancipationist, but the evidence so far seems thin.[66] No doubt Dessalines wished to see slave insurrection in the French

---

[60] C.O. 140/89, 111-113.

[61] Synnott says Cuffee was caught by the Maroons but offers no evidence of this ("Slave Revolts," 387).

[62] For example, the band manufactured musket balls by melting down lead in a pot and pouring the molten liquid down the hollow stalk of a plantain leaf to form a long strip. This was then cut into pieces that were rounded on machete handles.

[63] I discuss controversies among contemporaries and historians regarding the size of maroon bands, their relations with plantation society, and the motives prompting slaves to become fugitives in *Slave Resistance*, 4-10.

[64] Gabriel Debien and Pierre Pluchon, *Un plan d'invasion de la Jamaique* (*Notes d'Histoire Coloniale*, no. 186 [n.p., 1978]); "Letters of Toussaint Louverture and of Edward Stevens," *American Historical Review*, XVI (1910), 64-101.

[65] Jean Fouchard, "Quand Haiti exportait la liberté," *Revue de la société haitienne d'histoire*, CXLIII (1984), 42-45; below, n. 67.

[66] The French consul in Danish St. Thomas, a St. Domingue exile, reported that

colonies, but as he was as dependent on British commerce as Toussaint had been, it would seem unlikely that he had designs on Jamaica, any more than did his immediate successor, Henry Christophe. Conversely, the mulatto leader André Rigaud appears to have played a part in fomenting the 1795 and 1800 risings on Curaçao, which had close links with southern St. Domingue. Rigaud's lieutenant, Alexandre Pétion, actually participated in the 1800 insurrection, as had other free coloreds in an attempted rising in nearby Maracaibo the previous year.[67] It may be, therefore, that those who did most to export liberty from St. Domingue were not the ex-slaves but the former free coloreds and, of course, the Republican French. Certainly not until President Pétion in 1816 compelled Simón Bolívar to pursue an emancipationist policy in South America can one speak of the successful internationalization of the Haitian Revolution.

DISCUSSION: SLAVE RESISTANCE AND THE MILITARY

The impact of the St. Domingue Revolution on Jamaica's slaves appears to have been slight, in the sense that overt resistance in the 1790s was actually less than in most previous or subsequent decades. The slaves did not revolt; only one conspiracy was rumored; and, considering the disruption caused by the Maroon War, runaway activity was small. French agents had no apparent success in the colony, and there is no hard evidence that any operated there until 1799. Yet the initial reaction to the 1791 uprising had been one of excitement and admiration accompanied in some quarters by a desire to emulate it. Quite possibly planters covered up minor incidents on their own estates, and there can be no doubt that they wished to avoid giving an impression of public alarm that might damage their all-important commercial credit. Such considerations did not apply, however, to the governor's correspondence with London; from 1792 onward perhaps the most prominent leitmotiv in the letters of Williamson, Balcarres, and George Nugent is a smug confidence in the Jamaican slaves' "tranquillity."[68]

How is this to be explained? To begin with, it might be asked what impact one should expect the St. Domingue Revolution to have had on Jamaica. Just how influential were its several aspects—the slave revolt, free-colored equality, the emancipation decree, activity by French Repub-

---

local Haitians had attempted a landing on Martinique and then stirred up unrest on Trinidad in Dec. 1805. The evidence from Trinidad, however, suggests that the report was confused or mendacious. On Trinidad see Craton, *Testing the Chains*, 235-236. On Dessalines and other early heads of state see David Nicholls, *From Dessalines to Duvalier: Race, Colour and National Independence in Haiti* (Cambridge, 1979), 36-37, 46-47.

[67] Roberto Palacios, "Ansia de Libertad," *Lanternù*, I (1983), 20-27; José Salcedo-Bastardo, *Historia fundamental de Venezuela* (Caracas, 1977), 196. A plot against Jamaica hatched in southern St. Domingue was foiled by Christophe in 1806; see W. Harvey, *Sketches of Hayti* (London, 1827), 335-336.

[68] C.O. 137/89-113.

lican agents, and (not discussed here) the achievement of Haitian independence?

While the revolt of 1791 had far more influence on Jamaica than did the emancipation decree of 1794, the opposite was the case in Louisiana, Curaçao, South Carolina, Venezuela, and of course the other French colonies.[69] Both the revolt and the emancipation decree worried the British government considerably less than the spectacular attempts to spread from Guadeloupe the revolution begun by Victor Hugues[70]—but do these properly form part of the St. Domingue Revolution? In view of what happened in the British Windward Islands, in Venezuela (Coro rebellion, 1795, and Maracaibo conspiracy, 1799), in Brazil (Bahia conspiracy, 1798), in Cuba (Aponte conspiracy, 1812), and in the United States (Vesey conspiracy, 1822; perhaps also the 1811 revolt in Louisiana), one might argue that the Haitian Revolution had more impact on free coloreds than on slaves.[71] This could conceivably have been true of Jamaica as well. In the context of the island's colonial history, the free-colored petition of 1792 stands out as being more unusual and ultimately more effective than anything that happened in the slave community during this period.

Of course the St. Domingue slave revolt served as an example and inspiration to later rebels—Cuba, 1812, Barbados, 1816, and Jamaica, 1831, are well-known examples—but nowhere does its influence appear to have been at all critical. The British colonies most affected by the revolutionary crisis were the Windward Islands of Grenada, Dominica, and St. Vincent, none of which experienced actual slave rebellion. In each, an alienated Francophone population—free colored, white, and Carib—called in French forces from Guadeloupe and turned to the slaves for support.[72] We do find autonomous slave action in the 1801 conspiracy on Tobago, but it, too, was a formerly French colony and was then thought a likely bargaining counter in the forthcoming peace talks between France and England.[73] Tobago's slaves probably felt that revolt would ensure

[69] See Federico Brito Figueroa, *Las insurrecciones de los esclavos negros en la sociedad colonial venezolana* (Caracas, 1961), 64-81; "Rusticus" letters, Miscellaneous Papers, South Carolina Historical Society, Charleston; and notes 67, 74, 91.

[70] Geggus, *Slavery, War, and Revolution*, 150, 190-191.

[71] See below, notes 75, 89; Salcedo-Bastardo, *Venezuela*, 193-197; Kenneth R. Maxwell, *Conflicts and Conspiracies: Brazil and Portugal, 1750-1808* (Cambridge, 1973), 218-223; and Genovese, *Rebellion to Revolution*, 43-45. One might also include the Jean Kina revolt on Martinique in 1802 and the Morales conspiracy of 1795 in Cuba, but apparently neither was influenced by the example of St. Domingue; see David Geggus, "Manifestation de gens de couleur ou révolte d'esclaves manqué? La révolte de Jean Kina à Fort-Royal," *Annales des Antilles,* forthcoming, and Hugh Thomas, *Cuba: The Pursuit of Freedom* (London, 1971), 81.

[72] See above, n. 6, and below, n. 89.

[73] Keith Lawrence, "The Tobago Slave Conspiracy, 1801" (paper presented at the 13th conference of the Association of Caribbean Historians, Guadeloupe, 1981).

transfer to French rule and, with it, emancipation. The background to the Pointe Coupée conspiracy of 1795 in Spanish Louisiana was remarkably similar.[74] However, recent Spanish legislation on slaves and free coloreds may also have been a factor there, as it was in the almost simultaneous Morales conspiracy in Cuba and the Coro rebellion in Venezuela.[75]

In the Dutch colonies there was a different sort of "French connection." Forcibly allied to France at the beginning of 1795, their ruling classes split into pro- and anti-French factions, from which the slaves of Demerara and Curaçao immediately attempted to profit.[76] Five years later, forces from Guadeloupe and southern St. Domingue briefly invaded Curaçao and received support from slaves, it is true, but also from whites and free coloreds. Overall, the clustering of conspiracies and rebellions in the 1790s is impressive—and one could mention several more—but none can be viewed simply as reactions to events in St. Domingue.

In this light, the example of Jamaica seems rather less surprising. Still, it remains to be examined how others, then and since, have explained the dearth of autonomous slave resistance in the British Caribbean in these years. According to Jamaica's planters in their public pronouncements, the island's stability demonstrated the mildness of its slave regime.[77] There seems little doubt that slavery had become less brutal in the later eighteenth century, in response to changing sensibilities and rising slave prices, but this had been as true of St. Domingue as of anywhere else.[78] The historian of the Maroons, Robert Dallas, writing in 1803, thought the slaves' disunity guaranteed the island's safety, just as his fellow Jamaican Edward Long had observed thirty years earlier that Africans and creoles did not combine in revolt.[79] Similarly, in the work of Michael Craton, the factor inhibiting revolts in this period that receives most emphasis is the transition then taking place in the British Caribbean from African- to creole-dominated societies.[80] Africans and creoles, he argues, tended to

[74] Jack D. L. Holmes, "The Abortive Slave Revolt at Pointe Coupée, Louisiana, 1795," *Louisiana History*, XI (1970), 341-362.

[75] José Luciano Franco, *Las minas de Santiago del Prado y la rebelión de los Cobreros* (Havana, 1975), 69; John Lynch, *The Spanish American Revolutions, 1808-1826* (London, 1973), 192; Salcedo-Bastardo, *Venezuela*, 193. The reforming Codigo Negro Carolino of 1789 was withdrawn in 1794, but the legal position of free coloreds was improved early the following year.

[76] See above, n. 67, and Walter McGowan, "The French Revolutionary Period in Demerara-Essequibo" (paper presented at the 13th conf. of Assoc. of Caribbean Historians, Guadeloupe, 1981).

[77] Geggus, "British Opinion," in Walvin, ed., *Slavery and British Society*, 124.

[78] Geggus, *Slavery, War, and Revolution*, 26.

[79] Dallas, *Maroons*, II, 454-455; [Edward Long], *The History of Jamaica; or, General Survey of the Antient and Modern State of That Island . . .* (London, 1774), II, 444.

[80] Craton, "The Passion to Exist: Slave Rebellions in the British West Indies, 1650-1832," *Journal of Caribbean History*, XIII (1980), 11, and *Testing the Chains*, 165, 171.

stage different types of revolt, and, when the two communities were evenly balanced, tensions between them made it difficult to organize successful resistance.

There is much to be said for this argument. Rebels influenced by news of reforms or rebellions elsewhere were usually creoles. The new type of slave revolt linked to rumors of official emancipation, which was common in the nineteenth century[81] and which emerged in this period,[82] was closely associated with creole slaves. African rebellions, however, appear to have been more often of local inspiration, as in Santo Domingo in 1796 and in nineteenth-century Brazil.[83] Where creoles formed only a minority of the population, they rarely participated in insurrections, perhaps because they appreciated the difficulty of directing them. This seems to have been the case in Brazil at this time.[84] During the 1790s a huge upsurge in the slave trade to Jamaica was raising the number of Africans toward parity with creoles. This may have made creoles reluctant to try to act against the status quo. Contrarily, Africans still remained, despite massive annual importations, a minority in Jamaica, thus reducing the possibility of ethnically organized revolts. An additional factor may have been the high proportion of women and children in the Jamaican slave trade at this time. Also numerous were "Congo" and Ibo Africans, who were widely reputed to adapt least violently to slavery.[85]

Tensions between Africans and creoles, however, cannot provide an overall explanation of the relative dearth of rebellions and conspiracies in the British Caribbean during these years. As Craton points out, African and creole slaves did on occasion combine in revolt. St. Domingue itself is a classic case in point.[86] Furthermore, in many British colonies, such as

[81] Michael Craton, "Slave Culture, Resistance and the Achievement of Emancipation in the British West Indies, 1783-1838," in Walvin, ed., *Slavery and British Society*, 105-106.

[82] While earlier examples can be found (Virginia, 1730; Venezuela, 1749, 1770), the phenomenon first fully emerges with the rebellions on Martinique (1789), Tortola (1790), Dominica and St. Domingue (1791). See Geggus, *Slavery, War, and Revolution*, 30, 412; Brito Figueroa, *Insurrecciones*, 49-53, 59; Elsa V. Goveia, *Slave Society in the British Leeward Islands at the End of the Eighteenth Century* (New Haven, Conn., 1965), 334; Craton, *Testing the Chains*, 224-225; and [Pierre Dessalles], *Historique des troubles survenus à la Martinique pendant la Révolution*, ed. Leo Elisabeth (Fort de France, n.d.), 17-30.

[83] See above, n. 55, and Stuart Schwartz, *Sugar Plantations and the Formation of Brazilian Society* (Cambridge, 1986), chap. 18.

[84] Schwartz, *Sugar Plantations*, chap. 18.

[85] Sex ratio in the Jamaican slave trade was consistently 165:100 in the period 1764-1788 and fell to 161:100 in the 1790s; see *Two Reports from the Committee of the Assembly of Jamaica on the Slave Trade* (London, 1789), and *Proceedings of the Hon. House of Assembly of Jamaica on the Sugar and Slave Trade* (London, 1793). Blacks from Biafra and Central Africa accounted for more than 80% of Jamaican slave imports in the 1790s (Curtin, *Atlantic Slave Trade*, 160).

[86] See Geggus, *Slave Resistance*, 21-22.

Barbados, the Bahamas, and the Leeward Islands, the great majority of the slaves already were creole.

Of notable relevance, therefore, is another stabilizing factor mentioned by Craton and other writers. This is the creole slaves' growing sense of identification with their particular islands. Foreigners offering freedom, whatever color they were, were still foreign and likely to be perceived as disruptive outsiders rather than liberators.[87] The most striking example of small island chauvinism is doubtless that of highly creolized Barbados, whose slave population celebrated British military victories and was said to be actively Francophobe.[88] Yet even in recently settled St. Vincent and Dominica very few slaves rallied to the invading French in 1795, and, significantly, these tended to be those of resident French planters who rebelled with them. Even in the more successful Grenada insurrection of 1795-1797, slaves were far less prominent than the free coloreds and French whites. As Craton observes, Grenada and St. Vincent actually came to depend for their defense on black rangers who preferred to seek their freedom through military service, defending the slave regime.[89] In Jamaica, Governor Nugent reported in 1803 that the slaves "detested" the blacks brought there by refugees from St. Domingue.[90] Should the slaves have been any less xenophobic than their owners?

Nevertheless, the example of the three British Windwards clearly shows that the main factor here was not slave xenophobia but the presence or absence of disgruntled Francophone communities. In fact, in the whole Caribbean, the only colonies where the slaveowning class was seriously challenged in the 1790s (St. Domingue, Grenada, St. Vincent, Demerara, Curaçao) were those where it was divided by social and political tensions exacerbated by the French Revolution. These were also colonies where the white community was demographically and militarily weak.[91]

While most writers on slave resistance have recognized the importance of the strength and unity of the master class, few have given it its due weight, preferring instead to concentrate more on the rebel than on the forces that restrained him. In particular, the military factor has received very little attention at all. It may be that historians have discounted the importance of European troops because of their poor performance against slave rebels. However, this would confuse to some extent the rash blundering and indiscipline of colonial militias with the actions of the

[87] Craton, *Testing the Chains*, 165-168, and "Passion," *Jour. Caribbean Hist.*, XIII (1980), 11.

[88] H. Beckles, *Black Rebellion in Barbados* (Bridgetown, 1984), 60-61.

[89] Craton, *Testing the Chains*, 180-210, 227; Edward L. Cox, *The Free Coloreds in the Slave Societies of St. Kitts and Grenada, 1763-1833* (Knoxville, Tenn., 1984), 76-91.

[90] George Nugent to Joseph Sullivan, Feb. 5, 1803, C.O. 137/110.

[91] This was also true of the French colonies of St. Lucia and Guadeloupe, but black resistance there postdated the act of emancipation and was directed against foreign attempts to restore slavery. For psychological and military reasons, rather than narrowly legalistic ones, it cannot be considered "slave resistance."

European garrisons. It would also ignore the fact that it was usually regular soldiers who put down the rebellions. One need additionally note the deterrent effect, particularly of cavalry, which could pin down a slave population that lived for the most part, not in mountain fastnesses, but in coastal plains. While this military factor may seem obvious[92]—and certainly does not make for exciting social theory—it deserves emphasis for three reasons. First, it has been neglected by historians of individual revolts and of slave resistance in general.[93] Second, variations in garrison strength in the long or short term seem to have played a part in the genesis of numerous conspiracies and rebellions. Most important, the military factor provides a solution to our initial paradox, that slave resistance in the British Caribbean was at almost its lowest ebb during the Age of Revolution.

It was precisely during the years 1776-1815 that Britain's military presence in the region was at its peak. In his *History of Jamaica* (1774), Edward Long noted how the French West Indies (which had suffered fewer slave revolts than the British) were more strongly garrisoned and consequently dwelled "in full security."[94] Shortly thereafter the situation changed. The British colonial garrisons were boosted during the American War of Independence, and they were not cut back to prewar levels in 1783. They were successively strengthened during the war scares of 1788 and 1790, and again in 1791-1792 in reaction to the St. Domingue revolt. They were further reinforced during the struggle with Revolutionary France.[95] A succession of international crises ensured that, when the St. Domingue slave revolt broke out, there were already more soldiers in Jamaica than ever before in peacetime. The garrison then received substantial reinforcements, including cavalry. In the space of five years it almost doubled.[96] It is true that the transfer of troops to St. Domingue after 1793 on occasion considerably reduced the garrison, so it would be foolish to hold rigidly to some sort of military determinism. Nevertheless, it would seem self-evident that slaves meditating rebellion kept a weather eye on the arrival and departure of troops and acted accordingly.

[92] Craton, however, doubts the importance of the military garrisons because of the ease with which slaves were recruited in the colonies to fight black rebels ("Passion," *Jour. Caribbean Hist.*, XIII [1980], 11).

[93] A recent exception is Edward Cox. In explaining the Grenada insurrection of 1795, he contrasts the colony with peaceful and better-defended St. Kitts and notes that the Grenada garrison was cut down to only 192 men during the two years preceding the revolt (*Free Coloreds*, 78-86). Of the 100 or more peasant revolts that took place in 18th-century Peru, Leon G. Campbell observes that their incidence was lower in regions where local garrisons had been strengthened or reorganized ("Social Structure of the Túpac Amaru Army in Cuzco, 1780-81," *Hispanic American Historical Review*, LXI [1981], 676).

[94] [Long], *History of Jamaica*, III, 941.

[95] "Forces in Jamaica, Oct. 1791," C.O. 137/89; Dundas to Lord Effingham, Jan. 7, 1792, C.O. 137/90.

[96] Geggus, "Jamaica," *Americas*, XXXVIII (1981), 221.

Only after the end of the Napoleonic Wars were the West Indian garrisons reduced. In April 1816 the first major revolt in the British Caribbean in half a century broke out in Barbados, where the garrison had recently been cut by over half. This was in fact the only slave rebellion in the colony's long history, and the first instance of organized, violent resistance there since 1702. Between December 1814 and December 1815, the month the insurrection was planned,[97] the number of rank and file soldiers on the island fell from 3,289 to 1,414, while the proportion listed as sick rose from 7 percent to 21 percent.[98] Furthermore, the European troops remaining were merely the remnants of some twenty different corps, and almost half the garrison consisted of black, mainly Francophone soldiers, who the rebels wrongly thought would not attack them. During the three months before the rebellion, the garrison did receive 400 reinforcements, but it still mustered little more than half its wartime strength and the proportion in hospital remained high (16 percent).

Michael Craton and Hilary Beckles have shown that the 1816 insurrection was the product of several factors, but neither has noted this weakening in the forces of control. They do observe, however, that the major slave conspiracy in Barbados history, that of 1692, was specifically intended to profit from the departure of local militia on a wartime expedition. Two earlier attempts, they add, had been similarly timed but were abandoned owing to changes in the planters' plans and the arrival of naval and military forces.[99]

In Jamaica, both the Hanover conspiracy of 1776 and the Second Maroon War followed directly on the departure of regiments from the island.[100] With regard to the shadowy Ibo plot of December 1815, one cannot point to any major reduction of wartime troop levels, but garrison strength did decline by some 6 percent in the previous half year, while the number of troops present and fit for duty fell by over 10 percent.[101] It may also be relevant that the only other violent disturbances on Jamaican plantations during these four decades occurred in the postwar year of 1784.[102]

Much more striking is the background to the great Jamaican Christmas Rebellion, or Baptist War, of 1831. Apart from the St. Domingue uprising, this was the largest slave revolt in the history of the Americas. In the two years leading up to the rebellion, we find that the size of the Jamaica garrison was reduced by nearly 30 percent (more than 1,000 men) to what appears to have been its lowest level in over thirty years.[103]

[97] Beckles, *Barbados*, 92-93; Craton, *Testing the Chains*, 260-261.
[98] Garrison returns, W.O. 17/2503-2505.
[99] Craton, *Testing the Chains*, 111; Beckles, *Barbados*, 44.
[100] Craton, *Testing the Chains*, 174; above, n. 36.
[101] W.O. 17/2004-2006.
[102] Synnott, "Slave Revolts," 252.
[103] W.O. 17/2020-2021.

Numbers declined steadily through 1830-1831 but most rapidly in the spring and summer preceding the rebellion, when it is believed to have been organized.[104] Similar circumstances may also have attended the other great Jamaican insurrection, Tacky's Rebellion of 1760, which followed by just over a year the dispatch of militia and military forces to occupy the French colony of Guadeloupe. It is more certain, however, that the uprisings of 1765 and 1766 followed a major reduction in the Jamaica garrison. Wartime reinforcements had been withdrawn in 1764, and in the same year 14 percent of the new garrison died of disease.[105]

Any generalization about slave rebellions needs to be tested against the case of St. Domingue in August 1791. There we find that one of the two colonial regiments had been deported three months before the insurrection and that the other was nearly 200 men under strength. Two extra battalions had arrived in March, but in the governor's view they were actually dangerous, being politically radical, mutinous, and apt to fraternize with the slaves. More important, perhaps, is the fact that the rural police force in the region of the revolt had been disarmed the previous winter.[106]

Data from the Spanish Caribbean also point to the importance of troop levels in deterring slave resistance. At the time of the St. Domingue revolt, Cuba possessed probably the fastest-growing slave population in the West Indies.[107] However, its garrison of about 4,000 men was also the strongest in the Caribbean, both in absolute terms and relative to the colonial population.[108] Moreover, with the outbreak of war in 1793 this garrison was reinforced with two regiments from Mexico. Through the entire eighteenth century the island appears to have experienced little overt slave unrest until 1795. There then began a succession of revolts and conspiracies, culminating in the very extensive plot of José Antonio Aponte that reached fruition in March 1812.[109] During exactly the same

[104] Craton, *Testing the Chains*, 297-299.

[105] [Long], *History of Jamaica*, II, 308-312, 465, 471. The second largest revolt in the British Caribbean, the Aug. 1823 uprising in Demerara, occurred when garrison strength had fallen by 12% in six months. Troop levels had indeed been lower in the early months of 1821 but nonetheless were at their lowest level for almost two years. The revolt also followed two months of high morbidity (13%, 19%) (W.O. 17/2510-2512).

[106] Geggus, *Slavery, War, and Revolution*, 39, 413; Governor's Correspondence, Dxxv/46/431, Archs. Nationales; C9A/167, 98, 117.

[107] See the data in Kenneth F. Kiple, *Blacks in Colonial Cuba, 1774-1899* (Gainesville, Fla., 1976), 27-28.

[108] On the Cuban military see Allan J. Kuethe, *Cuba, 1753-1815: Crown, Military, and Society* (Knoxville, Tenn., 1986), 140-144; Jacobo de Pezuela, *Diccionario geográfico . . . de la isla de Cuba* (Madrid, 1863), II, 252-253.

[109] Fernando Ortiz, *Los negros esclavos* (Havana, 1975), 388-389; Alain Yacou, "Le projet des révoltes serviles de l'île de Cuba dans la première moitié du XIXe siècle" (paper presented at the 14th conf. of Assoc. of Caribbean Historians, San Juan, 1982), 3-9.

period, starting in 1793, the colonial garrison underwent a steady decline, as troops were sent to Santo Domingo, Florida, and Louisiana, and reinforcements from Europe dried up. By 1795, over half the garrison had been transferred outside Cuba. By 1810, the regular garrison had only 30 percent of its 1791 complement, while the two Mexican regiments sent to the island had lost 80 percent of their men.[110] Aponte began organizing his rebellion in the early months of 1811,[111] when it is probable that the colonial garrisons, cut off from war-torn Spain, declined even further. One might add that garrison strength rose during the years 1799-1804, which were free from internal strife.[112]

In Venezuela, as in Cuba, the years 1795-1799 saw a weakened garrison confront a remarkable upsurge in slave resistance. Not only did recruits from Spain cease arriving in the 1790s, but in 1793 militia and men from the Caracas Regiment were moved to Santo Domingo, where some remained until 1799. Moreover, in Maracaibo, where an attempted rising took place in May 1799, the garrison had been cut by more than half little over a year before.[113] As for Santo Domingo, scene of the New World's first slave insurrection in 1521, it apparently experienced no slave revolt at all in the eighteenth century, until the slaves on its largest sugar estate took up arms in October 1796.[114] The insurrection can be attributed to various factors, one of which was surely the reduction in troop levels that year, following Spain's surrender of the colony to France.[115]

Nineteenth-century Brazil provides further evidence. The long cycle of Bahian slave revolts in the period 1807-1835 was surprisingly interrupted by the civil war fought by the planters against the government in 1821-1823. João Reis argues that the slaves could not take advantage of the disruption because of the unprecedented mobilization of military forces.[116] Slaves did rebel during Venezuela's war for secession, but only during its early years, when royalist forces were extremely weak and,

[110] See above, n. 108. The earliest resistance dated from early July 1795 (Estado 5/15, Archivo General de Indias, Seville, Sp.). In May, additional troops had been rushed to Louisiana (Holmes, "Pointe Coupée," *La. Hist.,* XI [1970], 349).

[111] José Luciano Franco, *Las conspiraciones de 1810 y 1811* (Havana, 1977), 13.

[112] See Christon I. Archer, *The Army in Bourbon Mexico, 1760-1810* (Albuquerque, N.M., 1977), 255; Kuethe, *Cuba,* 141.

[113] See the data in Eleázar Córdova-Bello, *La independencia de Haití y su influencia en Hispanoamerica* (Caracas, 1967), 65, and Gary Miller, "Status and Loyalty in Colonial Spanish America: A Social History of Regular Army Officers in Venezuela, 1750-1810" (Ph.D. diss., University of Florida, 1985), 32. According to Córdova-Bello, Venezuela sent about 1,000 men to Santo Domingo.

[114] Carlos Esteban Deive, *La esclavitud del negro en Santo Domingo (1492-1844)* (Santo Domingo, 1980), II, 465-474.

[115] See Estado 5/61, 5/202, 11/59, 13/13 and 16/12, for details of both troop withdrawals and the rebellion.

[116] Reis, "Slave Resistance in Brazil, Bahia, 1807-1835," *Luso-Brazilian Review,* forthcoming.

deliberately encouraging such uprisings, declared slavery abolished.[117]

The cases of Brazil and Venezuela suggest an interesting parallel with Cuba. Between about 1805 and 1843, Cuban society went through a period of intense slave resistance, with a curious lull (scarcely noticed by historians) from 1813 to 1824.[118] These were not only years when the Spanish empire was rent by revolution, but also a period of extremely rapid expansion in the Cuban economy, when slaves came to bulk larger in the population than at any previous time. Slave imports into Cuba reached what was probably their peak, and the numbers involved outmatched any other example in the history of the Caribbean slave trade.[119] According to the criteria usually employed, this should have been a period of considerable slave resistance. Was it perhaps Havana's role between 1815 and 1824 as a military stronghold in Spain's war against its colonies that stemmed the tide of rebellion? Significantly, Spain's other military bastion, Puerto Rico, experienced its first major slave revolt in over a century in 1825 at the end of the war.[120] In this light, it seems that the dearth of slave conspiracies and uprisings in the British North American colonies during their own War of Independence might be explained not only by increased opportunities for flight and manumission but also by military factors.

Slave revolts were obviously multicausal phenomena. In none of the examples given above would I claim the weakening in the forces of control to have been the only, or even the decisive, factor at work. Yet it has been demonstrated, I think, that slaves paid closer attention to the troops who stood guard over them than have historians who have studied their behavior.[121] The coming and going of colonial regiments was highly visible. Military barracks and hospitals employed numerous slaves, and whites often remarked on the speed with which news could spread through slave communities. Of course, sudden reductions in troop levels

[117] Lynch, *Spanish American Revolutions*, 197-198; Jorge I. Domínguez, *Insurrection or Loyalty: The Breakdown of the Spanish American Empire* (Cambridge, Mass., 1980), 176-179.

[118] See above, n. 109.

[119] Accounts conflict; for import data I have followed David R. Murray, *Odious Commerce: Britain, Spain and the Abolition of the Cuban Slave Trade* (Cambridge, 1980), 80, 112, 212, and for population statistics, Kiple, *Cuba*.

[120] Luís M. Díaz Soler, *Historia de la esclavitud negra en Puerto Rico*, 4th ed. (San Juan, 1974), 201-214; Guillermo A. Baralt, *Esclavos rebeldes: Conspiraciones y sublevaciones de esclavos en Puerto Rico, 1795-1873* (Rio Piedras, P.R., 1981), 16-67. It should be noted, however, that the Cuban garrison actually increased considerably at the end of the war, although this brought with it the demise of the Cuban militia. A special mounted rural militia had been established in 1812 (Pezuela, *Diccionario*, II, 252-253).

[121] It is significant that at the end of the 18th century the carnival Jonkonnu character took on the appearance of a soldier in the British West Indies (Judith Bettelheim, "Jamaican Jonkonnu and Related Caribbean Festivals," in Margaret E. Crahan and Franklin W. Knight, eds., *Africa and the Caribbean: The Legacies of a Link* (Baltimore, 1979), 81, 86, 95.

did not necessarily produce revolts. The example of Jamaica itself after the departure of soldiers for St. Domingue in 1793-1794 makes this clear enough. However, the correlation revealed so far between military strength and the incidence of slave resistance certainly suggests that the topic is worth investigating further, preferably with regard to militia and police forces as well as troops.

Some may feel that this stress on the forces of control is another example of excluding the slaves from their own history, a denial of their ability to act independently. I prefer to see it as the best point of departure for the study of slave resistance. Avoiding the vagaries associated with theories of the "slave personality," it seems to identify one of the lowest common denominators shared by revolts and conspiracies in different types of slave society.

Sugar colonies were obviously in a class apart in this respect, but their tendency to generate rebellions could have stemmed less from harsh conditions than from organizational factors associated with large plantation units (ease of communication, for example). At present it is difficult to say if conditions of economic depression or expansion were the more conducive to resistance. Similarly, while the example of North America suggests that the demographic balance between black and white was of crucial significance, it is worth remembering that in the populations of nineteenth-century Brazil and Cuba the proportion of slaves was approximately the same as in the U.S. South. Newly arrived Africans clearly showed a propensity to rebel, but the largest revolts in the Caribbean tended to be those by creoles.[122] The proximity of rugged, uninhabited terrain probably encouraged rebellions, but perhaps more often it channeled resistance in the direction of *marronage*. The closing of such an internal "frontier" might stimulate all-out rebellion (as in eighteenth-century Jamaica)[123] or could stifle it entirely (as in eighteenth-century Barbados). The slave response to expanding and declining military garrisons appears much more clear cut.

The cultural factors emphasized by Craton were doubtless important in shaping modes of resistance, but the influence of libertarian ideas, to which Eugene Genovese gives great weight, seems less certain.[124] While surely no slave, before or after the French Revolution, lacked the concept of freedom, libertarian ideology clearly made a far greater impact on free coloreds, such as Toussaint Louverture, rather than on slaves.[125] Where

---

[122] Even in St. Domingue, in the northern plain where the 1791 revolt began, two-thirds of the slaves were creoles: David Geggus, "Les esclaves de la plaine du Nord à la veille de la Révolution française, partie 4," *Rev. soc. haitienne hist.*, CXLIX (1985), 16-51.

[123] Synnott argues that the Maroon treaties of 1739-1740 closed off Jamaica's hinterland to runaways, thus restricting options for resistance as in the small islands ("Slave Revolts," 234-235).

[124] Craton, *Testing the Chains, passim;* Genovese, *Rebellion to Revolution, passim.*

[125] On Toussaint's free status see D. Geggus, "Toussaint Louverture and the Slaves of the Bréda Plantations," *Jour. Caribbean Hist.*, XIX (1986), 30-48.

antislavery ideas and/or French libertarianism did shape slave resistance, I think it was less as inspiration than as evidence of divisions in the ranks of the whites and as a sign that concessions could be won. Hence, though the French Revolutionary period did see the appearance of a new type of slave revolt, linked to rumors of emancipation,[126] its ideological significance is questionable. It also owed at least as much to the Anglo-French antislavery movement as to the French Revolution itself.[127]

The most generally valid approach to slave resistance in the Age of Revolution is thus one that stresses the strength of the forces of control. If such an approach identifies occasions rather than causes, it is because resistance lay close to the surface of all slave societies. Another implication is that insurrections were more rationally calculated, less desperate affairs than they have often seemed.[128]

To expect slaves to have rebelled merely in reaction to events in St. Domingue is to suppose that the shackles of slavery were psychological rather than physical: it is to underestimate the problems involved. If the news of the slave revolution gave blacks in Jamaica a new sense of their potential strength and caused them to reassess the local balance of power, one should remember that the news from St. Domingue also included the slaughter of thousands of slaves like themselves. As always, the brutality and humiliations of bondage had to be weighed against the risks of resistance. In the absence of circumstances realistically favoring rebellion, slaves in Jamaica and many other places simply took pride, it seems, in what was happening in the French colony and showed their awareness by what whites everywhere called "insolence."[129] This in itself merits further study.

[126] See above, notes 81, 82.

[127] Note that the Martinique rebellion of Aug. 1789 was connected with rumors of royalist reforms and occurred before news arrived of the popular revolution in Paris (Elisabeth, ed., *Martinique,* 17-30).

[128] The point is also made in Craton, *Testing the Chains,* 15.

[129] See "Rusticus" letters, Miscell. Papers; Yacou, "Cuba," 5; Holmes, "Pointe Coupée," *La. Hist.,* XI (1970), 356; and above, n. 10.

25

The Saint-Domingue Slave Insurrection of 1791: A Socio-Political and Cultural Analysis

Carolyn E. Fick

The Saint Domingue slave insurrection of August 1791 was by no means a spontaneous or unmediated event, and in the context of the anti-colonial and anti-slavery struggles of the late eighteenth and nineteenth-century Atlantic world in which it occurred, its importance is paramount. This article will attempt to provide closer insights into the political and military organisation, the social composition of the leadership, and the cultural and ideological components of that momentous historical event.

One of the most prodigious and certainly one of the most respected writers on French Caribbean slavery was the late Gabriel Debien, who, in his monumental work, *Les esclaves aux Antilles françaises: XVIIe au XVIIIe siècle*, published in 1974, stated that no study had yet been made of the origins, the chronology, or the geographic development of the August 1791 Saint Domingue slave insurrection.[1] This article is a modest and, given the limited number of testimonies and eyewitness accounts, unfortunately only a partial attempt at providing a schematic record of what actually happened and how.[2] Specifically, the article will address controversial issues regarding the mode of organisation and the political and cultural content of the slave gatherings that preceded the insurrection, as well as the logistics of its outbreak and of its subsequent geographic movement. It will attempt to identify the leaders and their relationship to the plantation regime and will examine the relationship of marronage (or the flight of slaves from the plantations under a variety of circumstances) to the organisation and the unfolding of the insurrection, as well as to the character of the insurgency. Finally, it will begin to look at the developing cleavage— inevitable in all revolutions—between the behaviour of the leadership and the mentality and aspirations of the popular forces.

It should be remembered, however, that the Saint Domingue revolution did not begin by slave rebellion. Rather, the slave insurrection of August 1791 broke out in the midst of a colonial revolt

2   *Carolyn E. Fick*

against the metropolis, whose political foundations themselves were being challenged. And so it was in an environment of revolutionary upheaval in France and of the consequent and ubiquitous breakdown of the ruling order in the colony, from 1788-89 onward, that the aspirations of the slaves found concrete expression and became both militarily and politically expedient.

As a significant portion of the colony's white planter elite had begun, in the name of free trade and local sovereignty, to rebel against the economic and political constraints of the crown's mercantile policy, Saint Domingue's free coloureds, in their turn, openly rebelled against the colonial and metropolitan politics of white supremacy to obtain full civil equality. It was amid these upheavals that slaves of Saint Domingue were inauspiciously preparing to strike out on their own. Those in the colony's North Province had in fact been organising themselves, with purpose and deliberation, for several weeks before that fateful night of 22nd August 1791, a date which marked the beginning of the end of one of the greatest wealth-producing colonies the world had ever known.

On Sundays during the month of August, slave representatives from the major plantations in the region had been meeting clandestinely to lay the plans for general insurrection, but it was on the night of the fourteenth, one week before the actual outbreak, that the final scheme was drawn up and the instructions given out. Numbering some two hundred in all, consisting of "two delegates each from all the plantations of Port-Margot, Limbé, Acul, Petite-Anse, Limonade, Plaine du Nord, Quartier-Morin, Morne-Rouge, etc., etc." covering the entire central region of the North Province, they were assembled to fix the date for the revolt that had been in the planning for some time.[3] They met on the Lenormand de Mézy plantation in Morne-Rouge, and all of the delegates were upper-strata slaves in whom the masters had placed their confidence, most of them slave foremen, or *commandeurs*, whose influence and authority over the field slaves were considerable. Upon a given signal, the plantations would be systematically and methodically set aflame and a general slave insurrection set afoot. To dissipate any hesitation or equivocation, a statement was read by an unknown mulatto or quadroon to the effect that the king and the National Assembly in France had decreed three free days per week for every slave, as well as the abolition of the whip as a form of punishment. They were told that it was the white masters and the colonial authorities who refused to consent and that royalist troops were on their way from France to execute the decree by force. The news was of course false, but it represented the nearest thing to freedom the

The Slave Insurrection of 1791   3

slaves had ever known, and it served as a rallying point around which to galvanize the aspirations of the slaves, to solidify and channel these into open rebellion.

Although the majority of the delegates agreed in principle that they should await the arrival of these royalist troops, the slave representatives from some of the plantations in Limbé and Acul insisted upon instigating the war against the whites at whatever cost, with or without the troops. In the end, they nearly agreed to begin the revolt that very night, but then went back on this decision as the considered it inopportune to carry out, on the spot, a general insurrection for which the plans had been finalised only that evening. The majority of the slaves decided to wait, and the date was fixed for the 22nd.

The early leaders forming the core of this movement were Boukman Dutty, Jeannot Bullet, Jean-François, Georges Biassou. The first two, according to one source, were to take charge of the initial stages of the movement, while Jean-François and Biassou were to take over first and second command of the insurrection once under way. Toussaint Louverture, who was to emerge as supreme leader of the revolution years later, served, inauspiciously at this point, as the link between these leaders and the system, carefully dissimulating his actual participation.[4] Although he remained on the Bréda plantation where he served as coachman for the manager, Bayon De Libertas, he had been a free black, or *affranchi*, for well over a decade.[5] With a pass signed by the governor, Toussaint was thus permitted to circulate freely and to frequent other plantations; but he was also in communication with influential elements of the royalist faction who hoped to profit from, and who even helped stimulate, the brewing slave insurrection by invoking a common cause—the defense of the king who had, they rumoured, granted the slaves three free days per week. Once they had used the slave insurrection to defeat the rival colonial autonomist faction, known as the patriots, and once power was restored in royalist hands and the king securely on the throne of France, the blacks, they no doubt believed, could then be persuaded by their leaders to return to the plantations and be duped back into slavery. Undeniably, links between the slave leaders and certain royalists in the early stages were important, but for the latter to have assumed that the slave insurrection would, in the end, amount to little more than a traditional jacquerie was, in the context of impending revolution and imperial wars, a grave mistake.[6]

Of the leaders, it was Boukman who was to give the signal for the revolt. He had been a *commandeur* and later a coachman on the Clément plantation, among the first to go up in flames once the revolt

4   *Carolyn E. Fick*

began. While his experience as commandeur provided him with certain organisational and leadership qualities, the post as coachman no doubt enabled him to follow the ongoing political developments in the colony, as well as to facilitate communication links and establish contacts among the slaves of diverse plantations. Reputedly, Boukman was also a voodoo priest and, as such, exercised an undisputed influence and command over his followers, who knew him as "Zamba" Boukman. His authority was only enhanced by the overpowering impression projected by his gigantic size.[7]

Once the conspirators had reached agreement on the date, set for the 22nd, the accord was solemnized by a voodoo ceremony held in a thickly wooded area known as Bois-Caiman, not far from the Lenormand plantation.[8] According to one account, the ceremony was officiated by Boukman and a voodoo high priestess, an old negress "with strange eyes and bristly hair," just as terrifying as her counterpart.[9] Amidst raging streaks of lightning and violent bursts of thunder, as the account goes, accompanied by high winds and the torrential rains of the storm that had broken out that night, the high priestess raised her knife to kill a sacrificial pig, the blood of which was passed round for all to partake. As she began to invoke the deities, Boukman rose to deliver an impassioned oration to the assembled slaves. It was, in essence, a call to arms:

> The Good Lord who created the sun which gives us light from above, who rouses the sea and makes the thunder roar—listen well, all of you—this God, hidden in the clouds, watches us. He sees all that the white man does. The god of the white man calls him to commit crimes; our god asks only good works of us. But this god who is so good orders revenge! He will direct our hands; he will aid us. Throw away the image of the god of the whites who thirst for our tears and listen to the voice of liberty which speaks in the hearts of all of us.[10]

Couté la liberté li palé nan coeur nous tous: "Listen to the voice of liberty which speaks in the hearts of all of us." It was a refrain that would later recur under Boukman's leadership during the early days of the insurrection as he would exhort the insurgent slaves under his command to attack.[11]

The story of this ceremony has long since passed into legend, rendering all the more difficult the separation of actual fact from the elaborate mythology that later developed around the event.[12] Contemporary evidence is sparse; in fact, there is no mention of it at all in the archival documents that recount the conspiracy and are based largely on the testimony of a few slaves. But then, given the imperative of utmost secrecy in voodoo ceremonies, it is hardly surprising that no detailed contemporaneous accounts exist. This hardly justifies, on the other hand, dismissing the various accounts that do exist as pure fabrication. In fact, certain nineteenth-century Haitian family papers clearly identify one of the participants in the Bois-Caiman ceremony as Cécile Fatiman (that family member's own grandmother), a green-eyed mulatto woman with long silken black hair, the daughter of a Corsican prince and an African woman. She was herself a *mambo*, a voodoo high priestess.[13]

But in the absence of additional detailed documentation, many questions may still be raised concerning this event. Did all of the Morne-Rouge slave delegates participate in the Bois-Caiman ritual ceremony? Or conversely, were the participants in the Bois-Caiman ceremony the same individuals as those whose political views were expressed at the Morne-Rouge assembly earlier that evening? Certainly Boukman, as one of the chief leaders of the revolt and orator who delivered the Bois-Caiman speech, would have been present at both. Here then, the often-assumed antipathy of elite creole slaves toward voodoo, and toward African-born slaves practising it, may be brought into question as well. All or nearly all of the slave delegates were from the upper ranks of slave society usually filled by creole slaves. Cécile Fatiman, though a creole mulattress, was nonetheless a *mambo*. But was she actually the officiating priestess described quite dissimilarly in the one account as "an old negress with strange eyes and bristly hair?" As to so many questions pertaining to clandestine slave practices and activities in Saint Domingue before and during the revolution, where hard evidence is lacking, the answers will necessarily remain conjectural ones. What we can safely say, however, is first, that the Bois-Caiman ceremony did occur following the Morne-Rouge assembly; second, that the oration delivered was authentically Boukman's and that the ceremony was, after all, a voodoo event.

Even more important, though, is the historical significance of the 14th August assemblies, and this can be viewed on both an ideological and a political level. First, the Morne-Rouge gathering was a thoroughly organised affair and constituted in every sense a revolutionary political assembly, where issues were discussed, points of view and differing strategies presented, where a final agreement was reached, and a call to arms issued. That agreement was then confirmed and solemnised during the ritual ceremony at Bois-Caiman by a blood pact (and the symbolic drinking of the blood is mentioned in the account of the contemporary writer, Antoine Dalmas) that committed

6   *Carolyn E. Fick*

the participants to utmost secrecy, solidarity, and a vow of revenge.[14] In this sense, voodoo provided a medium for the political organisation of the slaves, as well as an ideological force, both of which contributed directly to the success of what became a virtual blitzkrieg attack on the plantations across the province.

Equally controversial in relation to the general framework and early stages of the conspiracy is the role of marronage, the desertion or running away of slaves from their plantations for diverse reasons and for varying lengths of time. Whether the August revolt was actually planned and organised in marronage, or by slaves in privileged positions within the plantation system, will no doubt remain a matter of dispute. What is probably closer to the truth is that the two elements worked hand in hand. Some evidence suggests that Jean-François was a maroon at the outset of the revolt and that Boukman was chronically maroon.[15] The report of the French civil commissioner, Roume, states that "for several weeks slave delegations had assembled on Sundays to work out together the plans for this destructive project."[16] As these slave delegations all came from different plantations throughout the North, from "Port-Margot, Limbé, Acul, Petite-Anse, Limonade, Plaine du Nord, Quartier-Morin, Morne-Rouge, etc. etc.," attendance at the meetings would have necessitated some sort of fairly regular small-scale marronage, or at least numerous and frequent leaves of absence without permission, unless of course each and every one of them held a Sunday market pass.[17] Even so, such passes were notoriously forged by even minimally literate slaves.

On the other hand, it is known that Toussaint was in close communication with Jean-François, Biassou, and Boukman even though he remained on his plantation and did not officially join the ranks until nearly three months later. We also have the statement of a slave *commandeur* from the Degrieux estate (referred to below) revealing that coachmen, domestics, and other trusted slaves of the surrounding plantations, in addition to the *commandeurs*, were involved in the conspiracy.[18] There is also the statement of an old Gallifet slave, Ignace, who was "distinguished from the other slaves by his exemption from any sort of work," who held the secret of the conspiracy for a long time and who had received instructions from a free black.[19] In fact, another of the core ringleaders was Jean-Baptiste Cap, a free black said to be possessed of substantial income and property.[20]

An incredibly vast network had been set afoot and facilitated by the interaction of several elements. These were African, as well as creole, and included the dynamics of marronage, as well as the subversive activities of *commandeurs* and of house slaves, and even a restricted segment of the free blacks, whose mobility and closer relationship to white society afforded them access to news, rumour, and information on the political situation in the colony. To separate any one element from the others, as if they are by nature mutually exclusive, will invariably leave the vital questions about the revolutionary organisation and capacities of these black masses perpetually unanswered.

The 14th August conspiracy was an ingenious plan, and it would have been perfect were it not for the premature activities of a few slaves in the Limbé district, who either misunderstood the final instructions or who impatiently insisted, in spite of the accord, upon beginning the revolt before the designated date. On 16th August, two days after the Morne-Rouge affair, some slaves were caught setting fire to one of the buildings on the Chabaud estate, in which the bagasse, or straw residue of the sugar cane, was stored. One of them, armed with a sabre, was the *commandeur* from the Desgrieux plantation. A physical battle ensued and, though wounded, the slave was arrested, put into irons and interrogated. Upon questioning, he revealed that the *commandeurs*, coachmen, domestics, and other slaves whom the masters trusted from the neighboring plantations had formed a conspiracy to burn the plantations and kill all the whites. He named as leaders a certain number of slaves from the Desgrieux plantation, four from the Flaville plantation in Acul, and Paul, a *commandeur* on the Blin plantation in Limbé.[21]

Upon confirming the declaration of the Desgrieux *commandeur*, the municipal authorities of Limbé issued a warning of the impending danger to the planters of the district and suggested to the manager of the Flaville estate that he apprehend those of his slaves who were denounced by name. Incredulous and unsuspecting, the Flaville manager convoked his slaves and offered his own head, in exchange, if the denunciations of the Desgrieux *commandeur* proved true. They all categorically denied any truth to the *commandeur's* statement, as did Paul Blin, who was also questioned and who also replied that the accusation brought against him was "false and slanderous," and that, filled with gratitude for the continual benevolence of his master, one would never see him involved in plots hatched against the whites or their property. A few days later (on the 20th) another conspirator, a mulatto slave, François, from the Chapotin estate was arrested and put to questioning for his part as accomplice to the arson committed at the Chabaud plantation. It was he who finally revealed the details of the Morne-Rouge assembly on the 14th. The following day the cook from the Desgrieux plantation was also to be arrested as one of the named conspirators, whereupon he managed to escape and went off to warn Paul Blin; together they joined the other ringleaders to prepare "the iron and the torch" for the execution of their dreadful projects. The general insurrection broke out on the following night as scheduled.

At ten o'clock, the slaves of the Flaville-Turpin estate in Acul, under the direction of one Auguste, deserted en masse to make their way to the Clément plantation, where they joined Boukman and combined their forces with the rest of the slaves there. Their numbers reinforced, they immediately set out to the Tremes estate; having narrowly missed the resident carpenter with their bullets, they took him prisoner and proceeded to the Noé plantation, where a dozen or so of these slaves had killed the refiner, his apprentice, as well as the manager. The only whites spared were the doctor and his wife, whose services they deemed might prove to be of great value to them.[22] By midnight the entire plantation was aflame, and the revolt had effectively begun.[23] The troops, by now consisting of the slaves from the Turpin-Flaville, Clément, and Noé plantations, returned with the three prisoners to the Clément estate, methodically assassinated M. Clément and his refiner, and left the prisoners there under guard. Armed with torches, guns, sabres, and whatever makeshift weapons they were able to contrive, they continued their devastation as they carried the revolt to the surrounding plantations. By six o'clock the next morning, both the Molines and Flaville plantations were totally destroyed, along with all of the white personnel; of all the plantations in the Acul district, only on two did some of the slaves refrain for the time being from participating in the revolt.[24]

From Acul, these slaves proceeded westward that same morning, the 23rd, toward the immediately adjacent Limbé district, augmenting their forces, by now close to two thousand,[25] as they moved from plantation to plantation and established military camps on each one as they took it over. One horrified colonist wrote at this point that "one can count as many rebel camps as there were plantations."[26] Making their way into Limbe via the Saint-Michel plantation, they were immediately joined by large numbers of slaves in the district where the premature beginning of this insurrection had been seen a week earlier. Within these few hours, the finest sugar plantations of Saint Domingue were literally devoured by flames. A resident merchant of le Cap remarked how, "like the effect of epidemical disease," the example set by slaves on one plantation communicated itself throughout the quarter of Limbé, and "in a few hours that immensely rich and flourishing country exhibited one vast scene of horror and devastation."[27] Nor was there

The Slave Insurrection of 1791   9

much tolerance in these crucial hours for slaves, and especially *commandeurs*, who hesitated or who offered opposition, for "wherever they have committed their ravages," the writer notes, "[the practice was] to seduce or oblige the Negroes on different plantations to join their party. . . . Those who discovered a reluctance or [who] refused to follow and assist in their designs [if they could not escape] were cut to pieces."[28]

Continuing westward, the slaves attacked Port-Margot in the early evening of the 24th, hitting at least four plantations, and by the 25th, the entire plain of this district had been devastated. The slaves took care to destroy, as they did from the very beginning and would continue to do throughout the first weeks of the revolution, not only the cane fields, but the manufacturing installations, sugar mills, tools and other farm equipment, storage bins, slave quarters; in short, every material manifestation of their existence under slavery and its means of exploitation. Insufficiently armed and totally unprepared, the planters could do little to oppose the rebels, and nothing to stop the fires that lasted for three days. The residents of Port-Margot believed for a long time that their slaves had had no part in the revolt, "but almost all the *ateliers* in the lower quarter ended up participating in it."[29] Coordinating their forces with insurgent slaves of the plantations situated in the hills and mountainous region bordering on Limbé and Plaisance, they completed their near-total destruction of the parish, leaving only the central area intact.[30]

As these slaves attempted to penetrate Plaisance on the 25th, they met with armed resistance, the first they had encountered, from a group of inhabitants who managed to drive them back into the Limbé plain, whereupon they divided up and returned by two different routes the following day.[31] Having terrorised the inhabitants upon their re-entry, having pillaged and then burned dozens of plantations, they took possession of the Ravine Champagne, where they set up military outposts and fortified their troops. Here, they held out for over three weeks while the planters, disorganised and badly armed, having already suffered serious casualties, awaited aid from the neighboring parishes. Yet whatever aid the whites managed to muster remained insufficient, for when strategically encircled or militarily overpowered, the slaves would disband and retreat into the mountains, only to attack again at different points with replenished and reorganised troops.[32]

At the very moment that these slaves were carrying out their depradations and defending their positions to the west of Acul, which appeared to have been the centre or hub from which the revolt would

10   *Carolyn E. Fick*

spread in all directions, slaves in the parishes to the east rose, torch in hand, with equal coordination and purpose. The movement of the revolt was indeed spreading like wildfire, and within these first few days, from the 22nd to the 25th, the plantations of the Petite-Anse, Quartier-Morin and Plaine du Nord parishes surrounding le Cap, as well as those of Limonade, all to the east of Acul, went up in flames as swiftly and as methodically as had those to the west.[33] The slaves on one of the Gallifet estates in Petite-Anse, however, had prematurely begun to revolt either on the 20th or the 21st by attempting to assassinate the manager, M. Mossut.[34] It is not surprising that it was on the smaller of the three Gallifet estates, on La Gossette, that this incident occurred. Of Gallifet's three sugar plantations, it was here that the slaves' conditions were harshest;[35] in fact, two years earlier, in 1789, 20 of these slaves had organized a "strike," or work stoppage, in the form of collective marronage, by remaining in the woods for two months in order to have the *commandeur* removed.[36] The account of the incidents from 20th to 24th August, presented by Antoine Dalmas, offers a small glimpse at some of the logistical difficulties involved in actually carrying through and strategically coordinating each part of the revolt. Particular circumstances over which the slaves had no control, such as the presence of key white personnel on the specified day, or other factors, like the degree of accord or dissidence between the *commandeur* and the slaves, or the role of the domestics, or simply the degree of impatience among the slaves, varied from one plantation to another.

For a reason that is unclear, the slaves at La Gossette had decided to begin before those in Limbé and Acul, and some 20 of them (perhaps some of the same that had deserted in protest in 1789) attempted to kill the manager during the night of his return from le Cap on the 20th or 21st. It was also on the 20th and 21st that two of the key conspirators, the slave François and the Desgrieux cook, were arrested in Limbé, and while the latter got away, François was taken to le Cap, put to the question, and revealed a major conspiracy. The La Gossette slaves, if they had received word of the arrests, may have deemed it unsafe to wait any longer. Whatever the case, their attempt on M. Mossut's life was unsuccessful, and the *procureur*, or plantation agent, M. Odeluc, along with several other whites from the main plantation, came to investigate. The *commandeur*, Blaise, who was the instigator of the assassination attempt, had already fled to warn the other leaders on the main plantation, La Grande Place, for when Odeluc returned there later that night, he found the gate wide open and the lock broken: "It was the work of the leader of the revolt who, seeing that the attempt at La

The Slave Insurrection of 1791   11

Gossette had failed, ran with all his might to hold off the other conspirators." Several fires had, however, already broken out in the immediate area. The Gallifet slaves did not move until Boukman's band, or a section of it, arrived from Limbé on the 24th. Dalmas relates that, on the night of the 23rd, the rebel bands, "leaving the Plaine du Nord parish behind them," entered Petite-Anse and began their attack, not on the Gallifet, but on the Choiseuil plantation. From there they advanced on the Pères de la Charité, Bongars and Clericy plantations, killing the managers and setting the bagasse sheds ablaze, after which they entered the Quartier-Morin parish. Here, according to Dalmas, they met with some resistance from several *ateliers*, or slave gangs, who were opposed to the revolt, and then retreated en masse to La Gossette. It was here that Odeluc had concentrated the few forces of whites available who, upon sight of the band, fled, leaving Odeluc prey to his trusted coachman, Philibert. As Odeluc pleaded for his life and reminded Philibert that he had always been kind to him, the coachman replied: "That is true, but I have promised to kill you," and then did so.[37] By the 24th, the insurgents had already established themselves at Gallifet to form a major military camp.[38] Effectively, on the 24th, as two deputies who had hastily been dispatched by Governor Blanchelande to solicit military aid from the United States prepared to sail, "the village of Petite-Anse had [already] been destroyed, and the light of the flames was visible in the night in the town."[39]

Earlier that day, while the insurgents had begun to penetrate Quartier-Morin, a battalion of citizen-volunteers set out around noon to contain them. While Dalmas claimed, on the one hand, that the slaves of Quartier-Morin "displayed as much disdain and horror toward the rebels as they did zeal and attachment for their masters" and pushed them back,[40] a participant in the volunteer battalion provides quite a different picture. He writes, on the 24th:

> Having arrived at the Quartier-Morin, which had yet received no injury, we saw the fire upon the plantation Choiseuil [the other one being in Petite-Anse], which is at the foot of Morin. We ran on towards the place, at the rate of three leagues in two hours. We were made to perform bad maneuvers; our commander got drunk, and 5 or 600 negroes who were there got clear by flight. Arrived at the plantation we found the overseer killed, his body mangled, and marks of teeth on several parts. A few negroes remained with about 40 negro women; we killed 8 or 10 of the number and the remainder got off.[41]

The following day, the 25th, he writes that all, or nearly all, was ablaze in the parish.[42] On four plantations (perhaps those to which Dalmas referred) the slaves did not take part, but in less than two weeks they "who hitherto had remained quiet, yesterday [5th September] revolted, in the engagement at Petite-Anse, and joined the body of insurgents."[43]

What these two apparently contradictory accounts appear to indicate, then, is the dispersal of the insurgents into diverse bands that must have struck several places at once upon their entry into the parish on the 24th. At a few plantations, they were pushed back by slaves, while at others, such as Choiseuil, where they had amassed some five to six hundred cohorts, they obviously enjoyed the complicity of the *ateliers*. In fact, this seems to have been the general pattern of the revolt from the beginning, as the one or two thousand that they were on the first day split into bands to attack the designated plantations, automatically increasing their numbers as well as their strategic superiority. By midnight, the conflagration had already spread to neighboring Limonade, and almost simultaneously, on the 25th, the Plaine du Nord parish was hit. In this latter parish, situated directly between Acul and Petite-Anse (and apparently circumvented on the 24th), rebel slaves arrived at the Robillard plantation and, joined by most of Robillard's *atelier*, began by assassinating the *commandeur* who refused to take part in the rebellion. What followed was a scene typical of those seen on plantation after plantation during these first days of insurrection. The rebels set fire to Robillard's three bagasse sheds, as well as the boiler house, the curing house, the mill house, and all of the cane fields. Thirteen of his boilers had been destroyed, along with the rest of the sugar manufacturing equipment, including the mill. In addition to Robillard's own house, they burned down the lodgings of the cooper, the carpenter, and the *commandeur* whom they had just killed. "In a word," wrote Robillard, "all that was left of my property was part of the shed for the hand trucks, which the brigands spared along with two large tables to take their meals. Everything, all the other buildings, all my furniture, as well, were totally consumed by flames." And once they had achieved their destruction, they set up a military camp, having spared their own quarters for the purpose.[44]

What appears to emerge from these accounts, then, is a brilliantly organised and strategically maneuvered plan of revolt that, had it succeeded in its entirety, conceivably would have enabled the slaves to take possession of the entire North Province very rapidly. For within three days, by the 25th, once all of the major parishes concentrated in the upper North Plain region had been hit and communication links between them severed,[45] a junction was to take place between insurgent bands from these areas surrounding le Cap and fellow rebels in the capital (See Map on next page).

The very first rumours of a plan to burn the capital were uncovered on the 22nd, immediately prior to the outbreak of violence in Acul and Limbé. Writing to the minister of the marine a little over a week after the insurrection began, Governor Blanchelande relates that, having been invited by the Provincial Assembly of the North on the 22nd to hear the declarations of various persons arrested the day before, "I was convinced that a conspiracy had been formed, in particular against the city of le Cap, without being able to determine precisely whether it was fomented by whites, mulattos or free blacks, or, even yet, by the slaves."[46] Then, referring to the sequence of events, Blanchelande goes on to say, "There was some talk of setting fire, on the night of that day (the 22nd), to the plantations neighboring around le Cap; fire would then break out in this city and would serve as the signal to assassinate the whites."[47] As the revolt in Acul grew awesome in dimensions, as *ateliers* from one plantation to another joined the revolt in succession, fear for the defense of le Cap, whose inhabitants included some eight to ten thousand male slaves, caused Blanchelande to recall the detachment he had sent out early on the 23rd to aid the planters of Acul.[48] Le Cap was now the seat of colonial government and already sheltered a good number of whites who had managed to escape the vengeance of their slaves. Fears of a conspiracy were confirmed as, wrote Blanchelande, "we had successively discovered and continue daily to discover plots that prove that the revolt is combined between the slaves of the city and those of the plains; we have therefore established permanent surveillance to prevent the first sign of fire here in the city which would soon develop into a general conflagration."[49]

Other indications that the burning of le Cap was an integral part of the original strategy are revealed in various letters of colonists and other residents writing at the moment the events were occurring. Mme de Rouvray, whose husband the marquis de Rouvray, had commanded a part of the military operations against the revels, wrote to their son-in-law of the insurrection that had just burst open. She relates that it was because of the impatience of the Desgrieux *atelier*, "more ferocious than the others," who began to revolt several days before the intended

14   *Carolyn E. Fick*

From Carolyn E. Fick, *The Making of Haiti The Saint Domingue Revolution From Below* (Knoxville: The University of Tennessee Press, 1990), 101. Used by permission.

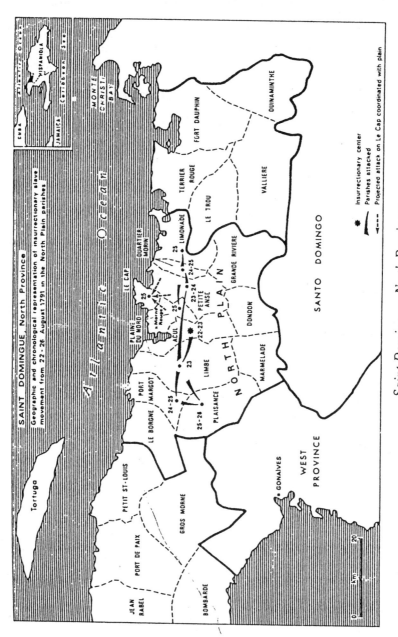

Saint Domingue, North Province:
Geographic and chronological representation of insurrectionary slave movement, 22–26 August 1791.
(*Map by Lucien J. Goupil.*)

date, that the measures conceived by the others "to burn le Cap, the plantations, and to massacre the whites all at the same time," were revealed. The impetuous and premature activities of the Desgrieux slaves had apparently given the planters of the surrounding parishes enough time to become informed of the revolt but, though some of them managed to escape the carnage, nothing could save their plantations from the rebel torches.[50]

From another resident we learn that after the first plantations had been set ablaze on the 24th and a score of whites assassinated, "the rebels dispersed and then came up to set fire to the city. They have been repelled and, in spite of their rage to advance on the city, we are certain their attempts will be in vain as it is guarded by the camp at Haut du Cap, which is the only point through which the rebels can penetrate the city."[51] According to another report, after the slaves had revolted on the Chabaud plantation in Limbé, "they advanced toward le Cap, and most of the slaves on the plantations along the way joined them. . . . The rebels marched without stopping and came within two miles of le Cap; we believe they were that night already 1,500 strong."[52] A resident merchant of le Cap also states that "on the 25th, the band from Limbé. advanced into this neighborhood."[53] Another writes on 26th August: "Since the 23rd every entrance to the city and every part of the neighborhood has been guarded with the greatest care. For these two days past, a camp of 300 men has been formed in the upper part of the city. The negroes are at a distance of one league, and frequently approach in numbers to bid defiance. Many of them are killed by our cannon. They, notwithstanding, come up unarmed."[54]

Finally, confirmation that the conspiracy against le Cap (coordinated with the revolt in the plains) had been scheduled for the 25th was obtained when, because of concentrated security around le Cap, an attempt was made at the end of the month, on the 30th and 31st, to take the upper part of the city.[55] An anonymous observer, having kept a journal account of the disturbances, relates: "Yesterday [on the 30th] some indications of a conspiracy had been discovered; several negroes have been taken and confined, some executed. It appears that the plot is to set fire to the city in 400 houses at once, to butcher the whites, and to take the city in the night by escalade. It appears that the revolted negroes have chiefs in town and who correspond with those in the plains."[56] Referring to this discovery on 30th-31st August of the renewed plot against le Cap, another writes that "thousands of these scoundrels are going to fall under the iron hand of justice."[57] One of them, sentenced to be broken on the wheel, was the free black, Jean-

Baptiste Cap, an organiser and a key leader of the insurrection. In fact, as it was the practice of the insurgents to elect titular heads, a king and queen whom "they treated with great respect" in each quarter that they occupied, Jean-Bapiste Cap had been chosen as "King of Limbé and Port-Margot."[58] It was as he incited the slaves on one plantation immediately outside the city of le Cap to revolt that he was denounced by its *commandeur*, seized and interrogated, no doubt under severe physical duress.[59] From him the authorities learned that "on the night of the 25th [August] all the negroes in the plain were to attack the city in different parts at once."[60] He further declared that "in every workshop in the city there were negroes concerned in the plot."[61] For logistical reasons and because of tightened security around the capital, it seems the plan had been postponed to the end of August.

It was on this occasion, the first of three unsuccessful attempts to capture le Cap,[62] that Boukman was cited as leading the band of insurgents, by now close to 15,000, that had come to lay siege to the capital.[63] The citing of Boukman is referred to in an account compiled from letters written by the nuns of the Communauté des Religieuses Filles de Notre-Dame du Cap-Français (an educational order for young girls in the colony) as they witnessed, from the window of their convent, the events that were occurring.[64] They spoke of a former pupil, a mulattress later known as the princess Améthyste, head of a company of Amazons; she had been initiated into the voodoo cult and had inveigled a good number of her companions to follow.[65] They would leave the convent at night to participate in ritual dances to an African chant, the words of which were inexplicable to the whites. The chant, in the Kikongo language as cited by the eighteenth-century writer, Moreau de Saint-Méry, went as follows:

> Eh! eh! Bomba, hen! hen!
> Canga bafio té
> Canga moun dé lé
> Canga do ki la
> Canga li[66]

The Slave Insurrection of 1791   17

It might be translated in this way:

Eh! eh! Mbumba (rainbow spirit = serpent)
Tie up the Ba Fioti (a coastal African slave-trading people)
Tie up the whites (i.e. Europeans)
Tie up the witches
Tie them.[67]

In other words, the chant was an invocation to the rainbow serpent, Mbumba, who occupies a predominant place in the religious belief system of the ancient Kongo, for protection against the evil powers of the "whiteman," the "slavetraders," and the "witches," who, among other forces, may also be the Ba Fioti, dreaded for their believed powers of witchcraft.[68] The schoolmistresses noticed a certain agitation among the Negresses that increased particularly after they sang this round, adopted to the exclusion of all others. The reason for this agitation, as Père Adolphe Cabon remarks in his own comments on the narrative, became clear when "at the end of August 1791, le Cap faced the uprising of Boukman, the fires on the plantations at the edge of the city, and the devastation of the plain. From the convent, the nuns saw the insurgents at the gates of le Cap, heard their death cries, witnessed their dances; they felt the terror that had struck the soul of the whites upon hearing of the massacres and destruction that was carried out in the countryside."[69] The narrator of the account relates that the king of the voodoo cult had just declared war on the colonists; they were marching to the assault on the cities and had come to lay siege to le Cap: "Amidst the rebels was Zamba Boukman inciting them to attack the barracks and the convent, which lodged a good number of young girls and other colonists." Then, in what amounts to a paraphrase of Boukman's Bois-Caiman oration, the writer notes how Boukman, "in his poetic Improvisations, reminded the insurgents that the whites were damned by God because they were the oppressors of the slaves, whom they crushed without pity, and [how] he ended each refrain with these words: *Couté la liberté li palé coeur nous tous.*"[70]

The relationship between voodoo and the insurrection, or the spirit of insurrection, is certainly not a gratuitous one, but nor is it, on the other hand, entirely intangible. The "Eh! eh! Mbumba" voodoo invocation dated back to at least the mid-eighteenth century in colonial Saint Domingue, when, as part of the initiation ceremony for a neophyte, it was a call for protection against the dreaded forces of those who had enslaved them and, as such, a form of cultural and spiritual

18   *Carolyn E. Fick*

protest against the horrors of their New World environment. On the eve of the slave insurrection, however, in the midst of what would be a difficult and dangerous liberation struggle to actually rid themselves of their enslavers, the incantation certainly must have taken on a more specific, a more political if still fetishistic, meaning, for the individual rebel would now need, more than ever before, a great deal of protection and, perhaps even more, luck in the annihilative endeavors that lay ahead. Similarly, Boukman's Bois-Caiman oration—by no means a voodoo incantation in its strictest sense—may nonetheless have been an exhortation for the slaves to rely on the governing forces of the Supreme Being found within nearly all African animistic religions, as opposed to the "false" Christian god of the whites. In other words, they must draw from within themselves, from their own beliefs, and their belief in themselves, for success.

Though the colonists managed to spare le Cap from destruction by the rebel armies, there was nothing they could do to save the plantations. One colonist wrote from le Cap: "We had learned . . . that a large attack was afoot, but how could we ever have known that there reigned among these men, so numerous and formerly so passive, such a concerted accord that everything was carried out exactly as was declared?"[71] Another wrote that "the revolt had been too sudden, too vast and too well-planned for it to seem possible to stop it or even to moderate its ravages."[72] The several frantic dispatches that were sent off to Jamaica, Cuba, Santo Domingo, and the United States for military aid were, with the single exception of a plea for assistance from a few American ships and crew at harbour, to no avail.[73] Finally, they accepted the offer of a body of mulattoes and free blacks in le Cap to take up arms and assist the whites in fighting the slaves. Within eight days, the slaves had devastated seven parishes and completely destroyed 184 sugar plantations throughout the northern province; in less than one month the count rose to over 200, to which would be added nearly 1200 coffee plantations.[74] An early estimate placed the loss in productive value for the sugar plantations alone, at nearly 40 million livres.[75] By September, all of the plantations within 50 miles on either side of le Cap had been reduced to ashes and smoke; 23 of the 27 parishes were in ruins, and the other four would fall in a matter of days.[76]

If during the first few days of the revolt the slaves were roughly ten to fifteen hundred strong, perhaps even 2,000 by one account of 23rd August, their numbers continued to swell with astonishing rapidity as they were joined by masses of slaves that deserted or were otherwise swept from their plantations, one after another, throughout the countryside.[77] On 24th–25th August, by the time de Touzard, commander of the local militia, arrived at the Dufour and Latour plantations in Acul, where the slaves appeared to have concentrated a part of their forces just two days after the revolt began, their numbers here had already reached three to four thousand.[78] Indeed, according to a report of the 27th, "they are now reckoned ten thousand strong, divided into three armies, of whom seven or eight hundred are on horseback, and tolerably well armed; the remainder are almost without arms."[79] And though at first their losses were heavy by conventional standards, "their numbers," wrote one colonist, "unfortunately increase one hundred fold in proportion."[80] In less than two weeks, the original core of ten to fifteen hundred had increased over tenfold to fifteen, some claimed twenty, thousand, one-third of them fully equipped with rifles and ammunition pilfered from the plantations, the rest armed with sabres, knives, farm implements, and a whole host of other contrivances that served them as weapons. Fear and panic among the whites spread almost as rapidly as the insurrection itself, causing some to believe that there were, at this point, as many as forty or fifty thousand slaves in revolt, a number the rebels did, however, achieve by late September or early October, and the number may even have reached a near eighty thousand toward the end of November.[81] The total number of slaves in the North Province was roughly 170,000.[82]

Here then, within the initial lightning stage of the insurrection, within the first eight to ten days, were 15,000 slaves (a number that continued to multiply) who had deserted their plantations, by will or by force, or by the sheer thrust and compulsion of events purposefully set in motion by the activities of a revolutionary core. Had this phenomenon occurred anywhere else but revolutionary Saint Dominigue, it quite reasonably would have been called a maroon war, and under the pre-revolutionary colonial regime, the colonists characteristically would have designated these slave troops as marauding, ravaging maroon bands with their chosen leaders. But if the maroon wars that broke out in Jamaica and elsewhere had occurred in a context of revolution, had they assumed the same magnitude and degree of political complexity, the circuitous question of whether the slaves were maroons or revolutionary rebels, or some combination of both, would no doubt have played its role in the historiography of slave rebellion in these plantation societies as well. It should be sufficient to say, as the noted sociologist of slavery and slave rebellion, Orlando Patterson, has so lucidly pointed out, that all armed slave rebellion necessarily takes on a maroon dimension.[83] Here in Saint Domingue, the entire situation had radically changed; the past colonial context in which colonists could try to reassure themselves by seeing armed maroons and fugitive slaves as entities outside the plantation system— troublesome, to be sure, but not enough to threaten the foundations and institutional viability of slavery—had now fallen into a million pieces and reposed, literally, on little more than a pile of ashes.

In this whole process, caught up in the web of events that were taking place, many slaves became maroons by deserting their plantations, perhaps having killed the master, the overseer or even their own *commandeur*, perhaps having set fire to a cane field or a shed. Once maroon, they then found themselves in an irreversible position with little choice but to defend their lives with arms. The transformation of the fugitive slave or deserter into a hardened, armed rebel, fighting for freedom, is one that occurred, no doubt to varying degrees, within the consciousness of each individual slave; but equally, this transformation was accelerated by collective rebellion in a context of revolutionary social and political upheaval.

The example of some slaves on the Vaudreuil plantation in the Plaine du Nord parish, just prior to the outbreak, may provide a small glimpse into these very elusive circumstances. Situated at Morne-Rouge, it was very near the Lenormand plantation where the 14th August conspiratorial gathering had first taken place.[84] Around the 20th, at about the same time as a few of the Limbé conspirators were being arrested and interrogated, and just before the revolt prematurely broke out at Gallifet's estates, the *commandeur* at Vaudreuil was caught setting fire to a part of the cane field. Apparently the slaves here were divided in their support for the insurrection that was to take place. Seeing the manager in battle with the *commandeur*, some of the slaves came to the aid of the manager and caught the *commandeur*, who, according to one letter, revealed that he had been influenced by a free mulatto; but then, according to another letter, 28 of the Vaudreuil slaves had also gone maroon. Three of them were captured in Limbé and revealed the conspiracy.[85]

Here one may ask whether the Vaudreuil maroons were actually involved in the revolt, as was the *commandeur*, or whether, having knowledge of the conspiracy, they ran away to flee the impending destruction. If the latter were the case, however, there would have been no need to flee since they would have had the support of the rest of the *atelier*, as well as the protection of the manager, whom these had just saved. More likely, they were in complicity with the *commandeur*, and, as he had just been apprehended with the aid of the other slaves, their own turn undoubtedly would be next. One may also find it significant that at least three of them ran away to Limbé, where the insurrection was to break out. Once having become maroons, though, it was now only a matter of days before the other 25 would be swept along into the larger body of insurgent slaves as a constituent part. It is perhaps at this conjuncture that slave deserters, who in ordinary times were called maroons or fugitives (and up to this point they still are by their unsuspecting masters), become, by the very nature of the circumstances, insurrectionaries, brigands, and rebels. They had in fact embarked on a collective struggle never before waged in such a manner, or on such a scale, by colonial slaves anywhere, and their activities were now inscribed within an irreversible revolutionary situation. The real significance of their movement, in the early days as throughout the revolution, was the profound impact of self-mobilisation, of the popular organisation and the obtrusive intervention of these slaves—on a revolutionary process already several years in motion.

During those first weeks of revolution, the slaves destroyed the whites and their property with much the same ruthlessness and cruelty as they had suffered for so many years at the hands of their masters. The scenes of horror and bloodshed on the plantations, as whites hopelessly tried to defend themselves or, at best, to flee from the unleashed terror and rage of their former slaves, were only too reminiscent of the brutality they had themselves endured under the plantation regime. Yet as atrocious as they were, these acts of vengeance were surprisingly moderate, in the opinion of one of the best known historians of that revolution, compared with those of cold-blooded, grotesque savagery and sadistically calculated torture committed by their oppressors throughout the past.[86] These were impassioned acts of revenge, of retribution, and were relatively short-lived.[87]

The uncontrolled explosions of vengeance and suppressed hatred that marked the beginning of the revolution constituted, however, only a temporary stage. Once expiated, these destructive energies were progressively channeled into military strategy, tactical maneuvers, and political alliances as the slaves gained territory and began to stabilise their positions. They had no experience in the use of military weaponry, and though their losses in the early engagements were heavy,[88] they learned quickly enough. A le Cap resident who participated in the militia observed how, "in the beginning of the insurrection, the negroes made their attacks with much irregularity and confusion, and their weapons were mostly their instruments of labor, but . . . they now come on in regular bodies, and a considerable part of them are well armed with muskets, swords, etc., which they have taken and purchased."[89] In this respect, as well as in discipline, in the opinion of the militia recruit, they were growing more formidable.[90] When they repelled an attack by the whites on one of their outposts, they would make off with cannons and other equipment left behind with which to wage their struggle.

During these first months, the blacks continued to defend their positions across the province through tactical guerrilla warfare. They retreated into the hills when it was to their advantage, organised their forces for counterattacks, and often continued to burn and ravage the nearby plantations in reprisal. One general described their tactics and sense of military organisation in this way:

> They established themselves nearly everywhere on the lower cliffs and on the slopes of high mountains to be within better range of their incursions into the plains, and to keep the rear well protected. For this, they always had behind them nearly inaccessible summits or gorges that they were perfectly familiar with. They established communication links between their positions in such a way that they were able mutually to come to each other's aid whenever we partially attacked them. They have surveillance posts and designated rendezvous positions.[91]

These were in fact maroon tactics, and they were utilised and refined in much the same way by maroons in colonies throughout the Caribbean, wherever their resistance had turned into protracted warfare.

What the slaves lacked in military hardware, they compensated for with ruse and ingenuity. They camouflaged traps, fabricated poisoned arrows, feigned cease-fires to lure the enemy into ambush, disguised tree trunks to look like cannons, and threw obstructions of one kind or another in the roads to hamper advancing troops; in short, any means they could invent to psychologically disorient, frighten, demoralise, or otherwise generally confuse the European units in order to defend their own positions.[92] On their flag was inscribed a motto calling for death to all whites. They marched to African martial music and would begin an engagement with considerable order and firmness, crying out victory. But they would retreat in what whites could only understand as "confused precipitation."[93] To disperse a prodigious body of slaves advancing on le Cap, Blanchelande's troops had "fired three times, but without the least effect," as each man had devised for himself a kind of light mattress stuffed with cotton as a vest to prevent the bullets from penetrating, "and thus stood the fire without showing any signs of fear," as one observer noted.[94]

When caught by their pursuers, they could convincingly invoke past affective ties with whites during the old plantation days in a plea for pardon, as one slave who claimed to be the loving godson of his assailant's mother. Taken off-guard by these sentiments, the pursuer dismounted as the slave, meanwhile, had recharged his gun, shot and narrowly missed his opponent. Even then, he claimed he had not seen correctly and loved his godmother's son too much to kill him. But when contradicted by witnesses who had seen the entire incident, he admitted: "Master, I know that is true. It is the devil who gets inside of this body of mine." Though his fate was sealed as he was bound to a tree to be shot, he furiously reviled his captors through laughter, song, and joke, and jeered at them in mockery. He gave the signal for his own execution with neither fear nor complaint. In the end, the contents of his pockets revealed more about the mentality, the beliefs, the unarticulated ideals, and fighting spirit of the slaves than any grandiloquent declaration their leaders might make about emancipation and "liberty or death" to the colonial whites. In one of his pockets, the slave's captor relates, "we found pamphlets printed in France [claiming] the Rights of Man; in his vest pocket was a large packet of tinder and phosphate of lime. On his chest he had a little sack full of hair, herbs, bits of bone, which they call a fetish . . . and it was, no doubt, because of this amulet, that our man had the intrepidity which the philosophers call Stoicism."[95]

The slaves were organised in bands, as European armies were organized in regiments, and although inter-band rivalry and divisions were not uncommon, the internal discipline of each band or camp was maintained with an iron hand by the individual leaders. In the camps, the least sign of insubordination or slightest evidence of uncertainty was often met with unimaginably harsh treatment and, on occasion, even death.[96] In the first weeks, their main camps were concentrated westwardly at Limbé, Morne-Rouge, and Gallifet in Petite-Anse. Following the Gallifet defeat in September, major strongholds had already formed, by October, in the eastward districts of Grande-Rivière and Dondon;[97] by November, Fort-Dauphin and Ouinaminthe at the eastern extremity of the province near the Spanish border, where participation of the free coloreds was particularly evident, were under rebel control.[98] It was under the military command of Jean-Baptiste Marc, a free black, seconded by Cézar, a recently emancipated free black, that they gained control of Ouinaminthe. Jean-Baptiste Marc, in particular, was described as one who ruled with the air of an army general (and who was also well known in Fort-Dauphin for thievery.)[99] Through intrigue, skillful duplicity, and brilliant maneuvering, they had feigned desertion from the rebels and allied themselves with government forces under de Touzard, who graciously supplied them with as much military armament as they needed or requested, allowing them to hold complete control for over three months. De Touzard had nothing but praise for Cézar, whom he credited with having saved the entire district from the "brigands" and promised to write the Colonial Assembly to recommend that he receive a handsome recompense for his services. Cézar absconded to Dondon, having first taken the precaution of hiding three of the best cannons in the cane fields. Within two days, he was back fighting with his black comrades in the attack on Marmelade.[100] Shortly thereafter, Jean-Baptiste Marc, having obtained replenished munitions to fight a few brigands, turned on the garrison and converged with rebel forces who took control of the district.[101]

The revolution had, in fact, produced hundreds of local leaders, for the most part obscure ones, slaves as well was free blacks like Jean-Baptiste Marc or Cézar, who held military posts on the plantations, organised raids, and maneuvered with France's enemies, with royalists and Spaniards, for ammunition, military supplies, and protection. Certainly the most revered of the early leaders, however, was Boukman. It was in November, during an attack by the Cap regiment in the Acul plain, that he was killed, the first of the original leaders to fall, while defending a rebel post at Fond Bleu.[102] Upon his death, it was Jean-François and Biassou who were to coordinate the activities and assume the direction of the New World's first colonial liberation struggle of its kind: Jean-François now officially assumed the rank and responsibility of general, while Biassou, as lieutenant-general, was second in command, and Jeannot in charge of the black troops in the east.

As a political leader, Jean-François was ambitious; as a general, he was outwardly pompous and unabashedly flaunted his ego by decorating his uniform with an abundant assortment of medals and other impressive military trinkets, not the least among them being the Cross of Saint-Louis. Yet he was a man of exceptional intelligence for one who had spent the greater part of his life as a slave; he was highly respected and especially well liked by those mulattos and free blacks under his command, as well as the "better subjects" among the slaves.[103] Biassou was of a far more fiery disposition. He was, according to Haitian historian, Thomas Madiou, a fervent voodoo adept and kept himself surrounded by *houngans,* or voodoo priests, from whom he frequently sought advice.[104] He was impulsive and forever ready, at the first sign of personal insult or political deception on the part of his white enemies, to take revenge on the prisoners in his camp. He would have killed them all were it not for the judicious interventions of Jean-François or Toussaint, who at this stage served as Biassou's secretary and as physician of the black army.[105] Jeannot, as well as being commander in the east, had also received the title of judge, giving him undisputed authority over the life or death of his prisoners.[106] He was a man of insatiable vengeance who thrived on torturing the white prisoners in as barbaric a manner as that of those masters who, in the past, had known no bounds.[107] His tyranny did not stop here, but extended equally to the blacks under his command. Following a crushing defeat in Limbé by the combined forces under General Blanchelande, Jeannot immediately suspected treason, and Paul Blin was the victim. Knowing that he had earlier helped some white masters to escape, Jeannot had him burned alive on the pretext that he had removed the bullets from their cartridges.[108]

By November, the political situation in the colony had changed with the arrival of civil commissioners from France. Negotiations would soon be under way between the rebel leaders and the French representatives. Upon being informed of Jeannot's excesses, Jean-François, a man of humanity in spite of his arrogance, and possessing a sense of common decency, was revolted by such atrocities. He also realized that this executioner was a liability to the revolution; more than that, his uncontrolled barbarism could seriously jeopardize the imminent negotiations with the white authorities. The black general had him tried and gave him a military execution at about the same time that the whites, who had killed Boukman in battle, cut his head off and garishly exposed it on a stake at the public square in le Cap with the inscription: "The head of Boukman, leader of the rebels."[109]

News of Boukman's death had in fact produced a profound effect in the rebel camps. There the slave leaders went into mourning and ordered solemn services to be held in honour of their deeply revered comrade.[110] But within the ranks of the slaves, the immediate reaction was quite different; their only wish was to assassinate, on the spot, every white prisoner to atone for their leader's death. Finally, they turned the event to their own advantage, extolled their abilities and successes on the battlefield, derided the whites for their cowardice, and celebrated with dance for three days.[111]

A far more serious differentiation between the mentality of the mass of slave rebels and that of their chief leaders, however, evidenced itself during the period of negotiations that had brought about a temporary cease-fire, as well as a set of demands formulated by Jean-François and Biassou. It was under these circumstances that the first signs of division appeared between the aims of those who had become the official leaders of the revolution, and the aspirations of the black masses. Together they had practically annihilated an entire province; that they were fighting to free themselves can hardly be denied. But neither Jean-François nor Biassou, nor even Toussaint for that matter, knew what to do at this point. While Toussaint mediated and kept the peace within their camp, the difficult and unfortunate responsibility of officially representing the revolutionary slave masses in negotiation with French authorities fell to Jean-François.

The whole scope of the revolution, only three months under way but rapidly taking on wider and graver proportions, had gone far beyond his capacities as the political leader of a people engaged in revolutionary struggle. To negotiate the outright abolition of slavery would be absurd; no ruling class ever negotiates away the economic foundations of its own power. Jean-François knew this as well as anyone. When asked about the real causes of the insurrection by one of his white prisoners—it was M. Gros, a le Cap lawyer who served as the general's personal secretary—Jean-François eventually answered, after brushing earlier questions aside, "that they have not taken up arms to obtain a liberty which, even if the whites chose to grant it, would be for them nothing more than a fatal and venomous gift, but at least they hoped for an amelioration of their condition."[112]

Gros published an account of his captivity shortly thereafter, in which he relates somewhat differently that, while refusing to explain himself categorically, Jean-François nevertheless gave as his reply to this question:

> It is not I who have installed myself as general over the slaves. Those who had the power to do so have invested me with this title: in taking up arms, I never claimed to be fighting for general emancipation which I know to be an illusory dream, as much in terms of France's need for the colonies as the danger involved in procuring for these uncivilised hordes a right that would become infinitely dangerous for them, and that would indubitably lead to the annihilation of the colony. [Moreover], if the owners

The Slave Insurrection of 1791   27

had all stayed on their plantations, perhaps the
revolution may never have occurred.[113]

But following this statement, the slave leader unleashed his animosity
toward the plantation agents and the stewards, and wanted included as a
fundamental article of their demands that these men should no longer
exist in Saint Domingue.[114]

In spite of his personal respect for Gros, Jean-François was
nevertheless speaking to the enemy. Moreover, he knew he would
eventually have to answer to the French authorities for the tremendous
devastation of property and lives by the rebels. It was now an
impossible situation in which the one plausible alternative may have
been precisely to blame it all on the royalists, while putting forward a
reasonably limited set of demands for themselves. Under the
circumstances, the best Jean-François could do was to demand, by
dispatching a formal address to the Colonial Assembly with de Touzard
as mediator, an unconditional amnesty for all slaves who had
participated in the revolt, freedom for 50 of the leaders and several
hundred of their officers, as well as an amelioration of conditions for
the slaves (the abolition of the whip and the *cachot* as forms of
punishment). In exchange for this, he promised to use his influence
over the slaves to encourage them to return to their respective
plantations and agreed to deliver the remaining prisoners, on the
condition that his wife, who was held prisoner by the whites in le Cap,
also be released. Although personally opposed to these limited
demands, Biassou finally agreed to subscribe to them, but demanded, as
well, the release of his own family. To charge Jean-François with the
deliberate and cold-blooded betrayal of his people at this stage in the
revolution, however, may perhaps be too premature a judgment. The
events of a revolution barely three months under way, but with rapidly
broadening dimensions, hardly afforded him the political experience
and fortitude of character necessary to see his way through at this point.
Yet someone had to do something, and Jean-François was the only one
in a position to do so.

Among the prominent leaders, it was now Biassou, the fiery and
impassioned voodoo adept who, in his more impulsive moments, best
incarnated the aspirations and mentality of the insurgent slaves. When
they learned of the death of Boukman, they, as Biassou, had been
enraged to the point of threatening to massacre all the white
prisoners.[115] In the camps, the black troops and local officers, already
irritated by the long delay in the Colonial Assembly's response to their
leaders' address, were determined to continue the war when they

28   *Carolyn E. Fick*

learned that de Touzard, commander of the white troops at Fort-Dauphin, had broken the temporary cease-fire to attack several of their camps. But they were under strict orders to refrain from all hostilities.[116] They became increasingly suspicious of the frequent contacts Jean-François and Biassou were having with various whites and swore they would exterminate all the whites, and even their own leaders, if these men dared to come to terms with the authorities.[117] Having gotten nowhere with the Colonial Assembly, the slave leaders had now turned to the newly arrived civil commissioners to be heard. The black troops soon learned of the impending negotiations and, near one camp, assembled themselves and "appeared ready to break by force any negotiation that would conduce their return to the plantations."[118] Of these slaves, Gros remarked that "it is useful to point out to those who are so good natured as to believe their slaves are being forcibly detained and that their [real] dispositions are peaceful ones, that, out of a hundred of these, generally speaking, if there are four whose intentions are good, it would be a lot; all of them, rather, breathe forth nothing but the total destruction of the whites."[119]

At the Gallifet camp in Grande-Rivière, the slave troops and especially their commander, Jean-Baptiste Godard, openly affirmed that the French civil commissioners were representatives without any powers and without a mandate, that it was not the king who had sent them, and that if they proposed peace, it was to trick them into submission before killing them all off.[120] It was not the whole truth, but it was not too far from it. Some of them even began murmuring that it was all because of the mulattos that their leaders had entered into relations with the whites of le Cap.[121] If a few of the white prisoners tried to convince these slaves that their revolt was pure folly, that the king had never granted them three free days per week, and that only the Colonial Assembly could legislate on such matters, they pretended not to listen and said that the government would give them what they wanted or they would continue the war to the bitter end. In their midst was a priest, Abbé de la Porte, who tried to frighten them by describing the might and power of the combined forces of France, Spain and Britain, and all the other kingdoms of Europe that would unite to exterminate them if they did not give up their arms and go back to the plantations, but his words, as he said, went in at one ear and out at the other.[122]

By a proclamation of 28th September 1791, decreed by the National Assembly of France and sanctioned by the king, amnesty was granted to all free persons in Saint Domingue charged with "acts of revolution." Biassou received a copy of it and had it read to his troops who could not have cared less. They wanted war and *bout à blancs*—an end to the whites. Most of all, they wanted their three free days per week, and as for the other three days, they would see about those in due course.[123] At this point Toussaint rose, demanded that the proclamation be reread, and delivered such a moving speech in creole that the slaves' attitudes suddenly changed to the point where they were even willing to go back to their various plantations if that was what their leaders wanted.[124] Already Toussaint's qualities of leadership were beginning to take shape, and he knew more than anyone else what they really wanted. He had been discreetly involved in the 14th August affair from the very beginning and carefully observed all that went on before finally deciding in November to join with Biassou and Jean-François. Once the agreement was reached to surrender their prisoners, Toussaint accompanied them as escort to the bar of the Colonial Assembly.

But for the mass of armed slaves, this also meant their return to the plantations. They were now violently opposed to any settlement whatsoever with the whites, and, at the Tannerie camp along the way to the site designated for the exchange of prisoners, they besieged the delegation with sabres and threats of sending all their heads off to le Cap, swearing vehemently against peace and against their own generals.[125] "We were convinced this time of a great truth," wrote Gros, "that the slave would never return to his duties but by constraint and by his partial destruction."[126] It was the uninstructed mass of slaves, and not their leaders, who saw so clearly what was at stake, regardless of the cost. And if the price they were ready to pay was high, it was no greater than the human suffering they had already endured.

The Colonial Assembly disdainfully refused to accede to any one of their leaders' demands (except for a nominal agreement on the release of Jean-François's wife), even after the number of requested emancipations was reduced by Toussaint himself from 400 to 60.[127] He returned to their camp and told the slaves what they already knew. There was nothing to be gained, neither from the civil commissioners nor from the Assembly. Jean-François convoked his council, and it was unanimously decided to continue the war, to finish what they had begun.[128]

In the course of their collective struggle against slavery, however, Jean-François eventually gave himself over to sheer political opportunism, shamelessly betraying the cause of a people he was initially supposed to have been leading. It would take yet another two years before Toussaint would emerge from the political background to provide clear, vigorous, and decisive direction to the profoundly felt aspirations of these slave masses who had killed their masters and burned the plantations to be free.

NOTES

1. Gabriel Debien, *Les esclaves aux Antilles françaises: XVIIe au XVIIIe siècle* (Basse Terre: Société d'histoire de la Guadeloupe, 1974), 468.

2. The present essay, with some modifications, appeared previously in Carolyn E. Fick, *The Making of Haiti: The Saint Domingue Revolution from Below.* Copyright © 1990 by the University of Tennessee Press. Used by permission.

3. Documents and discussion of the events up to and surrounding 22 August 1791 are presented in *ibid.*, Appendix B, 260-66. Diverse elements in the above section of this article are taken from the documents contained therein. See also C. Fick, "The Black Masses in the San Domingo Revolution." Ph.D. Thesis. Concordia University, 1979.

4. Beaubrun Ardouin, *Etudes sur l'histoire d'Haiti*, 11 vols., ed. F. Dalencourt (Port-au-Prince, 1958), 1:51; also, Pauléus Sannon, *Histoire de Toussaint L'ouverture*, 3 vols., (Port-au-Prince: A Héraux, 1920), 1:88.

5. Jean Fouchard, Gabriel Debien and M.A. Menier, "Toussaint Louverture avant 1789," *Conjonction* 134 (Juin 1977): 65-80.

6. On the links between royalists and the slave insurrection, see Gérard Laurent, *Quand les chaînes volent en éclats* (Port-au-Prince: Imp. Deschamps, 1979), 42-46.

7. In "Notice historique sur la Communauté des religieuses filles de Notre-Dame du Cap Français (Saint Domingue) fondée en 1733," *Lettre annuelle de l'Ordre de Notre Dame* (Bordeaux: Imp. B. Coussan et F. Constalet, 1889), 204. The word *Nzamba* is Congolese and means "elephant." See John K. Thornton, "I Serve the King of Congo: African Political Ideology and the Haitian Revolution." Annual Conference of the African Studies Association of Canada. Toronto, 16-19 May 1991. In this light, *Zamba* may be both an affectionate and a respectful sobriquet for Boukman to whom references about his "colossal size" concern his head rather than his height. On this point, see D. Geggus, "Slave Resistance Studies and the Saint Domingue Revolution: Some Preliminary Considerations," Occasional Papers Series, no. 4 (Miami: Latin American and Caribbean Centre, Florida International University, 1983), 10. The writer of the "Notice historique" offers as a

The Slave Insurrection of 1791   31

translation of *Zamba*: "professional poet" or "strolling musician" (*ménétrier*), 204. For additional speculation see Fick, *The Making of Haiti*, Ch. 4, n. 5.

8. The term *voodoo* is used here to reflect the overall composite realities of African religious cult practices in Saint Domiguean slave culture, as described in *ibid.*, Ch. 1, n. 128 and Ch. 2, while further discussion of the role of voodoo in the Bois-Caïman ceremony and the preparations for the revolt is pursued in Appendix B, 264–66.

9. Sannon, *Histoire de Toussaint*, 1:89.

10. Translated by author from Sannon's French translation of the creole in *ibid.* Unless otherwise stated, all further translations from French are those of author. The very first citing of this speech at the Bois-Caïman assembly is found in Hérald Dumesle's *Voyage dans le Nord d'Haïti* (les Cayes: Imp. du Gouvernement, 1824, 88), which was the source for its reproduction by Victor Schoelcher in *Colonies étrangères et Haïti* (2 vols. [Pointe-à-Pitre: Desormeaux, 1973], 2:99), written in 1843. The "Good Lord" or, in creole, "Bon Dié" invoked by Boukman may well characterise the notion of a distant supreme being "hidden in the clouds" that is generally central to nearly all African cult religions.

11. In "Notice historique," 204-5.

12. Antoine Dalmas (*Histoire de la révolution de Saint Domingue*, 2 vols. [Paris: Mame Frères, 1814]), the first, if not the only directly contemporary historian to mention the Bois-Caïman ceremony (presumably writing in 1793), does not make reference to a priestess or to Boukman, as David Geggus rightly points out in his "Slave Resistance Studies," (18). Dalmas does, however mention the ritual killing of a sacrificial black pig (1:117), a symbol of utter discretion, in the opinion of anthropologist Alfred Métraux, since it proves itself uninquisitive by seldom looking to the sky. *Voodoo in Haïti*, trans. Hugo Chartiris (New York: Schocken Books, 1972), 42-43. The black pig is usually associated with petro rites in Haitian voodoo. See also Geggus, "The Bois Caïman Ceremony," this issue.

13. In Fouchard, *Les marrons de la liberté*, (Paris: École, 1972), 528. First cited by Etienne Charlier in *Apercu sur la formation historique de la nation haitienne* (Port-au-Prince: Les Presses Libres, 1954), 49.

14. See n. 8 above.

15. In Geggus, "Slave Resistance Studies," 10.

16. AN, DXXV, 3, 31. Précis historique de la révolution de Saint Domingue, 9.

17. On the significance of small-scale, or *petit* marronage and its potential for facilitating slave resistance, see Fick, *The Making of Haiti*, Ch. 2, n. 142. In a similar vein Robin Blackburn, in his recent book, *The Overthrow of Colonial Slavery* (London: Verso, 1988), writes that *petit* marronage ". . . would [nonetheless] produce a layer of slaves with outside knowledge, experience and contacts, yet a continuing presence

within the plantations, a combination that could, under the right conditions, lead to plantation revolts." (Ch. 5, n. 13).

18. , AN, DXXV, 66, 667. L'Assemblée Coloniale de la partie française de Saint Domingue à l'Assemblée Nationale, 3 nov. 1791. (See n. 21 below).

19. In Dalmas, *Histoire de la révolution*, 1:116.

20. "St. Domingo Disturbances," *Philadelphia Aurora*, 11 Oct. 1791. From a Journal kept there; entry for 4 Sept. 1791. (The first part of the Journal, ending with the entry for 31 Aug. 1791, is also published in Boston, *Independent Chronicle and Universal Advertiser*, 20 Oct. 1791.)

21. AN, DXXV 56, 550. Discours fait à l'Assemblée Nationale le 30 novembre 1791 par MM. les commissaires de l'Assemblée de la partie française de Saint Domingue. (A rough draft of the beginning of this address, with corrections and marginal insertions, is found in AN DXXV 66, 666. The completed address in proper manuscript form, is in DXXV 66, 667. It was delivered to the National Assembly in France on 30 November 1791 and exists in printed form in DXXV 56, 550. All future references to this document will use the latter archival reference.) In the original manuscript draft, the slave conspirator's name is clearly written throughout the document as Paul Belin, although in its printed form, the name is written first as Blin and later, in reference to a subsequent incident, as Belin. He is also sometimes referred to as the slave, Paul à Belin, presumably belonging to the Belin estate in Limbé. Extract of a letter from Cape Français of 2 November received by the brig James, Capt. Row . . ., Boston, *Independent Chronicle and Universal Advertiser*, 8 Dec. 1791. Also AN, DXXV 78, 772. Liste des sucreries incendiées à Saint Domingue dont on a eu connaissance jusqu'au 30 septembre 1791, n.d. (oct. 1791?). The correct spelling of the name could possibly even be the latter of the two.

22. AN, DXXV 78, 772. AA 148. La partie du Nord, paroisse de l'Acul. DXXV 78, 772. AA 183. Deposition dated le Cap, 27 Sept. 1791. DXXV 56, 550. Discours.

23. AN, DXXV 46, 432. Copies de différentes lettres sur les événements de Saint Domingue extraites de la gazette anglaise et transmises à Paris, Kingston. M. Tausias à M. Camuzat, le Cap, 1 sept. 1791.

24. These were the Caignet and Busson plantations. AN, DXXV 78, 772. AA 183. Deposition, le Cap, 25 Sept. 1791. DXXV 78, 772. AA 148. Partie du Nord. DXXV 78, 772. KK 175. La paroisse de l'Acul, signed by M. Caignet. The latter plantation was burned, in any event, at some point before the end of the following month. DXXV 78, 772. Liste des sucreries incendiées, n.d. (oct. 1791?). The *ateliers*, or slave gangs, leading the revolt in Acul were, according to Caignet, those of the Molines, Flaville, Plaigne, Sacanville and Pillat plantations. DXXV 78, 772. KK 175. La paroisse de l'Acul.

The Slave Insurrection of 1791   33

25. "St. Domingo Disturbances," Boston, *Independent Chronicle and Universal Advertiser*, 20 Oct. 1791. Entry for 23 Aug. 1791.

26. AN, DXXV 78, 772. KK 178. Renseignements sur la position actuelle du Limbé, le Cap, 7 Oct. 1791.

27. "A letter from James Perkins, Esq., resident at Cape François, 9 Sept. 1791," Boston, *Independent Chronicle and Universal Advertiser*, 20 Oct. 1791.

28. *Ibid.*

29. AN, DXXV 78, 772. KK 179. Paroisse de Port-Margot, signed by Traynier and Palmis, n.d. (Sept.–Oct. 1791?).

30. *Ibid.*

31. AN, DXXV 78, 772. KK 161. Plaisance, signed by Manan, fils, Ch. Escot, A. Touvaudais, le Cap, 27 Sept. 1791.

32. *Ibid.* Also DXXV 47, 443. M. de Blanchelande à M. le président du Congrès de l'Amérique, le Cap, 24 août 1791.

33. "St. Domingo Disturbances," Boston, *Independent Chronicle and Universal Advertiser*, 20 Oct. 1791. Also, "Letters from James Perkins, Esq., resident at Cape François," in *ibid.*; DXXV 46, 432. Copies. M. de Blanchelande à M. Bertrand, Ministre de la Marine, le Cap, 2 Sept. 1791. MM. Foäche, Pierre Morange et Hardivilliers du Cap en date du 25 sept. 1791 à MM. Foäche, frères, du Havre. Lettre de M. Nicoleau, habitant de Saint Domingue, le Cap, 3 Sept. 1791. M. Tausias, Négociant du Cap et habitant de la plaine du Nord à Mme. Camuzat, 1 Sept. 1791.

34. Dalmas, *Histoire de la révolution*, 1:116-21. AN, DXXV 56, 550. Discours. See also, D. Geggus, "Les esclaves de la plaine du Nord à la veille de la Révolution française," RSHH 144 (sept. 1984): 25, 36. While Dalmas places the date of the incident on the twentieth, Geggus fixes it on the twenty-first.

35. See Geggus, "Les esclaves de la plaine," RSHH 14: 24-36.

36. *Ibid.*, 32.

37. AN, DXXV 56, 550. Discours. Geggus, "Les esclaves de la plaine," RSHH 144:36. Dalmas, on the other hand, attributes Odeluc's assassination to an unidentified slave, Mathurin, "the fiercest of them all." *Histoire de la révolution*, 1:123.

38. Sannon, *Histoire de Toussaint*, 1:91.

39. "Insurrection of the Negroes in the West Indies," Boston, *Independent Chronicle and Universal Advertiser*, 22 Sept. 1791.

40. Dalmas, *Histoire de la révolution*, 1:123-24.

41. "St. Domingo Disturbances," *Philadelphia Aurora*, 10-11 Oct. 1791. Entry for 24 Aug. 1791.

42. *Ibid.* Entry for 25 Aug. 1791.

43. *Ibid.* Entry for 6 Sept. 1791.

44. AN, DXXV 78, 772. Déclaration que fait M. Robillard habitant à la Plaine du Nord des désastres arrivés sur son habitation . . . ," le Cap, 29 sept. 1791. The details were related to Robillard by two mulattoes who

34   *Carolyn E. Fick*

later attacked the camp, killing four of Robillard's slaves and, to prevent the plantation being used again as a camp, burned the slaves' quarters.

45.   AN, DXXV 46, 432. Copies. Tausias à Camuzat, le Cap, 1 sept. 1791. DXXV 78, 772. AA 183. Deposition, le Cap, 27 Sept. 1791.
46.   AN, DXXV 46, 432. Copies. Blanchelande à Bertrand, le Cap, 2 sept. 1791. M. de Rouvray claimed that Blanchelande had been warned of the plot as early as the 19th, but was too inept to crush it in its beginnings. M.E. McIntosh and B.C. Weber, eds., *Une correspondance familiale au temps des troubles de Saint Domingue* (Paris: Larose, 1957), 41. M. de Rouvray to C^lesse de Lostanges, 6, 7 Dec. 1791.
47.   AN, DXXV 46, 432. Copies. Blanchelande à Bertrand, le Cap, 2 sept. 1791.
48.   *Ibid.* DXXV 78, 772. AA 183. Deposition, le Cap, 27 Sept. 1791.
49.   AN, DXXV 46, 432. Copies. Blanchelande à Bertrand, le Cap, 2 sept. 1791.
50.   *Une correspondance familiale,* 29. Mme de Rouvray to Cte de Lostanges, le Cap, 8 Sept. 1791.
51.   AN, DXXV 46, 432. Copies. Lettre de M. Nicoleau, le Cap, 3 Sept. 1791.
52.   AN, DXXV 46, 432. Copies. Rapport de M. Bagnet. Extrait de la gazette anglaise transmise à Paris, Kingston, Ile Jamaïque, 2 Sept. 1791.
53.   "Letter from James Perkins," Boston, *Independent Chronicle and Universal Advertiser,* 20 Oct. 1791.
54.   "St. Domingo Disturbances," *Philadelphia Aurora,* 10 Oct. 1791. Entry for 26 Aug. 1791.
55.   *Ibid,* 10-11 Oct. 1791. Entries for 31 Aug. – 1 Sept. 1791.
56.   *Ibid.* Entry for 31 Aug. 1791.
57.   AN, DXXV 46, 432. Copies. Tausias à Camuzat, le Cap, 1 Sept. 1791.
58.   "St. Domingo Disturbances," *Philadelphia Aurora,* 11 Oct. 1791. Entry for 5 Sept. 1791. Other evidence of this practice is revealed in various accounts of the subsequent engagements, in which blacks were taken prisoners: "The day before yesterday . . . we took the camp of Limbé . . .and took the King Jean-Louis and the Queen alive"; "The 16th October we captured one of his head men who calls himself King"; "We have in prison a priest who was taken at the capture of Gallifet, also the Queen of that quarter." Extract of a letter from Cape Français, 3 Nov. 1791, *Philadelphia Aurora,* 15 Dec. 1791; Extract of a letter from a gentleman in Cape Français, 1 Nov. 1791. Boston, *Independent Chronicle and Universal Advertiser,* 15 Dec. 1791, respectively. Boukman, of course, was also known and respected as a chief king.
59.   "St. Domingo Disturbances," *Philadelphia Aurora,* 11 Oct. 1791. Entry for 1 Sept. 1791. For his loyalty to the whites in denouncing Jean-Baptiste Cap, the slave Jean, *commandeur* of the Chaperon de la Taste plantation, situated behind the Pères de l'Hôpital of the city, was

The Slave Insurrection of 1791   35

granted freedom and a life pension of 300 livres per year. The owner received an indemnity for his slave from the colonial government. AN, DXXV 60, 595. Extrait des registres de l'Assemblée Générale de la partie française de Saint Domingue, 2 Sept. 1791.

60. "St. Domingo Disturbances," *Philadelphia Aurora,* 11 Oct. 1791. Entry for 2 Sept. 1791.

61. *Ibid.*

62. A second attempt was made during September and a third at some point before early October. Boston, *Independent Chronicle and Universal Advertiser,* 13 Oct. 1791. Extract from the schooner Peggy, Capt. White, 6 Oct. 1791.

63. AN, DXXV 46, 432. Pemerle to his brother, les Cayes, 31 Aug. 1791. Here the writer states that "the 15,000 insurgent slaves had taken the route toward le Cap." Another letter, dated 22 October, relates news that had arrived in France from a boat leaving the colony on 1 September: "There is a revolt of 15,000 slaves in Saint Domingue; they appeared at the city of le Cap. The planters armed themselves and attacked. They killed some and dispersed the others." DXXV 46, 432. Extrait d'une lettre de Bordeaux datée du 22 octobre, envoyée à M. de Lartigue.

64. The account is contained within a history of the Communauté (see n. 5 above) and, although compiled at a later date, is based nonetheless on the original correspondence of the nuns, as well as information related by other contemporary writers. So while some details may have somewhat gratuitously been attributed to the nuns by the reporter, the information is still based on fairly contemporaneous sources. See A. Cabon, "Une maison d'éducation à Saint Domingue: 'les religeuses du Cap'," RHAF 3 (déc. 1949): 417-19. Relevant passages of the text are translated from the original by author and presented in *The Making of Haiti,* Appendix B, 265-66; they are also cited by J. Fouchard in *Les marrons du syllabaire* (Port-au-Prince: Imp. Deschamps), 39-40.

65. Upon the initiative of a nun, later to be known as Mère de Combolas, whose wish was granted when le Cap was spared destruction from a British fleet threatening to attack in 1744, classes were opened for instruction to young black girls in the colony. Cabon, "Une maison," RHAF 3 (juin, 1949): 77-78. That a good number of these ended up in the voodoo cult toward the eve of the revolution reflects perhaps as much on the laxity of European mores in late eighteenth-century colonial society as the tenacity of African traditions and beliefs.

66. In M.E.L. Moreau de Saint-Méry, *Description topographique, physique, civil, politique et historique de la partie française de l'isle de Saint Domingue,* 3 vols. ([reprinted ed.] Paris: Société de l'histoire des colonies françaises, 1959), 1:67; also cited in Mgr. J. Cuvelier, *L'ancien royaume de Congo* (Brussels: Desclée de Brouwer, 1946), 290.

36 *Carolyn E. Fick*

67. For this translation by anthropologist John M. Janzen and further interpretation of the chant see Fick, *The Making of Haiti*, 58, esp. nn. 58-61. On Mbumba as rainbow serpent, see also Georges Balandier, *Daily Life in the Kingdom of the Kongo: From the Sixteenth to the Eighteenth Century*, Trans. Helen Weaver (New York: Meridian Books, 1968), 248.

68. See n. 67 above.

69. Cabon, "Une maison," RHAF 3 (déc. 1949): 418–19.

70. See n. 45 above.

71. AN, DXXV 78, 772. AA 183. Deposition, le Cap, 27 Sept. 1791.

72. AN, DXXV 56, 550. Discours.

73. Boston, *Independent Chronicle and Universal Advertiser*, 20 Oct. 1791. *Philadelphia Aurora*, 10-11 Oct. 1791. AN, DXXV 46, 432. Copies. Blanchelande à Bertrand, le Cap, 2 Sept. 1791.

74. Debien, *Les colons de Saint Domingue et la révolution: essai sur le Club Massiac* (Paris: Armand Colon, 1953), 334. AN, DXXV 46, 432. Copies. Extrait d'une lettre du Cap français en date du 25 sept. 1791. Also, DXXV 80, 787. Liste des habitations sucreries incendiées (dans l'espace de quinze jours) dont les noms sont parvenus jusqu'à ce jour, le Cap, 30 Sept. This list indicates 165 sugar plantations of the seven parishes hit during the first few days: Port-Margot, Limbé, Acul, Plaine du Nord, Petite-Anse, Quartier-Morin, and Limonade and estimates the loss in productive value at 39,800 *livres*. (It is a recapitulation of the same list as that cited in n. 21 above.) Another list, including the parishes of Dondon, Marmelade, Grande-Rivière, and Ste. Suzanne, and therefore drawn up somewhat later, lists 172 sugar, 1185 coffee, and 34 indigo plantations burned during the first month or two of the revolt, making a total of 1,391 plantations. DXXV, 63, 635. Liste des habitations incendiées, dépendance du Nord, n.d. (oct. 1791?). Obviously, figures vary from one source to another, making it nearly impossible to arrive at an exact count. Generally, however, colonists spoke of close to two hundred sugar plantations burned during the first week, and over two hundred by at least mid-September.

75. See n. 74 above.

76. AN, DXXV 46, 432. Copies. M. l'Ambassadeur à MM. les colons de l'Hôtel Massiac, 4 nov. 1791. Letter from Kingston, 17 Sept. 1791. Lettre de M. Nicoleau, le Cap, 3 sept. 1791. The four remaining districts, not including le Cap, were Ouinaminthe, Fort-Dauphin (including Terrier-Rouge), le Trou, and Dondon.

77. AN, DXXV 46, 432. Copies. Tausias à Camuzat, le Cap, 1 sept. 1791. See also Rapport de M. Bagnet, in *ibid.*; "St. Domingo Disturbances," *Philadelphia Aurora*, 10 Oct. 1791. Entry for 23 Aug. 1791.

78. AN, DXXV 78, 772. AA 183. Partie du Nord. DXXV 56, 550. Discours.

79. "St. Domingo Disturbances," *Philadelphia Aurora*, 10 Oct. 1791. Entry for 27 Aug. 1791.

The Slave Insurrection of 1791   37

80. AN, DXXV 78, 772. AA 183. Deposition, le Cap, 27 Sept. 1791. The facility with which the slaves were able to recruit additional forces was also remarked by Mr. Henry, a merchant captain, in a letter to his brother from le Cap, 27 Sept. 1791. DXXV 78, 772.

81. AN, DXXV 46, 432. Copies. Extrait d'une lettre de M. William Collann [?] à M. Thomas Collann [?] du Havre, en date du 28 octobre daté de Londres. Lettre de M. Guilhem de Bordaux, propriétaire au Cap, 28 oct. 1791 (?). Lettre au Général Melville d'un officier d'artillerie en garnison à la Jamaïque, le Cap, 24 sept. 1791. Extrait d'une lettre du Cap Français en date du 25 sept. 1791. See also J. Ph. Garran-Coulon, *Rapport sur les troubles de Saint Domingue,* 4 vols. Commission des Colonies (Paris: Imp. nationale, 1797-99), 2:215. Boston, *Independent Chronicle and Universal Advertiser,* 22 Sept., 13 Oct., 24 Nov. 1791. *Philadelphia Aurora,* 2 Oct, 14 Nov. 1791.

82. Cited in Arlette Gautier, *Les soeurs de Solitude: la condition féminine dans l'esclavage aux Antilles du XVIIe au XIXe siècle* (Paris: Editions Caraïbéennes, 1985), 239.

83. In "Slavery and Slave Revolts: A Socio-historical Analysis of the First Maroon War: 1665-1740," *Maroon Societies: Rebel Slave Communities in the Americas,* ed. Richard Price (Garden City, New York: Anchor Press, 1973), 279.

84. Geggus, "Les esclaves de la plaine," RSHH 136:12.

85. AN, DXXV 46, 432. Lettre écrite par M. Testard à M. Cormier, contenant l'extrait de deux lettres qu'il a reçues du Havre, le Cap, 26 oct. 1791, cited in Fick, "The Black Masses in the San Domingo Revolution." Geggus also cites the second of these two letters: AN Arch. Col., CC9A. Extrait d'une lettre anonyme, 20 août 1791, in "Les esclaves de la plaine," RSHH 136:12. Also see Fick, *The Making of Haiti,* Appendix B, n. 13.

86. C.L.R. James stated the case quite forcefully when he wrote that the crimes committed in the name of "property and privilege are always more ferocious than the revenges of poverty and oppression." *The Black Jacobins* ([1938] 3d ed., London: Allison & Busby, 1980), 88-89. Eugene Genovese has also gone to great lengths to defend this point in *From Rebellion to Revolution: Afro-American Slave Revolts in the Modern World* (Baton Rouge: Louisiana State University Press, 1979), 104-10.

87. The same may be said of the Haitian masses today as they are engaged in another struggle for liberation and for the basic principles of democracy and human dignity, indeed for the bare essentials of human survival. Any such violent expiation of repressed frustrations, hatred, and suffering as has occurred in the course of this struggle has been selective and relatively short-lived, compared with nearly thirty years of duvalierist repression and its aftermath.

88. While some estimates by colonists and other residents situate the number of insurgents killed at somewhere between three to four

38 *Carolyn E. Fick*

thousand in the first few months, others claim that in one of the attacks on le Cap alone, they suffered 2,000 killed and 1,500 taken prisoner, of which every tenth man was decapitated; another states that in Port-Margot alone, from 1,200 to 1,500 were slain. The figures given out by the whites for these single encounters, if they are not grossly inflated, would, in contradiction, largely surpass the generally-cited overall figure of three to four thousand. One report of 13 September claims that, thought upwards of 3,000 blacks had been killed, it would still require another 1,000 to 1,200 more killed before the slaves could be subdued. If, indeed, close to two thousand blacks were killed by white units at one single engagement, the reporter, then, would have been naïvely optimistic, for, by another report, although "about 3,000 insurgents have been killed, they are still strong and have fortified themselves in two or three different parts of the country." Extracts from the schooners Hardy, Peggy, 6 Oct. 1791; "Letter from James Perkins," le Cap, 9 Sept. 1791, Boston, *Independent Chronicle and Universal Advertiser*, 13, 20 Oct. 1791. "St. Domingo Disturbances," *Philadelphia Aurora*, 11 Oct. (entry for 13 Sept.); 14 Nov. 1791. An, DXXV 46, 432. Copies. Lettre écrite au Général Melville, le Cap, 24 sept. 1791.

89. "St. Domingo Disturbances," *Philadelphia Aurora*, 14 Nov. 1791.
90. *Ibid.*
91. In G. Laurent, *Chaînes*, 28. For a vivid example of maroon organisation and fighting tactics during the Jamaican maroon wars, see the descriptions in Miltin C. McFarlane, *Cudjoe of Jamaica: Pioneer for Freedom in the New World* (Short Hills, N.J.: Ridley Enslow Publ., 1977), passim.
92. Laurent, *Chaînes*, 29-31. Also, "St. Domingo Disturbances," *Philadelphia Aurora* 14 Nov. 1791.
93. *Ibid.* "Letter from James Perkins," Boston, *Independent Chronicle and Universal Advertiser*, 20 Oct. 1791.
94. Boston, *Independent Chronicle and Universal Advertiser*, 29 Sept. 1791.
95. In Althéa de Peuch Parham, trans. and ed., *My Odessey: Experiences of a Young Refugee from Two Revolutions, by a Creole of Saint Domingue* (Baton Rouge: Louisiana State Univ. Press, 1959), 32-34.
96. AN, DXXV 56, 550. Discours
97. AN, DXXV 46, 432. Copies d'une lettre de M. de Blanchelande au Ministre de la Marine, du Cap le 22 oct. 1791.
98. An, DXXV 20, 198. Mémoire fait par un habitant d'Ouinaminthe sur . . les événements arrivés à cette paroisse jusqu'au 15 janvier 1792, certifiée par Alexandre la Fosse, le Cap, 22 sept. 1792. DXXV 65, 662. Faits et événements relatifs à M. Wanderlinden, capitaine du régiment du Cap, lorsqu'il est venu au Fort Dauphin . . . , oct.–nov. 1791.
99. AN, DXXV 20, 198. Mémoire fait par un habitant d'Ouinaminthe. In addition to the command posts held at Ouinaminthe by Cézar and Jean-

The Slave Insurrection of 1791   39

Baptiste Marc were those held by Noël, a black slave, and Jean-Simon, a free black. Their nominal general was Sieur Gérard.

100. *Ibid.*
101. *Ibid.* Also DXXV 65, 662. Faits et événements relatifs à M. Wanderlinden; and Parham, *My Odessey,* 69-71.
102. On the death of Boukman, see the letter of M. de Cambefort recounting the incident, cited in full in Fouchard, *Marrons de la liberté,* 530-32. Also Boston, *Independent Chronicle and Universal Advertiser,* 15 Dec. 1791. Sannon, *Histoire de Toussaint,* 1: 92-93; Dalmas, *Histoire de la révolution,* 1: 132.
103. BPL, Gros, *Isle de St. Domingue, Province du Nord. Précis historique* . . . (Paris, 1793), 17, 26.
104. *Histoire d'Haïti,* 3 vols., 2d ed., Département de l'Instruction Public (Port-au-Prince; Edmond Chenet, 1922), 1:105.
105. AN, DXXV 63, 635. Déclarations. Déclaration de M. Guillaume Moulient. BPL, Gros, *Précis.* 25-26. See also Lacroix, *Mémoires,* 1: 153-54.
106. AN, DXXV 1, 2. Adresse à l'Assemblée Générale . . . par MM. les citoyens de couleur de la Grande-Rivière, Sainte-Suzanne et autres quartiers . . . n.d. (nov. 1791?).
107. BPL, Gros, *Précis,* 8-9.
108. Lacroix, *Mémoires,* 1: 1:2-13. See also Dalmas, *Histoire,* 1: 216-17. Extract of a letter from Cape Français of 2 Nov. ..., Boston, *Independent Chronicle and Universal Advertiser,* 8 Dec. 1791. Fick, *The Making of Haiti,* 108-9. (On Paul Blin's role in the organisation of the 22 August outbreak see the chronology of events presented earlier in this article).
109. Sannon, *Histoire de Toussaint,* 1: 93.
110. BSL, Gros, *Précis,* 14. Madiou even states that Boukman was mourned by his companions for several months. *Histoire d'Haïti,* 1: 106.
111. BSL, Gros, *Précis,* 14.
112. AN, DXXV 46, 439. Journal rédigé par M. Gros. Entry for 17 Nov. 1791.
113. BPL, Gros, *Précis,* 17. It appears evident here Gros, writing from his Journal notes two years after his captivity, took a good deal of liberty to embellish Jean-François' words and feelings.
114. *Ibid.*
115. AN, DXXV 46, 439. Journal rédigé par M. Gros. Entry for 11 Nov. 1791. BPL, Gros, *Précis,* 14.
116. *Ibid.* 21.
117. *Ibid.* AN, DXXV 46, 439. Journal rédigé par M. Gros. Entry for 17 Nov., 5 Dec. 1791. DXXV 46, 439. No. 300. M. de Rouvray to M. de Blanchelande, 8 Jan. 1792.
118. BPL, Gros, *Précis,* 21.
119. *Ibid.* In his observations, Gros made a distinction, however, between the slaves of mountainous regions (where the somewhat less labour-

40   *Carolyn E. Fick*

intensive coffee estates predominated) and those of the plains (where sugar production was concentrated); the former were far less ferocious than the latter, in Gros' opinion, and even seemed grieved over the fate of their maters.

120. AN, DXXV 60, 600. Extrait des registres. Suite de la déposition du Sieur Laroque, 21 janv. 1791.
121. BPL, Gros, *Précis*, 22.
122. AN, DXXV 79, 779. Extrait d'une lettre par M. Abbé de la Porte à M. l'Archevesque Thibaut, Vallière, 25 mars 1792.
123. The three free days per week had become a generalised demand throughout this early period; one exaggerated version of it even claimed that the slaves would be paid an average salary of three livres per day for the other three days. AN, DXXV 78, 772. Mr. Henry, capitaine du navire *la Charlotte* à son frère, le Cap, 27 sept. 1791.
124. AN, DXXV 63, 635. Déclarations. Déclaration de M. René Guillemeton. Déclaration de MM. René Cossait *et. al.*
125. BPL, Gros, *Précis*, 27.
126. *Ibid.*
127. Sannon, *Histoire de Toussaint*, 3: 18.
128. BPL, Gros, *Précis*, 28.

ABBREVIATIONS

AN	Archives Nationales (Paris)
BPL	Boston Public Library
RHAF	Revue d'histoire de l'Amérique française
RSHH	Revue de la Société Haïtienne d'histoire

Index

Please note: Page numbers which appear in italics are references to tables or illustrations.

Abenakis, Native Americans, attitudes toward
    Europeans, 198
abolitionism
  in Britain, 655, 658
  in France, 655
  in Saint Domingue, 659, 706–7
Abraham, Jacob, merchant peddler, 636
acculturation, definition of, 120
Acosta, José de, S.J., missionary, 234, 241,
    386, 393
Acosta, Josefa de, 557
Acosta, Tomás de, Inca chief, 365
Acul plantations, Saint Domingue revolution
    and, 683, 687–8
Adanson, Michel, botanist, 576–7
Adas, Michael, historian, 331
adoption, among Iroquois, 600–1, 607, 612
adultery
  among Iroquois, 596
  among Lebou people, 585–6
  in Brazil, 511, 522, 527
  and witchcraft accusations, 537, 548
  Woloff women and, 583–4
Aenons, Huron politician, 205, 228–9
Africa, transportation in, waterways and, 275–
    7, 283, 289–90; *see also* Lagos
Africans; *see also* free blacks
  versus Afro-Americans, 120, 147, 150
  as artisans: in Carolinas and Georgia, 138;
    in Chesapeake region, 148
  in Brazil: infant mortality among, 521; and
    sexual relations, 506
  in Carolinas and Georgia, 138, 141–2
  in Chesapeake region, 146–8
  female, *see* women, African
  in Mexico City, 492–5
  relations with Native Americans, 174–5
  slave culture of, 127–9
  and slave resistance, 671–2, 679
  in Spanish America, 80–1, 86–7
  tribes of, slaveowner stereotypes of, 134
Afro-American(s), 127–9, *see also* creole(s)
  versus Africans, 120, 147, 150
  in British North America, 119–53
  in Chesapeake region, 142–50, 152
  definition of, 120
  diversity among, 120, 152–3
  and politics, 129

afterlife
  in Christian theology, 216–19, 223–4
  in Montagnais theology, 223–4
Agamudaiyars, 334–5
agriculture
  in Carolinas and Georgia, 131–2
  in India, 333–42, 348
  Native American, 594–5; haciendas and,
    72–4, 77–8, 82–9, 92–3; Spanish
    impact on, 77–8, 81–9
  in New England, 100–1; slavery and, 121–3
  in Yucatán, 429, 441–2
Aguiar, João de Mattos de, philanthropist,
    531
Aguilar, Sanchez de, priest, 439
Agustina, accused witch, 555–6
Agwachimagan, Algonquin politician, 223
Aiyaz, Malik, official in Diu, 311
Akbar, Mughal emperor, 314
Akinsemoyin, *Oba* of Lagos, 298
Alagiyawanna, poet, 324–5
Albornoz, Cristóbal de, extirpator, 371, 402
Albornoz, Rodrigo de, *contador*, 494
Albuquerque, Afonso de, Portuguese governor
    of India, 312
alcohol, Native Americans and, 203
Aleman, Juan (Henche), merchant, 483
Alexander VI, pope, 237, 256
Alexander, William, colonist, 265
Alfonce, Ian, chronicler, 283
Algonquian-speaking Native Americans
  religion of, and view of Europeans, 200–1
  women of, *see* Iroquois women
Algonquins, Native Americans
  theology of, 225
Ali, Hyder, ruler of Mysore, 334–5, 339
Alibamos, Native Americans, 260
Allada, 276, 282, 285–6, 289–94
Allouez, Claude, priest, 198–9
Almeida, Francisco de, Portuguese viceroy,
    318
Almeida, Lourenço de, Brazilian official, 513
Almeida, Lourenço de, Portuguese captain,
    318, 323–4
Alonso, African slave, 493
Alonso, Hernando, blacksmith, 482, 488
Altman, Ida, historian, 471
Alva, Klor de, historian, 377